HYMNS OF THE
ROMAN
LITURGY

HYMNS OF THE ROMAN LITURGY

BY

THE REV.
JOSEPH CONNELLY, M.A.

ORIGINALLY PUBLISHED BY
THE NEWMAN PRESS
WESTMINSTER, MARYLAND

REPRINTED BY
PRIESTLY FRATERNITY OF ST. PETER, INC.

ORIGINALLY PUBLISHED BY

THE NEWMAN PRESS
WESTMINSTER MD USA

REPRINTED BY

PRIESTLY FRATERNITY OF ST. PETER, INC.
Elmhurst PA USA

Library of Congress Catalog Card Number 57-6438

ISBN: 0-9760370-8-4

First Published 1957
Reprinted 2006

NIHIL OBSTAT
THOMAS E. BIRD, S.T.D., PH.D.
Censor Deputatus

IMPRIMATUR
✠ FRANCISCUS J. GRIMSHAW
Archiepiscopus Birmingamiensis

BIRMINGAMIAE
die 10a Decembris 1954

REPRINTED BY
THE COVINGTON GROUP
KANSAS CITY, MISSOURI

CONTENTS

How This Book is Arranged

THE 154 hymns are divided into four main sections within which there are further subdivisions. Each group of hymns is preceded by a short introduction. Then follow the Latin hymns with adjacent English translations in prose and further notes on details of each hymn with references to individual lines of the Latin.

For the convenience of users, the typographical layout has been arranged with the principal object of ensuring that, as far as is practicable, both the English translation and the notes shall appear on the same page-opening as that part of the Latin text to which they refer. This has made necessary a slightly unusual typographical layout in which the following are the main points to be noted:

1. *Invariably* the completion of the entire material connected with any hymn is indicated by a rule across both pages of the book, even at the foot of a page. Where no rule occurs at the foot of pages this means that some part of the material is continued on the next page-opening.

2. *Frequently* the introduction to each group of hymns is continued on the right-hand page in a position level with that occupied on the left-hand page (*e.g.* pp. 2–3, 58–59). An arrow indicates the continuation of the introductory matter on to the right-hand page, only when the left-hand page ends with the completion of a paragraph.

3. *Occasionally,* owing to the length of some notes, it has been necessary to continue them from a right-hand page to a *left*-hand page first, and then on to the following right-hand page as usual (*e.g.* pp. 111–113). In such cases warning is given at the appropriate point.

Where, in the Breviary itself, portions of a whole hymn are used as separate hymns, the divisions are here shown in the Latin texts by an asterisk at the beginning of the first line of Latin text (and at the opening of the corresponding paragraph of English translation) and similarly in the index of first lines.

Where a new paragraph appears in the English translation, this is placed opposite the equivalent Latin passage.

PREFACE

THIS book is the outcome of some private classes that I used to take on the Breviary hymns. When for various reasons the classes had to be given up, I began to elaborate my notes with a view to their publication. But the work had to be put aside completely two or three times for quite long periods, and it was only recently that I was able to return to it and complete it. Thus in one sense the book has been long in the making, but the length of time was due to circumstances and spent in hope rather than in preparation of the book. So it may be that the notes are not as full nor always as up-to-date as a full-time hymnologist would expect, but I hope readers will pardon any deficiency in this respect. The circumstances in which the book was written and the requirements of a good number of those who may use it have prompted the plan of the book and the form and contents of the commentary.

Originally no translations of the hymns were provided, but those whose judgment I respect thought that their addition would make the book more useful. As the work of translation had to be done quickly, there was little time for the reflection and revision that translations of this kind seem to require, and I can only hope that my English versions have not suffered too much as a result.

In a work like the present book incorrect references are a nuisance to the reader but hard for the writer to avoid. I am therefore very grateful to those who went through the original manuscript and removed all such mistakes. But the providing of translations made many of the notes, in whole or in part, unnecessary and a revision of the notes had to be undertaken. It is no fault of those who checked the original if there are now any incorrect references; they will have occurred in the process of the later revision.

I also wish to thank all who helped in the work of typing, especially of the translations, and to all others who, each in their own way, have made the production of the book possible. I hope the book may prove useful and so bring a sense of reward and satisfaction to all these helpers for their work and patience.

FOREWORD

by THE MOST REV. F. J. GRIMSHAW

A GOOD hymn is a religious poem; and if the dictionary is correct when it describes a poem as a metrical composition expressing the powerful emotions which arise from the contemplation of the beautiful and the sublime, then a good hymn is one which clothes with beautiful language our thoughts about the Blessed Trinity and our heavenly Father's love for us.

Such indeed are the hymns of the Liturgy. They speak of the love of God, of the consecration of each hour of our waking day to Him, of our abiding sorrow for the sins we have committed against Him. They invite us, at the end of the day, to take our rest secure through our trust in Him. They express worthily sentiments which we cannot always find words to express at all. They are poetry. But they are also prayers.

They are intended to be recited, not merely read, and to be recited with attention. And even if that were not true by the nature of things, it would remain true by the Holy Father's expressed desire, that the hymns of the Divine Office, like the psalms and the lessons, should be read in such a manner as to yield up their ideas to the minds of those who take part in this public worship of God by the Church.

But the pity of it is that they occur, many of them, precisely at that place in our daily office where attentive recitation is most difficult. We hurry past them, conscious that there are many more pages to turn before our duty of prayer is done; and before there is leisure to turn back again the next instalment of this never-ending obligation is upon us.

This book is one which will commend itself to those of us already ordained who have often longed to know more about these poem-prayers but have found little leisure in which to do it. To those who are new to the recitation of the Office or who are not yet bound by its obligation but hope to be one day, it hardly needs commendation. It is the sort of commentary, I feel, that makes all the difference between early comprehension and the lack of it.

The table of contents is broad and comprehensive, and was planned to include some mention of as many as possible of the hymns most frequently recurring. It is not a book that will be read straight through by very many, I imagine. Rather it is the sort of book that finds a place on the bedside table, to be dipped into and browsed upon, now here, now there, as the pattern of the day's Office may indicate.

All of us who are priests or who are preparing to be priests welcome anything that will help us to understand more fully the liturgy that is put into our hands to perform. This book should help us all very much. I commend it heartily.

✠ FRANCIS, ARCHBISHOP OF BIRMINGHAM
2 November 1955

LIST OF BOOKS AND ABBREVIATIONS

Blakeney   = *Twenty-four Hymns of the Western Church,* by Edward Henry Blakeney (Eric Partridge, 1930). Text, translation and notes.

B   = *The Hymns of the Breviary and Missal,* by Dom Matthew Britt, O.S.B. (Benziger Brothers, 1936). Text, translation and notes. B refers to the treatment in that book of the hymn under discussion; B followed by a number refers to the hymn of that number in B, not to a page.

Byrnes   = *The Hymns of the Dominican Missal and Breviary,* by Rev. Aquinas Byrnes, O.P. (Herder, 1943). References as in B.

Daniel   = *Thesaurus Hymnologicus* (Leipzig, 1855–6), in five volumes. Reference by volume and page.

Fitzpatrick   = *Hymns from the Liturgy,* by Rev. John Fitzpatrick, O.M.I. (Burns, Oates and Washbourne, 1924). Metrical translation without Latin text or notes. References as in B.

Julian   = *A Dictionary of Hymnology,* edited by John Julian; revised edition (Murray, 1908). In the 1908 edition there are, in addition to the main Dictionary, two Appendices and a New Supplement—each in alphabetical order, and together adding 250 or so pages to the work.

            Julian without a number refers to the discussion of the hymn in the main Dictionary. Julian with a page number refers *either* to another heading in the main part of the work *or* to the hymn under discussion in one of the Appendices or in the Supplement.

Mulcahy   = *The Hymns of the Roman Breviary and Missal,* by Very Rev. Canon Mulcahy (Browne and Nolan, Dublin, 1938). Metrical translation without Latin text or notes. References as in B.

Oxford Medieval = *The Oxford Book of Medieval Latin,* compiled by Stephen Gaselee (Oxford, 1937). References as in B.

Phillimore   = *The Hundred Best Latin Hymns,* by J. S. Phillimore (Gowans and Gray, 1926). Latin text only. References as in B.

Pimont   = *Les Hymnes du Bréviaire Romain,* by S. G. Pimont (Paris, 1874). References as in B.

Raby   = *A History of Christian-Latin Poetry from the beginnings to the close of the Middle Ages,* by F. J. E. Raby (Oxford 1927 and 1953).

Schuster   = *The Sacramentary: Historical and Liturgical Notes on the Roman Missal,* by

Cardinal Ildefonso Schuster. English translation in five volumes (Burns, Oates and Washbourne, 1924), to which reference is made by volume and page.

Trench   = *Sacred Latin Poetry,* by Richard Chevenix Trench, third edition (Macmillan, 1874). References usually by *page.*

W   = *Early Latin Hymns,* by A. S. Walpole; edited for publication, after Walpole's death, by A. J. Mason (Cambridge Patristic Texts, 1922). References as in B.

To find a hymn in W is sometimes a difficulty, as he gives the un-revised text, and the changing of the first lines of so many hymns by the revisers under Urban VIII causes confusion. In case of doubt, hymns which are ascribed with practical certainty to an author will be found in the first part under the author's name. Hymns which are anonymous are from hymn *41* to the end of the book, and are grouped according to hours and seasons.

This collection of hymns does not contain medieval or later hymns.

Books which are only mentioned occasionally are given their full title whenever they are quoted.

Biblical quotations are mostly given in Latin, for they usually illustrate or explain the *text* of the hymns. Moreover the Latin Bible has the same relation to Christian Latin as the English Bible has to our own language. References to the Psalter must necessarily be to the Vulgate text, and quotations from the New Psalter are clearly indicated. The numbering of the psalms is according to the Vulgate (Douai) and not according to the Hebrew (A.V.).

Patristic quotations are, as far as possible, given by reference to the Breviary, since most users of this book will have a Breviary. When a text is not (or cannot be recalled as being) in the Breviary, the reference is to Migne's *Patrologia Latina,* indicated by PL followed by the volume and column numbers.

References to the Breviary are usually to the season or feast to which the hymn under discussion belongs, and the meaning to be attached to, e.g. 'second nocturn' or 'lesson 8' ought to be clear from the context. In the cases of octaves, an abbreviated form of reference is sometimes necessary. An example is the Octave of Corpus Christi, and the method of reference used is explained in the introduction to the hymns for that feast.

The regulations of 23 March 1955 about the simplification of the rubrics of the Breviary have not, up to the present, made any change in its text. References, therefore, to feasts, octaves and vigils are to the existing text of the Breviary, even if the particular feast or octave has now disappeared. The only changes made in this book as a result of the regulations are in the last paragraph of the introduction to the hymns of the Days and Hours and in the *Iste Confessor, 87,* 3–4.

INTRODUCTION

1. The Purpose of the Book

THE Latin hymns of the Roman liturgy cover a period of sixteen centuries, the first ones being written by Saint Ambrose and the latest ones in recent years for the new feast of the Assumption. They are of great religious and literary interest. In the history of literature they are important for the way in which classical forms were adapted to Christian uses, for the medieval development of Christian Latin poetry and for a still later development, though this time for the worse, in the Renaissance period. Their religious value and interest lies in the fact that their contents are a witness to the faith of the Church and illustrate Christian devotion through the centuries. Moreover they have a particular value in their liturgical setting inasmuch as they are one of the points in the Church's prayer where the hour, season or festival is mentioned explicitly and so help us to recall the particular purpose of the Office or of one of its parts.

But the hymns also have their difficulties and so are not always appreciated as they deserve. Perhaps one of the reasons for the neglect of these metrical prayers is that books about them are not numerous, though the literature on Latin hymns as a whole is enormous. As there is obviously a place for a commentary on the hymns of the liturgy, it is hoped that this book will go some way to satisfying such a need and that as a result the great spiritual treasure to be found in the hymns will be better appreciated and their value as prayers more clearly seen.

However, it is easier to state the purpose of the book than to find a good way of effecting it, for the things to be explained are so diverse and the potential users of the book so varied. In the matter of Latin, for instance, practically everybody at some time or another has found awkward lines, while to some the Latin is a serious and fairly permanent difficulty. Some have had a good classical education and others, coming to Latin later in life, have had to content themselves with a more utilitarian approach. And almost everybody, whatever his grasp of the language, must work out the hymns for himself. Something similar is found in relation to the contents of the hymns, with some people already knowing or being quick to perceive the important place hymns have in public worship and others needing some mental stimulus before due appreciation comes to life in their souls. The only way of dealing with this is to follow the advice that Saint Gregory gives in one of the Breviary lessons, namely to aim at giving instruction to those who need it without boring those who do not. With all this in mind, the plan of the book is as follows.

A prose translation is given of each hymn and linguistic points are considered in the notes. A word ought to be said about the translations. They are an attempt, however imperfect, to express in ordinary everyday English the thought and the words of the Latin text. 'Literal' translations are never elegant and seldom really helpful, and translations of religious texts are often so remote because they abound in the archaic and the exclamatory. But whatever merits the translations in this book may have, they are only aids for the study of the Latin; for it is the Latin that has to be understood as a text and eventually used as a means of prayer.

The subject-matter of the hymns is dealt with in two ways. The sectional introductions suggest rather than elaborate the main points of the hymns and their relation to the Church's prayer, while individual points are considered in the notes. As the commentary deals with doctrinal, liturgical and historical details as well as with linguistic and textual ones, there was always the danger of it getting overloaded or that its different elements would get confused. The total commentary is relatively long, but individual notes must for the most part be brief and can do little more than suggest lines of thought and interpretation.

The authorship of each hymn is given briefly, though in a few cases a longer discussion seemed necessary or desirable. A brief biographical note is given of the more important writers. The section on the metres of the hymns is relatively long for the sake of those who have had little chance of knowing about such things. The section on Accent and Rhyme may be of more general interest.

Two works in particular have been of great help in the making of this book, as almost every page bears witness. They are: *Early Latin Hymns* (Cambridge Patristic Texts) by A. S. Walpole, and *The Hymns of the Breviary and Missal* by the American Benedictine, Dom Matthew Britt. So often are these books referred to that they are indicated respectively by the letters W or B.

2. HYMNS AND DOXOLOGIES

St Augustine describes a hymn as the praise of God in song. '*Hymnus scitis quid est? Cantus est cum laude Dei. Si laudas Deum, et non cantas, non dicis hymnum. Si cantas, et non laudas Deum, non dicis hymnum. Si laudas aliud quod non pertinet ad laudem Dei, etsi cantando laudes, non dicis hymnum. Hymnus ergo tria habet, et cantum, et laudem et*

Dei. Laus ergo Dei in cantico, hymnus dicitur' (In Ps. 148, 17). St Ambrose wrote his hymns to be sung, and so have most hymn-writers since. To read a hymn is like reading a libretto; the composer is not justified and the reader is not satisfied. Unfortunately the regular choral celebration of the Office, through many different circumstances, became the exception and private recitation became the rule so that now the Breviary hymns are mostly read and seldom sung. This change of custom coupled with a pseudo-classicism led people to forget the claims of music, and revisers and poets of recent centuries do not seem to have considered this essential element of song. The results have been most unhappy, and some of them are noted in the course of this book.

The Psalms are rightly called hymns, for they are the praise of God in song; but the name 'hymn' is now usually restricted to works of human composition. The *Gloria in excelsis* and other such compositions are also rightly called hymns, but the term is now usually applied only to verse compositions. Inasmuch as hymns sing the praise of God, they might also be called doxologies, but this term now has a special meaning.

A doxology is a formula of praise, such as the *Sanctus,* the *Gloria Patri,* the *Gloria in excelsis* and *Alleluia.* Of these the *Gloria in excelsis* is known as the Greater Doxology. The *Gloria Patri,* or Lesser Doxology, is the specifically Christian formula which was added to the psalms in the Office and at Mass. When hymns were added to the Office, it was thought fitting that these 'private psalms' should end with a metrical equivalent of the *Gloria Patri,* and such endings are called doxologies. The text of these doxologies is not given in this book unless they were composed as an integral part of a particular hymn or have some point of interest, as in *4* and *68–70.* The usual types, for iambic hymns, are *Praesta, Pater piissime* or, for most feasts of our Lord, a variant of *Jesu tibi sit gloria,* though *Deo Patri sit gloria* is used for Easter (and for Pentecost).

3. THE ORIGIN AND DEVELOPMENT OF THE LATIN HYMN

The real father of Latin hymnody is St Ambrose, though St Hilary was also composing hymns about the same time. St Jerome mentions a book of hymns by Hilary, which was known only by this reference until a MS of them was found at Arezzo last century. But they were 'lost' almost as soon as they were written, for they are intricate and obscure and so ill-suited to public singing. St Hilary said that the Gauls were not very clever in singing hymns, presumably in comparison with the East where he had heard hymns sung. But the Gauls might have retorted that their bishop was not very clever at writing hymns which they could sing. St Ambrose and the Milanese had no such difficulties. They were only too ready to sing what he composed, and the choice by Ambrose of the iambic metre was the element of the unexpected which genius always turns to success.

The story of the Arian troubles at Milan which provided the occasion for Ambrose to write hymns is too well known to need detailed description here. If the Arians were going to press poetry and music into the service of heresy, St Ambrose would do the same for the cause of the true faith and at the same time provide the faithful with a way of beguiling the time of their siege. 'His hymns', says Mulcahy, 'are easy to understand, easy to remember, and are easily sung'. He gave the faithful in his *Splendor paternae gloriae, 12,* for instance, a statement of Catholic faith which they could easily understand and use in the defence of their faith. It could easily be remembered, for of all forms the iambic quatrains are the easiest to recall. It could easily be sung. All that was needed was a good tune, and they seem to have had no difficulty about that in those days. It may perhaps be that he did not write his hymns for strictly liturgical use, but it was not long before hymns were being used in the liturgy, so that he is rightly styled the 'Father of liturgical hymns'.

Thus with St Ambrose began the long line of writers of Latin hymns—Prudentius, *13,* Sedulius, *38,* Fortunatus, *52,* Adam of St Victor, the two Thomases, of Celano, *154* and of Aquino, *71,* to mention a few of those whose names are known, as well as a host of anonymities. Short notes are given on the main writers in the course of the book, and one particular aspect of the development of Latin hymnody is given in the section on Accent and Rhyme. For further information other books must be consulted.

The success of St Ambrose also produced many imitators, the results being called *Ambrosiani* because written *in similitudinem Ambrosii.* Very many of the Breviary hymns belong to this anonymous class, and many have been incorrectly ascribed to the saint through a misunderstanding of the term *ambrosiani.*

Customs varied about the admission of metrical compositions into the official worship of the Church. The monks seem to have used them in this way before the time of St Benedict, for he is able to direct the use of an *ambrosianum* at different Hours without further specification. Among the secular clergy hymns were in use in some places and not in others, and at Rome they were not finally admitted for secular use in the basilicas until the twelfth century. Eventually they were given a fixed place in the Breviary of the Curia of the thirteenth century from which, after many vicissitudes, the Roman Breviary of today is descended.

Monastic usage, different local breviaries and the collections of the hymns of different writers brought into being different hymnals. The treatment of this question falls outside the scope of this book, though a word must be said about what W calls the Old Hymnal and the Later Hymnal.

Caesarius of Arles (470–543) drew up a rule for monks, before he was bishop, and republished it, with various changes, for nuns after he became bishop. Both are said to be based on the customs of Lérins. His successor, Aurelian (died 553), revised both rules. Each bishop directed the use of hymns and the first lines of very many of them are given—the two lists being identical, except for two hymns that Aurelian added. The list of hymns obtained by comparing the two rules and the relevant MSS gives substantially a hymnal. But MSS, roughly from the tenth century onwards, show that many of these hymns have gone out of use and that others, more numerous than those that had been removed, have been admitted. This gives a second hymnal, called by W the Later Hymnal, its predecessor being called the Old Hymnal.

The Jesuit scholar, Blume, in 1908 focused attention on this question by asserting that the Old Hymnal was essentially the original Benedictine one and that the Later, of northern origin, gradually supplanted the Old through the liturgical changes connected with the name and court of Charlemagne. This is contrary to the traditional view which makes the Benedictine and the Roman hymnals to be essentially one, the Later being a development, not a supplanter, of the Old. The arguments for both sides are given in W, pp. xi–xix and by Raby (*A History of Christian-Latin Poetry*, pp. 36–40). W adopts Blume's position as being 'now generally accepted by all scholars', but Raby, writing five years after W, preferred the traditional view. Other points connected with this problem are dealt with in books and articles mentioned by W and Raby, and also in histories of the Breviary.

Whatever the origin of the hymnal, it is quite certain that, when formed, it came under fire from the Humanists. It was, in their eyes, a tasteless thing and its Latin inelegant and barbarous. A revision of the hymns was made by Ferari (or Ferreri)' and Clement VII allowed its use in the private recitation of the Office; but it does not seem to have had a very long life. The unrevised text of the hymns was used by Quignon in his Breviary and also in the Breviary of Pius V. But the desire for reform was still present and the seventeenth century saw the desire fulfilled.

This revision, now universally admitted to have been a great mistake, was set on foot by Urban VIII and carried out vigorously by him in his double capacity of pope and poet. Associated with him were four Jesuits, Famiano Strada, Tarquinio Galuzzi, Girolamo Petrucci and Matthias Sarbiewski—all well able to produce elegant imita-

B

tions of classical models and the last-named being likened by his contemporaries to Horace. How far their private feelings about exercising their gifts on the hymns and their spirit of obedience coincided is a matter of dispute, but it is quite clear that the driving force was from Urban, the last of the Humanist Popes. He personally considered all the changes suggested, and added his own—his, sometimes, being more radical than theirs. If hymns were needed for new feasts, he himself wrote them. It is probably due to the fact that he had such a large part in the revision that the results go far beyond the original plan. (Cf. Pastor, *History of the Popes*, XXIX, pp. 16 ff.; Batiffol, *History of the Roman Breviary*, pp. 221–3 and 233–5; etc.).

The immediate purpose of the revision was to make the hymns more classical in expression and metre. To do this '952 *corrections* were made in the 98 hymns then in the Breviary. Eighty-one hymns were corrected: 58 alterations were made in the hymns of the Psalter (i.e. *1* to *33* of this book), 359 in the Proper of the Season, 283 in the Proper of the Saints and 252 in the Common of the Saints. The first lines of more than 30 hymns were altered. The *Jam lucis orto sidere,* the *Ave maris stella,* the hymns of St Thomas Aquinas and a few others were spared. Some hymns were practically rewritten, others were scarcely touched', B, p. 24. The result of this was that many thoughts and ideas of the original text were obscured, changed or discarded altogether and many a good prayer spoiled. An equally bad result has been that these corrected hymns have furnished a style of hymn-writing that has been followed ever since. Moreover, the revision brought about a divorce between the music and words of the hymns, as was mentioned above and will often be referred to in the commentary. It is said that when the new edition of the Church's plainsong was being prepared, a request was made that the old text of the hymns be restored so that the music could be used with the words for which it was intended. (The old text still remains in the *Graduale* for Good Friday, and both sets of words are given for the Corpus Christi procession. For some reason this distinction between the Mass and Office texts is not observed in the *Liber Usualis,* only the new text being given.) Some notice was taken of this request, but no change has so far been made. The revision did not affect such Breviaries as those of the Benedictines and Dominicans, nor have St Peter's or the Lateran ever adopted it. Indeed some of the bitterest opposition to the new text, when it was first published, came from the Roman basilicas.

4. The Metres of the Hymns

The verses of a hymn are made up of lines in which the feet are ordered in metres according to a definite plan.

Feet

A foot consists of two or more syllables of defined quantity and may be contained in one word, two or more words or in parts of words.

A foot of *two* syllables may be a *pyrrhic,* two short syllables; a *spondee,* two long ones; a *trochee* (or *choree*), one long, one short; or an *iamb,* one short and one long.

A foot of *three* syllables may be a *tribrach,* three short syllables; a *molossus,* three long ones; a *dactyl,* one long and two short; an *anapaest,* two short and one long; a *cretic,* one long, one short and one long; or a *bacchius,* one short and two long.

A foot of *four* syllables may be one of sixteen forms; of these only the *choriamb,* i.e. a choree (trochee) plus an iamb, is found in the Breviary.

Lines

A line has a number of feet in a definite order. The following points are necessary for the understanding of the names of lines:

(*a*) In dactylic verse one foot equals one metre, while in iambic and trochaic *two* feet make up *one* metre.

(*b*) A line with the stated number of complete metres is *acatalectic.* If the last metre be short by one syllable, the line is called *catalectic;* if by two, *brachycatalectic.* But if there be one or two syllables *after* the last complete metre, the line is *hypercatalectic.* This occurs regularly in certain systems of verse.

Hypercatalectic is not the same as *hypermetric.* A hypermetric line is one in which the number of syllables is increased *in* or *before* the last foot. There are many examples of this in the Breviary, especially since the revision.

(*c*) Some lines are named after their inventor or first user, usually a Greek lyric poet; e.g. Archilochus, *cir.* 700 B.C.; Alcaeus and Sappho, *cir.* 600 B.C.; Pherecrates, *cir.* 450 B.C.; Asclepiades and Glycon, date unknown.

(*d*) Lines of more than two metres have a break (*caesura*) caused by the *end* of a word of two or more syllables occurring at the *middle* of the third foot, so that words and feet do not always coincide. In trochaic lines, however, the break normally comes at the *end* of the fourth or fifth foot so that words and feet coincide. In the Breviary it always occurs after the fourth foot; cf. e.g. 53 and 71.

(*e*) As a long syllable is equal to two short ones, a spondee sometimes takes the place of a dactyl or anapaest, and an iamb or trochee is resolved into a tribrach.

Further, a spondee is used, sometimes necessarily, sometimes optionally, in place of a trochee, dactyl, iamb or anapaest. St Ambrose, like the classical poets, sometimes uses a spondee for an iamb in the first or third foot of an iambic dimeter; e.g. *Aeterne rerum conditor,* or, *Aeterna Christi munera.*

The names and characteristics of the lines in the hymns are:

1. *Dactylic hexameter catalectic.* Six feet (or metres), of which the first four are either dactyls or spondees, the fifth a dactyl and the sixth always a trochee or a spondee. Caesura occurs in the middle of the third or fourth foot.

2. *Dactylic tetrameter acatalectic.* Four dactyls. This metre is not found in the Breviary, unless the accentual *Sacris solemniis, 72,* be so interpreted.

3. *Adonic,* i.e. *dactylic dimeter catalectic.* Dactyl with trochee or spondee. Only used with other lines, e.g. with Sapphics (11, below).

4. *Lesser Archilochius,* i.e. *dactylic dimeter hypercatalectic.* Dactyl and choriamb. Only used with other kinds of line.

5. *Dactylic pentameter,* i.e. *two dimeter hypercatalectics* (4). A spondee may occur in the first foot, and a molossus in the second. Regular caesura after the first choriamb. Frequently used alternately with hexameter lines (1).

6. *Trochaic tetrameter catalectic,* i.e. seven and a half trochees. Regular caesura after the fourth foot in the Breviary, which is emphasised by rhyme in 71.

7. *Trochaic trimeter catalectic,* i.e. five and a half trochees.

8. *Trochaic dimeter acatalectic.* Four trochees, i.e. the first half of 6.

9. *Trochaic dimeter catalectic.* Three and a half trochees, i.e. the second half of 6.

10. *Trochaic dimeter brachycatalectic,* i.e. three trochees.

Eight was not used classically; 9 and 10 were never used by themselves.

11. *Lesser Sapphic.* A line of five feet based on trochees, but with a dactyl always in the third foot and a spondee usually in the second. Usually combined with an Adonic (3).

12. *Pherecratian.* A dactyl between two dissyllables (trochees or spondees). Only used with other lines.

13. *Glyconic.* Trochee or spondee followed by two dactyls or by a dactyl and cretic.

14. *Lesser Asclepiad.* Spondee, choriamb and two dactyls. Others analyse as spondee, two choriambs and an iamb.

15. *Iambic trimeter acatalectic.* Six iambs. A spondee or, rarely, a dactyl may occur in the first, third or fifth foot and a tribrach in any foot but the last. Caesura in the middle of the third or fourth foot.

16. *Iambic dimeter acatalectic.* Four iambs, for the first or third of which a spondee is often substituted; cf. (*e*) above. Classically this line was only used in combination with others.

(For further information any good classical grammar may be consulted, e.g. *Revised Latin Primer,* by B. H. Kennedy.)

Verses

If the verses are composed of lines of the same metre, the metre gives its name to the verses. If, however, they are composed of a fixed order of different metres, they are usually named either after the metre which is most used, e.g. Sapphic, or after the one which gives it its special character, e.g. Archilochian.

The following are the verse systems used in the hymns, the numbers in brackets referring to the names of lines above and the other numbers to the hymns which use the metre:

Dactylic hexameter catalectic (1); *30.*

Dactylic tetrameter acatalectic (2); *?72,* the fourth line being Glyconic (13).

Trochaic tetrameter catalectic (6); *53, 55, 71, 76, 119, 134.*

Trochaic trimeter catalectic (7); *75.*

Trochaic dimeter acatalectic (8); *31,154.*

Trochaic dimeter catalectic (9); *67.*

74 uses trochaic dimeter acatalectic and catalectic in various groupings, and *109* in fixed groupings.

Trochaic dimeter brachycatalectic (10); *94.*

Iambic trimeter acatalectic (15); *77, 98, 99* (five-lined), *124.*

Iambic dimeter (16), known as the Ambrosian metre or, in English Hymnals, as the Long Metre. All hymns in this book are in this metre, unless otherwise stated.

Elegaic. Couplets, (1) and (5) alternately; *54, 61.*

Second Asclepiad. Three Lesser Asclepiads (14) and the fourth line a Glyconic (13); (*?72), 84, 100, 106, 118, 133, 136.*

Third Asclepiad. Two Lesser Asclepiads (14), one Pherecratian (12) and the fourth a Glyconic (13); *110.*

First Sapphic. Three Sapphics (11) and the fourth line an Adonic (3); *1, 10, 47, 87, 91, 103, 104, 107, 108, 112, 117, 121, 131, 132.*

Third Archilochian. Three-lined verses with one iambic trimeter (15), one Archilochian (4) and one iambic dimeter (16). The second and third lines are often treated as one line and then called an elegiambus; *123.*

5. ACCENT AND RHYME

Classical poetry was quantitative, that is based on the length or shortness of syllables, as described in the preceding section. But popular poems and songs, which existed side by side with the quantitative ones, were accentual. St Ambrose wrote his hymns for the people and so had to make them popular. To do this, he did not desert the quantitative system, in which he was well versed. Instead he formed verses of iambic dimeter, which the classical writers only used in combination with other lines, and so used it that the long syllables were often also the accented ones. The popular welcome given to his hymns showed how happy his compromise had been. The Ambrosian metre was used for most of the early hymns, quantitative with traces of accentual (cf., e.g. introduction to *38*), until at last the element of quantity was entirely ignored. The new system, called accentual, was based on the accent of syllables, whatever their quantity; for accent and quantity may or may not coincide. Thus a dactyl, in the accentual system, consists, not of a long and two short syllables, but of an accented and two unaccented ones, e.g. *gaudia* and a trochee of an accented and an unaccented syllable, e.g. *dies*. The iambic line *Rerum Deus tenax vigor* is trochaic, if considered accentually.

The Passiontide *Pange lingua, 53,* is trochaic, quantitative, but the Corpus Christi one, *71,* is accentual. The *Sanctorum meritis, 84,* is a Second Asclepiad, quantitative, though the accents fall fairly regularly on the first, fourth, seventh and tenth syllables. But the *Sacris solemniis, 72,* is an accentual composition and therefore, so it would seem, ought to be classed as dactylic and not, as is often stated, as Asclepiad. An Asclepiad must *begin* with a spondee, which is impossible in accentual poetry since two succeeding syllables cannot be accented. Its fourth line is a Glyconic (*12*), accentual.

Roughly speaking, hymns down to the Middle Ages are quantitative, the medieval ones are accentual and rhymed, and the post-medieval are mostly quantitative.

But besides the change from quantity to accent there was brought about another change, namely a conscious and consistent use of rhyme. Rhyme is not foreign to the Latin tongue, as the fragments of early Latin poetry show. There are examples of its use in the writings of all the great Latin poets of classical times and also in the early hymns; cf., e.g. *38* and the second verse of *52*. But writing in quantitative metre meant that rhyme could only occur by accident or when rhyme and quantity did not disagree, for the endings of lines, like the lines themselves, were governed by the laws of quantity, with certain legitimate substitutions.

The purpose of hymns gave them a special character, which eventually caused a new consciousness of the ends of lines. Hymns were instruction and praise in the form of poetry and not, if it may be so expressed, merely poetry. They were meant to be sung and therefore had to have a well-defined tune which would fit all the verses;

they were also meant to be sung by group answering group and, as it is humanly impossible to sing a verse without a pause, one major pause was allowed for in verses of iambic dimeter and two in those of trochaic tetrameter. The pause, however, had to be so arranged that it did not make nonsense of the words. A verse therefore need not be a complete sentence but it must have completed sense as a recognisable part of the complete sentence, and at each major pause there would be at least a 'sense-pause'. St Ambrose and the early writers and centonists always kept to this rule; cf., e.g. *Splendor paternae gloriae, 12,* where the exception in the eighth verse is due to the revisers. This indicates one of the differences between a poem and a hymn, and by this standard most of the modern hymns and the revisions of old hymns in the Breviary stand condemned.

Such an arrangement of lines gave a new importance to the ends of lines. Now the writers of accentual hymns, while keeping in general the old idea of pauses 'and sense-pauses', found a special difficulty in the treatment of the ends of lines. The last syllable of a Latin word is never accented and therefore cannot be the accentual equivalent of a final long syllable. Length and accent being thus eliminated for the last or the last two syllables, there remained only the music of sounds with which to embellish the endings. And perhaps it was the difficulty of beginning as well as that of ending accentual lines that brought it about that the greatest accentual hymns of the Middle Ages were written in the trochaic or dactylic metre, and the difficulty of ending such lines that caused them to be rhymed.

It is clear that the above remarks do not profess to be a history of the origins and development of rhyme. They are no more than suggested reasons why it was used and developed by Christian writers until it became, like the Ambrosian metre before it, a speciality and glory of Christian poetry. Accent and rhyme formed an appropriate means of expressing doctrinal truths in the hymns of St Thomas, pathos and pity in the *Stabat Mater,* the terrors of the judgment in the *Dies irae* and the consolation of the Holy Ghost in the *Veni sancte spiritus.*

With the end of the Middle Ages came the end of the poetical and popular elements of Christian Latin hymns; and, though many metrical compositions have been added to the Breviary since that time, scarcely any *hymns,* in the true sense of the word, have been added. Ambrose and Prudentius took something classical and made it Christian; the revisers and their imitators took something Christian and tried to make it classical. The result may be pedantry, and sometimes perhaps poetry; but it is not piety. *Accessit Latinitas, discessit pietas.*

I

HYMNS OF THE DAYS

AND THE HOURS

THE hymns of this section are the foundation on which the others are built, for the language and thoughts which are appropriate to the individual seasons and feasts are worked into a vocabulary already fixed. God is our creator, our redeemer and our judge—these are the themes of all sacred song, whether in the Bible or of human inspiration. That God is our redeemer and our judge is, naturally, a point to which the hymns of the seasons and of the saints constantly return, though these early hymns mention it but seldom. But that God is our creator is an idea which runs right through the hymnal. It is, however, the constant and peculiar theme of the hymns of the days and hours, which are but metrical variations on the text *Adjutorium nostrum in nomine Domini, qui fecit caelum et terram.*

Of all the gifts of the creator, the one which is hymned everywhere, from Matins to Compline, is that of light—the physical light which suggests the light of grace, so that the writers pass imperceptibly from the one to the other. The ideas then of creation and of light are the foundation of all the hymns, and the development of the imagery of light and its opposite, darkness, gives unity to the explanation of the hymns.

At Matins we pray that night will give way to day, and at Lauds we welcome its coming. The Christ to whom we pray at Matins as *lux ipse lucis et dies* is the *Aurora* of Lauds. At Prime we pray, now that the day has come, that the effects of this spiritual light will be with us through the day, and this prayer is with us always, adapted in its form to the different hours of the day. In this way we are reminded daily and throughout each day that our Lord said: 'I am the light of the world. He who follows me can never walk in darkness; he will possess the light which is life', John 8, 12; but 'he who journeys in darkness cannot tell which way he is going', John 12, 35. When Judas left the Supper, 'it was night'.

These hymns will repay much study and their value as prayers is very great. Hitherto the opportunities for using the week-day hymns at Matins, Lauds and

Vespers have been very few, but the simplification of the rubrics of the Breviary, introduced by Pope Pius XII, has increased their use and perhaps the future will see a further increase.

I. MATINS

The name Matins is a later and not very apt name for what is a *night* office. Its divisions are still called Nocturns and each of its hymns (in this section) makes mention of the night. The old name for this night office was *Vigilia,* to which the first hymn refers in its opening words *Nocte surgentes vigilemus omnes.*

The essence of the vigiliary office was that there was public prayer at dead of night, the *Nox atra* of Thursday's hymn, but its length and the hour at which it began seem to have varied. As will be seen from the notes, it is not possible to say who wrote the Matins hymns, nor can their date be settled beyond the fact that they were already in use, and perhaps had long been in use, by the ninth century. They cannot therefore be used with much precision to illustrate the history or development of Matins. The most that can be said is that the writers seem to have had in mind people who had been to bed and then rose for the night office.

The idea of rising to pray is found in all these hymns, except perhaps the Thursday

---

Hymn 1
Sunday Matins (a)

Nocte surgentes vigilemus omnes,
Semper in psalmis meditemur, atque
Voce concordi Domino canamus
   Dulciter hymnos,

5 Ut pio regi pariter canentes
Cum suis sanctis mereamur aulam
Ingredi caeli simul et perennem
   Ducere vitam.

Praestet hoc nobis Deitas beata
10 Patris ac Nati pariterque Sancti
Spiritus, cujus resonat per omnem
   Gloria mundum.

Now that we have risen while it is still night, let us all keep watch, fixing our attention always on the psalms and in pleasing unison singing our hymns to the Lord. So may it be that we who, as a group and in union with His saints, sing to the loving King, may be counted worthy to enter heaven's court, there to live for ever. May the blessed God, whose glory resounds through all creation, Father, Son and likewise the holy Spirit, grant us this.

one. The Christian casts off sloth and sleep and rises to sing God's praises and to implore His help and pardon. The praise of God is to be the first action of the day, *3, 5,* and the inspiration of the day's work, *3,* 8. As is natural, the spiritual imagery suggested by night, darkness, sleep, sloth and their opposites is also to be found here, except in the first hymn; e.g., *3, 9–12; 4, 5–8; 6, 9–12.* To be occupied with spiritual duties at night suggested also a comparison with sentinels, *excubantes, 7,* 4 and *excubent, 8,* 11, alert and guarding the whole church by their prayers at a time when God is most likely to hear them, *2,* 13–16.

Matins has a long, solemn prelude made up of the *Venite* and the hymn. The *Venite* joins together the psalmist's invitation to praise God with a special reason found in the season or feast of the day. The hymn then puts these sentiments in verse form, most of the emphasis being on the feast or season. These eight hymns, however, not being peculiar to any particular period, find their inspiration in the special circumstance of praise being offered to God at night. And in general this marks the difference between the hymns assigned for the days and the hours and those for the seasons or for saints' days.

Matins ends, except on certain days, with the *Te Deum*—the culmination of all the praise given to God at Matins and a fitting prelude to Lauds.

Notes on Hymn 1

Author. Unknown. W suggested Alcuin (735 to about A.D. 804) as the author of this and *10.* A Carolingian date seems probable, and Alcuin did write some sapphics whose thought and style are not unlike these two hymns.

Metre. First Sapphic.

Use. From the fourth Sunday after Pentecost until the end of September.

2. *meditemur,* reflect, ponder over; cf. *meditabor in mandatis tuis,* Ps. 118, 47.

5. *pariter,* together. This word and *cum suis sanctis* are connected in thought with *canentes* and *mereamur.* Breviaries mostly have a comma after *canentes.* But if one is needed, after *sanctis* seems a better place. The verse is a prayer that those who as a group on earth are praising God in unison with the Saints may be reunited with one another and united with the Saints in heaven.

6. *mereamur. Mereri* means, according to the context, win, succeed in gaining, be counted worthy, merit. It is usually found with the accusative or with *ut;* the infinitive, as here, is rare.

9. *Praestet,* grant. Here and in *71,* 15 *praestare* is used with the accusative, but it is often found without an object expressed, as in *4,* 13.

10. *pariter,* likewise, no less; cf. line 5.

11. *cujus* refers to *Deitas. Resonat,* resounds.

Hymn 2

Sunday Matins (b)

Primo die quo Trinitas
Beata mundum condidit,
Vel quo resurgens conditor
Nos, morte victa, liberat,

5 *Pulsis procul torporibus,*
Surgamus omnes ocius
Et nocte quaeramus Deum—
Propheta sicut praecipit—

Nostras preces ut audiat
10 *Suamque dextram porrigat,*
Et expiatos sordibus
Reddat polorum sedibus,

Ut quique sacratissimo
Hujus diei tempore
15 *Horis quietis psallimus,*
Donis beatis muneret.

Jam nunc, paterna claritas,
Te postulamus affatim,
Absint faces libidinis
20 *Et omnis actus noxius,*

Ne foeda sit vel lubrica
Compago nostri corporis,
Ob cujus ignes ignibus
Avernus urat acrius.

25 *Mundi redemptor, quaesumus,*
Tu probra nostra diluas
Nobisque largus commoda
Vitae perennis conferas,

Quo carnis actu exsules,
30 *Effecti ipsi caelibes,—*
Ut praestolamur cernui—
Melos canamus gloriae.

On the first day of the week, the day when the blessed Trinity created the world and the risen creator conquered death and brought us freedom, let us cast aside all slothful feelings, rise even more readily than on other days and, as the prophet commands, seek God by night. May He heed our prayers, stretch out to us His right hand, cleanse us from our sins, restore us to our home in heaven and then reward with the gift of unfailing bliss all of us who, assembled at the hallowed part of the present day, sing His praises during the hours of quietness.

And now in this very hour we address an urgent prayer to You, the glory of the Father: Let all that would move us to sin as well as sin in any of its forms be far from us, so that this body of ours, which You have so marvellously knit together, be not shamefully defiled by sin or brought perilously near to it; for if the fires of passion burn in us now, the fires of hell will for that reason burn all the more fiercely. We beg You, redeemer of the world, wash away our shameful sins and of Your bounty grant us the blessings of everlasting life so that being absent now from fleshly activity and becoming hereafter like the angels in heaven, we may—as we humbly hope—sing the song of Your glory.

Notes on Hymn 2

Author. Unknown. W thinks this may be two hymns joined into one, because the style of the original text is different in the two halves, because of the length, because *Jam nunc* was a favourite way of beginning hymns and because, it may be added, lines 13–16 are as probable an ending as *8, 13–16.* If that be true, we must look for two authors.

The date of the supposed joining is not known, but the hymn appears in its present form by the time of the earliest MSS of the Later Hymnal. The reason for the joining is not known, unless it be that the new arrival, *Nocte surgentes, 1,* threatened the survival of the somewhat uncouth *Jam nunc paterna claritas.*

Use. From October to Lent, Advent and the Christmas season excepted.

1. *Trinitas.* The reference to the Trinity and to the *first* day of creation is due to the revisers. The original *Primo dierum omnium/Quo mundus exstat conditus* refers to our Lord (*conditus* of line 2 and *conditor* of line 3 being connected) and to the *eighth* day, i.e. to the first day after the day of rest. The day after the Sabbath was also the day of the Resurrection. The unrevised text thus explains the *Lord's* day, as St Gregory did: *Dies dominicus, qui tertius est a morte dominica, a conditione dierum numeratus octavus,* In Ezech., II, iv, 2. The line *Octava prima redditur* of an Easter hymn has the same meaning.

2. *mundum;* cf. *8, 2,* note.

3. *vel,* and; a common meaning in late Latin; cf. *25, 9.*

6. *ocius,* comp. of *ociter,* with greater speed—because it is the *Lord's* day.

8. *praecipit. In noctibus extollite manus vestras,* Ps. 133, 2.

10. *porrigat.* The imagery may be suggested by the healing of the leper, Mt. 8, 2–3.

11. *expiatos,* sc. *nos;* purified, cleansed from.

12. *polorum,* of heaven; cf. *11,* 10, note.

13. *ut quique,* that all of us who . . . *Quisque* was commonly used in late Latin for *quicunque. Sacratissimo,* because prayer at night was always so thought of, and here also because it is the *Lord's* day.

The first four verses form one sentence in the Latin.

17. *paterna claritas.* This *could* refer to the Father or to the Son; but it more probably refers to the Son; cf. *Mundi redemptor* in line 25. *Paternae gloriae, 12,* 1 and *paterna gloria, 85,* 25, refer to the Father.

18. *affatim* (= *ad* and *fatim,* to satiety or fatigue), incessantly, urgently, until God is fatigued with our prayers.

19. *faces libidinis.* Flames of lust, B; or, metaphorically, incitement to sin.

20. *noxius,* guilty, sinful; cf. *omne noxium, 22,* 15 and *noxa, 3,* 14.

21. *lubrica. Lubricus* always connotes danger, and is applied in the hymns to sin, its occasions and to desires leading to sin; cf. *12, 12,* etc.

22. *compago,* structure, fastening together. Lest our body so marvellously knit together, W.

23. *cujus,* i.e. the body; *ignes,* passions.

24. *Avernus,* a lake near Cumae in Italy. The name was adopted from Virgil by Christian writers to denote hell.

30. *caelibes,* unwedded; like the angels in heaven.

31. *ut,* as; *cernui;* cf. *71,* 13.

32. *melos,* song, hymn.

Lines 29–32, not used in the Roman Breviary, explain the end of the preceding verse.

Hymn 3
Monday Matins

Somno refectis artubus,
Spreto cubili, surgimus;
Nobis, Pater, canentibus
Adesse te deposcimus.

5 Te lingua primum concinat,
Te mentis ardor ambiat,
Ut actuum sequentium
Tu, sancte, sis exordium.

Cedant tenēbrae lumini
10 Et nox diurno sideri,
Ut culpa, quam nox intulit,
Lucis labascat munere.

Precamur idem supplices
Noxas ut omnes amputes,
15 Et ore te canentium
Lauderis omni tempore.

With our bodies refreshed by sleep, we rise from our bed with alacrity and ask You, Father, to assist us as we sing Your praises. Let our tongue magnify You first of all and our soul most fervently seek out Your help so that You, holy One, may be the starting-point of all else we do in the day. Oh that the soul's darkness would give place to light and night to day so that the sin which night brought may lose its hold through light's action. We also ask and pray You to prune away all our sins and to grant that we who now sing of You, may praise You through eternity.

Hymn 4
Tuesday Matins

Consors paterni luminis,
Lux ipse lucis et dies,
Noctem canendo rumpimus;
Assiste postulantibus.

5 Aufer tenebras mentium,
Fuga catervas daemonum,
Expelle somnolentiam
Ne pigritantes obruat.

Sic, Christe, nobis omnibus
10 Indulgeas credentibus,
Ut prosit exorantibus
Quod praecinentes psallimus.

Sharer of the Father's light, Yourself light of light and source of man's light, we break night's silence with our sung praise; hear us with favour as we make this prayer. Dispel the darkness from our souls; put to flight the bands of evil spirits; drive away sloth that it may not overwhelm us, liable as we are to inertia. Grant pardon, Christ, to all of us believers so that the praise we sing in Your presence may win for our earnest prayers a favourable

Notes on Hymn 3

Author. Unknown. It is not in the Ambrosian tradition or style, and Biraghi, the authority on the hymns of St Ambrose, excludes it from the list of genuine hymns of the saint. Daniel thinks it to be of the seventh or eighth century.

1. *artubus* (*artus*, 4), joint, limb; cf. *8*, 11; *87*, 8.

2. *Spreto cubili*, abl. absol; *spernere*, spurn, scorn, despise etc.

4. *deposcimus*, pray earnestly; here with infinitive instead of the more usual *ut* clause.

6. *mentis*, soul—its usual meaning in the hymns. *Ardor;* here in a good sense, as in *19*, 8. *Ambiat;* (1) to take every possible means to find God; or (2) to solicit, pray to, as in Hor. *Od.* I, 35, 5 and Prud. *Perist.* II, 491.

8. *exordium*, beginning, starting-point of the acts to follow, *actuum sequentium;* cf. the collect *ut cuncta*

nostra oratio et operatio a te semper incipiat.

9. *cedant;* an optative. *Tenēbrae;* the second syllable is normally long in poetry and short in prose. The darkness and light are spiritual; cf. Eph. 5, 8.

10. *diurno sideri*, the sun; cf. *14*, 8. Here spiritually of the sun of righteousness.

12. *labascat* (from *labascere*, 3, inchoative of *labare*), totter, waver, give way, yield; *munere*, by the gift of; or, better, by the office, working of light.

13. *idem*, also. *Idem* is the old form of the nom. plur. and the reading of the MS. The Breviary *iidem* should be scanned as *idem*.

14. *noxa*, guilt, sin. *Amputes*, prune away; cf. *amputa opprobrium meum*, Ps. 118, 39.

15–16. Cf. *ut viventes laudemus nomen tuum, Domine, et ne claudas ora te canentium*, Esther 13, 17.

Notes on Hymn 4

Author. Unknown. For the reasons given in *3*, it cannot be St Ambrose. 'The doxology is so insistently contained in all MSS, that I have printed it as an integral part of the hymn', W. 7 is the only five-verse hymn in the Matins series, and W wondered if *7*, 17–20 originally belonged to this hymn.

This doxology is now one of the common ones in the Breviary, but it did not become such until Clement VIII when it was substituted for the form: *Praesta Pater omnipotens,/Per Jesum Christum Dominum,/Qui tecum in perpetuum/Regnat cum sancto Spīritu.*

1. *Consors;* for the sense cf. *12*, 1. Cf. lines 1–2 with *12*, 1–4.

2. *ipse;* for the masculine with a feminine noun, cf. *11*, 15, note.

3. *rumpimus*, break in upon, interrupt; cf. *5*, 8; *8*, 14; *13*, 14.

4. *assiste*, stand by, i.e. hear with favour; cf. *adesse* in *3*, 4; cf. also *112*, 19.

5. *tenebras;* cf. *3*, 9, note. *Mentium;* cf. *3*, 6.

6. *catervas*, bands; cf. *signum quod ipse nosti/Damnat tuam catervam*, Prud. *Cath.* VI, 147–8.

8. *pigritantes* (from *pigritari*, intensive of *pigrari*), to be given to laziness. W suggests 'lingering' and compares *ne pigriteris venire usque ad nos*, Acts 9, 38.

9. *Sic* is answered by *ut* in line 11.

11. *exorantibus*, praying earnestly; more usually, gaining requests.

12. *Prae* of *praecinentes* is local; *prae* of *praecinit*, *13*, 2, is temporal.

Praesta Pater piissime
Patrique compar unice
15 *Cum Spiritu Paraclito*
Regnans per omne saeculum.

answer. Grant this most loving Father and You, the only Son, equal to the Father and, with the Spirit, the Paraclete, reigning through the ages.

Hymn 5
Wednesday Matins

Rerum creator optime
Rectorque noster, aspice;
Nos a quiete noxia,
Mersos sopore, libera.

5 *Te sancte Christe, poscimus,*
Ignosce culpis omnibus;
Ad confitendum surgimus
Morasque noctis rumpimus.

Mentes manusque tollimus,
10 *Propheta sicut noctibus*
Nobis gerendum praecipit
Paulusque gestis censuit.

Vides malum quod fecimus,
Occulta nostra pandimus,
15 *Preces gementes fundimus,*
Dimitte quod peccavimus.

Good creator of the world and ruler of mankind, look down on us and free us, buried in sleep, from sinful sloth. To You, holy Christ, we make our prayer; pardon all our sins. It is to own You as Lord that we have risen and now break upon the silence of the night. We raise up our hearts and lift up our hands in prayer, as the Psalmist commanded to be done at night and as Paul by his actions showed to be the right thing. You see the evil we have done, and we confess our hidden faults. With penitent heart we make this earnest prayer: Forgive us our sins.

Hymn 6
Thursday Matins

Nox atra rerum contegit
Terrae colores omnium;
Nos confitentes poscimus
Te, juste judex cordium,

5 *Ut auferas piacula*
Sordesque mentis abluas,
Donesque, Christe, gratiam
Ut arceantur crimina.

Night's pall has shrouded in darkness all the colours of creation. Acknowledging that we are sinners, we beseech You, just judge of man's heart, to take away our sin and wash away the soul's guilt. Give us, Lord Christ, the grace of being preserved from sin. Behold our soul lies

Notes on Hymn 5

Author. Unknown. It has been attributed to St Ambrose and to St Gregory.

3. *noxia,* sinful; cf. *2*, 20.

5. *sancte.* Very rarely used in the liturgy in this way of our Lord. Its purpose here is to contrast His holiness with our sinfulness.

7. *confitendum. Confiteri* has the idea of 'acknowledge' underlying all its uses in Christian Latin. (1) to acknowledge God's holiness, i.e. to *praise* Him; (2) to acknowledge our sinfulness, i.e. to *confess* our guilt; (3) to acknowledge God by death (*martyrs*); and (4) to acknowledge God by a holy life (*confessors*). Perhaps the second as well as the first meaning is implied here, for 9–12 illustrate the first and 13–16 the second.

8. *morasque noctis,* the spaces i.e. the hours of the night; *mora* = delay and *mora temporis* (Ovid) = space of time. Original: *morasque nostras,* i.e. we bring our delay to an end; cf. *rumpe moras,* Virg. *Georg.* III, 43.

Rumpimus; cf. *4,* 3, note.

9. *mentes;* cf. *3,* 6. *Manus.* The ancients prayed with hands uplifted and upturned. This posture suggested a cross: *Non ausa est cohibere poena palmas/in morem crucis ad Patrem levandas,* Prud. *Perist.* VI, 106.

10. *propheta,* i.e. psalmist; cf. *2,* 8, note.

12. *gestis censuit,* showed his approval (of the psalmist's advice) by his actions. *Media autem nocte Paulus et Silas orantes laudabant Deum,* Acts 16, 25.

13. *fecimus;* cf. *50,* 29. Original: *gessimus,* which is purposely contrasted with *gerendum* and *gestis,* i.e. sin at night with prayer at night. For such a use of *gerere* cf. *peccata vestra quae gessistis,* Deut. 9, 18.

14. *pandimus* (*pandere,* open; cf. *73,* 18), lay open, confess, acknowledge.

15. *preces gementes. Preces* is accusative and *gementes* nominative. Cf. *8,* 6; *11,* 28; *13,* 10 etc. for prayers and tears.

Notes on Hymn 6

Author. Unknown. Same conjectures as for 5.

1. *Nox atra;* cf. *rebus nox abstulit atra colorem,* Virg. *Aen.* VI, 272. For similar ideas, cf. *14,* 7–8 and *15,* 2. *Contegit,* as if darkness were a substantial pall; cf. *14,* 5 for a similar use of *caligo.*

3. *confitentes;* cf. *5,* 7, note.

5. *piacula,* sins; it usually means sin offerings. For

the meaning 'sin', cf. Virg. *Aen.* VI, 569 and *numquam . . . tam grande piaculum factum est in Israel,* Judges 20, 6.

5–8. Give the reason for the prayer—5–6 the repairing of the past and 7–8 the future results of grace. *Arceantur,* warded off.

c

Mens ecce torpet impia
10 *Quam culpa mordet noxia;*
Obscura gestit tollere
Et te, redemptor, quaerere.

Repelle tu caliginem
Intrinsecus quam maxime,
15 *Ut in beato gaudeat*
Se collocari lumine.

motionless in its wickedness and the grip of guilty sin holds it fast. Yet its desire is to put away the works of darkness and to seek You, its Redeemer. Dispel completely the inner darkness of our soul so that it may rejoice to find itself in the light of happiness.

Hymn 7

Friday Matins

Tu Trinitatis Unitas,
Orbem potenter quae regis,
Attende laudis canticum
Quod excubantes psallimus.

5 *Nam lectulo consurgimus*
Noctis quieto tempore
Ut flagitemus omnium
A te medelam vulnerum,

Quo fraude quidquid daemonum
10 *In noctibus deliquimus,*
Abstergat illud caelitus
Tuae potestas gloriae,

Ne corpus astet sordidum
Nec torpor instet cordium,
15 *Ne criminis contagio*
Tepescat ardor spiritus.

Ob hoc, redemptor, quaesumus,
Reple tuo nos lumine,
Per quod dierum circulis
20 *Nullis ruamus actibus.*

Lord God, one and three, all-powerful ruler of the world, receive the hymn of praise that we sing as we keep watch. For we have risen from our beds during the silence of the night to ask You earnestly to heal the wounds our sins have caused so that the might of Your heavenly glory may wash away whatever sin may have befallen us at night through the craft of evil spirits. Thus our body will not be defiled from sin nor sluggishness of soul be sin's immediate result; thus our soul's eagerness will not grow colder under sin's evil influence. Wherefore we ask You, Redeemer, fill us with Your light so that no actions of ours may cause us to fall.

10. *mordet.* Besides meaning to bite, *mordere* may mean to bite into, take fast hold of and also to sting, pain. Interpretations of *mordet* in this line vary.

11. *gestit,* is eager, yearns, desires.

14. *intrinsecus,* an adverb used almost as an adjective; dispel the inner darkness (of our soul).

15. *gaudeat* sc. *mens.*

16. *se collocari,* to establish oneself, live permanently in. In such cases the pronoun is often omitted; cf. *24, 15.*

Notes on Hymn 7

Author. Unknown. Same conjectures as for *5.*

2. *quae,* sc. *Unitas.* MSS have *qua* or *qui.* If *qui* is read, the construction is similar to *lux ipse, 4, 2.*

3. *Attende;* usually followed by the dative or by a preposition. Here, as occasionally in the Vulgate, the accusative is used.

4. *excubantes,* keeping watch; cf. *vigilemus, 1, 1.*

10. *Noctibus:* the plural in such cases denotes that no particular night (or day, *diebus*) is meant.

11. *Caelitus,* an adverb, used almost as an adjective; cf. *6, 14.*

13. *astet,* originally *adsit;* both = *sit.*

14. *instet* suggests that this is an immediate result of the preceding line; cf. *perennis instet gloria, 21, 8.*

15. *contagio* (*contagium,* a touching, contact, generally in a bad sense), pollution, defilement, infection, contamination etc. Cf. *arcens mali contagium, 83, 7* and *diabolica vitare contagia,* collect Seventeenth Sunday after Pentecost.

17. *Ob hoc.* W suggested that 17–20 are an addition to this hymn (cf. intro. to *4*), and certainly the *Ob hoc* is abrupt. The first four verses are addressed to *Trinitatis Unitas,* but this one to the *Redemptor.*

19. *per quod,* sc. *lumen;* i.e. if we are helped by this light.

20. *nullis ... actibus,* no actions of ours may cause us to fall, W. An intransitive followed by an ablative is classical. The sense is that of John 11, 9–10.

Hymn 8

Saturday Matins

Summae Parens clementiae
Mundi regis qui machinam,
Unius et substantiae
Trinusque personis Deus,

5 Nostros pius cum canticis
Fletus benigne suscipe,
Ut corde puro sordium
Te perfruamur largius.

Lumbos jecurque morbidum
10 Flammis adure congruis,
Accincti ut artus excubent,
Luxu remoto pessimo,

Quicunque ut horas noctium
Nunc concinendo rumpimus,
15 Ditemur omnes affatim
Donis beatae patriae.

Fount and source of infinite mercy, ruler of the world's structure, God, one in nature and three in persons, in Your love graciously receive our 'mingled penitence and praise' so that with our soul free from sin we may more fully enjoy You. Burn away with healing flames what is unhealthy in our affections and thoughts so that with loins well girt and all sinful desires cast out we may keep our prayerful vigil. May all of us who break the silence of the night with songs of praise be abundantly enriched with graces from heaven.

Hymn 9

Te Deum laudamus, te Dominum confitemur.
Te aeternum Patrem omnis terra veneratur.
Tibi omnes angeli, tibi caeli et universae potestates,
Tibi Cherubim et Seraphim incessabili voce proclamant
5 'Sanctus, sanctus, sanctus, Dominus Deus sabaoth.
Pleni sunt caeli et terra majestatis gloriae tuae'.
Te gloriosus apostolorum chorus,
Te prophetarum laudabilis numerus,
Te martyrum candidatus laudat exercitus.
10 Te per orbem terrarum sancta confitetur ecclesia
Patrem immensae majestatis,
Venerandum tuum verum et unicum Filium,
Sanctum quoque Paraclitum Spiritum.

We praise You as God; we acknowledge You as Lord.

The whole earth reverences You, the eternal Father. All the angels, the heavens and the whole body of heavenly powers, Cherubim too and Seraphim, cry aloud unceasingly: 'Holy, holy, holy Lord God of hosts. Your glory and majesty fill heaven and earth.'

The choir of Apostles, of glorious fame, the band of prophets, worthy of our praise, the array of martyrs, in their robes of white—all give praise to You. The holy Church in all parts of the earth acknowledges You, the Father of boundless majesty, Your adorable, true and only Son, and also the holy Spirit, the Paraclete.

Continued

Notes on Hymn 8

Author. Unknown.

1. *Parens*. As the hymn is addressed to the three Persons, line 4, 'Father' for *Parens* is ambiguous. Fount and Source of . . . .

2. *mundi. Quem κόσμον Graeci nomine ornamenti appellaverunt, eum nos a perfecta absolutaque elegantia mundum*, Plin. II, 1, 4.

machinam, i.e. fabric, structure; cf. *moles et machina mundi*, Lucr. V, 96; also *63, 9; 95, 3. Machina* may also mean scheme, plot, as in 3 Nov., lesson 9 (St Augustine).

This line originally was *mundique factor machinae*. The idea of creation would have been better left in; for *factor* cf. *50*, 8.

6. *fletus;* cf. *5*, 1 5 note; *benigne* may be a vocative, not an adverb, W; i.e. gracious God.

7. *corde puro;* MSS also *corda pura. Sordium;* but MSS *sordibus,* the more usual construction after *purus* and such words.

8. *largius* (adv. comparative), more fully, more abundantly.

9. *jecur*, liver; regarded as the seat of the passions and affections; *morbidum*, diseased, in a moral sense.

10. *adure*, burn away (as with cautery); cf. the collect, *Ure igne sancti Spiritus renes nostros et cor nostrum. Congruis*, fitting, appropriate, meeting the occasion; cf. *si congruam poenitentiam agant* and *congruas poenas* (Ambrosiaster). Here the flames would meet the occasion if they *cured* the diseased part; healing flames.

11. *accincti* with the accusative *artus* (cf. *3*, 1). In the original *accincti* referred back to *lumbos*. In either case cf. *sint lumbi vestri praecincti*, Lk. 12, 3 5. *Excubent;* cf. *7*, 4.

14. *rumpimus;* cf. *4*, 3, note.

15. *ditemur*, be enriched; *affatim*, abundantly; cf. *2*, 18.

Notes on Hymn 9

Author. Probably St Nicetas of Remesiana in Dacia (335–415). In this province Greek and Latin were in daily use, and Nicetas seems to have had Greek models in mind when he wrote the *Te Deum*. It is in rhythmical prose, and is endowed 'with a majesty and freedom that no other hymn of the Latin Church possessed' (Raby, *Secular Latin Poetry*, I, p. 53).

Use. It is used at the end of Matins on all Sundays except those of Advent and Lent and on feastdays.

1. *Deum* and *Dominum* are accusatives, not vocatives; as God, or, for You are God; as Lord, or, to be the Lord.

5–6. A direct quotation after *proclamant*.

9. *candidatus*, white-robed; cf. *152*, 14 and Apoc. 7, 13. Lines 7–9, cf. St Cyprian, *de Mortalitate* (8 Nov., lesson 6).

12. *et unicum;* another version is *verum unigenitum*.

Tu rex gloriae, Christe, Tu Patris sempiternus es Filius.

15 *Tu ad liberandum suscepturus hominem, non horruisti Virginis uterum.*

Tu, devicto mortis aculeo, aperuisti credentibus regna caelorum.

Tu, ad dexteram Dei sedes in gloria Patris; judex crederis esse venturus.

Te ergo quaesumus, tuis famulis subveni, quos pretioso sanguine redemisti.

Aeterna fac cum sanctis tuis in gloria numerari.

20 *Salvum fac populum tuum, Domine, et benedic haereditati tuae.*

Et rege eos et extolle illos usque in aeternum.

Per singulos dies benedicimus te,

Et laudamus nomen tuum in saeculum et in saeculum saeculi.

Dignare, Domine, die isto sine peccato nos custodire.

25 *Miserere nostri, Domine, miserere nostri.*

Fiat misericordia tua, Domine, super nos, quemadmodum speravimus in te.

In te, Domine, speravi; non confundar in aeternum.

You, the king of glory, Christ, are the Father's everlasting Son. Yet, when for man's salvation You were about to assume man's nature, You did not shrink from entering the Virgin's womb.

You drew out death's poisonous sting and opened for believers the kingdom of heaven.

You sit at God's right hand; You will, as we believe, come again as Judge.

We therefore ask this favour of You: come to Your servants' aid, for You redeemed them at the price of Your blood. Bring it to pass that they be numbered with Your saints in everlasting glory.

Save Your people, Lord, and bless Your inheritance.

Be a shepherd to them and bear them up for ever.

Day by day we bless You, and we praise Your name for ever and ever.

Deign, Lord, today to keep us without sin.

Have mercy on us, Lord, have mercy on us.

May Your mercy, Lord, be upon us, as we have hoped in You.

In You, Lord, have I placed my hope; never let me be put to shame.

---

2. LAUDS

When the name Matins was given to the vigiliary office, it could no longer be used for the morning service, whose former name was *Matutini* or *Laudes Matutinae.* From the second of these titles there was accordingly formed the new name of *Laudes,* Lauds. But the office did not thereby lose its character of being a morning one, as the hymns in this section clearly show.

The morning office was the normal completion of the night office and followed it without break or with but a slight break. The references in these hymns to rising must therefore be interpreted either as a continuation of the mention of this at Matins or in a spiritual sense. But the writers may well have thought, in some cases at least, of the normal sense of 'rising'. This would certainly be true of *13, 14* and *15,* which were not written for the Office but were formed out of longer hymns and then inserted into the prayer of the Church.   →

15. When you were about to take upon you (*suscepturus*) human nature (*hominem*) so as to deliver man (*ad liberandum sc. hominem*). The versions 'When you took . . .' derive from the reading *suscepisti. Horruisti,* variously rendered as fear, abhor, disdain, shrink from, etc.

16. *devicto;* cf. *devicta morte,* collect Easter Sunday; *aculeo,* sting, dart, of death; cf. 1 Cor. 15, 55–6.

17. *sedes.* Probably this ought to be *sedens,* with a comma after *Patris. Crederis,* pass; you are believed.

18. *Quos.* Some join the *quos . . . redemisti* to the following verse *Aeterna . . . numerari.*

19. *numerari.* The alternative reading *munerari,* to be rewarded, seems more likely.

20. *Salvum fac.* The verses from here to the end are an addition to the original composition, and various other endings are found. All these endings give the *Te Deum* an air of supplication and a penitential character, and it seems that 'in the Middle Ages it was chanted in times of great calamity, whilst on joyous and solemn occasions the *Gloria in excelsis* was sung' (Schuster, II, p. 283). This character is very evident in the verse translation 'Holy God, we praise thy name', where the last verse begins 'Spare thy people, Lord, we pray'. (Cf. *Westminster Hymnal,* 187, which gives verses 1, 2, 4 and 8 of this translation.)

20–27 are sentences from various psalms. The sudden transition to the singular in the last verse suits neither the *Te Deum* as a whole nor 20–26. Some editors therefore, e.g. Phillimore, omit it from the text.

Two ideas are prominent in these hymns. Cock-crow is the theme of *Aeterne rerum conditor, 11,* by St Ambrose and of *Ales diei nuntius, 13,* by Prudentius. Who is it, asks God of Job, that has 'put wisdom in the heart of man? Or who gave the cock understanding?' (Job 38, 36). St Ambrose, following this idea, sees a manifestation of God's wisdom and power in the division of day and night and in the God-given instinct of the cock to announce this division. And on that simple fact joined with the story of St Peter's denial he builds up one of the most beautiful hymns of the Breviary. For simplicity and sublimity it has few rivals. However beautiful the *Ales diei nuntius* may be, in its full or shortened form, it pales beside the other.

Prudentius in one place likens our Lord to the cock. He is the *excitator mentium, 13, 3,* as the cock is to the sun, *11,* 9, or to those still in bed, *11,* 18. But if He is the awakener of men's souls, He is also their light, as all these hymns testify. The Matins hymns were more concerned with light in the darkness, but these think of the light which ends the darkness. There is, for instance, Prudentius' breathless *Lux intrat, albescit polus,/Christus venit—discedite, 14, 3-4,* and St Ambrose's *Aurora cursus provehit,/Aurora totus prodeat, 12, 29-30,* note, and hymn *17* which carries the idea right through to the Last Day.

The first hymn of the Lauds series, as was the case in the Matins series, differs from the rest in spirit as well as in metre. It is an appeal to worship God with all one's strength at the morning service of praise. The other hymns have in them the note of vigilance. *Vigilate ergo; nescitis enim quando dominus domus veniat: sero, an media nocte, an galli cantu, an mane. . . . Quod autem vobis dico, omnibus dico: Vigilate,* Mark 13, 35-7. This idea of vigilance is developed in two ways. The first is through the story

---

Hymn 10
Sunday Lauds (a)

Ecce jam noctis tenuatur umbra
Lux et aurorae rutilans coruscat;
Supplices rerum Dominum canora
   Voce precemur,

5 *Ut reos culpae miseratus, omnem*
Pellat angorem, tribuat salutem,
Donet et nobis bona sempiternae
   Munera pacis.

Behold night's darkness is lifting and dawn's blushing light is gleaming in the sky. In humble prayer and with melodious voice let us beseech the Lord of creation to have mercy on those guilty of sin, to banish all trouble of mind, to bestow health and to give us the good blessings of everlasting peace.

Hymn 11
Sunday Lauds (b)

Aeterne rerum conditor,
Noctem diemque qui regis
Et temporum das tempora
Ut alleves fastidium,

5 *Nocturna lux viantibus*
A nocte noctem segregans,
Praeco diei jam sonat
Jubarque solis evocat.

Eternal creator of the world, You govern night and day and give changes of time and season to relieve man's boredom. And now the bird that has been like a light to travellers during the night and marked off for them the night-watches, is heralding the day and calling

of St Peter, *11*, but the other is found in *12–17* as a commentary on Romans 13, 11–14, from which is taken the Chapter for weekday Lauds. This passage, to which many references are made in the notes, is as follows: *Hora est jam nos de somno surgere… Nox praecessit, dies autem appropinquavit. Abjiciamus ergo opera tenebrarum, et induamur arma lucis. Sicut in die honeste ambulemus: non in comessationibus et ebrietatibus, non in cubilibus et impudicitiis, non in contentione et aemulatione: sed induimini Dominum Jesum Christum.*

The morning office of Lauds, so full of joy that light and *the* Light are coming, ends fittingly with the *Benedictus* which daily recalls the *Oriens ex alto*, Who has come *illuminare his qui in tenebris … sedent.*

Notes on Hymn 10

Author, Metre and Use. Cf. *1*, which is its counterpart at Matins.

1. *tenuatur* (*tenuo*, 1), make thin or small; diminish.

2. *rutilans* (*rutilo*, 1), make or be reddish; blushing; cf. *59*, 1, note.

3. *rerum Dominum*, the Lord of creation; *canora*, melodious, not only musically but as springing from a heart aflame with love of God. The original *Nisibus totis rogitemus omnes* and the original *Viribus totis* of *1*, 3, mean with all our strength and effort, both referring to *ex omnibus viribus tuis* of Lk. 10, 27.

6. *angorem*, anguish, torment, trouble, etc. Original *languorem*, i.e. sickness as contrasted with health, *salutem*. For this use of *languor* (and *languidus*), cf. *sanans omnem languorem*, Mt. 4, 23, and *34*, 7 and *81*, 15. For the doxology *Praestet*, cf. *1*, 9–12.

Notes on Hymn 11

Author. St Ambrose (cf. Introduction § 3, and introduction to *13*). That St Ambrose is the author is mentioned by St Augustine in *Retract.* I, 21: *qui sensus etiam cantatur ore multorum in versibus beatissimi Ambrosii, ubi de gallo gallinaceo ait: Hoc ipsa petra ecclesiae/Canente, culpam diluit.*

A passage in St Ambrose's Hexaemeron is a good commentary on this hymn and, in spite of its length, is worth quoting. It was probably written after the hymn.

Est etiam galli cantus suavis in noctibus, nec solum suavis sed etiam utilis; qui quasi bonus cohabitator et dormientem excitat et sollicitum admonet et viantem solatur, processum noctis canora voce protestans. Hoc canente latro suas relinquit insidias, hoc ipse lucifer excitatus oritur caelumque illuminat. Hoc canente maestitiam trepidus nauta deponit omnisque crebro vespertinis flatibus excitata tempestas et procella mitescit; hoc devotus affectus exsilit ad precandum, legendo quoque munus instaurat. Hoc postremo canente ipse ecclesiae petra culpam suam diluit, quam, priusquam gallus cantaret, negando contraxerat. Istius cantu spes omnibus redit, aegri relevatur incommodum, minuitur dolor vulnerum, febrium flagrantia mitigatur, revertitur fides lapsis, Jesus titubantes respicit,

Hoc excitatus lucifer
10 *Solvit polum caligine;*
   Hoc omnis erronum cohors
   Viam nocendi deserit.

   Hoc nauta vires colligit
   Pontique mitescunt freta;
15 *Hoc, ipsa petra ecclesiae,*
   Canente, culpam diluit.

   Surgamus ergo strenue:
   Gallus jacentes excitat
   Et somnolentos increpat;
20 *Gallus negantes arguit.*

   Gallo canente spes redit,
   Aegris salus refunditur,
   Mucro latronis conditur,
   Lapsis fides revertitur.

25 *Jesu, labantes respice*
   Et nos videndo corrige;
   Si respicis, labes cadunt
   Fletuque culpa solvitur.

   Tu lux refulge sensibus
30 *Mentisque somnum discute;*
   Te nostra vox primum sonet
   Et vota solvamus tibi.

on the sun to shine. When the cock crows, the sun wakes up and frees the skies from darkness; when he crows, all night-prowlers leave the path of sin. At cock-crow the sailor again finds courage, the angry seas become calm. It was at cock-crow that the very Rock of the Church washed away his sin.

Let us then rise promptly. The cock awakes the sleepers, loudly upbraids the sleepy and puts to shame the lie-abed. When he crows, hope comes back, a feeling of health returns to the sick, the robber sheathes his sword and trust makes its way back to sinful souls. Look on us, Jesus, when we waver and with a glance correct us; for if You look on us, our sins fall from us and our tears wash away our guilt. Be a shining light to our minds and drive sloth away from our souls. May our tongue's first act be to praise You; so may we discharge our promises to You.

errantes corrigit. Denique respexit Petrum et statim error abscessit; pulsa est negatio, secuta confessio. (W.)

Use. From October to Lent, Advent and the Christmas season excepted.

1. *conditor;* our Lord, as in *2, 3* and *53, 11.* Because of the Arians, St Ambrose naturally stressed the divinity of the Second Person.

3. *Temporum* are the fixed periods of day and night, and the fixed seasons; *tempora* the fixed times at which they change.

4. *fastidium;* probably boredom (from monotony), which would result if there were no such changes.

5. *nocturna lux,* like a lamp at night, i.e. serving as a guide, and giving heart to the traveller; cf. *viantem solatur* in the prose passage.

6. *Nox = vigilia;* cf. *processum noctis* in the prose passage.

7. *Praeco diei;* cf. *13,* 1 and 'The cock that is trumpet to the morn', *Hamlet* I, 1, 150. *Praeco diei* is the subject, *nocturna . . . segregans* being in apposition.

8. *jubar,* ray. This non-Ambrosian line is due to a misunderstanding of *lucifer* in line 9.

5–8 in the original are: *Praeco diei jam sonat,/noctis profundae pervigil,/nocturna lux viantibus/a nocte noctem segregans.* This the revisers ruined by inverting the order of the lines and by omitting the most expressive line. The Church, because of its unbroken public prayer, may also be said to be *noctis profundae pervigil.*

9. *Hoc.* Here and in lines 11, 13 and 15 (and in the prose passage) supply *canente* from 16. The rhetorical repetition of *hoc, gallus* and *tu, te* and *tibi* is Ambrosian; cf. W.

excitatus lucifer, the sun is awakened. In the hymns *lucifer* sometimes means the sun, sometimes the day-star as in *16,* 9.

10. *polum* (Greek πόλος), vault of heaven. *Polus =* (1) pivot, especially of the earth, 'the pole'; (2) the vault of heaven, as here and in *nec lucidus aethra/siderea polus,* Virg. *Aen.* III, 585–6; and (3) heaven, as in *2, 12.*

11. *erronum (erro, -nis),* vagabond, wanderer, night-prowler—a word introduced into the Roman Breviary in 1632 and adopted by many editors for the MSS *errorum;* cf. W and Trench. Ambrose is apparently referring to roving demons *(errorum)* not to evil men *(erronum),* the connection being between the physical darkness, *caligine,* and the powers

of spiritual darkness, whose leader is Lucifer. *Errorum* is the equivalent of the *vagantes daemones* of Prudentius, *Cath.* I, 37 and both passed into the 'extravagant and erring spirit' of *Hamlet* I, 1, 154.

cohors. All MSS have *chorus;* cf. *quodam nequitiarum choro circumfusum,* Ambr. *de Cain,* I, 14, for a similar use by Ambrose.

15. *ipsa.* Thus in very many MSS, in Breviaries and in St Augustine's quotation above. In the prose passage it is *ipse*—a favourite usage of Ambrose; cf. *aurora totus, 12, 29,* note.

16. *diluit,* washed away; cf. Mt. 26, 75.

18. *excitat.* Note the climax: *excitat,* awakens, *increpat,* rebukes, *arguit,* denounces, convicts of.

The cock is a symbol of the Resurrection; *inde est quod omnes credimus/illo quietis tempore/quo gallus exsultans canit/Christum redisse ex inferis,* Prud. *Cath.* I, 65–8.

It is also an emblem of the preacher: *quia et gallus iste, quem pro exprimenda boni praedicatoris specie in locutione sua Dominus assumit, cum jam edere cantus parat, prius alas excutit, et semetipsum feriens vigilantiorem reddit; . . . prius se per sublimia facta excutiant (sc. praedicatores), et tunc ad bene vivendum alios sollicitos reddant.* Greg. *Regula Pastoralis,* III, 40.

For a medieval summary of the symbolism of the cock, cf. *Oxford Medieval,* 97.

22. *refunditur,* pours, flows back. *Fundere* and its compounds are favourite words of Ambrose.

25. *labantes (labare, 1),* tottering, wavering, about to fall. For the whole verse cf. *Et continuo . . . cantavit gallus. Et conversus Dominus respexit Petrum . . . Et egressus Petrus flevit amare,* Lk. 22, 60–2.

27. *labes,* stains, sins. Probably *lapsus* (cf. *26,* 11) should be read. MSS vary between *lapsos, lapsi* and *lapso.* For *lapsus* in Ambrose's prose, cf. lessons 5 and 6, Fifth Sunday after Pentecost.

29. *lux refulge,* blaze forth as a light. It seems more likely that *lux* is predicative here rather than the vocative which the Breviary punctuation suggests. Our Lord, as *lux,* is likened to the cock which is a *nocturna lux viantibus. Sensibus,* thoughts, mind—the usual meaning in the hymns.

30. *somnum,* slothful negligence, lethargy; *mentis,* cf. *3,* 6; *discute,* dispel; cf. *13,* 13.

31. *primum;* cf. *3,* 5.

32. *vota solvamus,* discharge our vows (by singing God's praises). In *12,* 9, *votis =* prayers.

Hymn 12
Monday Lauds

Splendor paternae gloriae,
De luce lucem proferens,
Lux lucis et fons luminis,
Diem dies illuminans,

5 *Verusque sol illabere,*
Micans nitore perpeti,
Jubarque sancti Spiritus
Infunde nostris sensibus.

Votis vocemus et Patrem—
10 *Patrem potentis gratiae,*
Patrem perennis gloriae—
Culpam releget lubricam,

Confirmet actus strenuos,
Dentes retundat invidi,
15 *Casus secundet asperos,*
Agenda recte dirigat,

Mentem gubernet et regat,
Sit pura nobis castitas,
Fides calore ferveat,
20 *Fraudis venena nesciat.*

Christusque nobis sit cibus
Potusque noster sit fides;
Laeti bibamus sobriam
Profusionem Spiritus.

25 *Laetus dies hic transeat,*
Pudor sit ut diluculum,
Fides velut meridies,
Crepusculum mens nesciat.

Aurora lucem provehit,
30 *Cum luce nobis prodeat*
In Patre totus Filius,
Et totus in Verbo Pater.

Radiance of the Father's splendour that brings light from light, come as the light of light, the source of light, the day that gives the days their light and the true sun that shines with everlasting brilliance. Direct on to our thoughts the light of the holy Spirit.

In our prayers let us also ask the Father—the Father of might and grace, the Father of eternal glory—to banish sin and its attractions, to inspire us to ready action, to hold in check the devil's malice, to turn our ill-fortune to good, to give right direction to our way of life, to control and rule our soul and to grant that our purity remain untarnished and that our faith, like a fire, burn bright and hot and be unaffected by the poison of false doctrine.

Let Christ be our soul's food, and faith its drink. Let us joyfully accept from the Spirit the drink that soberly overpowers our soul. Let this day pass for us in joy. Let our purity be clear as the dawn, our faith strong like the noonday sun, and our soul unacquainted with the twilight regions of sin. Dawn is bringing the light of day. With the light may there come to us the whole Son in the Father, and the whole Father in the Son.

Notes on Hymn 12

Author. St Ambrose. St Augustine alludes to the hymn, without claiming Ambrose as the author: *Veni Mediolanum ad Ambrosium episcopum ... cujus tunc eloquia strenue ministrabant adipem frumenti tui et laetitiam olei et sobriam vini ebrietatem populo tuo,* Conf. V, xiii, 23. St Fulgentius, however, twice quotes the hymn as Ambrose's: *Beatus Ambrosius in hymno matutino splendorem paternae gloriae Filium pronuntiat;* and, *hujus nos postulare gratiam ebrietatis edocuit, dum dicimus: Laeti bibamus sobriam/ebrietatem Spiritus,* Ep. XIV, 10 and 42.

1. *splendor;* cf. *qui cum sit splendor gloriae ejus,* Heb. 1, 3; *candor est lucis aeternae,* Wisdom 7, 26; also *2, 17,* note. The sun represents the Father, and the rays issuing from it the procession of the Son. But there is no inequality of nature, for the Son also is *verus sol;* and cf. *11,* 1, note.

4. *diem.* All early MSS have *dies dierum illuminans, dierum* being genitive after *illuminans*—a common construction with participles used as adjectives. *Diem* is due to a misreading of the contracted form of *dierum,* and the revisers changed the order to *diem dies.*

5. *verusque.* The *que* seems to indicate that lines 3 and 4 are a predicate along with *verus sol,* W. Come as the light . . . , the day . . . , the true sun; cf. *11,* 29. Some translate as vocatives, but *verus* cannot be a vocative, and *que* needs explanation. *Illabere* (imp. of *illabor,* 3, dep.), steal into—of the quiet coming of dawn and of God's grace. Cf. *animis illabere nostris,* Aeneas to Apollo, Virg. *Aen.* III, 89.

6. *perpeti* (from *perpes*), lasting, continual, everlasting; cf. *88,* 2.

7. *jubar;* cf. *11,* 8 and, for the Holy Ghost, *lucis tuae radium, 67,* 3.

8. *sensibus;* cf. *11,* 29.

9. *votis,* prayers; cf. *11,* 32; *et,* also, i.e. as well as the Son. *Patrem;* for repetitions in Ambrose, cf. *11,* 9, note.

10. *potentis.* Breviaries invert the original order of 10 and 11, and so obscure the sense. The Father should be first addressed as *perennis gloriae,* as a continuation of *paternae gloriae* in 1, and then be invoked as *potentis gratiae,* of which the following lines are an elaboration.

12. *releget,* banish. The subjunctives from here to 20 are indirect jussive, dependent on *vocemus.* Let us call on the Father . . . to banish . . . to strengthen. The subjunctives from 21 to 28 are precative. *Lubricam;* cf. *2,* 21, note. Its position at the end of the line brings out the idea of danger.

13. *confirmet,* encourage, animate, strengthen. It replaces a favourite word of Ambrose, *informet,* i.e. may He shape our actions into energy, W, *strenuos* being predicative.

14. *dentes,* envy, ill-will, rage; *retundat,* blunt, restrain, check; *invidi,* referring to the devil. *Invidia autem diaboli mors introivit in orbem terrarum,* Wisdom 2, 24.

15. *casus,* misfortunes. *Casus;* lit. a falling, and so (1) error, moral fall, etc.; and (2) occurrence, event, accident, chance, misfortune.

secundet, change for the better, turn to good; cf. *eventus . . . secundet,* Virg. *Georg.* IV, 397.

20. *fraudis venena,* the poison of wrong doctrine. *Fides* is the subject of *nesciat.*

21–22. The divinity of Christ and the faith of the Christian are the two main subjects of the hymn. The Arians denied the divinity of our Lord and replaced the nourishment of faith by *fraudis venena. Christus* therefore must mean the divinity of Christ, the foundation of all our other beliefs (the Eucharist included). To accept that is to be fed (*cibus*) and not to be poisoned. But we accept it by faith, which is likened to a drink and explained by *laeti bibamus . . . Spiritus.* Indeed *potus,* in late Latin, could mean a drinking-cup; cf. Lewis and Short.

Commentators who see in 21 and 22, singly or together, an exclusive reference to the Eucharist, surely break Ambrose's order of thought and insert a new idea. Chandler's version 'And Christ shall be our daily food,/Our daily drink His precious blood' in effect substitutes *sanguis* for *fides.* It was St Thomas, not St Ambrose, who wrote *Caro cibus, sanguis potus, 74,* 40.

24. *profusionem,* the revisers' substitute for *ebrietatem*—probably the most inept emendation in the whole history of literature. The supposed metrical reason for the change is non-existent for, as W notes, 'the accent falls on the *i* and tends to lengthen

Notes continued on p. 22

it'. Moreover the Fathers, and not least Ambrose, used *ebrietas, inebriare*, etc. as meaning fill, stimulate, give soul to, etc; cf. Newman's 'Blood of Christ, fill all my veins', *inebria me*. In any case *profusio* is not a Pentecostal term; cf. *19, 4*, note.

The juxtaposition *sobriam ebrietatem* was suggested by the account of the first Pentecost. This influenced St Paul's *nolite inebriari vino . . . sed implemini Spiritu sancto*, Eph. 5, 18, which is the immediate inspiration of these lines. For *inebriari*, cf. *109, 50*.

25. *laetus*, predicative or the equivalent of an adverb; joyfully, full of joy.

26. *diluculum*, dawn; probably referring to the →

Hymn 13
Tuesday Lauds

Ales diei nuntius
Lucem propinquam praecinit;
Nos excitator mentium
Jam Christus ad vitam vocat.

5 *'Auferte', clamat, 'lectulos,*
Aegro sopore desides,
Castique, recti ac sobrii
Vigilate, jam sum proximus'.

Jesum ciamus vocibus
10 *Flentes, precantes, sobrii;*
Intenta supplicatio
Dormire cor mundum vetat.

Tu Christe somnum discute,
Tu rumpe noctis vincula,
15 *Tu solve peccatum vetus*
Novumque lumen ingere.

The bird that heralds the day is crowing his warning that dawn is near; now Christ the soul's awakener, is calling us to life. 'Away', He cries, 'with your beds, you lazy slaves of enervating sleep. Be pure, upright, sober and alert, for now I am near.' Repentant, sincere and recollected, let us with voice upraised summon Jesus to our aid. Prayer that is sincere keeps the pure soul from slumbering. Lord Christ, dispel our sloth; break the bonds of night; unfasten the sins of the past and give us the grace of new light.

purity of the first rays of dawn. Cf. line 18.

27. *fides* delights in the heat and light of noon; cf. line 19.

28. *crepusculum*, dusk, used here for darkness.

29–30. *Lucem* and *cum luce* seem to refer to the light of day. Original: *Aurora cursus provehit,/*

Aurora totus prodeat,/In Patre etc., where the symbolism of dawn is clear. The natural dawn is coming; may *the* Dawn come—and in His entirety. *Totus* is explained by the next two lines and by *ego in Patre et Pater in me est*, John 14, 10. The hymn ends where it began—with the divinity of Christ.

Notes on Hymn 13

Author. Prudentius, 348–413.

This and the next two hymns have been formed from two long poems by the Spaniard Aurelius Prudentius Clemens, namely from the first two of his collection of twelve poems known as the *Cathemerinon* or Hymns for the Day. Prudentius did not write them for use in church but as a way of consecrating his talents, in his declining years, to the praise of God and the explanation of the faith. That he had talents to consecrate is clear even to a casual reader of his poetry, and he has been called the 'Virgil and Horace of the Christians'. (Cf. also *54*, introduction.)

As a poet St Ambrose is inferior to Prudentius. The fame of Ambrose came partly from finding an occasion for the singing of hymns and from seeing the possibilities of iambic verse. But to Prudentius hymns were much more than occasional poetry. He worked with a variety of metres, and for his subject-matter turned to incidents of the Old Testament and to the mysteries of the New, in the *Cathemerinon* and the *Apotheosis*, to allegory in the *Psychomachia* and to the lives of the martyrs in the *Peristephanon*. The two pervading influences in his work were the example of his contemporary, St Ambrose, and the Christian art of the Catacombs.

His success with these subjects varies. At his lowest he is yet a skilful versifier; at his best he is capable of sustaining noble epic verse and inspired lyrics. His influence on the Middle Ages was profound, and at the Renaissance Erasmus singled him out as *unum inter Christianos vere facundum poetam*.

The *Cathemerinon* represents, perhaps, the best of his work, and from these lyrics were early formed some

hymns for public use, of which *13*, *14* and *15* are three. One or two others are also in the Breviary and still more were formed for the Mozarabic rite. The well-known *Corde natus ex parentis ante mundi exordium* is formed from the ninth poem of this work. (Cf. *55*, introduction.)

This hymn is from the first in the *Cathemerinon*, that *Ad galli cantum*, and comprises lines 1–8, 81–4 and 97–100 of the original.

1. *ales*, the winged messenger of the day; cf. *11*, 7, note.

2. *propinquam*, approaching; cf. *dies appropinquavit*, Rom. 13, 12. *Praecinit*, is announcing; and contrast 4, 12.

3. *excitator*, awakener; cf. *excitatus*, *11*, 9 and *ut a somno excitem eum*, John 11, 11, of the sleep of death.

6. *desides*, slothful—vocative of *deses*. W and most editors read *aegros, soporos, desides*, accusatives with *lectulos*; couches that are for the sick. . . .

7. *castique*; cf. Rom. 13, 13, in introduction to Lauds, above.

8. *vigilate*; cf. Rom. 13, 11, Mt. 24, 42, etc. and *sobrii estote et vigilate*, 1 Peter 5, 8.

9. *ciamus* (*cio*, 4, a less common form of *cieo*, 2), let us summon. The prayer 'must be aloud, *vocibus*, accompanied by repentance, *flentes*, it must come from the heart, *precantes*, apart from all worldly excitement, *sobrii*', W.

11. *intenta*, eager, earnest, intent, and not, as Prudentius says a few lines later, from a mind *vanis vagantem somniis*.

13. *discute*, dispel; cf. *11*, 30. *Somnus, nox* and *lumen* are of the spirit.

Hymn 14
Wednesday Lauds

Nox et tenebrae et nubila,
Confusa mundi et turbida—
Lux intrat, albescit polus,
Christus venit—discedite.

5 Caligo terrae scinditur
Percussa solis spiculo,
Rebusque jam color redit
Vultu nitentis sideris.

Te Christe solum novimus,
10 Te mente pura et simplici
Flendo et canendo quaesumus;
Intende nostris sensibus.

Sunt multa fucis illita,
Quae luce purgentur tua;
15 Tu vera lux caelestium
Vultu sereno illumina.

Night and darkness and clouds, all the world's confusion and disorder, be gone—light is piercing through; the sky is becoming bright; Christ is coming. The darkness which envelops the earth is torn open, pierced by the sun's ray; colour returns to the world at a glance from the shining sun.

You alone, Christ, do we know. To You, in purity and simplicity of soul, with tears and song, we make this prayer: Turn Your attention to our thoughts. Many things in our way of thought and life are coloured with the rouge of insincerity; may the light of Your grace restore them their true colour. True light of the heavens, shed Your bright light on us.

Hymn 15
Thursday Lauds

Lux ecce surgit aurea,
Pallens facessat caecitas,
Quae nosmet in praeceps diu
Errore traxit devio.

5 Haec lux serenum conferat
Purosque nos praestet sibi;
Nihil loquamur subdolum,
Volvamus obscurum nihil.

Sic tota decurrat dies,
10 Ne lingua mendax, ne manus
Oculive peccent lubrici,
Ne noxa corpus inquinet.

Behold the golden light of the sun is appearing. Let colourless darkness depart that has for a long time made us stray from the right path and brought us into danger. May this Light bring us fair weather and present us unharmed before Him. May no deceitful words come from our lips, no evil thoughts occupy our minds. So may the whole day run to its close that neither our tongue, ever ready to lie, nor our hand nor our restless eyes commit sin, nor any guilt defile our body. For God

Notes on Hymn 14

Author. Prudentius; cf. *13*.

This is a cento from the second hymn in the *Cathemerinon*, called *Hymnus matutinus*, and comprises lines 1–8, 48, 49, 52, 57, 59, 60, 67 and 68 of the original.

1. *Nox . . . turbida*, vocatives with *discedite* of line 4; *nubila*, clouds; neut. plur. of adj. used as a noun. The imagery of this verse is primarily spiritual, but in the next verse it is physical.

3. *lux . . . venit*. Three urgent reasons why night etc. should depart. *Albescit*, grows bright; cf. *ut primum albescere lumen/vidit*, Virg. *Aen.* IV, 586, 7; *polus*, cf. *11*, 10, note.

4. *discedite*; a common formula bidding the uninitiated or the unclean to depart from a sacrifice; cf. *Discede, Christus hic est*, Prud. *Cath.* VI, 145. Cf. also the use of *procul* in *procul o procul este, profani*, Virg. *Aen.* VI, 258 and *Procul o procul vagantium/Portenta somniorum*, Prud. *Cath.* VI, 137; cf. also *29*, 5.

5. *caligo*; cf. *6*, 1, note on *contegit*.

6. *spiculo*, ray; cf. *17*, 3.

7. *rebusque*; cf. *6*, 1, note on *nox atra*.

8. *vultu*; i.e. at the appearance of; *sideris*, star (of the day), i.e. the sun; cf. *3*, 10.

9. *te* with *novimus; te* in 10 with *quaesumus (dis-*cimus in Prudentius), which is followed by *intende* in direct speech instead of by *ut*. The sense of Prudentius has inevitably undergone some change by the putting together of disconnected lines.

10. *mente*; cf. *3, 6*.

11. *flendo, canendo*, instead of present participles—a classical construction which became very common in late Latin; cf. *44*, 12.

12. *intende*, sc. *animum*, with dative, as here, or with *in* or *ad* and the accusative; direct one's mind to, and so, help, bring help. *Sensibus*; cf. *11*, 29.

13. *fucis. Fucus*, a sea-weed from which a red dye was made; hence, red colour, 'rouge'; figuratively, pretence, disguise, deceit.

15. *vera lux caelestium*. Prudentius has *rex eoi sideris* and breviaries, other than the Roman, *lux eoi sideris. Eous* in Virgil and elsewhere means the rising sun, the dawn. If the revisers meant to put the same thought into different words, *caelestium* is a supposed equivalent of *eoi sideris*. Editors, by printing *caelestium* with a capital, presumably see a reference to the citizens of heaven.

16. *sereno*, bright. So Ambrose says that Easter day is *sancto serenus lumine*.

Notes on Hymn 15

Author. Prudentius; cf. *13*. Like *14* it is from *Cathemerinon* II, and comprises lines 25, 93, 94, 96–108 of the original.

2. *pallens*, colourless; for the idea, cf. *6*, 1–2 and *14*, 7. *Facessat (facesso*, 3) to do eagerly, despatch; intrans., as here, to go away, depart. The variant *fatiscat* means fail, give way. *Caecitas*, the equivalent of *caligo, tenebrae*.

3. *praeceps*, danger, destruction; used as a noun governed by *in*.

4. *devio* seems to be used actively, i.e. which leads from the right path; otherwise *errore devio*= devious tracks.

5. *lux*, i.e. Christ, because of *sibi* in the next line. *Serenum*, as a noun, fair weather; metaphorically, contentment, peace of soul; cf. also *14*, 16, note.

If *serenum* is taken here to mean bright, *puros* may suggest the result in us, namely freedom from sin.

6. *praestet*, make us, present us.

7. *subdolum*, deceitful.

8. *volvamus*, turn over in our minds; *obscurum nihil*, no dark thought; cf. *obscura* in *6*, 11.

9. *Sic* is explained by *ne* in 10; *decurrat*, run to its close.

10. *mendax*, prone to lie; for lines 10 and 11 cf. *18*, 5–8.

11. *lubrici*, in its literal sense of easily moving, cf. *2*, 21, note; for its position at the end of the line, cf. *12*, 12, note.

12. *ne* may be like *ne* in 10 or may be dependent on *ne peccent*. Cf. James 3, 6. *Noxa*, guilt; *3*, 14.

D

Speculator astat desuper,
Qui nos diebus omnibus
15 Actusque nostros prospicit
A luce prima in vesperum.

in heaven is like a watchman. He sees us and our actions from first light of the day until evening.

Hymn 16
Friday Lauds

Aeterna caeli gloria,
Beata spes mortalium,
Summi tonantis unice
Castaeque proles virginis,

5 Da dexteram surgentibus,
Exsurgat et mens sobria,
Flagrans et in laudem Dei
Grates rependat debitas.

Ortus refulget lucifer
10 Praeitque solem nuntius,
Cadunt tenebrae noctium;
Lux sancta nos illuminet,

Manensque nostris sensibus
Noctem repellat saeculi
15 Omnique fine temporis
Purgata servet pectora.

Quaesita jam primum fides
In corde radices agat,
Secunda spes congaudeat,
20 Qua major exstat caritas.

Eternal glory of heaven and blessed hope of earth, only Son of the most high Thunderer and Son of a pure Virgin, stretch out Your right hand to us as we rise. Let our soul rise up recollected and, zealous in God's praise, return Him due thanks. The morning star shines clear in the sky and announces the coming of the day; the darkness of night disappears. Do You, holy light, shine on us, dwell in our thoughts, drive out the night of sin and keep our hearts purified from all that would make the night return. First let the faith we have won take root in our hearts; let the second virtue, hope, rejoice with faith. But charity is greater than either.

Hymn 17
Saturday Lauds

Aurora jam spargit polum,
Terris dies illabitur,
Lucis resultat spiculum;
Discedat omne lubricum.

Now is the dawn spreading its light over the heavens, day is gradually coming to the earth; light's rays are mounting in the sky. Darkness and its attendant dangers, depart. Let the night's

13. *speculator*, watchman. *Quanto magis Deus, auctor omnium et speculator omnium, a quo nullum potest esse secretum ... interest ... cogitationibus nostris,* Min. Felix, *Octavius*, 32, 9. For the general idea cf. Ps. 138, 7–12 and *49*, *5*.

Notes on Hymn 16

Author. Unknown; perhaps of the fifth century.

It is an alphabetical hymn, though this device is not preserved in any breviary. As the Latin alphabet has only twenty-three letters, letters were sometimes doubled in these compositions. C was used for lines 3 and 4 of this hymn.

1. The hymn is addressed to Christ as God and man; line 3 further explains line 1, and line 4 explains line 2; cf. the opening of *46*.

3. *summi tonantis unice*, only-begotten of the most high (and) thundering, i.e. omnipotent, Father. Original: *celsitonantis unice*, i.e. of Him who thunders on high; cf. Ps. 17, 14 and Ps. 28.

6. *sobria*, thoughtful, recollected; cf. *13*, 9, note.

9. *Ortus;* in the original *Hortus* to make up the alphabet. H could be so used according to the vulgar pronunciation of Latin; cf. *insidias Arrius* (sc. *dicebat*) *hinsidias*, Catullus, 84, 2. *Lucifer*, the morning star; cf. *11*, 9, note.

10. *Praeitque.* MSS have *sparsamque*, which must be wrong. Some word with I is necessary; hence the suggestions *ipsamque*, Mone, and *jactamque*, W.

11. *cadunt*, fall away, disappear; cf. *labes cadunt*, *11*, 27. Original: *Kadit* (for *cadit*) *caligo noctium.*

13. *manensque, sc. lux sancta* of 12. The Breviary's full-stop at the end of 12 is not helpful.

15. *omnique.* Original: *omnique fine diei*, from any close of day, W; i.e. from any spiritual darkness or night. This gives a connection between *noctem* and *diei* and is like the related metaphors of *12*, 28 and *21*, 5–6. The revisers' *temporis* destroys this meaning and gives a text without any meaning. Probably the best thing is to interpret *temporis* as if it were *diei*. B's 'till the end of time' does not seem satisfactory.

17. *quaesita*, sought (and found), i.e. won; cf. *110*, 23.

18. *in corde.* Original, *radicet altis sensibus* (where *sensibus* may be a mistake for *mentibus*), take root in our inmost, deepest, thoughts (or, soul).

19. *secunda* answers *primum* of 17. *Congaudeat* is probably derived from *congaudet veritati* of 1 Cor. 13, 6, though there it is charity that rejoices.

20. *qua* must, in effect, refer to *fides* and *spes;* cf. 1 Cor. 13, 13. *Exstat=est*, is the reading of some MSS. But the form *Tunc major exstet caritas* is more frequent and better. An indicative seems out of place here.

Notes on Hymn 17

Author. Unknown, of date between the fourth and sixth century.

The hymn may be interpreted as a summary and completion of the previous Lauds hymns. Its first verse sums up the imagery of dawn and light and the second that of sin and darkness. The third verse looks forward to the dawn of the morning which will have no evening, and asks that it may be to us the beginning of an eternity of light. It is not without difficulties, especially in its revised form.

1. *Aurora.* The spiritual application is uppermost in this verse. *Aurora, dies* and *lucis spiculum* refer to

Notes continued on p. 28

5 *Phantasma noctis exsulet,*
  Mentis reatus corruat,
  Quidquid tenebris horridum
  Nox attulit culpae, cadat;

  Ut mane, quod nos ultimum
10 *Hic deprecamur cernui,*
  Cum luce nobis effluat,
  Hoc dum canore concrepat.

spectres be banished, the soul's guilt fall away and the soul be freed from whatever dark and horrible sin night has brought. Thus may the morning for which, as the last of all mornings, we here make humble supplication, issue forth with (eternal) light, as it resounds with this song of praise.

Notes continued from p. 27

Christ; *polum*, according to one commentator, may be thought of as referring to man's intellect or soul, and *terris* to mankind in general. For the whole verse cf. *14*, 1–8. *Spargit*; understand *lumine* or *rubore* or some such word; cf. *spargit lumine*, Lucr. II, 144, and *spargebat lumine*, Virg. *Aen.* IV, 584. *Polum*; cf. *11*, 10.

  2. *illabitur*; cf. *12*, 5, note.

  3. *resultat*, climb, mount, and, of Christ, is be-

coming clear; contrast *resultet*, *81*, 2. *Spiculum*, point, dart, ray, cf. *14*, 6, and, of Christ, character, outline, idea.

  4. *discedat*; cf. *discedite*, *14*, 4; *lubricum*; cf. *2*, 21 and *12*, 12.

  5. *phantasma*; sing. for plur.; cf. *noctium phantasmata*, *29*, 6. It may be understood of any form of spiritual deception; cf. *14*, 7–8 and 13–14. *Exsulet*, the revisers' substitute for *decidat*, is little more than a →

---

3. The Little Hours

From earliest times Christians were exhorted to pray during the day and, in particular, to sanctify the beginnings of the civil divisions of the day. This was a private devotion, with no fixed prayers. In later years the monks made prayer at these times of the day part of the public prayer, and in this way Terce, Sext and None received their present status. Prime, however, was of purely monastic origin, and was sometimes called, by the monks to whose laziness it put an end, *altera matutina*— not without some emphasis, probably, on *altera*. This too eventually passed into the Church's Office.

One of the pious customs connected with these Hours was the recalling of the Passion. At Prime our Lord, in the custody of the High Priest, offered Himself to the Father to undergo the crucifixion. At Terce—*Jam surgit hora tertia/qua Christus ascendit crucem*, says St Ambrose in one of his hymns. At Sext began the three hours on the cross, and there was darkness over the whole earth from then until, after pardoning the Good Thief, He died at None. →

synonym for *discedat* of line 4. The original is better. As the devils fell before the risen Christ, so may temptations of the devil fall away (*decidat*) at the rising of the Dawn. *Decidat*; cf. *21, 6*.

6. *mentis reatus*, i.e. the sense of guilt and liability for punishment, while the next two lines are about the stain of sin.

7. *quidquid. Culpae* is genitive after *quidquid*, which is further qualified by *tenebris horridum*; may whatever dark and horrible (*tenebris horridum*) sin (*culpae*) night has brought . . . , W. But B orders as: *quidquid horridum culpae nox attulit, tenebris cadat* (i.e. vanish with the darkness). B's seems rather unnatural and awkward. *Cadat*, cf. *16, 11*, note.

9–12. A difficult verse and 'very obscure', B. The following points should be noted. *Mane* has been taken as an adverb and as a noun; if as a noun, as referring to the last day of the week or to the Last Day. *Ultimum* has been taken as an adjective and adverbially (i.e. as the last Lauds of the week). *Hoc* has been interpreted as nominative with *mane* and ablative with *canore*. If the latter, 'this song' refers to praise of the Blessed Trinity, of which the doxology that follows is an example.

The original is:

> Ut mane illud ultimum,
> Quod praestolamur cernui,
> In lucem nobis effluat,
> Dum hoc tenore concrepat.

Here *Quod . . . cernui* might well be parenthetical, like *2, 31*. The first and third lines are clearly about the Last Day. The last line is difficult. Some MSS have *vox canora*, and many have *concrepet*. *Canore* of the Breviary does not seem to be in any MSS. *Hoc* could be ablative, but could easily be nominative in contrast with *illud*—the last day of the week with the Last Day.

B gives this anonymous translation from the Hymnal Noted:

> So that last morning, dread and great,
> Which we with trembling hope await,
> With blessed light for us shall glow,
> Who chant the song we sang below.

Though there is no direct reference to these events in the hymns, it is easy to make one. Prime is a public morning offering—an offering of the next step on the way to our death. At Sext the light and heat of the noonday sun may remind us, by contrast, of the darkness of Good Friday. At None, mindful of the Good Thief and of our Lord's death, we pray that our death may be a holy one. But if we look at their direct meaning, the prayer of Prime is the negative one that we be kept from harm while that of Terce is the positive one that the grace of the Holy Ghost will enable us to grow in love and zeal. At Sext we pray that God will temper the heat of temptation and at None we ask for the gift of perseverance.

The hymns of the Little Hours, both by their position and by their subject-matter, give a special character to this part of the Office. There is much matter for reflection in these short hymns and they are valuable as prayers outside the Office. Few prayers for the grace of perseverance are as beautiful as the *Rerum Deus tenax vigor* of None.

Hymn 18
Prime

Jam lucis orto sidere
Deum precemur supplices,
Ut in diurnis actibus
Nos servet a nocentibus.

5 Linguam refraenans temperet
Ne litis horror insonet;
Visum fovendo contegat
Ne vanitates hauriat.

Sint pura cordis intima,
10 Absistat et vecordia,
Carnis terat superbiam
Potus cibique parcitas;

Ut, cum dies abscesserit
Noctemque sors reduxerit,
15 Mundi per abstinentiam
Ipsi canamus gloriam.

Now that the sun has risen, let us as suppliants ask of God that in today's acts He preserve us from all that may hurt us. May He check and restrain our tongue so that it be not an instrument of discord and strife. May He screen and protect our eyes so that they do not drink in vanities. May our inmost soul be pure and the folly of impurity find in us no place; may moderation in food and drink wear down the body's pride so that when day has gone and night, as God planned, has returned, we may be found free from sin through our self-restraint and thus sing praise to Him.

Hymn 19
Terce

Nunc sancte nobis Spiritus,
Unum Patri cum Filio,
Dignare promptus ingeri
Nostro refusus pectori.

5 Os, lingua, mens, sensus, vigor
Confessionem personent;
Flammescat igne caritas,
Accendat ardor proximos.

Holy Spirit, one with the Father and the Son, deign at this hour to come down on us without delay and pour out Your graces over our soul. Let mouth, tongue, soul, thought and strength make Your praise resound. Let our love be set aflame by the fire of Your love and its heat in turn enkindle love in our neighbours.

Author. ?St Ambrose. This and the next two hymns are certainly by the same author. If it was not Ambrose, it must have been a very good imitator, for 'the prosody, the vocabulary, the concentrated force of the language, the thoughts, the theology, are all' Ambrosian. W.

1. *Nunc,* i.e. at the hour when the Holy Ghost came on the first Pentecost.

2. *unum Patri,* one (in essence) with the Father and the Son. *Patri;* the dative expressing relationship, as it →

Notes on Hymn 18

Author. Unknown. It is thought to be of the fifth or early sixth century, but some place it in the eighth century.

1. *lucis . . . sidere,* the sun; cf. *3,* 10.

3. *diurnis actibus,* the acts of the (coming) day; cf. *3, 7.*

4. *nocentibus,* from all that may hurt us; cf. *ut noxia cuncta submoveas,* Collect Seventh Sunday after Pentecost.

5. *refraenans;* cf. *non refraenans linguam suam,* James 1, 26; cf. also Ps. 33, 14 and 1 Peter 3, 10.

6. *ne litis;* that grating strife (harsh note of strife, Blakeney) may not resound on it (the tongue), W. *Insonet* understands the ablative *lingua,* as in *calamis insonare,* Ov. Met. 11, 161. *Litis;* cf. *unde bella et lites in vobis?,* James 4, 1.

7. *Fovendo,* instead of a present participle, cf. *14,* 11, and balancing *refraenans. Fovere* combines the ideas of nursing (*nutrit et fovet eam,* Eph. 5, 29) and of keeping warm (*tamquam si nutrix foveat filios suos,* 1 Thess. 2, 7) and so gives the more general meaning of protect.

8. *vanitatis;* cf. *averte oculos meos ne videant vanitatem,* Ps. 118, 37.

10. *absistat* = *absit; vecordia,* folly, madness, as often in Latin of O.T. The folly here is that of impurity; cf. *vecordem juvenem,* Prov. 7, 7.

12. *parcitas,* abstinence from, sparing use of.

14. *sors,* time in its allotted, ordered course; divine providence, ordinance.

15. *mundi;* probably an adjective like *mundum* in *13,* 12; but it could be genitive after *abstinentiam,* as in *ceterarum rerum abstinentiam,* Num. 30, 14. For the latter meaning, cf. James 1, 27; for the general meaning cf. 1 Thess. 4, 3 and 5, 22.

16. *ipsi;* either nominative, W, or dative, to Him, B.

Notes on Hymn 19

Continued from the foot of p. 30

does after *affinis, similis,* etc.

3. *promptus,* without delay; *ingeri,* practically equivalent to *infundi.*

4. *refusus;* a participle, but expressing the result of *ingeri,* namely the gradual working of the Spirit through us and 'taking possession' of our whole being, as explained in the next line.

Effundere is the scriptural word for the coming of the Spirit, Acts. 2, 33 and 10, 45; *diffundere* is the word used in Romans 5, 5 (cf. note on line 7) for the charity of God being poured over our souls. *Refundere* here is the equivalent of *diffundere,* but also hinting at the *sobria ebrietas* which results; cf. *11,* 22 and *12,* 24.

5. *Os . . . vigor.* Mouth, tongue, soul, thought and strength. The line refers to the effects of the first Pentecost and then to those desired by the singers— *os, lingua* being the external signs and results, *mens,* *sensus* the complete transformation of soul and mind, and *vigor* the zeal of the apostolate. It is the result of *refusus,* just as the ringing announcement of salvation (*personent*) by the Apostles followed on the coming of the Spirit.

6. *confessionem,* declaration of faith or thanks, cf. *5, 7,* note; thus the Apostles were *loquentes . . . magnalia Dei,* Acts 2, 11. For the accusative after *sonare* and its compounds, cf. *11,* 31 and *90,* 12—the former certainly and the latter almost certainly by Ambrose.

7. *igne;* cf. *linguae tamquam ignis,* Acts 2, 3; *fons vivus, ignis, caritas, 64,* 7. *Caritas:* cf. *Caritas Dei diffusa est in cordibus nostris per Spiritum sanctum, qui datus est nobis,* Rom. 5, 5.

8. *ardor,* in good sense; cf. *3,* 6, note.

'And love light up our mortal frame
Till others catch the living flame' (Newman).

Hymn 20
Sext

Rector potens, verax Deus,
Qui temperas rerum vices,
Splendore mane illuminas
Et ignibus meridiem,

5 *Exstingue flammas litium,*
Aufer calorem noxium,
Confer salutem corporum
Veramque pacem cordium.

Mighty ruler, faithful God, who arranges the successive changes in nature, giving bright light to the morning sun and burning heat at noon, put out the flames of strife and take away the heat of passion; grant us health of body and to our souls true peace.

Hymn 21
None

Rerum Deus tenax vigor,
Immotus in te permanens,
Lucis diurnae tempora
Successibus determinans,

5 *Largire lumen vespere,*
Quo vita nusquam decidat,
Sed praemium mortis sacrae
Perennis instet gloria.

Lord God, the strength which daily upholds all creation, in Yourself remaining unchanged and yet determining in due order the successive changes of the light of day; grant us light in the evening so that life may not decay at any point of its activity but everlasting glory be the immediate reward of a happy death.

---

4. VESPERS AND COMPLINE

The next division of the day after None is the hour when the sun sets, the evening star, *Vesper,* appears and the lamps are lit, *Lucernarium.* It thus marks the beginning of the first watch of the night, and the prayer of Vespers was once classed as a night one—St Benedict being the first to place it among the *day* Hours. This change was one of classification and did not change the essential character of Vespers. Lauds, after all, is a morning hour and yet, historically

Notes on Hymn 20

Author. See *19*.

1. *verax,* God of truth, faithful to His promises; cf. *Deus verax est,* John 3, 33. The promises are (1) such as that made to Noe in Gen. 8, 22 for the physical order and (2) those of help and grace in the spiritual order.

2. *rerum vices,* i.e. changes from morning to noon, from summer to winter; cf. *qui certis vicibus tempora dividis,* Prud. *Cath.* V, 2 and *11,* 3.

3. *splendore.* Original: *splendore mane instruis*—a poor line, where a short unaccented syllable is left unelided before a vowel. The revisers' *illuminas* suits *splendore* better than *ignibus.* W suggested *splendore mane qui instruis,* which is better, for *instruis* suits both nouns. *Mane;* noun as in *17,* 9 and *22,* 5.

5. *Exstingue.* The idea of *temperas* is applied in this verse to the life of grace in which, as in the physical order, God *is verax. Flammas litium;* suggested by *ignibus* above and *homo iracundus incendit litem,* Ecclus. 28, 11. *Litium;* cf. *litis, 18,* 6.

6. *calorem,* heat of passion; for *calor* in a good sense, cf. *12, 19.*

Notes on Hymn 21

Author. See *19*.

1. *Rerum . . . vigor.* O God who art the strength which sustains all creation from day to day, W; or, though with less emphasis on the element of time, 'O Strength and Stay upholding all creation'. *Rerum* after *tenax* like Horace's *tenacem propositi.*

2. *immotus,* unchanged, unmoved; cf. Ps. 101, 27; James 1, 17. *In te permanens;* cf. *(sapientia) in se permanens,* Wisdom 7, 27.

3. *tempora;* cf. *11,* 3.

4. *successibus,* progress, succession of time. Ambrose often uses this word in the plural.

5. *vespere,* adv., in the evening. Original: *largire clarum vespere,* where *vespere* is a noun as in *22,* 5.

6. *quo,* whereby, introducing *decidat* and *instet. Nusquam,* at no point in its activity. W. *Decidat,* fail, decay; cf. *17,* 5, note, and *vespere decidat* Ps. 89, 6.

Lumen and *vita* are thought of spiritually, but *vespere* seems to be taken in its ordinary meaning. B and the translation mentioned above interpret *vespere* of the evening of life, but this is implicit in the next lines.

7. *praemium . . . sacrae;* predicate after *instet,* as the reward of . . . .

8. *instet,* follow hard upon, immediately; cf. *7,* 14.

---

and chorally, it is the conclusion of the night office. In the same way Vespers could be considered either as the prayer which finished the day or the one which began the night. This point is of some importance in relation to the question of the authorship of these hymns. All of them, save that for Saturday, are attributed to St Gregory, a follower of St Benedict; and scholars, looking for signs of the author, have looked to see whether the author thought of Vespers as a day or night hour. The hymns which are said to have been written for Vespers as a *night* office are considered by some as variations on the lines of St Ambrose:

> *Ut cum profunda clauserit*
> *Diem caligo noctium,*
> *Fides tenebras nesciat*
> *Et nox fide reluceat.*

With such hymns they contrast those of the Breviary, and say that the latter make no mention of night or nightly rest. And yet perhaps a case could be made out that these hymns too, but in their own way, are variations on the same theme; cf. e.g. *22, 7; 23, 13; 25, 13.*

But, if they are variations, they are only so as far as the main subject of creation will allow. The opening verses give, in order, the work of each day of creation and, by their use at Vespers, suggest God looking back over each day's work and 'seeing that it was good'. Man also, as the Psalmist says, goes out each day to his work and labours until the evening, Ps. 103, 23. But when he comes to examine the day's work and sees its imperfections, he cannot, as God did, delight in it; moreover night and darkness, symbols of sin, are near at hand. He therefore turns to God for forgiveness and

---

Hymn 22

Sunday Vespers

Lucis creator optime,
Lucem dierum proferens,
Primordiis lucis novae
Mundi parans originem,

5 *Qui mane junctum vesperi*
Diem vocari praecipis,
Illabitur tetrum chaos;
Audi preces cum fletibus,

Ne mens gravata crimine
10 *Vitae sit exsul munere,*
Dum nil perenne cogitat
Seseque culpis illigat.

Caeleste pulset ostium,
Vitale tollat praemium;
15 *Vitemus omne noxium,*
Purgemus omne pessimum.

Beneficent creator of light, You brought forth the light of day, furnished the world at its start with the first beginnings of new light and commanded that morning joined to night be called Day. Night with all its fears is now coming down on us; hear our prayers and heed our sorrow that our soul does not become weighed down with sin and deprived of the grace of life while it has no thought for things eternal and entangles itself with sin after sin. Grant that the soul knock on heaven's gate and that it win life as its prize. May we avoid all sin and atone the evil we have done.

---

for help, and his aspirations are put into words in the last part of the hymns—this part being in each case a spiritual application of the opening verses. All are composed to the same pattern. The first seven or eight lines (in 25, the first twelve lines) are an address to God, with the main verb, an imperative, coming in the second part. Thus the Vesper hymns for Sunday to Friday form a series quite unlike those for Matins or Lauds, as they have unity of author and subject as well as unity of purpose and style.

The Saturday hymn is a short one in which we praise the Blessed Trinity and pray, that when the working week of our life is over, we may be privileged to sing God's praises for ever. It is not by the writer of the other Vesper hymns. Whether it displaced one of the series and, if so, what happened to the one displaced, are unsolved questions.

The name, Compline, is due to St Benedict, but the thing preceded him. It is of later origin than Vespers and began as monastic night prayer. St Benedict, in his Rule, gave it the form which we know, except that the Church has added to the non-monastic form the *Nunc dimittis*. The hymn suggests that some light still remained, *lucis ante terminum*, when Compline was said.

Notes on Hymn 22

Author. ?St Gregory. The common opinion favours St Gregory, but certainty on the point seems impossible at present.

As the Latin text of Genesis was the inspiration of the writer, the relevant part of Genesis 1, with the verse divisions, is given with each hymn.

In principio creavit Deus caelum et terram. 2. Terra autem erat inanis et vacua, et tenebrae erant super faciem abyssi; et Spiritus Dei ferebatur super aquas. 3. Dixitque Deus: Fiat lux. Et facta est lux. 4. Et vidit Deus lucem quod esset bona. Et divisit lucem a tenebris. 5. Appellavitque lucem diem, et tenebras noctem. Factumque est vespere et mane, dies unus. Gen. 1, 1-5.

2. *proferens;* cf. 12, 2.

3. *primordiis,* first beginning, because the luminaries were not yet created; *lucis,* i.e. the *lux* of Gen. 1, 3; *novae,* newly created

5. *mane* and *vesperi* (dative), nouns as in Gen. 1, 5; cf. 17, 9 and 20, 3.

7. *illabitur tetrum chaos,* the frightening and confused darkness (of night) is descending (*illabitur;* cf.

12, 5; 17, 2). *Tetrum* from *teter, tra, trum,* foul, loathsome, shocking. *Chaos:* (1) the state of the world in Gen. 1, 1; and cf. Ovid. *Met.* I, 5-7; (2) an image of night (frequently in Prudentius) and of hell; Virgil, *Aen.* IV, 510 personifies Chaos as one of the gods of the lower regions. Here, with *tetrum, chaos* signifies the darkness and terrors of the night; (3) the spiritual *chaos,* as suggested in lines 9-12.

8. *preces,* as given in the following lines—the purpose in 9-12 and the prayer in 13-16. *Preces cum fletibus;* cf. 13, 9-10.

10. *exsul,* deprived of the gift, *munere. Exsul* may govern an ablative, as here and in 2, 29, or a genitive.

11. *nil ... cogitat,* has no thought of eternity; 'thoughts and schemes of sense and time', Newman.

12. *illigat,* entangles; *funibus peccatorum suorum constringitur (impius),* Prov. 5, 22.

13. *pulset* (and *tollat*), sc. *mens.*

14. *vitale,* instead of *vitae* and answering *vitae* of line 10; *tollat,* may it receive, take, win.

Hymn 23
Monday Vespers

Immense caeli conditor,
Qui, mixta ne confunderent,
Aquae fluenta dividens
Caelum dedisti limitem,

5 *Firmans locum caelestibus*
  Simulque terrae rivulis,
  Ut unda flammas temperet,
  Terrae solum ne dissipent;

  Infunde nunc, piissime,
10 *Donum perennis gratiae,*
  Fraudis novae ne casibus
  Nos error atterat vetus.

  Lucem fides adaugeat;
  Sic luminis jubar ferat;
15 *Haec vana cuncta proterat;*
  Hanc falsa nulla comprimant.

Mighty creator of the firmament, You divided the streams of water that, if left together, would cause confusion, and made the firmament the line of division. You fixed a place for the waters of heaven and one for those of earth so that the burning heat, tempered by water, should not scorch the face of the earth. Pour into us now, most gracious God, a stream of never-failing grace that the wrong of past days may not be repeated and wear our virtue away. Let faith increase the light in our souls. O that faith would bring its radiant light. May faith trample under foot all vanity and let nothing that is false suppress our faith.

Hymn 24
Tuesday Vespers

Telluris alme conditor,
Mundi solum qui separans,
Pulsis aquae molestiis,
Terram dedisti immobilem.

5 *Ut germen aptum proferens,*
  Fulvis decora floribus,
  Fecunda fructu sisteret
  Pastumque gratum redderet,

Loving maker of the world who, by separating the soil of the earth and banishing the troublesome waters, set the land firm so that it may produce seeds of different kinds, be beautiful and bright with flowers, abundant in fruit and yield desirable food—cleanse with the

Notes on Hymn 23

Author. As *22.*

6. *Dixit quoque Deus: Fiat firmamentum in medio aquarum, et dividat aquas ab aquis.* 7. *Et fecit Deus firmamentum, divisitque aquas quae erant sub firmamento ab his quae erant super firmamentum. Et factum est ita.* 8. *Vocavitque Deus firmamentum caelum.* Gen. 1, 6–8.

1. *caeli,* i.e. the firmament, here and in line 4; cf. Gen. 1, 8. The firmament or vault of heaven is thought of as solid.

2. *mixta,* nominative, and referring to *fluenta* in line 3; *confunderent,* make confusion, W or, perhaps, mingle together, B. It does not seem to be the equivalent of *vastarent,* as has been suggested.

3. *fluenta; fluentum,* neut., river, stream.

4. *dedisti,* sc. *fluentis; limitem,* as their boundary, line of division.

5. *firmans,* establishing; suggested by *firmamentum* and texts such as *verbo Domini caeli firmati sunt,* Ps. 32, 6; *caelestibus,* sc. *rivulis* of next line, and = *quae erant super firmamentum,* Gen. 1, 7.

6. *terrae,* answering *caelestibus; quae erant sub firmamento,* Gen. 1, 7.

7. *flammas = aestus,* burning heat. It describes a creative act preparatory to the creation of the dry land, *24,* and of the sun, *25.*

8. *terrae solum,* the soil, face, of the earth; cf. *24,* 2. *Dissipent,* sc. *flammae,* destroy, waste. A better reading is *dissipet,* sc. *unda;* for such a use of *dissipare,* cf. *neque erit deinceps diluvium dissipans terram,* Gen. 9, 11.

11–12. Various interpretations are given. *Vetus error* has been taken as the devil and *fraudis* to *casibus* as the fresh disguises under which he appears; or *vetus error* as Adam's sin which is repeated in subsequent sins; or *vetus error* as some former personal sin which would beguile us in new ways. The basic idea of 11–16 seems to be that, by God's grace, our soul should be firmly established, a spiritual firmament dividing the lower and the higher desires.

Casibus, cf. *12, 15,* note, is purposely contrasted with the single *error,* but its meaning is hard to determine; and cf. *perpetuae mortis eripuisti casibus,* Collect of Second Sunday after Easter.

Atterat, wear away, exhaust; contrast *24, 12.*

13. *lucem fides;* cf. *12, 27.*

14. *sic;* O that it may .... Each of lines 13–16 is a new petition, and the *sic* does not connect this line with the preceding.

15. *haec* and *hanc,* of 16, seem to refer to the same thing, namely to *fides,* B; but W refers *haec* to *lux* and *hanc* to *fides. Proterat,* trample down, defeat. MSS vary between *terreat* and *conterat.*

16. *falsa nulla,* perhaps the devil and his emissaries, W; others take it as plural for singular, no falsehood.

Notes on Hymn 24

Author. As *22.*

9. *Dixit vero Deus: Congregentur aquae, quae sub caelo sunt, in locum unum, et appareat arida. Et factum est ita.* 10. *Et vocavit Deus aridam Terram, congregationesque aquarum appellavit Maria. Et vidit Deus quod esset bonum.* 11. *Et ait: Germinet terra herbam virentem et faaientem semen, et lignum pomiferum faciens fructum juxta genus suum, cujus semen in semetipso sit super terram. Et factum est ita.* 12. *Et protulit terra herbam virentem, et facientem semen juxta genus suum, lignumque faciens fructum, et habens unumquodque sementem secundum speciem suam. Et vidit Deus quod esset bonum.* Gen. 1, 9–12.

1. *Telluris,* the earth—apparently as the planet; but commentators differ greatly.

2. *mundi,* the earth as an ordered thing of beauty; cf. *8,* 2, note; *solum,* earth, i.e. the soil which, after the action described in line 3, became *arida,* Gen. 1, 9, and was called *terra, ib.* 10.

3. *aquae molestiis;* troublesome waters, W, or troubling waters, Newman, rather than troubled waters, B. The waters are troublesome if dry land and its vegetation are wanted. It is explained by *separans* of 2 (or the much better *eruens* of the original) and by 5–8.

4. *terram,* i.e. *aridam;* cf. note on line 2. *Dedisti*

Mentis perustae vulnera
10 *Munda virore gratiae,*
Ut facta fletu diluat
Motusque pravos atterat.

Jussis tuis obtemperet,
Nullis malis approximet,
15 *Bonis repleri gaudeat*
Et mortis ictum nesciat.

freshness of Your grace the wounds of our sin-parched soul that it may wash away in sorrow its evil deeds and wear down the power sin has to attract us. Let our soul obey Your commands and keep far away from anything evil; let it be thankful that it is filled with good and may it never be struck down by death.

Hymn 25
Wednesday Vespers

Caeli Deus sanctissime,
Qui lucidas mundi plagas
Candore pingis igneo,
Augens decoro lumine,

5 *Quarto die qui, flammeam*
Dum solis accendis rotam,
Lunae ministras ordinem
Vagosque cursus siderum,

Ut noctibus vel lumini
10 *Diremptionis terminum,*
Primordiis et mensium
Signum dares notissimum,

Expelle noctem cordium,
Absterge sordes mentium,
15 *Resolve culpae vinculum,*
Everte moles criminum.

Most holy God of the firmament, You adorn with resplendent radiance the lightsome regions of the universe and enhance them with beauty and light. When You kindled the sun's fiery disk, You also gave the moon her orbit and the stars a speedy course, thus marking a line of separation for night and day and affording an easily recognisable sign for the beginnings of the month. Drive out the darkness from our hearts, wash away defilement from our souls, loosen the chain of our guilt and remove completely the heavy burden of our sins.

immobilem, set the earth to be immovable; cf. *dedisti* in *23,* 4.

5. *aptum;* the poet's way of describing the different kinds of flower and tree, Gen. 1, 11. Note the climax *germen, flos, fructus* and *pastus.* The subject of 5–8 is *terra.*

6. *fulvis,* bright ('brilliant-hued', Newman), without its usual reference to yellow, golden, etc. Note the alliteration here and in 7 and 11.

7. *sisteret,* be, become.

8. *pastum,* normally food for beasts, but here for men as well.

9. *perustae (perurere,* burn through and through), burnt up, parched. W thinks it a reference to *arida* of Gen. 1, 9 'but with exaggerated emphasis'.

10. *virore,* by the freshness, power, vigour, of grace; cf. *virentem* of Gen. 1, 11. There are various MSS readings here.

11. *diluat,* wash away its (evil) deeds, *facta.* The subject of *diluat* and of all verbs to the end is *mens,* from *mentis* of 9.

12. *atterat,* wear away, weaken; cf. *23,* 12.

14. *approximet,* draw near, approach; a late Latin verb for *appropinquare,* twice used in the Vulgate; *non approximabunt* and *non approximant,* Ps. 31, 6 and 9.

15. *repleri,* sc. *se;* cf. *6,* 16, note.

16. *ictum,* stroke of (eternal) death, or, of sin. Original: *actum,* action of eternal death; cf. *actu, 2,* 29.

Notes on Hymn 25

Author. As *22.*

14. *Dixit autem Deus: Fiant luminaria in firmamento caeli, et dividant diem ac noctem, et sint in signa, et tempora, et dies, et annos,* 15 *ut luceant in firmamento caeli, et illuminent terram. Et factum est ita.* 16. *Fecitque Deus duo luminaria magna: luminare majus, ut praeesset diei, et luminare minus, ut praeesset nocti, et stellas.* 17. *Et posuit eas in firmamento caeli, ut lucerent super terram,* 18. *et praeessent diei ac nocti, et dividerent lucem ac tenebras.* Gen. 1, 14–18.

1. *Caeli,* i.e. the firmament, as in Gen. 1, 14 and in *23,* 1.

2. *lucidas . . . plagas,* lightsome regions of the universe, B. Distinguish *plăga,* region, from *plāga,* blow. Original: *lucidum centrum poli,* i.e. the shining centre of the sky, the place, that is, where the sun is fixed.

3. *pingis,* pick out, adorn, embellish, as in Virg. *Ecl.* II, 50 and *Aen.* IX, 582, and *polum . . . pinxisse,* Prud. *Cath.* V, 6.

4. *augens . . . lumine,* enhancing with beauteous light, W; cf. *lunae pars ignibus aucta,* Lucr. V, 722. The sense of *augens* being unusual, there are many MSS variants.

5. *flammeam,* the fiery disk, *rotam,* of the sun; cf. Lucr. V, 433 and 565.

6. Original: *Solis rotam constituens,* and MSS vary in the next line between *ministrans* (which means no verb in the relative clause) and *ministras.* The re-

visers introduced *dum* and a new verb, *accendis,* in 6 and chose *ministras* as the verb for *qui* in 7.

7. *lunae . . . ordinem,* did appoint a path, orbit, for the moon. The better reading probably is *lunae ministra(n)s ordini/vagos recursus siderum.* This implies that the stars return at their appointed time and wait upon their mistress, the moon.

8. *vagos,* rapid, speeding, not, as B, wandering; cf. *pede vago,* Catull. 63, 86 and, of the sun, *qua vagus oceanas exit et intrat aquas,* line 4 of *Tempora florigero rutilant distincta sereno,* cf. intro. to *61.*

9. *vel,* and; cf. *2, 3.*

10. *diremptionis terminum,* a line of separation; a limit. *Terminum,* acc. after *dares;* likewise *signum* in 12.

11. *primordiis,* the beginnings (of the months); cf. *22,* 3.

12. *signum;* cf. *signa,* Gen. 1, 14; *notissimum,* conspicuous, easily recognisable. The rising and setting of the sun are meant in 9 and 10, the changes of the moon in 11.

13. *Expelle;* original: *Illumina cor hominum.* A direct mention of light, such as *illumina,* is required, for this is the point to which the hymn about the creation of the luminaries has been leading.

16. *everte,* overturn, overthrow, destroy completely; *moles,* heap, load. Cf. *tanta mole curarum,* Tac. *Ann.* XII, 66, and *peccati mole gravide pressos* in a Mozarabic hymn.

Hymn 26
Thursday Vespers

Magnae Deus potentiae,
Qui fertili natos aqua
Partim relinquis gurgiti,
Partim levas in aera,

5 Demersa lymphis imprimens,
Subvecta caelis erigens,
Ut stirpe ab una prodita
Diversa repleant loca.

Largire cunctis servulis,
10 Quos mundat unda, sanguinis,
Nescire lapsus criminum
Nec ferre mortis taedium,

Ut culpa nullum deprimat,
Nullum efferat jactantia,
15 Elisa mens ne concidat,
Elata mens ne corruat.

Most powerful God, You leave in the deep some of those born of the fruitful water and raise others into the air. You set down in the sea those plunged in the waters and raise up to the heavens those that have been brought up from below and so, though they own one common element, they find their home in sea or sky. Grant to all Your servants whom water and blood have cleansed, not to suffer any fall into sin or to experience sin's loathsomeness. So may it come to pass that none be depressed by his guilt or exalted by pride, that the despondent does not lie defeated or the proud fall headlong to destruction.

Hymn 27
Friday Vespers

Hominis superne conditor,
Qui cuncta solus ordinans,
Humum jubes producere
Reptantis et ferae genus,

5 Et magna rerum corpora,
Dictu jubentis vivida,
Per temporum certas vices
Obtemperare servulis,

Repelle quod cupidinis
10 Ciente vi nos impetit,
Aut moribus se suggerit
Aut actibus se interserit.

Heavenly creator of mankind, to whom alone belongs the ordering of the universe, Your decree is that the earth bring forth reptiles and beasts and that the mighty animals, called into life by Your word, obey Your servants at the fixed changes of time and season. Drive away the violent assaults of passion which assail us, whether as an idea which seeks a place in our way of thought or as an act which finds

Notes on Hymn 26

Author. As *22.*

20. *Dixit etiam Deus: Producant aquae reptile animae viventis, et volatile super terram sub firmamento caeli.* 21. *Creavitque Deus cete grandia, et omnem animam viventem atque motabilem, quam produxerunt aquae in species suas, et omne volatile secundum genus suum.* 22. *Benedixitque eis, dicens: Crescite et multiplicamini, et replete aquas maris; avesque multiplicentur super terram.* Gen. 1, 20–2.

2. *Fertili,* because water is the common source of fishes and birds; *natos,* obj. of the two verbs through the restricting adverb *partim.* Original: *qui ex aquis ortum genus;* cf. Gen. 1, 20. *Relinquis* in 3 is a colourless substitute for *remittis.*

5–6. *Lymphis* and *caelis,* datives with *imprimens* and *erigens* (for the original *irrogans,* assigning, which better explains the dative), but also to be taken with *demersa* and *subvecta.* Line 5 explains line 3, and 6 explains 4.

7. *stirpe . . . prodita,* coming from, owning, one common element, cf. line 2; *prodita* from *prodire.*

10. *sanguinis* is probably the equivalent of *sanguis,* i.e. whom water *and* blood cleanse. For a case other than the nominative used, *metri gratia,* as a nominative, cf. *vincis sapore nectare* (for *nectar*), *52, 26.* For the sense, cf. *unda manat et cruor* (original: *sanguis, unda profluit*), *53, 20*—where a double subject has, as here, a singular verb. The reference here and in *53* is to John 19, 34. If *sanguinis* is a genitive, it excludes the idea of water, which one would expect to be mentioned in a hymn about things born of water.

11. *nescire;* cf. *nesciat, 12, 20; lapsus,* falls; cf. *11, 27,* note.

12. *taedium,* i.e. loathsomeness; or perhaps, malice.

13. *ut . . . nullum;* final, and equals *ne quemquam; deprimat,* submerge, and cf. *imprimens* in 5.

14. *efferat,* exalt; cf. *erigens* of 6.

15. *elisa,* the crushed, despondent, soul, and cf. *demersa* of 5; for *elisos* cf. *Dominus . . . erigit elisos,* Ps. 145, 8.

16. *elata;* cf. *subvecta* of 6; *ne in superbiam elatus, in judicium incidat diaboli,* 1 Tim. 3, 6.

Notes on Hymn 27

Author. As *22.*

24. *Dixit quoque Deus: Producat terra animam viventem in genere suo, jumenta et reptilia, et bestias terrae secundum species suas. Factumque est ita . . . 26. Et ait: Faciamus hominem ad imaginem et similitudinem nostram; et praesit piscibus maris, et volatilibus caeli, et bestiis, universaeque terrae, omnique reptili quod movetur in terra.* 27. *Et creavit Deus hominem ad imaginem suam.* . . . 28. *Benedixitque illis Deus, et ait: Crescite, et multiplicamini, et replete terram, et subjicite eam, et dominamini piscibus maris, et volatilibus caeli, et universis animantibus, quae moventur super terram.* Gen. 1, 24–8.

3. *humum;* referring to *terra* of Gen. 1, 24; *jubes* governs *producere* and *obtemperare* in 8.

4. *reptantis . . . genus,* the race of creeping things and that of beasts. *Reptantis* and *ferae,* sing. for plur., and = *reptilia* and *bestiae* of Genesis.

5. *magna . . . corpora,* (and orders) the mighty forms, *corpora,* of things, *rerum,* i.e. the *bestiarum* and *jumentorum* of Genesis, to be subject to . . . , *obtemperare.*

6. *dictu . . . vivida,* called into life, *vivida,* sc. *corpora,* at the bidding of your command, *dictu jubentis.* This use of the ablative of a verbal substantive is very rare; hence the suggested emendation *dicto.*

7. *per . . . vices,* through the determined changes of time and season. *Temporum,* cf. *11, 3; vices,* cf. *20, 2.* Original: *ut serviant per ordinem,* which also echoes *ordinans* of 2.

8. *servulis.* The diminutive here serves to emphasise man's insignificance in relation to God and his smallness in relation to the *magna rerum corpora;* cf. *89, 3,* note. Cf. Gen. 1, 26 and 28, and Ecclus. 17, 4.

9. *repelle.* Drive away from us whatever, *quod,* attacks, *impetit,* us . . . Or, according to others,

E

Da gaudiorum praemia,
Da gratiarum munera,
15 Dissolve litis vincula,
Astringe pacis foedera.

itself a place in our actions. Grant us the reward of heavenly joy and the gift of grace on earth. Unfasten the chain of strife and give us the peace you promised.

Hymn 28

Saturday Vespers

Jam sol recedit igneus,
Tu lux perennis Unitas,
Nostris, beata Trinitas,
Infunde lumen cordibus.

5 Te mane laudum carmine,
Te deprecamur vespere,
Digneris ut te supplices
Laudemus inter caelites.

The fiery sun is already going down. Do You, light unending, blessed Godhead, three in one, bring light to our hearts. We made humble prayer to You this morning when we sang Your praise, and we do so now at eventide. Graciously grant that we, Your suppliants, may praise You for ever in the company of Your saints.

Hymn 29

Compline

Te lucis ante terminum,
Rerum creator, poscimus,
Ut pro tua clementia
Sis praesul et custodia.

5 Procul recedant somnia
Et noctium phantasmata,
Hostemque nostrum comprime
Ne polluantur corpora.

Before the day is finished, creator of the world, we earnestly ask of You that, in keeping with Your mercy, You be our protector and defence. May no 'ill dreams', no 'nightly fears and fantasies' come near us. Hold in check our enemy that our bodies be not defiled.

cupidinis as genitive after *quod*, i.e. any evil desire.

10. *ciente vi*, i.e. violent, *vi*, emotion (or even, invitation, incitement) of passion, *cupidinis*. *Ciente*, cf. *13, 9*, note, carries the idea of calling, summoning. The idea of the force of passion is derived from the overpowering strength of the *magna rerum corpora*.

Original of 9–10: *Repelle a servis tuis/Quidquid per*

immunditiam. This fits into the construction of the next two lines, but unkindly confuses size and *immunditiam*.

16. *astringe*, draw closer; or perhaps, confirm, secure. *Pacis foedera*, bonds of peace, B; better, promise of peace; cf. *foedus pacis meae non movebitur*, Is. 54, 10, and *percutiam illis foedus pacis*, Ezech. 37, 26.

Notes on Hymn 28

Author. Unknown, though it has been ascribed to St Ambrose. The fact that it has not been received into the Ambrosian use, the constant use of rhyme and, one would think, its length seem to indicate that it was not written by St Ambrose. (For arguments on either side, cf. W, Julian and Daniel IV, 48). The fact that the hymn is so short has been the source of many interpolations in the MSS.

The unrevised text makes it clear that the hymn is addressed to the Blessed Trinity. The first verse is:

> *O lux beata Trinitas,*
> *Et principalis Unitas,*
> *Jam sol recedit igneus,*
> *Infunde lumen cordibus.*

5. A verb must be supplied out of *deprecamur*, such as worship; *laudum;* this word is 'at least on its way to becoming "Lauds" ', W.

6. *deprecamur*, pray, rather than pray that something be averted. In the revised text it governs *ut* in the next line.

8. *laudemus*, the continuation in eternity of the *laudum carmine*. It echoes the sentiments of the Saturday Lauds hymn, *17, 9–12*. The prayer of petition, *deprecamur*, will eventually give way to that of praise, *laudemus*.

Notes on Hymn 29

Author. Unknown, probably of the seventh century.

The hymn is in daily use at Compline, and displaced the older and longer *Christe qui lux es et dies*. This latter hymn is still in use among the Dominicans for Compline during Lent (cf. intro. to Lent).

3 *pro*, according to, by virtue of.

4. *praesul*, leader, protector, cf. *88, 2*.

5. *procul*, cf. *14, 4*, note. The body is thought of as a temple, in which uncleanness has no place.

6. *noctium phantasmata*, cf. *17, 5*, note.

7. *hostem*, the devil; the *invidi* of *12, 14* and the *diabolus* of 1 Peter 5, 8—the passage with which Compline begins.

5. THE ANTIPHONS OF THE BLESSED VIRGIN

As their name implies and their musical setting shows, these are not hymns. But they are often included in collections of hymns, and in any case two of them are metri-

---

Hymn 30

Alma Redemptoris mater, quae pervia caeli
Porta manes et stella maris, succurre cadenti,
Surgere qui curat, populo. Tu quae genuisti,
Natura mirante, tuum sanctum genitorem,
5 *Virgo prius ac posterius, Gabrielis ab ore*
Sumens illud 'Ave', peccatorum miserere.

Loving mother of the Redeemer, open door to heaven and star of the sea, come quickly to the aid of your people, fallen indeed but striving to stand again. To nature's astonishment you were the mother of your holy Creator without ceasing to be a virgin, and heard from Gabriel that greeting 'Hail'. Have pity on us sinners.

Hymn 31

Ave regina caelorum,
Ave domina angelorum;
Salve radix, salve porta,
Ex qua mundo lux est orta.

Hail, queen of heaven; hail, mistress of the angels; hail, root of Jesse; hail, the gate through which the Light rose over the earth.

5 *Gaude virgo gloriosa,*
Super omnes speciosa;
Vale, o valde decora
Et pro nobis Christum exora.

Rejoice, virgin most renowned and of unsurpassed beauty.

Farewell, lady most comely. Prevail upon Christ to pity us.

cal—though the original form of the *Ave Regina* seems not to have been metrical.

John of Parma, in 1249, mentions these four antiphons in a letter he sent to the Friars Minor about the use of the Breviary of Aymo, and Pius V made their recitation obligatory. (For further details, see histories of the Breviary etc.)

Notes on Hymn 30

Author. ?Hermann the Cripple (*Hermannus Contractus*). According to Raby, the evidence is insufficient to prove his authorship. Hermann (1013–54), a monk of Reichenau, was a cripple 'who passed a life of pain and trial, and though he could hardly raise his voice above a whisper, he was able to make his mark as a teacher and a man of universal learning' (Raby, p. 225). He was the composer of some sequences.

Metre. Hexameter.

Use. From the beginning of Advent to 2 February.

1. *pervia,* passable, affording a passage through and, here, with the further idea of affording entrance to all, accessible to all. *Fit porta Christi pervia/Referta plena gratia.* In these lines of a fragmentary hymn our Lady is styled *pervia* as the one through whom the Saviour came to men; here she is so called as the one through whom all men may approach God.

2. *manes;* i.e. is (the gate of heaven and the star of the sea). The *Alma* borrows many ideas from the *Ave maris stella, 94. Cadenti* with *populo,* fallen rather than falling.

3. *curat,* strives; *genuisti;* it is hard to re-produce in English the play on *genuisti* and *Genitorem. Genitor* is used of God the Father in *71,* 16 and of an earthly father in *110,* 13. Here the Son is *Genitor* as being Mary's, *tuum,* Creator.

Notes on Hymn 31

Author. Unknown. It is a metrical adaptation of the antiphon: *Ave regina caelorum, ave domina angelorum, salve radix sancta ex qua mundo lux est orta; gaude gloriosa, super omnes speciosa. Vale, valde decora, et pro nobis semper Christum exora.* (Cf. Daniel, II, 319.)

This antiphon seems to have been used in some places in the twelfth century as the antiphon for None on the feast of the Assumption. For this the titles given to our Lady are most appropriate, and the last lines, with their *Vale* and *exora,* peculiarly so. (Dom B. Capelle, in *Les Questions Liturgiques et Paroissiales,* March 1950, pp. 33–5). The Collect after the *Ave regina* suggests such a connection as, with *memoriam agimus* for *festivitatem praevenimus,* it is the same as the Post-Communion of the Vigil of the Assumption. The *Ave* was later put into its present form and used as one of the seasonal antiphons. It must be admitted that it is not so well suited to its season as the others are to theirs.

Metre. Trochaic dimeter, accentual, though the first two lines are dactylic.

Use. From Compline of 2 February to Wednesday in Holy Week.

3. *radix;* cf. *97,* 7, note. Our Lady is called *radix* as the representative of the house of Jesse and David from whom was born the Saviour, *the* Root of Jesse.

4. This line is closely connected in the antiphon with *radix,* which the added *porta* rather hides. The reference here is to Is. 11, 10 and in line 3 to Is. 11, 1 as well.

Porta creates something of a difficulty. Our Lady is usually called the gate of heaven, as in *30,* 2, and such an interpretation is often given of this line. But some prefer to think of our Lady here as the gate of morning, and perhaps that makes *porta* and *orta* go together better.

Hymn 32

Regina caeli laetare, alleluia,
Quia quem meruisti portare, alleluia,
Resurrexit sicut dixit, alleluia.
Ora pro nobis Deum, alleluia.

Queen of heaven rejoice, alleluia. The Son whom it was your privilege to bear, alleluia, has risen as He said, alleluia. Pray God for us, alleluia.

Hymn 33

Salve regina, mater misericordiae,
Vita, dulcedo et spes nostra, salve.
Ad te clamamus, exsules filii Hevae,
Ad te suspiramus gementes et flentes
5 In hac lacrimarum valle.
Eja ergo, advocata nostra,
Illos tuos misericordes oculos ad nos converte,
Et Jesum, benedictum fructum ventris tui,
Nobis post hoc exsilium ostende.
10 O clemens, o pia,
O dulcis virgo Maria.

Hail, queen and mother of mercy. Hail, our life, comfort and hope. Exiled sons of Eve, with loud voice we call upon you. As we journey in sorrow and lament through this 'Valley of Tears', we sigh and long for your help. Come then, our advocate, and turn those eyes of pity towards us now. When this time of exile is past, show us Jesus, the blessed fruit of your womb, gentle, loving and kind virgin Mary.

Notes on Hymn 32

Author. Unknown. It is thought to be an adaptation of the Christmas antiphon: *Maria Virgo semper laetare, quae meruisti Christum portare, caeli et terrae conditorem, quia de tuo utero protulisti mundi salvatorem*. According to the famous Jesuit hymnologist Blume, the earliest copy of the *Regina* is in an antiphonary in the Vatican Library, whose date is between 1170 and the early years of the next century and in which it occurs as an antiphon of the ordinary paschal Vespers.

At the present day it still figures in the Breviary as an antiphon, in the Little Office of our Lady.

It was used by the Franciscans as one of the seasonal antiphons as early as 1249. Its use as a substitute for the *Angelus* dates from Benedict XIV in 1743.

The supposed connection of the Regina with St Gregory is a myth. (Cf. Thurston, *Familiar Prayers*, pp. 146–51).

Use. During the Paschal season.

Notes on Hymn 33

Author. ?Hermann; cf. *30*.

As the author of the words seems also to have been the author of the music, Hermann could well have been its composer; but there is no direct, early evidence to prove this.

Another candidate is Peter, bishop of Compostella (died 1000); but there is apparently little justification for this.

The date of the early MSS shows that St Bernard cannot have been its author, and the state of the MSS proves that he is not responsible for adding the last two lines to a composition already in existence. All copies have these two lines.

The last suggested author, of any importance, is Aimar or Adhémar, bishop of Le Puy (died 1098). There are two or three independent sources which connect the *Salve* with him so that it is sometimes called the *antiphona de Podio,* the antiphon of Le Puy. But, once again, the evidence is inconclusive. (Cf. Thurston, *Familiar Prayers*, pp. 115 ff.)

This antiphon of our Lady has always been greatly loved. Many medieval translations of it are to be found, and many elaborations of it in Latin verse were written. One of these, ascribed to St Bonaventure, is printed in Daniel, II, 323–6. In modern times also, many prayers and hymns owe their inspiration to the *Salve*.

Use. From Trinity Sunday until Advent.

1. *mater* is an addition to the original *Salve, regina misericordiae*. Dreves, *Analecta Hymnica*, I. p. 319, thought it was added in the sixteenth century, but it is found in a *Horae* of about the year 1340, now in the Bodleian. As the *Salve* is entirely about our Lady's mercy, it is a pity to lose the title Queen of mercy or to delay the mention of mercy.

2. *vita*. Another version, which the Carthusians use, is *vitae dulcedo*.

5. *lacrimarum valle;* cf. Ps. 83, 7. The *Salve* describes our life as an exile and ourselves as exiles. This line implies that our exile is also a pilgrimage, for the Psalm in the Vulgate text is about the pilgrim who goes through the Valley of Tears to reach Jerusalem. St Peter addressed his readers as 'strangers and exiles', 1 Pet. 2, 11.

9. The version mentioned above adds *benignum* after *ostende*.

11. *virgo*, like *mater* in line 1, is an (early) addition and, like *mater*, tends to blur the picture. The children of Eve are sorrowful, the Child of Mary is blessed. The two mothers are mentioned by name only, and Mary receives at the end attributes which recall the opening titles. *Virgo* is an element foreign to the original unity.

II

HYMNS OF THE SEASONS

Christe, salus rerum, bone conditor atque redemptor . . .
Tu satis es nobis, et sine te nihil est. (Fortunatus.)

THE hymns of the days and the hours have as their foundation the praise of God as the creator, and not least as the creator of light. With this goes the praise of our Lord as the light of the world. The hymns of the seasons, however, reverse the process. Their first concern is with the mysteries of our redeemer, though at each season we are also reminded that the redeemer is likewise our creator. Just as we would not exist, unless God gave us our being and sustained us in being, so we would not enjoy the life of the sons of God unless our redeemer gave it to us and, with our co-operation, sustained us in it. *Deus qui humanae substantiae dignitatem mirabiliter condidisti et mirabilius reformasti.* . . . This is the constant theme of the hymns of this section, presented in a variety of forms, of which the most frequent is again the image of light.

Eternity is a completeness of being and of possessing such as we find hard even to imagine. It belongs to our Lord, as God, necessarily; and it belongs to Him as man as a result of the Resurrection and Ascension. But when He was on earth, He was subject to the conditions of time. The feasts of the seasons are the Church's way of relating the two opposites of time and eternity and of interpreting one in terms of the other.

Each year is a *complete* cycle in terms of time and may be considered as some sort of natural image of the completeness which is eternity. It is a *totum,* if not a *totum simul.* In like fashion a man's life, from birth to grave, is one complete thing—a sort of likeness of eternity as well as a preparation for it. Our Lord's mortal life was one such totality, and He came to His death when He had *completed* His life on earth—*tempus implens corporis,* as Fortunatus puts it, *53, 16.* The parts which went to its making, the mysteries, that is, of His birth, hidden life, public life and passion together with the Resurrection and Ascension, are divided among the seasons which make up one complete year, so that we may sanctify the years by re-living these

48

mysteries and thus prepare for eternity. Just as the natural seasons have their own functions and characteristics, so have the different mysteries of our Lord's life. For this reason it is necessary for us to think about each of them and, as mystery follows mystery in the Church's year, to approach our Lord in prayer and petition and so be enlightened. Nothing less would suffice; nothing more is necessary. *Tu satis es nobis et sine te nihil est.*

One thing remains to be mentioned. The important thing in these hymns is the mystery being celebrated, and the idea of the hours at which the hymns are used comes second, if indeed it comes at all. The ideas suggested by Vespers or Matins cannot be expected in a hymn which is used at both these Hours, as *44* is at the Epiphany. Nor can they be expected, apart from a happy accident, in centos which were made up purposely to be short hymns about the feast itself, of which *44* and *45* may serve as examples. However, if hymns are composed to be used at a given hour of a given feast, then mention ought to be found of the feast and of the hour. There is an example of this in the hymns of the Holy Family, *46–8*, and an altogether remarkable one in those of Corpus Christi, *71–3*.

I. ADVENT

Advent and Christmas may be likened to Lauds and Prime—Advent to the longing for the coming of the Day and to the first dawn of His coming and Christmas to the actual coming. So it may be more than a coincidence that the passage from Romans, which is the Scripture reading for ferial Lauds and the inspiration of its hymns, should also be the Scripture reading for the first Sunday of Advent and, together with the gospel of that day, namely Luke 21, 25–33, should be the inspiration of the Lauds hymn for Advent. Christ, the *lux* and *aurora* of the Lauds hymns, appears in the Advent ones as *Creator siderum, lux credentium* and *sidus novum*. He shines forth from heaven, *36, 4* and we ask Him to bring light to our souls, *35, 5.* His opposite at Lauds is *Nox et tenebrae et nubila, 14, 1*; the opposite is described in Advent as *obscura quaeque, 36, 2* and the very punishment of the deeds of darkness is described in terms of blackness, the *nigros turbines* of *35,* 13–14.

To greet the dawn we must be awake. So we must put aside spiritual sloth, as *36,* 1–8 tells us, if we would sincerely welcome our Lord. *Non enim dormientibus,* says St Ambrose, *divina beneficia, sed observantibus deferentur.* Likewise we must travel light, leaving earthly baggage behind—*cor caduca deserens, 35,* 7, and go out eagerly and with speed. *Nescit tarda molimina,* St Ambrose again reminds us, *sancti Spiritus gratia* (Ember Friday, Advent, lesson 1).

The advent of Christ is often said to be threefold; that of the past, in the flesh and in weakness, that of the present, in spirit and in power, and that of the future, in glory and in majesty. The three may be found in these hymns; the past in *intacta prodis victima, 34, 12* as well as in *35, 3–4* and *36, 7–10*; the present in *defende nos ab hostibus, 34, 20* and the future in *35, 9–12*.   →

Hymn 34

Creator alme siderum,
Aeterna lux credentium,
Jesu, redemptor omnium,
Intende votis supplicum.

5 *Qui, daemonis ne fraudibus*
Periret orbis, impetu
Amoris actus, languidi
Mundi medela factus es.

Commune qui mundi nefas
10 *Ut expiares, ad crucem*
E virginis sacrario
Intacta prodis victima.

Cujus potestas gloriae
Nomenque cum primum sonat,
15 *Et caelites et inferi*
Tremente curvantur genu.

Te deprecamur ultimae
Magnum diei judicem,
Armis supernae gratiae
20 *Defende nos ab hostibus.*

    Jesus, loving creator of the heavenly bodies, eternal light of the faithful and redeemer of all men, hear Your suppliants' prayers. For, urged on by generous love, You became a healing power to a sick world to prevent it being, through the devil's wiles, sick even to its death. You went forth as a sinless victim from Mary's sacred womb to die on the Cross to atone for the sin of all mankind. The might of Your glory and the reverence which the very mention of Your name inspire are so great that heaven and hell tremble and adore. We beseech You, our mighty judge at the last day, defend us with the arms of heavenly grace from our enemies.

Hymn 35

Verbum supernum prodiens
E Patris aeterni sinu,
Qui natus orbi subvenis,
Labente cursu temporis,

    Heavenly Word, proceeding from the eternal Father's bosom, by Your birth You came to man's help when time's course was

The Vesper hymn is built round the idea of *siderum,* the Matins one is a good summary of the chief ideas of Advent and the Lauds one is inspired by the message of the Baptist. They were greatly altered, to their disadvanatge, by the revisers, especially the Vesper one, of which only one line 'was left unaltered, and only twelve words of the original were retained', B.

Notes on Hymn 34

Author. Unknown. Perhaps of the seventh century.
Use. Vespers of Advent.

1. *siderum,* i.e. the heavenly bodies, including the sun and moon. 'The word strikes the keynote of the hymn, forecasting the light which Christ, Himself the eternal light, was to bring into the world', W.

7. *Languidi,* sick; cf. *curavit lauguidos eorum,* Mt. 14, 14, and *10, 6,* note. The revisers ruined this as a *hymn.* At 5-6 and 10-11, if the words are phrased properly, the music is ruined; if the music is given first place, the sense has gone.

8. *medela,* healing, cure; cf. *confer medelam languidis, 49, 12.*

9-12. The revisers changed the main idea from *sponsus* to *victima,* though *sponsus* is connected with the *motif* of the heavenly bodies through the *sol* of Ps. 18, 6. They also took out the reference to Vespers contained in the original line 9, *Vergente*

mundi vespere. This *mundi vespere* is balanced by *labente cursu temporis, 35,* 4, itself a variant of the original *cursu declivi temporis.*

11. *sacrario,* sacred womb; lit. shrine, sacristy, secret place.

13-14. *Cujus=cujusmodi;* supply *est. Nomenque;* the *que* joins 13 and 14, both leading to 15. In 15 the first *et,* strictly, should be *ut.*

15. *caelites,* especially with the capital normally printed in Breviaries, must mean those in heaven. But the original is *caelestia, terrestria,* where *caelestia* means the sun, moon, etc. thus keeping the unity of *siderum* of line 1. Some MSS have an extra verse after 16 which explains *caelestia* as: *Occasum sol custodiens,/Luna pallorem retinens,/Candor in astris relucens/Certos observans limites.* Revisers and editors are fond of changing stars into angels and saints; cf. e.g. *14, 15.*

Notes on Hymn 35

Author. Unknown. Variously dated as fifth, seventh, eighth and even eleventh century. The last one is certainly wrong.
Use. Matins of Advent.

1. *supernum,* heavenly; cf. *Ego de supernis sum,* John 8, 23. *Prodiens . . . sinu* of the eternal generation of the Son. In the original, the comma must come after *prodiens,* the line then being the equivalent of O

5 *Illumina nunc pectora*
  Tuoque amore concrema,
  Ut cor caduca deserens
  Caeli voluptas impleat;

  Ut, cum tribunal judicis
10 *Damnabit igni noxios*
  Et vox amica debitum
  Vocabit ad caelum pios,

  Non esca flammarum nigros
  Volvamur inter turbines,
15 *Vultu Dei sed compotes*
  Caeli fruamur gaudiis.

drawing to its close. Shine Your light into our hearts now and inflame them with Your love so that heavenly desire and joy may take possession of a heart emptied of earth's fleeting desires. And thus, when the Judge on His throne sentences sinners to hell and a welcoming voice calls the saints to the heaven promised them, may it be that we are not cast into the black whirlpool as food for the flames but that we be granted the vision of God and possess the joys of heaven.

Hymn 36

En clara vox redarguit
Obscura quaeque personans;
Procul fugentur somnia,
Ab alto Jesus promicat.

5 *Mens jam resurgat torpida*
  Non amplius jacens humi;
  Sidus refulget jam novum
  Ut tollat omne noxium.

  En Agnus ad nos mittitur
10 *Laxare gratis debitum;*
  Omnes simul cum lacrimis
  Precemur indulgentiam,

  Ut, cum secundo fulserit
  Metuque mundum cinxerit,
15 *Non pro reatu puniat*
  Sed nos pius tunc protegat.

The Baptist's message of rebuke rings loud and clear through all the world of darkness: Away with dreams of darkness. Jesus, the light, is shining in the sky. Let the slothful soul now arise and no longer lie earth-bound, for a new sun is now shining, Christ, Who will take away every sin. Behold the Lamb is sent to us to pay freely the debt we owe. Therefore let all of us together, with tears of sorrow, ask for His pardon so that when He comes in glory at the end of time and causes fear in all hearts, He will not then punish us, as our sins deserve, but in His pity be our protector.

---

2. THE CHRISTMAS SEASON

Jam lucis orto sidere we sing at Prime, and the same words could well be used to describe the feast of Christmas. The Light of the world has appeared, the Redeemer has come. The two themes of redemption and light are found right through the

Sapientia, quae ex ore Altissimi prodiisti; cf. *73*, 1, note.

4. *labente*, drawing to its close; not, as B, fleeting. It is a revision of *cursu declivi* (sloping) *temporis*, as if time were falling, setting, towards its evening—the Incarnation being thought of as coming in the evening of the world's history; cf. *34, 9*, note.

6. *concrema*, inflame, B and W. But W also suggests that it may mean 'and in thy love *burn* them *up*', which better suits the usual meaning of *con-*

cremare. The hymn is one long sentence, *illumina* and *concrema* being the main verbs.

11. *amica*, welcoming; *debitum*, due, because promised by Christ, to those who use His grace well, Mt. 25, 34.

13. *esca flammarum*, predicate after *volvamur*.

15. *compotes*, having gained, having been granted, the vision, *vultu*, of God. *Compotes* usually governs a genitive, as in *vultus compotes, 62, 15*, but here it has an ablative—classical, but rare.

Notes on Hymn 36

Author. Unknown. Probably of the fifth century.
Use. Lauds of Advent.

1. *clara.* If *vox* refers to the Baptist's message, *clara* means unambiguous, forthright, loud. But if *vox* be taken as referring to the person of the Baptist as in *Ego vox clamantis in deserto*, John 1, 23, *clara* would refer to a personal quality, e.g. the famous Baptist. The unrevised line *Vox clara ecce intonat* could easily mean that.

redarguit, contradicts, refutes, rebukes.

2. Some make *obscura quaeque* the object of *redarguit, personans* then meaning loudly resounding, filling the world with the message. Others interpret *redarguit* absolutely, *obscura quaeque* then being taken after *personans. Quaeque*, everything; cf. *2*, 13. *Personans*; cf. *19, 6*, note.

The rest of the hymn is the Baptist's message.

5-6. Some take *torpida* with *jacens*, prostrate in sloth; others take it with *mens*, the slothful soul, the soul that once was slothful.

7. *sidus* may refer to the *star* of Jacob, Num. 24, 17, to the *sun* of justice, Mal. 4, 2 or to the *stella splendida et matutina* of Apoc. 22, 16.

8. This line and the next refer to John 1, 29.

10. *laxare=solvere*, pay our debt. *Gratis*, freely; cf. *justificati gratis per gratiam ipsius*, Rom. 3, 24.

13. *secundo fulserit* in contrast with *refulget* of line 7. *Fulserit*, shine or, if the equivalent of *fulgens advenerit*, comes in glory.

14. *cinxerit*, girdles the world with fear. Unrevised: *mundumque horror cinxerit*.

15. *pro reatu*, in proportion to, according to, our guilt; cf. *29, 3*.

Christmas liturgy, and no full appreciation of these hymns is possible except against the background of the Missal as well as of the Breviary, for the hymns are rather reticent, especially on the theme of light.

The feast of the birth and the feast of the Epiphany stand at either end of this season; the former thinks more of God becoming *man* and the latter of the *God* who became man. The Epiphany is the inevitable climax of the season, not a pale reflection of the feast of the birth.

'And the Word was made flesh.' The Babe is the *lumen et splendor Patris, 37, 5,* the equal of the Father in glory, *37, 3* and the *rerum conditor, 37, 9.* Such is He who took our flesh, *37, 10–12,* and we praise Him *natalis ob diem tui, 37, 23.* Likewise in *38,* He is God the creator, *5, 8, 24* and *28;* but He is also man, newly-born and helpless, *4* and *23.* There is, however, a great difference in the approach of the writers of *37* and *38.* The heavenly Father and the divinity of the Son who became man are to the fore in *37,* while the Mother of the God-man and the helplessness of the new-born Child inspired Sedulius in *38.*   →

Hymn 37

Jesu redemptor omnium,
Quem lucis ante originem
Parem paternae gloriae
Pater supremus edidit.

5 *Tu lumen et splendor Patris,*
Tu spes perennis omnium,
Intende quas fundunt preces
Tui per orbem servuli.

Memento, rerum conditor,
10 *Nostri quod olim corporis*
Sacrata ab alvo virginis
Nascendo formam sumpseris.

Testatur hoc praesens dies,
Currens per anni circulum,
15 *Quod solus e sinu Patris*
Mundi salus adveneris.

Hunc astra, tellus, aequora,
Hunc omne quod caelo subest,
Salutis auctorem novae
20 *Novo salutat cantico.*

Et nos, beata quos sacri
Rigavit unda sanguinis,
Natalis ob diem tui
Hymni tributum solvimus.

Jesus, redeemer of all men, You were begotten by the mighty Father, before light was created, as His equal in glory. Do You, the Father's light and radiance and man's unfailing hope, accept the prayers of Your servants the world over. Remember, creator of the world, that long ago, at Your birth, You took our body's form from the Virgin's holy womb. The present day, as it comes round every year, bears witness to this—that You, the only-begotten of the Father, have come to be man's salvation. The heavens, the earth, the sea and every creature under heaven greet Him with a new song as the author of new salvation. And we too, cleansed by the redeeming stream of Your holy blood, make this gift of a hymn of praise on Your birthday.

'And we have seen his glory'—the glory of the divinity, *44, 1–2* and 8; *45, 8* and 13, and the glory of the miracles which pointed to the divinity for the Magi, *44, 5–8*, and at the beginning of the public life, *44, 9–16*.

Between Christmas and the Epiphany come the hymns for the Holy Innocents and the Holy Name. Of these, the *Salvete flores martyrum, 40,* is famous for its artless simplicity, and the hymn for the Holy Name is important enough in the history of hymns to have a special introduction.

Finally, in the Octave of the Epiphany comes the feast of the Holy Family with an office which betrays its modern origins at every turn. The hymn for Matins, *47,* is rather unlike a hymn and not too easy, but the hymns for Vespers and Lauds, *46* and *48*, are better suited to their purpose in form and words.

Notes on Hymn 37

Author. Unknown. Probably of the sixth century.

Use. At Vespers and Matins of Christmas. In some other Breviaries, St Ambrose's *Veni redemptor gentium* is used at Vespers.

3. *parem*, agreeing with *quem*; both accusative after *edidit*. *Paternae gloriae*; for this and *splendor Patris* in line 5, cf. *12, 1*, note.

9. *conditor*; cf. *resurgens conditor, 2, 3*. Original: *Memento, salutis auctor*—the writer wishing to stress the birth of the *Redeemer*, as the opening words show. *Salutis auctor; Decebat enim eum . . . auctorem salutis eorum per passionem consummare*, Heb. 2, 10. Cf. note on line 17.

10. *quod . . . sumpseris = te sumpsisse;* likewise *quod . . . adveneris* in 15–16 = *te advenisse. Olim*, once, formerly; or, perhaps, long ago, in contrast with the date of its annual celebration; cf. *prisca, 121, 15*.

11. *alvo*, from *alvus, -i*, fem; hence *sacrata*. Some make this line dependent on *nascendo*, others on *formam sumpseris;* the latter seems more probable.

12. *formam*, as in *formam servi accipiens*, Phil. 2, 7.

13. *Hoc* explained by *quod . . . adveneris*. Other MSS readings are *sic* or *hic;* if the latter, the present day (Christmas), recurring, *currens*, in the year's cycle, W.

15. *quod;* cf. note on 10. *Solus;* some take this to mean that only the Second Person became man, and others that it is a poetical version of *Et non est in alio aliquo salus*, Acts 4, 12.

17. *Hunc*, in the Breviary text, must refer to our Lord whom the stars, etc. greet as their creator. In the original it must refer to the *day* of Christmas— the witness of *praesens dies* in verse 4, creation praising the day in verse 5 and the redeemed, *Et nos*, in verse 6; so W.

The text seems always to have caused trouble, and the number of variants is large. The revisers made things no better by substituting here *salutis auctorem* (*novae*) from 9 in place of *auctoris adventu sui* (i.e. at the coming of their *creator*). Moreover the change from the second person, *adveneris*, to the third, *hunc*, and back to the second, *tui*, is awkward.

24 *hymni;* original, *hymnum novum*, probably with reference to the new canticle already mentioned in 20. The repetition of ideas here and in lines 3 and 5 is not found in the unrevised text.

Hymn 38

A solis ortus cardine
Ad usque terrae limitem,
Christum canamus principem,
Natum Maria virgine.

5 *Beatus auctor saeculi*
Servile corpus induit,
Ut carne carnem liberans,
Ne perderet quos condidit.

Castae parentis viscera
10 *Caelestis intrat gratia;*
Venter puellae bajulat
Secreta quae non noverat.

Domus pudici pectoris
Templum repente fit Dei;
15 *Intacta nesciens virum*
Concepit alvo Filium.

Enititur puerpera,
Quem Gabriel praedixerat,
Quem ventre matris gestiens
20 *Baptista clausum senserat.*

Foeno jacere pertulit,
Praesepe non abhorruit,
Et lacte modico pastus est
Per quem nec ales esurit.

25 *Gaudet chorus caelestium*
Et angeli canunt Deo,
Palamque fit pastoribus
Pastor, creator omnium.

Let all the world, from East to West, sing of Christ the King, the virgin Mary's Son. The blessed maker of the world assumed a servant's form so as to free man by becoming man and not to lose those whom He had created. Heavenly grace enters the chaste mother and a virgin's womb carries a secret of which she had no previous knowledge. The home of her pure womb instantly becomes the temple of God, and she, undefiled and not knowing man, conceived a son. In childbirth she brought forth the one that Gabriel had foretold and that the Baptist, jumping with joy in his mother's womb, had recognized as being in Mary's womb. He deigned to have hay for a bed, and did not refuse the shelter of a manger. He does not suffer even a bird to hunger, and yet He was fed with a little milk. The heavenly choir rejoices and angels sing to the glory of God, and the Shepherd, the creator of all, is made known to the shepherds.

Notes on Hymn 38

Author. Caelius Sedulius. This poet is not to be confused with the Irish poet of the ninth century, known as Sedulius Scotus or Sedulius of Liége, of whom it has been said that 'he combined a lively humour with an adequate amount of piety', Raby, p. 193.

Caelius Sedulius lived in the fifth century, probably being born at Rome, and taught philosophy at Rome and in Achaia. It seems that he was converted by a certain Macedonius and that he then turned his talents to the cause of Christianity. Some state that he was always a layman, while others think that he was ordained priest.

But if little is known of his life, his writings have always been very well known and popular. His greatest work, the *Carmen Paschale*, was intended to replace to some extent the old classics and their mythology. For this purpose he gathered together the miraculous events of the Bible and presented them with much allegory and symbolism. His language is predominantly didactic, without much striving after effect, though at times it rises to great heights.

Nothing of the *Carmen Paschale* has passed into the liturgy, except five lines in honour of our Lady, namely:

Salve, sancta parens, enixa puerpera regem
Qui caelum terramque tenet per saecula; and

Gaudia matris habens cum virginitatis honore,
Nec primam similem visa es, nec habere sequentem.
Sola sine exemplo placuisti femina Christo.

Of these quotations, the first is used, with slight verbal changes, as the Introit for the Common of feasts of our Lady. The first two lines of the second are part of the second antiphon of Christmas Lauds, and the third line is part of the Magnificat antiphon on the feast of the Presentation of our Lady.

Besides the *Carmen Paschale* only two of his hymns survive, of which one is the *A solis ortus cardine*. This hymn is quantitative, though it tends sometimes to be accentual. It also uses rhyme, though not consistently. These two tendencies foreshadow what the Latin hymn was to become in later centuries. It is also an acrostic or alphabetical hymn, each verse beginning with the next letter, while *16* is alphabetical by lines. Verses A to G make up the present hymn,

and verses H, I, L and N are used for Vespers of the Epiphany. For an alphabetical translation, see *Westminster Hymnal*, 8 and 9.

Use. At Lauds of Christmas.

1-2. From the point of sunrise to the boundary of the earth, i.e. from East to West, W. *Ortus* is a genitive and, with *solis*, may be thought of as a compound noun like the English 'sunrise'; cf. *a solis ortu usque ad occasum*, Ps. 112, 3. *Cardo*, pivot, 'pole' on which the earth turns.

3. *principem. Princeps* or *Rex* is often used of Christ by Fortunatus and Prudentius; cf. e.g. *39*, 2.

6. *servile;* cf. *formam servi accipiens*, Phil. 2, 7.

7. *ut . . . ne;* the *ut* is redundant. The other reading is *ut . . . non. Carne carnem*, freeing flesh by flesh, i.e. freeing man by becoming man; cf. the use of *caro* in *63*, 15-16.

11. *bajulat*, carries. *Bajulare quis dicitur quae suo corpore fert*, says the grammarian Festus. The word is formed from *bajulus*, porter, labourer, an equivalent of *operarius*; cf. *95*, 4.

12. *noverat*, which she knew not; i.e. the full significance of which she knew not, W; or, which she had not thought of, B. The next verse continues the thought.

14. *templum*, because it is the presence of God which makes a temple.

13-16 are part of the fifth and eighth responsories of the Circumcision, the fourth line being the unrevised *Verbo concepit Filium. Verbo* refers to the angel's message at the Incarnation and to Mary's acceptance of it; cf. *95*, 9-12. MSS vary between *concepit* and *creavit*, the latter being preferable. Such a use of *creare* is rare, but is found in Virgil and elsewhere in Sedulius. Either form is preferable to the revised one.

17. *Enititur;* an emendation of the rather uncouth *enixa est;* cf. *enixa puerpera*, Carm. Pasch. 2, 63.

19. *Gestiens;* contrast *gestit*, 6, 11.

22. *abhorruit*, did not shrink from; cf. *horruisti*, *9*, 15.

24. *Nec*= not even, as in *nec Salomon*, Mt. 6, 29.

26. *Deo*, sing to (the glory of) God. Other MSS have *Deum*, sing of (the birth of) God.

27. *palamque fit;* and to the shepherds the Shepherd is displayed, *palam fit*. The two words are almost a compound verb.

F

Hymn 39

Audit tyrannus anxius
Adesse regum principem,
Qui nomen Israel regat
Teneatque David regiam.

5 Exclamat amens nuntio:
'Successor instat, pellimur.
Satelles, i, ferrum rape,
Perfunde cunas sanguine'.

Quid proficit tantum nefas?
10 Quid crimen Herodem juvat?
Unus tot inter funera
Impune Christus tollitur.

The uneasy tyrant is told of the coming of the King of Kings to rule over the people of Israel and to ascend the throne of David. Beside himself at the news, he cries out: 'He is here to take my place. I am dethroned. Guards, go, sword in hand, and drench the cradles with the babies' blood.' Of what avail is so great an outrage? How does this monstrous wickedness benefit Herod? Though so many were put to death, yet one, Christ, escapes unharmed.

Hymn 40

Salvete, flores martyrum,
Quos lucis ipso in limine
Christi insecutor sustulit,
Ceu turbo nascentes rosas.

5 Vos prima Christi victima,
Grex immolatorum tener,
Aram sub ipsam simplices
Palma et coronis luditis.

Hail, martyr flowers. On the very threshold of your life Christ's persecutor destroyed you, as a whirlwind does the budding roses. You, Christ's first fruits, a flock of tender sacrificial victims, now play with your palms and crowns right up by the very altar.

HYMNS 41-43

The Dulcis Jesu Memoria

The *Dulcis Jesu memoria*, to give it its correct title, is the subject of an enormous literature. This introduction pretends to be no more than a mere summary of some of the main conclusions of scholars and is, in particular, indebted to the article of nearly three hundred pages by Dom Wilmart in the *Ephemerides Liturgicae* of 1943.

→

Notes on Hymn 39

Author. Prudentius; cf. *13.*

This hymn and the next, for the feast of the Innocents, are from the twelfth hymn of the Cathemerinon, called the *Hymnus Epiphaniae.*

The section for Matins, *39,* consists of lines 93–100 and 133–6 of the original, and the Lauds section, *40,* of lines 125–132. The order of thought in Prudentius is: Herod receives the news, 93–6; his rage and his orders, 97–108—reduced in the Breviary to the verse *Exclamat;* the carrying out of the orders—omitted in the Breviary; the poet's salute to the Martyrs, 125–132=Lauds hymn; and the poet's reflection on Herod's act, 133–140—reduced in the Breviary to the verse *Quid proficit.* The original has gained rather than lost by the abbreviation, though perhaps the Matins section may seem to come to its last part rather abruptly.

Use. Hymn for Matins of the Holy Innocents.

3. *nomen,* i.e. the people of Israel.

4. *regiam,* sc. *sedem;* cf. *Et dabit illi Dominus Deus sedem David,* Lk. 1, 32.

5. *amens,* mad with rage at the news, *nuntio. Amens, insanus* etc. are often applied by early writers to the persecutors; cf. *85,* 16.

6. *instat,* is upon (us); cf. *instet, 21,* 8.

7. *satelles;* sing. for plur. *Satelles* is a guardsman, an officer attached to the personal service of a prince.

11. *unus=solus,* alone.

Notes on Hymn 40

Author. Prudentius. See introduction to previous hymn.

Use. Hymn for Lauds and Vespers of the Holy Innocents.

1. *flores martyrum,* flowers of the martyr band, W, *martyrum* being a partitive genitive. *Qui jure dicuntur flores martyrum, quos in medio frigore infidelitatis exortos, velut primas erumpentes Ecclesiae gemmas, quaedam persecutionis pruina decoxit* (End of sixth lesson of Matins, in a sermon ascribed to St Augustine).

2. *lucis ... limine,* on the very threshold of life, *lucis.* Cf. *infantumque animae flentes in limine primo,* Virg. *Aen.* VI, 427; *in limine vitae,* Lucan, II, 106.

5. *victima;* this and *grex* are in apposition with *vos.*

7. *sub;* original, *ante.* Under the very altar, or, at the side of.

8. *palma.* The palm and the crown, tokens of victory among the pagans, were adopted by the Christians as tokens of the martyrs' triumphs.

Author

It seems unlikely that St Bernard, who died in 1153, was the author since (1) the earliest MSS are early thirteenth century and one perhaps of the end of the twelfth, so that the date of composition is probably 1170/80–1200; (2) the hymns to St Victor and St Malachy are the only ones which can be positively ascribed to St Bernard; and (3) the name of St Bernard is not found in the MSS until the fifteenth century.

As the first and most reliable MSS are English and as the use of the poem spread from England, it is reasonable to conclude that it was written in England. The anonymous English writer was probably a Cistercian. Whoever he was, he was well versed in the Scriptures and their liturgical uses and applications, and acquainted with the writings of St Bernard and with his use of the Scriptures, especially of the Psalms and the sapiential books. These reasons suggest a Cistercian.

Text

The original poem was of forty-two verses, the text of which can be found in the *Oxford Medieval* and, with slight changes, in Wilmart. However, copyists and adapters changed the order of verses, omitted, altered and added verses, as they wished. Altogether the MSS show eighteen new verses and nineteen doxologies or quasi-doxologies. These make a composite text of seventy-nine verses—apart from twenty-five variations of original or added verses which in the process have become almost new verses. This confusion in the MSS was not detected for some time so that Mabillon's edition, for instance, and the compilers of this Office in 1721 treated as original some of the additions. If Roman numerals are used for the verses of the original and Arabic for the additions, the Breviary hymns are made up as follows:

> *41:* verses I, II, III, V and 74;
> *42:* verses IX, 14, IV, XII and 79;
> *43:* verses XVIII, XVI, XXIII, X and XXXI.

Only in *41* are the verses chosen in anything like a consecutive order, and *42* is a very mixed affair. Hymn *129* for the Transfiguration is also derived from this poem. But there the centoist strung together not verses but unconnected lines and in so arbitrary a fashion that the relation to its source would scarcely be suspected. The revisers made the relationship even more remote.

The subject of the poem

The poem describes the soul's search for Jesus—a search which is continuous, progressive and ends only in heaven. Different moments in this search and different feelings which accompany it are described in groups of verses. For instance, the search is the subject of the first three verses and the object of the search, Jesus, is hymned in the next seven verses. No delineation of the character of our Lord is attempted, but one emerges very clearly. No incidents in His life are related, except the tomb and the Resurrection, and these are used only as illustrating the difficulties and the joys of the search. The poem is not a haphazard collection of verses, as a casual reading might suggest, and the regroupings of verses in some of the MSS and in centos completely ruin the composer's plan. Unity is given to the different parts by the constant mention of the object of the soul's search, and the name, Jesus, is found in about thirty of its forty-two verses. Hence its name 'Jubilus on the name of Jesus'.

The relentless procession of rhymed quatrains, which some find tedious, is very much to the writer's theme and purpose. It matches the lover's relentless pursuit of God and suits the class of popular composition in which it should probably be placed, for it is mystical in thought and popular in form. The many repetitions likewise suit the thought and the form.

Though the poem is intensely personal, yet it has a universal appeal. This accounts for the different titles which are found in the MSS, for the different purposes which it has been made to serve and for the different objects which its author has been supposed to have had in mind. All these, when not merely fanciful, are applications and do not indicate the writer's real purpose. Thus to say, for instance, that it 'is a meditation on the Holy Communion and not on the Holy Name' is to confuse an application, already found in the MSS, with the primary purpose of recounting the search by the soul for its Beloved, whose name is Jesus. *Desiderate millies,/Mi Jesu, quando venies?*; and, *Quocunque loco fuero/Meum Jesum desidero.*

This universal appeal also explains why a composition so individual in feeling seems to find a natural place in the liturgical Office. Its use there renders it impersonal so that it may come to individual life again on the lips of those who sing it. Wilmart made the interesting suggestion that the whole poem in its original form should be used in the Office, with the verses in their proper order and the grouping of the verses respected. Whatever may be one's opinion about that, the vitality of the *Jubilus* is such that even in its dismembered form it still breathes life, love and light.

Hymn 41

Jesu dulcis memoria,
Dans vera cordis gaudia,
Sed super mel et omnia
Ejus dulcis praesentia.

5 *Nil canitur suavius,*
Nil auditur jucundius,
Nil cogitatur dulcius
Quam Jesus Dei Filius.

Jesu spes paenitentibus,
10 *Quam pius es petentibus,*
Quam bonus te quaerentibus—
Sed quid invenientibus?

Nec lingua valet dicere
Nec littera exprimere;
15 *Expertus potest credere*
Quid sit Jesum diligere.

Sis Jesu nostrum gaudium
Qui es futurus praemium;
Sit nostra in te gloria
20 *Per cuncta semper saecula.*

Sweet is the remembrance of Jesus, bringing man his heart's true joy; but sweet beyond honey and all created bliss is His presence. No theme is more agreeable in the singing, none more welcome in the hearing, none more comforting in thought than Jesus, the Son of God. Jesus, hope of penitent souls, how gracious You are to those that ask, how good to those that seek; but who shall say what You are to those that find? No tongue can tell this, nor pen express it; but the one who has experience of it can know in his heart what it means to love Jesus. Jesus, one day to be our reward, be our joy in this life. May our glory be in You through all eternity.

Hymn 42

Jesu rex admirabilis
Et triumphator nobilis,
Dulcedo ineffabilis,
Totus desiderabilis.

5 *Quando cor nostrum visitas,*
Tunc lucet ei veritas;
Mundi vilescit vanitas
Et intus fervet caritas.

Jesus, king most wonderful and conqueror most glorious, our consolation beyond all telling, 'nothing in You but awakes desire'. When You visit our heart, the light of truth shines there; then the world is seen to be foolish and worthless, and love of You burns strong

Notes on Hymn 41

Author. Unknown. Perhaps an English Cistercian. See introduction.

Use. At Vespers of the Holy Name.

1. *Jesu dulcis,* an inversion of the correct *Dulcis,* sc. *est, Jesu memoria. Dulcis* rightly comes first, for it is the keynote to the hymn, as is clear even from the opening lines. *Jesu,* whether in the first or second place, must be a genitive, not a vocative, as is clear from *ejus* in 4. 'Jesu, the very thought of thee' makes it both and turns *ejus praesentia* into 'And in *thy* presence rest'.

2. *cordis; cordi* is the better reading.

3. *mel. Spiritus enim meus super mel dulcis, et haereditas mea super mel et favum,* Ecclus. 24, 27.

4. *praesentia.* St Bernard, referring to *Memoria mea in generationes saeculorum,* Ecclus. 24, 28, says: *Hoc dicit quia ... non deerit electis consolatio de memoria, quibus nondum de praesentia plena refectio indigetur ... Memoria ergo in generatione saeculorum, praesentia in regno caelorum,* P.L. 182, 980; and *Dei ergo quaerentibus et suspirantibus praesentiam praesto interim et dulcis memoria est, non tamen qua satientur, sed qua magis esuriant ut satientur, loc. cit.;* and cf. note on line 12. Cf. also Gilson, *The Mystical Theology of St Bernard,* pp. 81–4.

6. *Nil auditur,* for the more correct *Auditur nil.*

9. *paenitentibus. Quoniam et Altissimus ... misertus est paenitentibus,* Ecclus. 12, 3; *paenitentibus autem dedit viam justitiae, ib.* 17, 20.

10. *petentibus. Petite et dabitur vóbis, quaerite et invenietis,* Mt. 7, 7.

11. *quaerentibus. Quaesivi quem diligit anima mea; quaesivi illum et non inveni,* Cant. 3, 1; and, *inveni quem diligit anima mea, ib.* 3, 4. And cf. next note.

12. The first three verses are closely connected, and this line brings us back to line 4. St Bernard, alluding to *Bonus est Dominus ... animae quaerenti illum,* Lam. 3, 25, says: *Si quaerenti, quanto magis invenienti? Si tam dulcis est memoria, qualis erit praesentia? Si mel et lac dulce est sub lingua, quid erit super linguam?,* P.L. 183, 552.

13. *valet,* instead of the correct *potest.*

15. Among the many variants of this line, the best reading seems to be *Expertus novit tenĕre. Tenĕre,* tenderly, is an adverb, qualifying *diligere.* Copyists took the word to be *tenēre,* the infinitive, and as this did not fit the line, they indulged in doubtful emendations.

17–20. One of the many doxologies added in the MSS and reserved in some to the Vesper portion. With *Tu esto* instead of *Sis Jesu* it is the unrevised doxology or, in some cases, the penultimate verse, of the Ascension hymn *Jesu nostra redemptio* (= *Salutis humanae sator, 62*).

Notes on Hymn 42

Author. See *41.*

Use. At Matins of the Holy Name.

1–4. The verse that precedes this in the full text is about the soul, in company with Mary Magdalen, looking for Jesus at the tomb. Our Lord is here addressed as *rex* and *triumphator* because of the Resurrection, and lines 3–4 express Mary's and the soul's joy at finding Him. The poem then goes on to the prayer *Mane nobiscum,* which is deferred in the Breviary until *43,* 13–16. *Totus desiderabilis,* from Cant. 5, 16.

Jesu dulcedo cordium,
10 *Fons vivus, lumen mentium,*
Excedens omne gaudium
Et omne desiderium.

Jesum omnes agnoscite,
Amorem ejus poscite;
15 *Jesum ardenter quaerite,*
Quaerendo inardescite.

Te nostra, Jesu, vox sonet,
Nostri te mores exprimant,
Te corda nostra diligant
20 *Et nunc et in perpetuum.*

within us. Jesus, consolation of all hearts, source of life and light of our souls, You surpass completely all the joys that man knows or desires. Let all men recognize Jesus and ask earnestly for His love; let them seek Him, their souls aflame with love, and become yet more on fire with love in their search for Him. May our voice, Jesus, sing Your praise, our way of life tell of You, and our hearts love You now and for ever.

Hymn 43

Jesu decus angelicum,
In aure dulce canticum,
In ore mel mirificum,
In corde nectar caelicum.

5 *Qui te gustant, esuriunt,*
Qui bibunt, adhuc sitiunt;
Desiderare nesciunt
Nisi Jesum quem diligunt.

O Jesu mi dulcissime,
10 *Spes suspirantis animae,*
Te quaerunt piae lacrimae,
Te clamor mentis intimae.

Mane nobiscum, Domine,
Et nos illustra lumine,
15 *Pulsa mentis caligine,*
Mundum reple dulcedine.

Jesu, flos matris virginis,
Amor nostrae dulcedinis,
Tibi laus, honor nominis,
20 *Regnum beatitudinis.*

Jesus, glory of the Angels, You are grateful music to man's ear, exceedingly sweet on man's lips and heavenly joy to his heart. Men taste You and still hunger, drink of You and are still unsatisfied; they are unable to desire anything except Jesus, their love's object. My sweet Jesus, hope and desire of my soul, in love and tears I seek You and my inmost soul cries out for You. Stay with us, Lord; shed Your light on us; dispel the soul's darkness; fill the world with Your consolation. Jesus, flower of the Virgin-mother, man's love and consolation, to You be praise, an honoured name and a kingdom of blessedness.

10. *Fons vivus* is an echo of *64, 7*. *Fons veri* is probably the correct text.

11. *excedens*. *Excedit* (and *Jesus* for *Jesu* in line 9) is probably the correct text, though *excedis* is possible.

13. Otherwise: *Experti recognoscite*.

14. *amorem ejus;* otherwise, *amorem pium*. Wilmart prefers *pascite* to *poscite*, and refers to *Indica mihi . . .*

ubi pascas, Cant. 1, 6; cf. also Cant. 2, 16 and 6, 2.

15. *ardenter; ardentes*, Wilmart.

17–20. The last in the series of additional doxologies. Its use at Matins apparently dates from the institution of this Office by Innocent XIII.

18. *mores*, way of life, life; for the idea cf. *72, 3–4* and *149, 23–4*.

Notes on Hymn 43

Author. See *41*.

Use. At Lauds of the Holy Name.

3. *mel*. *Jesus mel in ore, in aure melos, in corde jubilus*, St Bernard in lesson 6 of the feast.

4. *in corde*. Better: *Cordi* (or *corde*) *pigmentum caelicum*. *Pigmentum*, late Latin, a spiced and scented wine, and so fragrance, spice etc. *Nectar*, like *pigmentum*, suggests something that gives joy. The line paraphrases Bernard's *in corde jubilus*.

5. *esuriunt*. *Qui edunt me adhuc esurient, et qui bibunt me adhuc sitient*, Ecclus. 24, 29. *Gustant*, however, seems to be an echo of *Gustate et videte quoniam suavis est Dominus*, Ps. 33, 9. This in turn recalled the lessons of St Gregory where these words are quoted and commented upon, Sunday after Corpus Christi, lessons 7-9. This verse and the neighbouring ones in the original have many of the words and sentiments of St Gregory.

8. *diligunt*. *Sentiunt* preserves the rhyme and gives better sense than the substitute *diligunt*. It is explained by *gustant* and *bibunt*, *desiderare* by *esuriunt* and *sitiunt*.

9. *O Jesu*: Better, *Jesu mi dilectissime*.

10. *suspirantis*. *Fidelis anima et suspirat praesentiam inhianter* (cagerly) *et in memoria requiescit suaviter*, St Bernard, P.L. 182, 981; and cf. *41, 4*, note at the second quotation.

12. *Te;* better *Et*. This and the preceding line are perhaps an echo of *cum clamore valido et lacrimis*, Heb. 5, 7.

14. Originally: *Mane novum cum lumine*, where *mane* is a noun, in apposition with *Domine*. *Mane nobiscum* in 13 is from Lk. 24, 29.

15. *pulsa . . . caligine*, abl. absol., like *nocte pulsa* in *115, 1*. The reading *caliginem* treats *pulsa* as imperative of *pulsare*, in the sense of remove.

16. *reple;* otherwise, *replens*.

17–20. This verse is part of the original and not one of the added doxologies. *Flos;* cf. *ego flos campi*, Cant. 2, 1; *flos de radice*, Is. 11, 1; *97, 7*, note and *150, 9*.

19. *nominis;* original: *numinis*, divinity, godhead.

Hymn 44

Crudelis Herodes, Deum
Regem venire quid times?
Non eripit mortalia
Qui regna dat caelestia.

5 *Ibant magi quam viderant*
Stellam sequentes praeviam;
Lumen requirunt lumine,
Deum fatentur munere.

Lavacra puri gurgitis
10 *Caelestis agnus attigit;*
Peccata quae non detulit,
Nos abluendo sustulit.

Novum genus potentiae:
Aquae rubescunt hydriae
15 *Vinumque jussa fundere*
Mutavit unda originem.

Why, merciless Herod, are you afraid of God coming as king? The giver of heaven's kingdom does not usurp earthly ones. The Magi went on their way, following the lead of the star they had seen. By its light they go in search of the Light and their gift of incense owns Him to be God. The Lamb from heaven touched the Jordan's cleansing waters and, washing us, took away sins that were not His. A new kind of miracle. The water-jars redden, for the water, bidden to come out as wine, changed its nature.

Hymn 45

O sola magnarum urbium
Major Bethlem, cui contigit
Ducem salutis caelitus
Incorporatum gignere.

5 *Quem stella, quae solis rotam*
Vincit decore ac lumine,
Venisse terris nuntiat
Cum carne terrestri Deum.

Videre postquam illum magi,
10 *Eoa promunt munera*
Stratique votis offerunt
Thus, myrrham et aurum regium.

Regem Deumque annuntiant
Thesaurus et fragrans odor
15 *Thuris Sabaei, ac myrrheus*
Pulvis sepulchrum praedocet.

Bethlehem, singularly favoured, greater than the great cities, it was your good fortune to bring to birth in human form the heaven-sent leader of salvation. And a star that in beauty and brightness outshone the sun, gives the news that God has come in earthly flesh for earth's redemption.

When the Magi see Him, they unfold their gifts from the East and with reverent prostration offer Him incense, myrrh and royal gold. The treasure of gold and the sweet-scented Sabaean incense disclose that He is King and God, and the powdery myrrh foretells His tomb.

Notes on Hymn 44

Author. Sedulius. See *38*.

Use. Hymn at Vespers and Matins of the Epiphany.

1. The original *Hostis Herodes impie* may stand, since metrical liberties are necessarily allowed with foreign and proper names. Erasmus changed the line to *Herodis hostes,* which preserves the alphabetical device. The revisers had no interest in such things.

5. *Quam* is the reading of the later MSS and is based on *stella quam viderant,* Mt. 2, 9. Earlier MSS have *qua venerant,* i.e. following the lead of the star, by means of which they had come.

These three verses deal with the three manifesta-tions of our Lord which are the subject of the feast of the Epiphany.

8. *munere,* by the gift, i.e. of incense.

9. *puri;* cleansing or, according to others, cleansed (by Christ's baptism). *Gurgitis* is used of any great volume of water.

11. The Breviary text is that of most MSS, including some fairly old ones. Another version is *peccata qui mundi tulit. Sustulit* in the next line would then mean raised us up.

13. *Novum . . . potentiae,* as explained by the rest of the verse.

Notes on Hymn 45

Author. Prudentius. See *13* and *39*. It is made up of lines 77–80, 5–8, 61–4 and 69–72 of the 12th hymn of the *Cathemerinon.*

Use. Hymn at Lauds of the Epiphany.

1. *sola,* unique, singularly favoured. *Magnarum urbium,* genitive after *major,* instead of the usual ablative. Cf. Mich. 5, 2 and Mt. 2, 6.

5. *Quem,* sc. *ducem* of 3; translate as 'and' because of *Deum* in 8. Most modern editors give *Haec stella. Solis rotam;* cf. *25, 5,* note.

6. *vincit,* surpassed in beauty and brightness.

7. *terris;* according to some dative after *nuntiat,* and according to others after *venisse* as a dative of advantage.

9. *Videre*=*viderunt; illum,* Christ, for *quod* of the original—a change made necessary by joining un-connected verses.

10. *Eoa,* from *eous,* adj. Eastern; cf. *14, 15.*

11. *stratique votis*=*procidentes adoraverunt eum* of Mt. 2, 11.

14. *thesaurus,* i.e. the *aurum regium* of 12.

15. *Sabaei,* adj., from Saba, the chief city of Arabia Felix, renowned for its frankincense and myrrh. Also used because of *Reges Arabum et Saba dona adducent,* Ps. 71, 10—a psalm much used in the Epiphany Office.

16. *praedocet,* foreshadows. For lines 12–16, cf. *pretiosa munera obtulerunt: aurum, sicut Regi magno; thus, sicut Deo vero; myrrham, sepulturae ejus,* Bene-dictus antiphon, 7 Jan.

Hymn 46

O lux beata caelitum
Et summa spes mortalium,
Jesu, o cui domestica
Arrisit orto caritas:

5 *Maria, dives gratia,*
O sola quae casto potes
Fovere Jesum pectore,
Cum lacte donans oscula:

Tuque ex vetustis patribus
10 *Delecte custos Virginis,*
Dulci patris quem nomine
Divina proles invocat:

De stirpe Jesse nobili
Nati in salutem gentium,
15 *Audite nos qui supplices*
Vestras ad aras sistimus.

Dum sol redux ad vesperum
Rebus nitorem detrahit,
Nos hic manentes intimo
20 *Ex corde vota fundimus.*

Qua vestra sedes floruit
Virtutis omnis gratia,
Hanc detur in domesticis
Referre posse moribus.

Jesus, blest light of heaven and highest hope of earth, greeted at birth with the kindly smile of family love—Mary, rich in grace, singled out to nurse Jesus at your pure breast, feeding and kissing Him—and you, Joseph, chosen from Jews of former times to protect and watch over Mary and fondly addressed as 'Father' by the divine Child—listen to the prayers we offer at your altars, for you were born of Jesse's noble lineage for man's salvation. Here we remain, as the sun is setting towards evening and taking its light from the world, and from the bottom of our hearts pour out our prayers to you. Grant that we may be able to reproduce in our family life the grace of every virtue with which your home abounded.

Hymn 47

Sacra jam splendent decorata lychnis
Templa, jam sertis redimitur ara
Et pio fumant redolentque acerrae
Thuris honore.

5 *Num juvet summo Geniti Parente*
Regios ortus celebrare cantu?

Now are the holy temples filled with the beauteous light of lamps, the altar is garlanded and smoking censers with fragrant perfume pay their loving homage. Surely then this would be a fitting occasion to honour in song the royal ancestry of the mighty Father's Son;

Notes on Hymn 46

Author. Leo XIII.

Use. Hymn at Vespers of the Holy Family.

1. The first three verses are addressed to Jesus, Mary and Joseph in turn. The verb is *audite* in 15, with which *nati* in 14 agrees.

3. *cui*, with *orto* in 4, on whose birth; *orto* also with reference to our Lord as the light. *Domestica*, i.e. the mutual love of Joseph and Mary and their love of our Lord—the theme of the feast.

9. *vetustis patribus*, i.e. from the Jews of old; or, if there is reference to the familiar legend of the Apocrypha, from the contemporaries of St Joseph— God's choice being shown by the blossoming of Joseph's staff. The latter seems unlikely, but Byrnes favours it.

14. *nati . . . gentium.* Each member of the Holy Family was of the house of David, *de stirpe . . . nati*, and each had a special part to play in the work of man's salvation, *in salutem gentium.*

18. *rebus . . . detrahit*, deprives the world of light, brightness; cf. *6, 1* and contrast *14, 7.*

19. *hic*, i.e. before the altars of line 16.

21–24. The order is: *detur (nos) hanc (gratiam,* from *gratia* in 22) *referre posse . . . Detur* is a subjunctive of desire, unless it be taken as dependent on an implied *ut* after *vota. Moribus;* cf. *42, 18.* The verse gives the substance of the prayers mentioned in the previous verse.

Notes on Hymn 47

Author. Leo XIII.

Use. Hymn at Matins of the Holy Family.

Metre. First Sapphic

1–3. *lychnis; lychnus*, 2, light, lamp; *sertis; serta, -orum*, flowers, garlands; *redimitur, redimio*, 4, bind round, encircle; *acerrae*, incense-boxes, censers.

5. *Num juvet* suggests something which is to be turned down—as it is in the next verse.

6. The plural *ortus* perhaps signifies the eternal and temporal generations of Christ, both of which are royal.

Num domus David, decora et vetustae
    Nomina gentis?

Gratius nobis memorare parvum
10 *Nazarae tectum tenuemque cultum;*
   Gratius Jesu tacitam referre
    Carmine vitam.

Nili ab extremis peregrinus oris,
   Angeli ductu, propere remigrat
15 *Multa perpessus Puer, et paterno*
    Limine sospes,

Arte, qua Joseph, humili excolendus
   Abdito Jesus juvenescit aevo,
   Seque fabrilis socium laboris
20   *Adjicit ultro.*

'Irriget sudor mea membra', dixit,
   'Antequam sparso madeant cruore;
   Haec quoque humano generi expiando
    Poena luatur'.

25 *Assidet Nato pia mater almo,*
   Assidet sponso bona nupta, felix
   Si potest curas relevare fessis
    Munere amico.

O neque expertes operae et laboris,
30 *Nec mali ignari, miseros juvate*
   Quos reluctantes per acuta rerum
    Urget egestas.

Demite his fastus quibus ampla splendet
   Faustitas, mentem date rebus aequam.
35 *Quotquot implorant columen, benigno*
    Cernite vultu.

Sit tibi, Jesu, decus atque virtus,
   Sancta qui vitae documenta praebes,
   Quique cum summo Genitore et almo
40   *Flamine regnas.*

surely this the time to recall the glory of David's house and the famous names of that race of old. Nay rather, a sweeter theme would be the lowly house at Nazareth and its slender resources; sweeter to tell again in song Jesus' hidden life.

After many hardships the Child, under an angel's guidance, hastens back home—an exile from the distant banks of the Nile. Now safe under His father's roof, Jesus grows up in hidden seclusion, to be trained in Joseph's lowly trade. He gives Himself of His own free choice to be Joseph's companion in his work as a carpenter. 'Let sweat', He said, 'bathe my limbs before they drip with my out-poured blood. Let this penalty also be paid for the cleansing of man's guilt.' The loving mother sits beside her dear son, the good wife by her husband, content if her loving attention can ease and comfort them in their weariness.

You who knew both work and toil and were acquainted with misfortune, help in their misery those whom poverty sore afflicts as they struggle against life's hardships. Take from the rich that proud contempt with which abundant wealth bedecks itself and make their souls to be unruffled, whatever the state of their fortunes. Look down with kindly countenance on all who call upon the Most High for help.

Glory and praise be to You, Jesus, for You give us the example of a holy life and now reign with the sovereign Father and the loving Spirit.

7. *Domus* implies an accusative such as *gloriam*.

9. The theme chosen for the hymn sharply contrasts with those suggested in the previous verse and with the splendour, as depicted in the first verse, of the place in which the hymn is sung.

13. *peregrinus,* from foreign parts; an exile; cf. *103,* 14.

14. *propere,* adv. quickly; *remigrat, remigro,* 1, journey back, return.

16. *sospes,* in the passive sense of unharmed.

19. *fabrilis,* adj., of or belonging to an artificer; here of carpentry.

21. *irriget, irrigo,* 1, water, wet, moisten.

22. *madeant, madeo,* 2, to be wet, drip, flow with.

24. *poenam luere,* suffer, undergo punishment.

25. *assidet, assideo,* 2, sit by, near.

29. *operae et laboris,* genitive after *expertes; mali* in the next line, genitive after *ignari.*

31. *reluctantes, reluctor,* 1, dep., struggling, battling against; *acuta rerum,* violent, severe misfortunes of life; cf. *acuta belli,* Hor. *Od.* IV, 4, 76. But Byrnes joins *egestas* and *rerum,* want of things, poverty.

33. *fastus,* scornful contempt, disdain, pride.

34. *faustitas,* happy condition, favourable circumstances.

35. *columen,* i.e. most High; cf. *100,* 33.

Lines 29–32 are a prayer for the poor to the Holy Family who willingly accepted poverty; 33–4 are a prayer for the rich, for the Holy Family is an example of a noble family which has come down in its material fortunes; 35–6 apply to all, rich or poor, *quotquot.*

The prayer of 33–4 is that something will be taken from the rich, *demite,* and something positive and virtuous given them, *date.* A clue to this virtuous thing may perhaps be found in the fifth lesson of Matins from *Qui nobiles* to *posthabendae divitiae.* Translations mostly seem to introduce the equivalent of *nobis* after *date,* or else make *date* refer to rich and poor. But the punctuation seems to be against this, and virtue in the rich is not a mere absence of *fastus.*

38. *documenta,* precepts, examples, patterns; cf. *71,* 14.

Hymn 48

O gente felix hospita,
Augusta sedes Nazarae,
Quae fovit alma Ecclesiae
Et protulit primordia.

5 *Sol, qui pererrat aureo*
Terras jacentes lumine,
Nil gratius per saecula
Hac vidit aede aut sanctius.

Ad hanc frequentes convolant
10 *Caelestis aulae nuntii,*
Virtutis hoc sacrarium
Visunt, revisunt, excolunt.

Qua mente, Jesus, qua manu
Optata patris perficit!
15 *Quo Virgo gestit gaudio*
Materna obire munera!

Adest amoris particeps
Curaeque Joseph conjugi,
Quos mille jungit nexibus
20 *Virtutis auctor gratia.*

Hi diligentes invicem
In Jesu amorem confluunt,
Utrique Jesus mutuae
Dat caritatis praemia.

25 *Sic fiat ut nos caritas*
Jungat perenni foedere
Pacemque alens domesticam
Amara vitae temperet.

O venerable house of Nazareth, favoured in being the home of people so hospitable, Yours it was to foster and to introduce to men the loving beginnings of the Church. The golden sun looks down on the countries far below, but in all its time it has seen nothing more pleasing, nothing holier than this house. Messengers come constantly from the court of heaven; they visit, revisit, and pay honour to this hidden retreat of holiness. How carefully and skilfully Jesus carries out His father's wishes, and how joyfully Mary delights to perform her duties as mother. And always Joseph is at her side to share her loving responsibilities, while Jesus, from Whom all virtue comes, is ever gratefully strengthening the bonds of love between them. The love of Mary for Joseph and that of Joseph for Mary unite in their love for Jesus, and He rewards them both for their love of each other. May it happen to us in like fashion that love be the unbroken bond of our life, promote family peace and bring comfort in life's sorrows.

---

3. LENT

Quia promisit Dominus coronam vigilantibus, says the Church in the Lenten invitatory. Lent may be looked on as a prolonged *vigilia* in which the Christian, by prayer and penance, is more alert than usual in imitation of our Lord, *50,* 7, hoping for

Notes on Hymn 48

Author. Leo XIII.

Use. Hymn at Lauds of the Holy Family.

1–2. O venerable house of Nazareth, fortunate, *felix,* in the hospitable family, *gente,* (which lived in you). *Hospes* and *hospita* may be used as adjectives, meaning hospitable. *Hospita* must be abl. with *gente* and not nomin. with *sedes.* The members of the Holy Family, as explained in 3–4, were hospitable in that each of them, according to their office, looked after the beginnings of the Church (cf. *46, 14*), while the house itself, being the home of the God-man, was an image of the Church.

3. *Quae,* sc. *sedes,* but with some reference in thought to *gente;* cf. previous note. *Fovit;* cf. *18, 7,* note.

4. *protulit* probably means displayed, made known or public, though B and Byrnes translate as nourished. 'Where first the holy Church unfurled/Her banners o'er the expectant world', McDougall.

5. *pererrat,* travels over; or, looks down on, as in *totumque pererrat/luminibus tacitis,* Virg. Aen. IV, 363. The mention of the setting sun in *46, 17* and of the rising sun here suits the Hours for which they were written. The darkness of Matins is implied by the artificial light of the lamps, *47, 1.*

8. *Aede,* house, also suggests the idea of a temple, God's house.

11. *sacrarium,* hidden sanctuary. The word means both a holy place and a hidden one; cf. *34, 11,* note.

13. *mente,* care, good will; *manu,* skill, diligence.

15. *gestit,* is eager, glad, to; cf. *6, 11.*

16. *obire,* discharge, perform.

17. *Adest* governs *conjugi,* and *particeps* governs the genitives.

19. *mille,* i.e. always, ever.

20. *Gratia,* ablative used adverbially. It could be used here in its normal meaning of gratefully, in loving fashion, or in the more theological sense of as a grace, by His grace.

Hymns have always preached in song the truths of religion, the Incarnation, for instance, or the Eucharist. These hymns underline all that goes to make a good Christian family, namely mutual love and respect, hospitality. Lines 19–20 emphasise the place of the child as the link between the parents, and this is developed in the next verse.

21. *Hi,* i.e. Mary and Joseph, to whom *utrique* in 23 also refers.

28. *amara vitae;* cf. *acuta rerum, 47, 31.*

---

pardon for past offences, *49, 7–10* and *50, 21–4,* and preparing against future temptations. The basis of our prayer and penance is hope. The words *promisit coronam* remind us of this, and so does the use of the psalm *Qui habitat* during the Mass of the first Sunday and the constant use of some of its verses during the office up to Passion-

G

tide. Our hope is in the omnipotent God who made us, *49*, 1; *50*, 8 and 25–8, and in the omniscient God, *49*, 5. On both counts He knows how weak we are and so will be ready to pardon us, *49*, 5–8 and *50*, 21–32.

As the *vigilia* ends with the light of day and spring follows winter, so the life of the soul comes from mortification and eternity is the crown of time. The Lauds hymn therefore describes in such terms what we are working and hoping for during Lent, and so suits the hour as well as the season. We greet our Lord as the *sol salutis, 51*, 1. We look forward through the days of Lent to the day of Easter, *in qua reflorent omnia, 51*, 14, and through Easter to the final day when the just will enter into that unfading inheritance which is to be their everlasting reward (cf. 1 Peter, 1, 3–5). To appreciate this imagery it should be connected with that of some of the Easter hymns, not least with *61*.

Lauds then provides the only hymn in Lent which uses the theme of light, and its

---

Hymn 49

Audi, benigne conditor,
Nostras preces cum fletibus
In hoc sacro jejunio
Fusas quadragenario.

5 *Scrutator alme cordium,*
Infirma tu scis virium,
Ad te reversis exhibe
Remissionis gratiam.

Multum quidem peccavimus,
10 *Sed parce confitentibus;*
Ad nominis laudem tui
Confer medelam languidis.

Concede nostrum conteri
Corpus per abstinentiam,
15 *Culpae ut relinquant pabulum*
Jejuna corda criminum.

Praesta, beata Trinitas,
Concede, simplex Unitas,
Ut fructuosa sint tuis
20 *Jejuniorum munera.*

Bounteous creator, hear the prayers of repentance we offer You during the holy fast of forty days. Loving searcher of our heart, You know how feeble our strength is; give those who return to You the grace of pardon. We have sinned much, but spare us who confess our guilt; for Your name's honour bring healing remedy to the sick. Grant that our body be brought into subjection by fasting, that our hearts, unburdened by sin, may leave untouched anything that feeds sin. Blessed Trinity and undivided Unity, grant that the sacrifice of the fast may be fruitful to Your servants.

---

use there is much heightened by its absence at Vespers and Matins. But it could be introduced elsewhere, and the Dominicans still use at Compline during Lent, cf. *29, a* hymn which joins the ideas of light and the *vigilia.* Its first and fourth verses are:

Christe, qui lux es et dies,
Noctis tenebras detegis,
Lucifer lucem praeferens,
Lumen beatum praedicans . . .

Oculi somnum capiant,
Cor ad te semper vigilet,
Dextera tua protegat
Famulos qui te diligunt.

Notes on Hymn 49

Author. ?St Gregory.

Use. Hymn at Vespers during Lent.

2. *preces cum fletibus;* cf. *5,* 15, note.

5. *scrutator,* searcher; cf. *scrutans corda et renes, Deus,* Ps. 7, 10; and cf. *15,* 13, note.

6. For *infirma* with a genitive cf. *infirma nostri corporis, 64,* 15.

11. *laudem;* cf. the Lenten Tract *Et propter gloriam nominis tui libera nos,* Ps. 78, 9.

In German MSS and in one French lines 10–11 are: *Poenasque comparavimus,/Sed cuncta qui solus potes/ Confer. . . .* This better suits the general character of the metre; W, quoting Blume.

12. *languidis;* cf. *34,* 7, note.

16. The metaphor of 'fasting from sin' is a strange one, but common enough in the liturgical prayers; e.g. *sectando justitiam, a culpa jejunet,* collect of second Monday of Lent, and cf. St Leo at end of lesson 6 of the first Sunday. Perhaps all such uses go back to Isaias 58, esp. 5–6: *Numquid tale est jejunium quod elegi? . . . Numquid istud vocabis jejunium, et diem acceptabilem Domino? Nonne hoc est magis jejunium quod elegi?*

19. *tuis,* sc. *famulis,* though, according to Pimont, *muneribus* is to be understood.

20. *munera.* That the *sacrifice* of the fast may be fruitful to Thy servants, W; but, that the *rewards* of fasting . . . , B.

Munus is used in many senses in the hymns and liturgical prayers, one being that of a gift from man to God, of a sacrifice. This is common in the Secrets and seems to be the meaning here. The Lenten fast is looked on as a gift to God, as is expressed in another hymn: *ut expiati annuis/jejuniorum victimis.* The idea of reward, which is another meaning of *munus,* is already in *fructuosa.*

Hymn 50

Ex more docti mystico
Servemus hoc jejunium
Deno dierum circulo
Ducto quater notissimo.

5 Lex et prophetae primitus
Hoc praetulerunt, postmodum
Christus sacravit, omnium
Rex atque factor temporum.

Utamur ergo parcius
10 Verbis, cibis et potibus,
Somno, jocis; et arctius
Perstemus in custodia.

Vitemus autem noxia
Quae subruunt mentes vagas,
15 Nullumque demus callidi
Hostis locum tyrannidi.

Flectamus iram vindicem,
Ploremus ante judicem,
Clamemus ore supplici,
20 Dicamus omnes cernui:

'Nostris malis offendimus
Tuam Deus clementiam;
Effunde nobis desuper
Remissor indulgentiam.

25 Memento quod sumus tui
Licet caduci plasmatis;
Ne des honorem nominis
Tui, precamur, alteri.

Laxa malum quod fecimus,
30 Auge bonum quod poscimus,
Placere quo tandem tibi
Possimus hic et perpetim'.

As holy custom has taught us, let us keep this well-known fast of forty days. Moses and Elias originally revealed this period of forty days and in later times Christ, the king and maker of all seasons, hallowed it. Therefore let us give less time to talking, eating, drinking, sleeping and amusing ourselves and show a greater vigilance in our way of life. But let us avoid sin, for it undermines the unreflecting soul; let us yield no ground before our cunning foe's tyrannical demands. Let us appease God's avenging wrath, beg for mercy before our Judge, call upon Him in suppliant entreaty; let all of us most humbly offer this prayer. 'Our sins have offended Your divine mercy. Yet pour out on us from heaven the grace of pardon, for You are the forgiver of sins. Remember that, fallen though we are, we are Your handiwork. Do not, we beg You, give another the honour that is due to Your name. Pardon the evil we have done. Give in even greater measure the grace we ask for, so that at last it may come about that we are pleasing to You in this life and in the next.'

Notes on Hymn 50

Author. ?St Gregory.

Use. Hymn at Matins during Lent.

1. *Ex more,* by custom—an ablat. of instrument; or, perhaps, in accordance with custom; cf. W. *Mystico;* (1) referring to the number, forty; (2) referring to the mystery of fasting, as in *nil hoc profecto purius* (more cleansing) *mysterio* (i.e. of fasting), Prud. *Cath.* VII, 6; or (3) meaning holy.

3–4. In the well-known tenfold, *deno,* round of days reckoned, *ducto,* four times. *Deno* is the less probable reading for *denum = denorum* with *dierum;* cf. *12, 4,* note, for a similar misunderstanding of a contraction. *Circulo;* cf. *7, 19* and *37, 14.*

5. *Lex,* i.e. Moses, Exod. 34, 28; *prophetae,* Elias, 3 Kings 19, 8; these two passages are the Lessons for Ember Wednesday in Lent.

6. *praetulerunt,* displayed, revealed. 'But *praeferre* is used, though very rarely, in the sense of "to anticipate" ', W.

7. *sacravit,* hallowed, sanctified—in a special manner, for He is the ruler and maker of all the seasons, *temporum,* cf. *11, 3.*

11. *arctius (artius),* more attentively, with greater alertness.

12. *custodia,* on guard, like a sentinel. *Custodia* is the equivalent of *vigilia.* The hymn well suits Matins and is a commentary on the Lenten invitatory.

14. *subruunt,* undermine. *Vagas,* heedless, unheeding; contrast *vagos* in *25,* 8.

15–16. Another reading is: *callido/Hosti locum tyrannidis,* i.e. the advantage of tyranny to . . . *Callidi,* the serpent of Gen. 3, 1 who was *callidior cunctis animantibus. Locum dare* is a military metaphor in keeping with *custodia.* The line is based on *Nolite locum dare diabolo,* Eph. 4, 27.

17. *vindicem,* avenging; cf. *vindex in iram,* Rom. 13, 4 and *119,* 1.

20. *dicamus* introduces the next three verses.

25. *tui.* Some take it as a genitive singular, others as a nominative plural. We are of your creation, though a fallen one, *licet caduci;* or, We are yours, *tui,* though belonging to a fallen creation.

27. *honorem;* cf. *49,* 11, note.

28. *alteri,* i.e. the devil.

29. *laxa,* forgive, pardon; cf. *36,* 10.

31. *tandem,* at last, at length, emphasising *possimus.*

Hymn 51

O sol salutis, intimis,
Jesu, refulge mentibus,
Dum, nocte pulsa, gratior
Orbi dies renascitur.

5 Dans tempus acceptabile,
Da lacrimarum rivulis
Lavare cordis victimam,
Quam laeta adurat caritas.

Quo fonte manavit nefas,
10 Fluent perennes lacrimae,
Si virga poenitentiae
Cordis rigorem conterat.

Dies venit, dies tua
In qua reflorent omnia;
15 Laetemur et nos, in viam
Tua reducti dextera.

Te prona mundi machina
Clemens adoret Trinitas,
Et nos novi per gratiam
20 Novum canamus canticum.

Jesus, salvation's sun, shine bright in our inmost souls until night is driven away and day with its more welcome joys rises again.

Having given us this 'acceptable time', grant that we may purify by abundant sorrow the sacrifice we make of our heart and that our love may willingly consume the sacrifice in its flames. Tears of repentance will never stop welling up from our heart, the source of our past sin, if the rod of penance break its stubborn rock.

The day—Your day—is coming, when everything again begins to blossom. And when Your right hand has led us back to the way, may we too rejoice on that day.

May the world that You constructed humbly adore You, merciful Trinity, and may we, renewed by grace, sing a new hymn of praise.

---

4. PASSIONTIDE

Fulget crucis mysterium. Passiontide is a time of rejoicing as well as of mourning, of triumph as well as of defeat. The office of this season, apart from the hymns, is one of sorrow and mourning which comes to a fitting climax in the Lamentations. So is it also with the Masses of Passion and Palm Sundays whose musical settings in the *Graduale* are unrivalled for depth of feeling. Yet for all that St Paul, in the epistle of Passion Sunday, would have us enter with our High Priest into the sanctuary, and St John reminds us that He who is to suffer is truly God; 'before Abraham was, I am'. The epistle and gradual of Palm Sunday speak of the ultimate triumph of Him whose passion and death the gospel is to recall. *Attende gloriam crucis ipsius. Jam in fronte regum crux illa fixa est, cui inimici insultaverunt. Effectus probavit virtutem: domuit orbem non*

Notes on Hymn 51

Author. Unknown. Probably of the sixth century, though some give a very late date.

The original text has many difficulties. This caused many variants in the MSS and perhaps prompted the revisers to make a smoother text. The first verse in the Breviary is practically a new text, and in the second and third verses new ideas as well as new words have been introduced.

4. *dies* gives the main idea of the hymn. The coming of the natural day, made more welcome by grace, *gratior*, is answered by the coming of 'your day' in line 13.

5. *dans*, used as a past participle; having given. *Acceptabile*; 2 Cor. 6, 2. The use of 2 Cor. 6 for Lent was universal in the West from early times. It is the epistle for the first Sunday of Lent and the inspiration of St Leo's homily (2nd Noct., 1st Sunday) and of some of the antiphons and responsories of Lent.

7-8. The reference is to the victims of the Old Law, which were purified and then destroyed in whole or in part by fire.

9. *fonte*, i.e. the heart of man (*cordis* of line 7); cf. Mark 7, 21.

11-12. The reference seems to be to the striking of the rock by Moses, though the metaphors *conterat* and *rigorem* are not very apt.

13. The day is coming, your day, i.e. Easter Sunday. *Haec dies quam fecit Dominus; exsultemus et laetemur in ea*, Ps. 117, 24.

14. *reflorent*. The renewal of nature in spring is connected with the renewal in the order of grace at Easter. Cf. *61*, which the writer may have had in mind.

15. *laetemur;* cf. note on line 13.

16. *dextera*. The reference to God's right hand is due to the revisers, but it could be connected with the *dextera Domini* of Ps. 117, 16.

17-20. This doxology is used more than once in the Breviary, but this *may* have been its first appearance. *Machina*; cf. *8, 2*; *clemens Trinitas*, vocative; *novi*, made new.

---

ferro, sed ligno (St Augustine in the 6th lesson of Maundy Thursday). It is this triumph of the *Cross* as well as the triumph of its Victim which inspires these two most majestic hymns, *52* and *53* which are used for *feasts* of the Cross as well as at this season. *Fulget crucis mysterium*; the Cross and its mystery are indeed resplendent at this season through the presence of these hymns in offices which otherwise are so full of lament.

These two hymns, the *Vexilla Regis* and the *Pange lingua*, were written for a special occasion. The Emperor Justin II and his wife had sent a relic of the true Cross to Queen Radegunde for the convent at Poitiers. Fortunatus, who has a lifetime of writing occasional verse to his credit, was inspired by this occasion to poetry of supreme excellence in hymns which 'combine a deep sincerity and a fervour of poetic feeling and religious thought with high dignity, strength and skill of expression. They are indeed models of what Christian hymns should be,' W. Nor could he let the occasion pass without addressing a long elegaic poem to the Emperor to honour him for this gift.

The majesty of the opening verses of the two hymns recalls the robed Christ of early centuries, while other lines, such as 53, 19–20, point forward to the 'historical' crucifixes of later times. Neither the divinity nor the humanity of the Victim is lost sight of. The Cross moreover is a throne, an altar and the Master's chair, as the *Vexilla* suggests. The whole life of our Lord is a foreshadowing of the Cross, 53,

---

Hymn 52

It is easier to give the original text of this hymn and to put the variants of the Breviary text in the notes. Lines which belong to the original but have no place in the Roman Breviary are in (   ); lines which are in use but are no part of the original are in [   ].

Vexilla regis prodeunt,
Fulget crucis mysterium,
(Quo carne carnis conditor
Suspensus est patibulo.

5 *Confixa clavis viscera,*
Tendens manus, vestigia,
Redemptionis gratia
Hic immolata est hostia).

Quo vulneratus insuper
10 *Mucrone diro lanceae,*
Ut nos lavaret crimine
Manavit unda (et) sanguine.

Impleta sunt quae concinit
David fideli carmine,
15 *Dicendo nationibus*
'Regnavit a ligno Deus'.

Arbor decora et fulgida,
Ornata regis purpura,
Electa digno stipite
20 *Tam sancta membra tangere.*

The standards of the King appear, the mystery of the Cross shines out in glory—the mystery wherein the creator of man's flesh in His own flesh hung on the gibbet. Here the victim, His body pierced with nails, stretched out His hands and feet and was sacrificed for our redemption. And while He was still on the Cross, His side was wounded by the spear's cruel point, and poured out water and blood to wash away our sins. The words of David's true prophetic song were fulfilled, in which he announced to the nations: 'God has reigned from a tree.' Tree of dazzling beauty, adorned with the purple of the King's blood, and chosen from a stock worthy to bear limbs so sacred!

Continued

10–18. All this was to pass into the art and poetry of succeeding ages and, for its spiritual applications, into such passages as the twelfth chapter of the second book of the Imitation. *In cruce salus, in cruce vita, in cruce protectio ab hostibus . . . Non est salus animae nec spes aeternae vitae, nisi in cruce . . . Tota vita Christi crux fuit et martyrium.*

The purpose and character of the hymns for Palm Sunday and Maundy Thursday are sufficiently explained in the notes—*54* singing of our Lord as king, *55* as judge and redeemer and *56* as *caritas,* whose members we are, whose command we know (John 15, 12) and whose example is before us to follow (John 13, 15).

Notes on Hymn 52

Author. Venantius Fortunatus. He was born about the year 530 near Ravenna. After a colourful life, being everybody's friend at home and on his many travels, he settled at Poitiers at the court of Radegunde, wife of Clotaire I. He was ordained priest and eventually became bishop of Poitiers, where he died about 600.

Fortunatus, who has been called 'the last of the Roman poets', left a mass of poetry, serious, gay and frivolous, whose quality ranges from poor to exalted. His most famous religious poetry is found in three hymns in honour of the Cross and the poem from which hymn *61* is taken. Of the three hymns just mentioned, the *Crux benedicta nitet* has no place in the Breviary, but the other two are hymns *52* and *53.* The last two hymns certainly and the *Crux benedicta* in all probability were written for the reception of the relic of the Cross. (For further information on Fortunatus and on these hymns, cf. Walpole, Raby, Julian, and *The Wandering Scholars* by H. Waddell.)

Use. Hymn at Vespers during Passiontide and for the feast of the Cross on 3 May and 14 September. It was once in the Missal as a processional hymn on Good Friday, but has now been replaced by three antiphons from the September feast.

1. *prodeunt.* The first two lines seem to suggest a person seeing the procession come into view, the centre of all the pageantry being the rich reliquary of the Cross, as *fulget* implies. The relic recalls the mystery of the Cross, which is stated in lines 3–4. The rest of the hymn elaborates this short statement,

5–20 being about the Victim, 21–8 about the Cross, and 29–32 an address to the Cross and its Victim.

3. *quo* sc. *mysterio,* the mystery wherein or whereby; *carne,* in the flesh.

4. *patibulo;* literally, a yoke; used here for *cruce.*

3–4 in the Breviary are: *Qua Vita mortem pertulit,/ Et morte vitam protulit,* being lines 31–2 of the full text, with *protulit* for *reddidit. Qua* refers to *crucis* of line 2; *Vita* is our Lord; *pertulit,* suffered, cf. *38, 21.* For the idea, cf. first and third nocturns of 14 September and John 3, 14–15.

5. *confixa* refers to *hostia* of line 8; *viscera* is accusative of the thing affected and means here 'body'.

6. *vestigia,* i.e., feet.

8. *hic,* adv., here.

9. *quo,* sc. *patibulo* of line 4, which *hic* of line 8 has kept before the reader's mind. *Insuper,* whereon, governs *quo.* It may follow the word it governs. Others translate *insuper* as 'moreover'.

10. *mucrone,* sharp point; cf. *11, 23.*

9–12 in the Breviary are: *Quae vulnerata lanceae/ Mucrone diro, criminum/Ut nos lavaret sordibus,/ Manavit unda et sanguine. Quae* refers to *Vita* in line 3 of the Breviary text.

13. *concinit. Canere* and *concinere* are normally used of the prophets; cf. *117, 25*

15–16. A paraphrase of: *Dicite in gentibus quia Dominus regnavit,* Ps. 95.

16. The words *a ligno* are not part of the psalm, but are a very early Christian gloss on the text; cf. Justin, *Apol.* I, 41.

Beata cujus brachiis
Pretium pependit saeculi,
Statera facta corporis
Praedam tulitque tartari.

25 *(Fundis aroma cortice,*
Vincis sapore nectare,
Jucunda fructu fertili
Plaudis triumpho nobili.

Salve ara, salve victima
30 *De passionis gloria,)*
Qua vita mortem pertulit
Et morte vitam reddidit.

[O crux, ave, spes unica,
Hoc passionis tempore,
35 *Auge piis justitiam*
Reisque dona veniam.

Te summa, Deus, Trinitas,
Collaudet omnis spiritus;
Quos per crucis mysterium
40 *Salvas, rege per saecula.]*

How favoured the tree on whose branches hung the ransom of the world; it was made a balance on which His body was weighed, and bore away the prey that hell had claimed. From your bark issues fragrant spice, its taste more delicious than nectar. You rejoice in your fruit so full of promise, and clap your hands in glorious triumph. Hail, altar of the Cross, and hail, Victim on the Cross, because of the glory of the Passion in which Life suffered death and by that death gave life back to us.

Hail, Cross, our only hope. In this season of Passiontide give an increase of holiness to the good and pardon to sinners. Let every spirit praise You, God, mighty Trinity. Through all the ages be King of those that You saved through the mystery of the Cross.

Hymn 53

Pange, lingua, gloriosi lauream certaminis
Et super crucis trophaeo dic triumphum nobilem,
Qualiter redemptor orbis immolatus vicerit.

De parentis protoplasti fraude factor condolens
5 *Quando pomi noxialis in necem morsu ruit,*
Ipse lignum tunc notavit damna ligni ut solveret.

Hoc opus nostrae salutis ordo depoposcerat,
Multiformis proditoris ars ut artem falleret
Et medelam ferret inde, hostis unde laeserat.

Tell, my tongue, of the victory gained in glorious conflict, and sing a triumphal song about the trophy of the Cross, telling how man's redeemer offered His life and thus won the day.

The creator in grief at the harm done to the first man when, by eating of the fatal apple, he fell headlong to death, Himself at that moment marked a tree to undo the harm done by a tree. The plan of our salvation had demanded this work so that God's wisdom might outwit the craftiness of the betrayer and his many disguises and find a remedy in a tree just as the enemy had done hurt to man through a tree.

Continued

The first verse puts Christ before us as king and victim, the second verse considers the Cross as a place of sacrifice and this verse looks on it as a throne.

17. *arbor;* cf. *53,* lines 6 and 22, notes.

19. B takes *electa* with *tangere,* chosen to bear on thy worthy trunk. The idea is that of *53,* 6 and, in part, of *53,* 28.

23. *Statera,* a balance, scales, beam. *Facta sc. est.* 'The Cross was the scales on which the weight of human sin was counterbalanced by the weight of Christ's body on the other side, i.e. the Passion of Christ restored the balance between God and man; cf. Rom. 5, 10', Byrnes. This leads to and explains the next line. Cf. also Blakeney.

24. The MSS offer every possible combination of the words of this line, that of the Breviary being *Tulitque praedam tartari. Que,* wherever placed, joins 23 and 24. The abrupt change of metaphor caused the confusion and variety in the MSS. *Praedam;* cf. 'despoiling the principalities and powers', Col. 2, 15. For this use of *tartari* cf. *in tartarum tradidit cruciandos,*

2 Pet. 2, 4.

25. *aroma,* spice; *cortice, cortex,* 3, bark.

26. *vincis,* surpass; cf. *45,* 6. *Nectare,* ablative used as accusative; cf. *26,* 10 and *43,* 4.

27. *fructu* refers to our Lord, the *dulce pondus* of *53,* 24. *Fertili* applies to the fruit rather than to the tree.

28. *plaudis.* Cf. *omnia ligna regionis plaudent manu,* Is. 55, 12; also Ps. 97, 8.

30. *de,* because of.

31. *qua* refers to *passionis. Reddidit* in 32 is a much better word than the revisers' *protulit;* cf. note on line 4.

33-40. These two verses are an addition, though an old one, to the hymn. The Breviary text is a revision.

34. On 3 May this line becomes *In hac paschali gaudio* and on 14 September *In hac triumphi gloria.*

39-40. The unrevised ending has at least the merit of recalling the *crucis mysterium* of line 2 and *regis* of line 1.

Notes on Hymn 53

Author. Fortunatus. See *52.*

Metre. Trochaic tetrameter. This metre, familiar in Greek tragedy, was adopted by the Romans and became the rhythm of the marching song of Caesar's legions: *Milites ejus inter cetera carmina . . . etiam illud vulgatissimum pronuntiaverunt, 'Ecce Caesar nunc triumphat qui subegit Gallias',* Suet. *Div. Jul.* 49. St Hilary adopted the metre for a Christian hymn and Prudentius used it to good effect in the ninth poem of the *Cathemerinon;* cf. *55.* Fortunatus' hymn and its imitation by St Thomas, *71,* have become marching songs for the Christian legions.

Use. The first five verses are used at Matins and the second five at Lauds of Passiontide and for feasts of the Cross. The doxology, which is added to each section, is not part of the original. The hymn is also used at the Adoration of the Cross on Good Friday, with lines 22-4 as a refrain.

1. *Pange,* tell, relate, sing; cf. *71,* 1 and *84,* 2. *Lauream,* victory. Fortunatus used *proelium,* not *lauream,* as he was thinking of the struggle, not of its result.

2. *super=de,* about, with the ablat. *trophaeo. Trophaeo,* the trophy of (consisting in) the cross. The *trophaeum* was that on which were placed or carried the spoils of victory to recall the victory. The relic of the Cross, carried in procession, recalled Christ's victory. *Triumphum,* a song of triumph an exceptional meaning. Cf. *Dic tropaeum passionis, dic triumphalem crucem,/Pange vexillum, notatis quod refulget frontibus* Prud. *Cath.* IX, 83; also, *52,* 28.

3. *qualiter,* how, in what way.

10 *Quando venit ergo sacri plenitudo temporis,*
   Missus est ab arce Patris natus, orbis conditor,
   Atque ventre virginali carne amictus prodiit.

   Vagit infans inter arcta conditus praesepia,
   Membra pannis involuta virgo mater alligat
15 *Et Dei manus pedesque stricta cingit fascia.*

  **Lustra sex qui jam peregit, tempus implens cor-*
       poris,
   Sponte libera redemptor passioni deditus,
   Agnus in crucis levatur immolandus stipite.

   Felle potus; ecce languet; spina, clavi, lancea
20 *Mite corpus perforarunt; unda manat et cruor.*
   Terra, pontus, astra, mundus quo lavantur flumine.

   Crux fidelis, inter omnes arbor una nobilis,
   Silva talem nulla profert—fronde, flore, germine;
   Dulce ferrum, dulce lignum, dulce pondus sustinent.

25 *Flecte ramos, arbor alta, tensa laxa viscera,*
   Et rigor lentescat ille quem dedit nativitas,
   Et superni membra regis tende miti stipite.

   Sola digna tu fuisti ferre mundi victimam
   Atque portum praeparare arca mundo naufrago,
30 *Quam sacer cruor perunxit, fusus Agni corpore.*

   (Sempiterna sit beatae Trinitati gloria,
   Aequa Patri, Filioque; par decus Paraclito:
   Unius Trinique nomen laudet universitas.)

When therefore the time appointed by God came, the Son, the world's creator, was sent from heaven and, clothed in man's flesh, was born of a Virgin. The Infant cries as He lies in the narrow crib; the Virgin Mother wraps and envelops Him in the swaddling clothes, and a tight-drawn band fastens together the hands and feet of God.

*The redeemer had now completed thirty years and had come to the end of His earthly life, and then of His own free will He gave Himself up to the Passion. The Lamb was lifted up on to the tree of the Cross to be sacrificed. He tastes the gall; He swoons; the thorns, nails and lance pierce His tender body; water and blood flow out. In this stream the whole world, earth, sea and sky are purified. Faithful Cross, tree that is alone in its glory among all other trees; no forest ever yielded its equal in leaf, flower and fruit. Loving nails and loving wood bear a loving burden. Soften your branches, noble tree, relax your taut fibres and let your natural hardness give way to yielding suppleness, and so offer yourself as a gentle support for the body of the King of heaven. You alone were worthy to bear the victim of the world and, like the ark, to give a shelter to a shipwrecked world—an ark which the sacred blood, poured out from the body of the Lamb, has anointed.

Eternal glory to the blessed Trinity; equal glory to the Father, the Son and the Paraclete. Let the whole world praise the name of the one God in three Persons.

Hymn 54

Gloria, laus et honor tibi sit, rex Christe, redemptor,
   Cui puerile decus prompsit hosanna pium.

Israel es tu rex, Davidis et inclita proles,
   Nomine qui in Domini, rex benedicte, venis.

Glory, praise and honour be to You, Christ, king and redeemer. Long ago children in their winning way raised the loving cry 'Hosanna'. You are Israel's king and David's glorious son; You come, king most blessed, in the Lord's

4. *fraude,* the harm done to, or, done by; *proto-plasti,* first-made.

6. According to the legend the Cross came from the tree in Eden, a shoot of which Adam brought out from paradise; cf. lines 7–9 and *52,* 17 foll. *Paradisum nobis crux reddidit Christi. Hoc est lignum quod Adae Dominus demonstravit,* Ambr. in Ps. 35, 3. Cf. also 3 May, 3rd Resp.

7. The pluperfect, *depoposcerat,* shows that it was part of the eternal plan.

9. *inde . . . unde.* Cf. *ut unde mors oriebatur, inde vita resurgeret; et qui in ligno vincebat, in ligno quoque vinceretur,* Preface of the Cross. There may also be a reference to the *locality* of the Cross. Seth is supposed to have planted the shoot from paradise on Golgotha, which was so called because Adam was buried there.

10. *plenitudo;* cf. Gal. 4, 4. The final stage in God's plan began with the Incarnation.

13. *conditus,* hidden. The word is purposely contrasted with *conditor* of line 11.

14. *membra,* i.e. the body. *Pannis,* rags—used poetically to heighten the contrast between the real majesty and the apparent poverty. *Involuta,* enveloped, wrapped up, with *membra; alligat,* binds, wraps, up.

15. Some consider *stricta fascia* to be ablative, the subject of *cingit* then being *virgo mater.*

The Child's helplessness and his being bound up are put as a fore-shadowing of the Passion. The mention of God, *Dei,* and subsequent changes are due to the revisers.

16. *implens;* a present participle used as a past.

18. *stipite* for *stipitem*—a frequent usage in Fortunatus.

19. The unrevised text is: *Hic acetum, fel, harundo, sputa, clavi, lancea (harundo,* reed; cf. Mt. 27, 30 and 48). Both texts give a graphic summary of incidents of the Passion; there is no other connection between

Felle potus and *ecce languet. Potus, poto,* 1, drink.

21. *mundus* is the universe of which *terra* etc. are the parts. Fortunatus is fond of this threefold division; and cf. *95,* 1.

22. *fidelis,* as doing its duty and as opposed to the tree in paradise.

23. *silva nulla,* because this tree, according to the legend, was from paradise. The same reason explains *talem;* moreover no other tree was put to such a use.

24. The best of many variants seems to be: *Dulce lignum dulce clavo dulce pondus sustinet,* i.e. the Cross holds the weight of the body with the nails. This rightly puts *lignum* as the sole subject, while the revisers perversely added *ferrum* as a second subject and put it in the first place. The Missal is nearer: *Dulce lignum, dulces clavos, dulce pondus sustinet—clavos* and *pondus* being the object of the verb, though Byrnes makes them accusatives of exclamation. This is also the wording of the second and seventh Responsories of feasts of the Cross.

25. *Flecte* is usually translated as bend and *alta* as lofty, the words being explained as a way of expressing our Lord getting on the Cross. But perhaps the whole verse is an invitation to the wood to make itself more suitable for our Lord, especially if the correct *Ut . . . tendas* were put back in line 27; line 27 would then explain lines 25 and 26. Hence 'soften' is used in the translation, and cf. *67,* 22. For the same reason *viscera* refers to the tree, not to our Lord's body.

26. *Nativitas* for *natura;* cf. *vultum nativitatis suae,* James 1, 23.

28–30. The metaphors are mixed, and the revisers substituted *victimam* for *pretium* and *arca* for *nauta.* Perhaps they interpreted *nauta* as meaning a ship and so put *arca.* Julian 880 gives a similar interpretation of *nauta.* But some think *nauta* ought to be made *nata,* i.e. destined to be. *Quam* in 30 refers to *arca,* though *perhaps* in thought it goes back to *sola,* for the relative seems to be about the Cross itself.

Notes on Hymn 54

Author. St Theodulf, bishop of Orleans, who was born in Northern Spain about 760 and died about 821. His education was most comprehensive and, as a poet, he overshadowed his contemporaries. To find anyone approaching his excellence one must go back

to Fortunatus. Yet it was Prudentius, not Fortunatus, whom Theodulf looked on among Christian poets as *disertissimus atque christianissimus poeta.*

The text given above is of the opening lines of a poem, 78 lines in length, which Theodulf wrote

5 Coetus in excelsis te laudat caelicus omnis,
   Et mortalis homo et cuncta creata simul.

Plebs Hebraea tibi cum palmis obvia venit;
   Cum prece, voto, hymnis adsumus ecce tibi.

Hi tibi passuro solvebant munia laudis;
10 Nos tibi regnanti pangimus ecce melos.

Hi placuere tibi; placeat devotio nostra,
   Rex bone, rex clemens, cui bona cuncta placent.

name. The whole of heaven's assembly on high, mortal man and all created things, united, praise You. The Jewish people came to meet You with palms; now we are here before You with our prayers and hymns. They made their offering of praise to You on the eve of Your passion; we sing our joyful hymn to You now rejoicing in heaven. They pleased You then; may our devotion please You now. Good king, merciful king, all that is good pleases You.

Hymn 55

O Redemptor, sume carmen temet concinentium.

Audi, judex mortuorum, una spes mortalium,
Audi voces proferentum donum pacis praevium.

Arbor foeta alma luce hoc sacrandum protulit,
5 Fert hoc prona praesens turba salvatori saeculi.

Stans ad aram immo supplex infulatus pontifex,
Debitum persolvit omne, consecrato chrismate.

Consecrare tu dignare, rex perennis patriae,
Hoc olivum, signum vivum jura contra daemonum,

10 Ut novetur sexus omnis unctione chrismatis,
Ut sanetur sauciata dignitatis gloria.

Lota mente sacro fonte aufugantur crimina,
Uncta fronte sacrosancta influunt charismata.

Corde natus ex parentis, alvum implens virginis,
15 Praesta lucem, claude mortem chrismatis consortibus.

Accept, Redeemer of man, the hymn that in union of heart and voice we sing in Your honour.

Judge of the dead and only hope of those that are to die, listen to the prayers of those that are bringing the gift that leads to peace. The tree, fertilized by a kindly light, produced this gift for it to be consecrated, and we, here gathered together, humbly bring it to the saviour of the world. The bishop in his vestments, standing at the altar, yea and a suppliant, has completed his ritual action and consecrated the chrism. Do You, king of our eternal homeland, deign to consecrate this oil, this living sign against the powers of hell, so that man or woman may receive new life through anointing with chrism and our injured honour be healed. For when the soul is washed in baptism's water, sin is put to flight, and when the forehead is anointed, most sacred graces are received. Son of the Father's love and Son of a virgin-mother, grant the grace of light to all that

while imprisoned in a monastery at Angers. That much seems certain, but other details which are grouped round this fact are rather doubtful.

Metre. Elegaic.

Use. It is sung during the Palm Sunday procession. In the liturgy Jerusalem is a type of the Church, universal and local, as is seen, for instance, in the office of the Dedication. Here the church is a type of Jerusalem into which our Lord rode in triumph on the first day of Palms. This is shown by the last antiphon of the procession, the *Ingrediente Domino.*

Lines 1 and 2 are used as a refrain after each couplet.

1. *rex* is the key-word of the hymn. In these few lines it occurs five times and *regnanti* once.

2. *puerile decus* is the subject. *Puerile* is suggested by the antiphons *Pueri Hebraeorum* which in turn come from *pueros clamantes in templo et dicentes:*

Hosanna filio David, Mt. 21, 15.

4. *nomine. Benedictus qui venit in nomine Domini,* Ps. 117, 26 and Mt. 21, 9 and 15. In this line *benedictus* becomes the vocative *benedicte* with *rex.*

5–8. Cf. the antiphon *Cum angelis et pueris* which is sung just before this hymn.

9. *Hi,* i.e. the *plebs Hebraea* of line 7 and the *pueri Hebraeorum* of the antiphons. *Passuro,* about to suffer, so soon to suffer—answered by *regnanti* of line 10. *Munia,* n. pl., debt, gift.

10. *melos,* neut., hymn, song.

The *Oxford Medieval* gives the first 22 lines of this hymn, of which lines 21 and 22 are:

Sis pius ascensor, tuus et nos simus asellus,
Tecum nos capiat urbs veneranda Dei.

Be Thou, O Lord, the Rider, and we the little ass,
That to God's holy city together we may pass (Neale).

Notes on Hymn 55

Author. This hymn does not seem to be 'older than Carolingian times' (Raby), and is said by Phillimore to be the work of an unknown Irish poet. In this connection it is interesting to note that the trochaic metre is said to be the basis of most Irish metres (*Wandering Scholars,* Waddell, p. 15). The hymn is mostly a cento from *Cathemerinon* IX and *Peristephanon* II of Prudentius.

Metre. Trochaic tetrameter; cf. 53.

Use. This hymn is in the Pontifical for use on Holy Thursday at the blessing of the chrism, being adopted from the Gallican liturgy. The first line is sung as a refrain after each couplet. Lines 2–9 are sung while the oils are being brought in solemn procession for consecration, and lines 10–17 when the oils, now consecrated, are being taken back in procession. Thus, once again, the trochaic metre is used for a processional hymn.

2. *mortuorum.* Life and death are often mentioned in the hymn, always with the new attitude towards them which comes to the redeemed through baptism, the sacrament of life. The many titles given our Lord in these few lines must be thought of in the same way and in relation to the graces which come

through the sacred chrism.

4. *foeta alma luce,* fertilized by the light of grace, W. *hoc* sc. *donum.*

5. *prona,* humbly, reverently; rather like *cernui* in 2, 31.

6. *infulatus,* in his robes, vestments. The word is derived from *infula,* and passed into Christian language to indicate episcopal or even priestly vestments. It was eventually identified with *mitra.*

7. *debitum persolvit omne,* has paid his debt in full, i.e. has duly performed the rite. *Consecrato chrismate,* i.e. in the poet's thought, but not in the order of the ceremony; for these verses are sung in the procession before the consecration of the oils.

8. *rex.* The thought progresses from *arbor, turba, pontifex* to *rex* for Him to complete the work of the other three and to consecrate their gift. Parallel with the gift of oil is the gift of the singers; hence line 1 and *sacrata digna laude* in the last line.

9. *signum,* because all anointings are given cross wise, and *vivum* because counteracting the power of the devil and the terrors of the judgment. 'The men signed of the cross of Christ/Go gaily in the dark' sings Chesterton's King Alfred.

Sit haec dies festa nobis saeculorum saeculis,
Sit sacrata digna laude, nec senescat tempore.

chrism has made Your companions, and cut death off from them. May this day be one of festival for us throughout eternity; may it be consecrated with fitting praise, and may the memory of it live through the years.

Hymn 56

Ubi caritas et amor,   Deus ibi est.
Congregavit nos in unum   Christi amor.
Exsultemus et in ipso   jucundemur,
Timeamus et amemus   Deum vivum
5 *Et ex corde diligamus   nos sincere.*

Ubi caritas et amor   Deus ibi est.
Simul ergo cum in unum   congregamur,
Ne nos mente dividamur   caveamus.
Cessent jurgia maligna,   cessent lites
10 *Et in medio nostri sit   Christus Deus.*

Ubi caritas et amor   Deus ibi est.
Simul quoque cum beatis   videamus
Glorianter vultum tuum,   Christe Deus;
Gaudium quod est immensum   atque probum,
15 *Saecula per infinita   saeculorum.*

Where love and loving-kindness are together, God is in their midst. Christ's love has gathered us together in one company. Let us then rejoice and take delight in Him; let us fear and love the living God; let us without any reserve or deception love one another.

Where love and loving-kindness are together, God is in their midst. And so let us see that whenever we are gathered together in company, we are not divided from each other in our feelings. Let spite, quarrelling and strife give place and may Christ, Who is God, be in our midst.

Where love and loving-kindness are together, God is in their midst. May it be ours in company with the blessed, Christ our God, to see Your face in glory—happiness of immeasurable excellence, through unending ages of ages.

---

5. EASTER AND THE ASCENSION

Just as the Easter vigil is the *mater vigiliarum,* so the Easter season may be called the *mater octavarum,* for besides beginning with an octave of days, namely Easter week, it is also made up of an octave of weeks. Because of the symbolism of the number 8

10. *ut,* here and in the next line, gives the result of *consecrare. Omnis = uterque.*

11. *Et medetur* is as good a reading, if not better, and makes the line an independent statement, 'and our injured honour is healed'—*medetur* being used passively.

12. *lota fronte* is the better reading. As a result of the outward washing, *lota,* and anointing, *uncta,* of the head, *fronte,* at baptism, there comes death to sin and life to God. And so again the oil is the *signum vivum*—the chrism which christens us.

14. *corde.* Cf. *Tu Dei de corde Verbum* in St Hilary's *Hymnum dicat* and *Corde Patris genita est sapientia,* Prud. *Apoth.* (init). The heart is thought of as the seat of the affections. *Natus = Nate.*

15. *chrismatis consortibus,* probably derived from *unxit te Deus ... prae consortibus tuis,* Ps. 44, 8. Prudentius thinks of the Incarnation as the primary anointing with chrism when the Word anointed human nature by assuming it. Other anointings are part of the sacrament which makes us sons of God and Christ's companions in the Mystical Body. *Claude,* bring to an end, W; cut death off from.

16. *festa,* festal, full of joy, because of the graces which chrism brings to Christians and the eternity of happiness dependent on them.

17. *sacrata,* cf. note on line 8. *Digna laude,* abl. after *sacrata. Senescat,* let not (the memory of it) grow dim; cf. *senescit tempore,* Prud. *Perist,* I. 82.

Notes on Hymn 56

Author. Unknown, of the Carolingian era. A more recent suggestion is that Rufinus of Aquileia wrote it in 796 in connection with the Synod of Forum Julii.

Metre. Lines of twelve or thirteen syllables, with a division always after the eighth syllable.

Use. It is used at the *Mandatum* or washing of the feet on Maundy Thursday. The service takes its name from its first antiphon: *Mandatum novum do vobis ut diligatis invicem, sicut dilexi vos, dicit Dominus* (cf. John 15, 12). This hymn, of which these verses are only a part, seems to have been written for use at the monastic weekly *Mandatum* and later passed into the Pontifical. Of no great intrinsic value, compared with many other hymns, it is marked by a deep religious simplicity and has held its place through the centuries.

Raby gives the first line as *Ubi caritas est vera, Deus ibi est* and prints it as the fifth line of each verse.

1. *caritas et amor.* The immediate inspiration of the hymn is the text: *Ubi enim sunt duo vel tres congregati in nomine meo, ibi sum in medio eorum,* Mt. 18, 20. Each of these verses is about a gathering or company where Christ, God and Love, is present, and another verse says: *Clamat Dominus et dicit clara voce: Ubi fuerint in unum congregati. . . .*

The first line, as given above, thinks of *caritas* and *amor* as an example of 'two gathered together'; and so Christ must be there with them. *Caritas* and *amor,* as virtues, must be in people and practised in company, and each verse develops this idea.

5. *nos;* accus. after *diligamus.*

9. *jurgia,* quarrels, disputes.

12. The earthly gathering is to be matched and rewarded by the heavenly one—the love and presence of Christ being the cause of both.

13. *glorianter,* joyfully; or, in glory.

(cf. *2,* 1, note) and because of the use of the *alleluia,* which St Augustine calls the canticle of heaven, the whole paschal season is a symbol of eternity and a time of rejoicing because of our Lord's triumph.

During this period the Church commemorates the last two mysteries of our

H

Lord's life as well as the coming of the Holy Ghost. The resurrection and the ascension are here treated together because the ascension has somewhat the same relation to the resurrection as the epiphany has to the nativity. Pentecost, however, has its own section, partly because of the importance of its hymns.

Easter is the *solemnitas solemnitatum* and so gathers up and explains all the other feasts. Its hymns therefore remind us of our Lord's birth, *58, 13,* of the last supper, *57, 5–8,* of the cross, *58, 22* and of the burial, *58, 14–16* and *59, 9–12.* They recall too the paschal types of the Old Testament, the fall of Adam which made type and fulfilment necessary and also the sacrament of baptism by which we are joined to the new Adam.

The hymn *Aurora caelum purpurat, 59,* sings in particular of the triumph of the resurrection and of its effect on the Apostles. Because of the special place the Apostles had in the story of the resurrection and in preaching it, the Church has given them special hymns, formed from *59,* for their office at this season.

The mention of dawn in *59* as well as the many references to light in lines 33–40 make it a suitable hymn for Lauds, whether of Easter or of the Apostles. The *sol formosior* of *59, 34* is not the original wording but it may serve to connect this hymn with the beautiful *Salve festa dies, 61,* and with the Lent hymn *O sol salutis, intimis, 51.* Much of the imagery of these three hymns is drawn from the natural phenomena of light and the season of spring, and *61,* even in a short form, remains one of its best

---

Hymn 57

Ad regias Agni dapes,
Stolis amicti candidis,
Post transitum maris rubri,
Christo canamus principi,

5 Divina cujus caritas
Sacrum propinat sanguinem
Almique membra corporis
Amor sacerdos immolat.

Sparsum cruorem postibus
10 Vastator horret angelus;
Fugitque divisum mare,
Merguntur hostes fluctibus.

At the Lamb's royal banquet, clothed in white robes and with the journey through the Red Sea behind us, let us sing to Christ our King. His divine love gives us His sacred blood to drink and His love, priest-like, offers us His loving body as our sacrificial food. The destroying angel left alone houses that were marked with blood; the sea divided and fled to either bank; the enemy are drowned by the

representations. It is fitting that Fortunatus, the poet of the Cross, should also sing of the resurrection in such felicitous terms.

There remains for Easter only the dramatic *Victimae paschali, 60*, so beautiful in its own right and so important in the history of the sequence.

The hymns of the ascension, *62* and *63*, commemorate the glory of our Lord as He enters heaven and takes, as His due, the place at the right hand of the Father (especially *62*), and sing also of the future glory of the Christian. But this future glory is impossible unless, as the collect of the feast says, *mente in caelestibus habitemus;* and this is the point of *62*, 16–20 and *63*, 21–8.

Christmas has been called, rightly, a feast of light, but Easter surely is *the* feast of light both in the Scripture and in the liturgical splendour of the Easter vigil. This is typified in the continued use of the Paschal Candle until we commemorate the ascension of the Light of the world to become, as the Apocalypse says, the lamp of the heavenly Jerusalem. Yet though He has left this earth, He is still with us.

> *Sit nobis cum caelestibus*
> *Commune manens gaudium:*
> *Illis quod se praesentavit,*
> *Nobis quod se non abstulit.*

(From an ascension hymn, W. *112*, 25–8)

Notes on Hymn 57

Author. Unknown, of fourth to sixth century date. This hymn and *59*, according to W, 'may have been written by a younger contemporary of Ambrose—possibly by Niceta of Remesiana; but not by Ambrose himself'. (For Nicetas, cf. introduction to *9*.) The original text, which is rhymed almost throughout, was shamefully treated by the revisers, only lines 3, 4 and 13 remaining unaltered.

Use. At Vespers from Low Sunday to the Ascension. The Roman office for Easter week represents the form of the office before hymns were introduced. But in the monastic office, where hymns very early had a place, this hymn was used from Easter Sunday onwards.

1. The primary reference is to the newly-baptized, present for the first time at the *regias dapes. Ad,* at. *Agni* strikes at once the Paschal note.

2. *Stolis,* garments, from *stola,* a long upper garment. The use of the word for a stole is a mystery and a misnomer.

3. *maris rubri,* i.e. after their baptism; cf. *et omnes in Moyse baptizati sunt in nube et in mari,* 1 Cor. 10, 2.

4. *Christo ... principi;* cf. *38*, 3 and *39*, 2.

5. *cujus,* referring to *Christo principi,* and introducing *caritas* and *amor.*

6. *propinat,* gives us to drink—a post-classical use; classically, *propinare* means to drink a person's health.

8. *amor sacerdos,* and whose love, like a priest, offers in sacrifice....

Jam pascha nostrum Christus est,
Paschalis idem victima,
15 *Et pura puris mentibus*
Sinceritatis azyma.

O vera caeli victima,
Subjecta cui sunt tartara,
Soluta mortis vincula,
20 *Recepta vitae praemia.*

Victor, subactis inferis,
Trophaea Christus explicat;
Caeloque aperto, subditum
Regem tenebrarum trahit.

25 *Ut sis perenne mentibus*
Paschale, Jesu, gaudium,
A morte dira criminum
Vitae renatos libera.

returning waters. But now our Pasch is Christ. He is both the paschal victim and the pure unleavened bread of sincerity for pure souls. In very truth You are a victim from heaven, for You vanquished hell, unloosed death's bonds and regained for man life's rewards. Now triumphant, Christ displays the spoils of His victory over hell, opens the gates of heaven and drags the king of darkness at His chariot's tail. Free from sin's foul death those who have been born again unto life and so, Jesus, may You be our soul's unending paschal joy.

Hymn 58

Rex sempiterne caelitum,
Rerum creator omnium,
Aequalis ante saecula
Semper Parenti Filius,

5 *Nascente qui mundo faber*
Imaginem vultus tui
Tradens Adamo, nobilem
Limo jugasti spiritum,

Cum livor et fraus daemonis
10 *Foedasset humanum genus,*
Tu, carne amictus, perditam
Formam reformas artifex.

Qui, natus olim e Virgine,
Nunc e sepulcro nasceris,
15 *Tecumque nos a mortuis*
Jubes sepultos surgere.

Eternal king of the blessed, creator of all things and the Father's co-equal Son from all eternity, when the world was at its beginning You created Adam and gave him the image of Your own likeness, joining a soul of noble destiny with slime of the earth. But when an envious, deceitful enemy had covered mankind with the filth of sin, You clothed Yourself in man's flesh and, a creator once again, gave man back the beauty he had lost. Once You were born of a virgin. Now born from the tomb, You command us, buried in sin, to rise with

9–12. Cf. Exod. 12 and Exod. 14, 22–31. This verse and the next contrast the old and the new Paschs.

13. *Jam* and *nostrum* contrast the two Paschs, and so *Christus* must be predicative; and cf. 1 Cor. 5, 7–8, on which the whole verse is based.

18. *Cui=a qua,* sc. *victima;* supply *sunt* in 19 and 20. *Tartara;* cf. 52, 23, note.

21. *Victor,* in contrast with *victima* of 17; for the Victim who is also the Victor cf. *Victimae paschali, 60.*

22. *trophaea,* cf. 53, 2, note.

24. *trahit,* sc. *post se,* drags behind Him the king of darkness—like a captive in a triumphal procession; but the original metaphor of *tyrannum trudens vinculo* is better.

25–8. Original: *Quaesumus, auctor omnium,/In hoc paschali gaudio/Ab omni mortis impetu/Tuum defende populum.* This verse, which seems to have belonged to this hymn in the beginning, was added to the other Easter hymns (of the season and of Apostles) and is followed in most MSS by a doxology. The question is: what is the purpose of the verse? W thinks it is a 'kind of doxology'. It would be no argument against this to say that the verse is mostly a petition, for practically all doxologies have some element of petition, and the title *'auctor omnium'* could imply the Three Persons. But (as it is a hymn to Christ, cf. line 4) it is at least as probable that the verse is a petition, addressed to Christ, as *auctor omnium,* to give His people the special grace of Easter —*ab omni mortis impetu.* W's reasons would suit this hypothesis as well, if not better. The verse was mostly indicated in the MSS merely by its opening words, because it was well-known, and added to the other Easter hymns because most appropriate to the season.

Notes on Hymn 58

Author. Unknown, probably of the fifth century or early sixth. Both Caesarius (died 543) and Aurelian (died 555) legislate for the use of this hymn.

The original hymn is much longer and commemorates the whole redeeming work of our Lord. But 'from the tenth century onwards the first seven (or six) stanzas were taken by themselves to form an Easter hymn', W. The text of these verses has undergone extensive revision in the Breviary.

Use. Hymn at Matins from Low Sunday to the Ascension.

1. The first three verses form one sentence, the verb being *reformas* in line 12.

3. *aequalis,* with *Parenti,* equal with the Father; cf. *unum Patri, 19,* 2.

5. *nascente.* The insistence on the verb *nasci* here and in lines 13 and 14 is due to the revisers; but the ideas are in the original, and the word suits the frequent mention of baptism. *Faber,* maker, creator; cf. *fabrilis, 47, 19.*

8. *jugasti,* yoked, joined. *Formavit Deus hominem de limo terrae, et inspiravit . . . spiraculum vitae,* Gen. 2, 7.

9. *livor=invidia,* envy, malice; cf. *invidi, 12, 14.*

11. *carne amictus;* cf. *53,* 12.

12. *formam,* beauty. Sin, by destroying the *ordo* between God and man, also deprived man of the *splendor ordinis,* that is, of beauty. *Reformas,* restored, re-made. *Faber* in line 5 looks on our Lord as creator of the natural order; *artifex* here looks on Him as our Redeemer—redemption being like a second creation, which makes us a *nova creatura.* Cf. *Deus, qui humanae substantiae dignitatem mirabiliter condidisti et mirabilius reformasti,* second prayer at the Offertory.

13. *Qui=et tu;* also in lines 17 and 21.

Qui, pastor aeternus, gregem
Aqua lavas baptismatis;
Haec est lavacrum mentium;
20 Haec est sepulcrum criminum.

Nobis diu qui debitae
Redemptor affixus cruci,
Nostrae dedisti prodigus
Pretium salutis sanguinem.

You from the dead. As our eternal shepherd You wash Your flock in the waters of baptism, where souls are cleansed and sins are buried. And as our redeemer, fastened to the cross that we ought to have suffered, You gave Your blood to the last drop as the price of our salvation.

Hymn 59

Aurora caelum purpurat,
Aether resultat laudibus,
Mundus triumphans jubilat,
Horrens avernus infremit,

5 Rex ille dum fortissimus
De mortis inferno specu
Patrum senatum liberum
Educit ad vitae jubar.

Cujus sepulcrum plurimo
10 Custode signabat lapis,
Victor triumphat, et suo
Mortem sepulcro funerat.

Sat funeri, sat lacrimis,
Sat est datum doloribus;
15 'Surrexit exstinctor necis',
Clamat coruscans angelus.

*Tristes erant Apostoli
De Christi acerbo funere,
Quem morte crudelissima
20 Servi necarant impii.

Sermone verax angelus
Mulieribus praedixerat,
'Mox ore Christus gaudium
Gregi feret fidelium'.

Dawn gives its light to the sky, heaven re-echoes with praises, the world in triumph shouts aloud its joy and hell in terror roars out its rage as He, the king most mighty, comes from death's underworld cavern and brings in freedom the holy ones, there assembled, to light and life. His tomb was well guarded; a stone, sealed, covered its entrance. Yet He makes His way out in triumph, a conqueror, and His tomb becomes death's burial-place. Funeral rites, mourning and sorrow have had their day. 'Death's destroyer has arisen', proclaims the shining angel.

*But the Apostles were still grieving over Christ's bitter death that wicked servants had most cruelly inflicted on Him. A trustworthy angel had already told the women: 'Soon Christ will with His own lips bring joy to the faithful flock.' And while the women were

19. *haec*, sc. *aqua baptismatis;* also in next line.

20. *sepulcrum. Consepulti enim sumus cum illo per baptismum in mortem*, Rom. 6, 4. Cf. also lines 15–16.

21. *nobis diu . . . debitae . . . cruci*, to the cross that had long been the debt we owed.

For the last two verses in the Breviary, see 57, 25, note.

Notes on Hymn 59

Author. Unknown; cf. introduction to 57.

This long Easter hymn is divided in the Breviary, but it is well to read it in an unbroken text, if only so that the second section will not be judged as if *Tristes* were its ruling idea.

Use. Lines 1–16 at Lauds from Low Sunday to the Ascension; 17–32 at Vespers and Matins of Apostles during Paschaltide and 33–44 at Lauds of the same office. To each section are added 57, 25–28 and the doxology.

1. *purpurat.* Unless 'crimson' is meant, the idea is probably that of adorning, bringing light to. The exact meaning of *purpureus* and cognate words is often uncertain. The original text is: *Aurora lucis rutilat.*

2. *aether*, heaven; *resultat*; cf. *81*, 2.

5. *dum.* The action of the *dum* clause is contemporaneous with that of the first verse.

9–10. Cf. *munierunt sepulcrum, signantes lapidem cum custodibus*, Mt. 27, 66. *Signabat lapis* indicates the stone and the seal.

12. *mortem . . . funerat* is the revisers' idea.

13. *sat=satis. Datum est* goes with each of the nouns. *Funeri* here and *funere* in line 18 could mean death or burial, the use of *funus* in each case being due to the revisers.

17. *Tristes.* All reason to be sad and dispirited had gone with the Resurrection, lines 13–16, but until the Apostles knew that He *had* risen, they continued to be, *erant*, sad and bewildered.

18. *funere*, death. The unrevised line is *de nece sui Domini*, which is clearly about the death and which contrasts *Domini* with the *servi impii* of line 20.

21. *verax*, truthful. The message proved to be true and was from God who is *verax*, 20, 1, note. The original is *Sermone blando angelus*, where *blando* thinks of the comforting words 'Fear not . . .', Mt. 28, 5.

23. *ore*, by word of mouth, i.e. in person.

25 *Ad anxios apostolos*
Currunt statim dum nuntiae,
Illae micantis obvia
Christi tenent vestigia.

Galilaeae ad alta montium
30 *Se conferunt apostoli*
Jesuque, voti compotes,
Almo beantur lumine.

**Paschale mundo gaudium*
Sol nuntiat formosior,
35 *Cum luce fulgentem nova*
Jesum vident apostoli.

In carne Christi vulnera
Micare tamquam sidera
Mirantur, et quidquid vident
40 *Testes fideles praedicant.*

Rex Christe clementissime,
Tu corda nostra posside,
Ut lingua grates debitas
Tuo rependat nomini.

running with this message to the troubled Apostles, they meet the radiant Christ and clasp His feet. The Apostles betake themselves to the mountains of Galilee where, their desire satisfied, they rejoice in Jesus' love and light.

*The sun shining with unwonted beauty tells the world of the Easter joy when the Apostles see Jesus glorified in new brightness. They are amazed at the wounds in Christ's body that shine like stars, and as true witnesses they proclaim all they saw. Do You, Christ, king most merciful, take possession of our hearts that our tongue may repay You our debt of thanks.

Hymn 60

Note on Sequences

The *Victimae paschali, 60,* is the first example in this book of a Sequence, and a note about this class of composition will not be out of place.

Sequentia was the name given to the *jubilus* or musical prolongation of the last vowel of the word *alleluia*. The *jubilus* is divided into small sections, and to these parts separately as well as to the whole melody the name *sequentia* could be applied. The custom gradually came into being of adding words or a *Prosa* to the music of the *jubilus*. At first, perhaps in the eighth century, a text was added to some of the sections, the last vowel of such texts being, in some places, always the vowel *a* to which the next wordless section could be sung. Later on a text was added to the whole melody and so began what is now generally called a Sequence or, less generally, a Prose. Its full name would properly be *Sequentia cum prosa*.

27. *micantis* and *micare* in line 38, shining, radiant. *Obvia* with *vestigia*, the feet coming to meet.

28. *vestigia*, feet; cf. *52, 6.* For the whole verse see Mt. 28, 8–9.

29. *Galilaeae.* The message of Mt. 28, 7 and 10 is that the Apostles should go into Galilee, and this verse refers to the appearance in Galilee of Mt. 28, 16. This part of the hymn deals with the completion of the message to the women when the Apostles saw our Lord in Galilee, and their passage from being *Tristes* to *beantur.* The apparitions of Easter day in Jerusalem are summarized in 33–40.

ad alta montium = ad altos montes; cf. *in montem ubi constituerat illis Jesus,* Mt. 28, 16.

31. *compotes;* cf. *35, 15,* note.

34. *formosior,* with more beautiful (or, purer) light—partly because the sun was darkened at His death and partly as if the sun itself told men of the Easter joy by shining with a clearer light. In the original *mundo* is an adjective with *radio.* Cf. *gratior dies, 51, 3–4,* note, and *61, 24.*

35. Our Lord, the *verus sol, 12, 5,* and the *sol salutis, 51, 1,* also appears more beautiful as He comes resplendent in the new light of His glorified body.

39–40. The fact of the true bodily Resurrection and the fact that they were witnesses of it were the basis of the Apostles' preaching.

Just as the sung liturgical texts of the Mass are mostly prose, not poetry, so the earliest Proses were, as their name indicates, unmetrical, their structure being dictated by the length and shape of the melody. The first use of such texts is connected with the name of Notker *Balbulus,* the Stammerer, who was born about 840 and died as a monk of St Gall in Switzerland in 912. But whether such a connection is rightly asserted and, if rightly, what compositions are to be ascribed to him, are matters of great dispute. As time went on, the words were not attached to an existing melody but words and music were composed together. This made for rhythmical structure in prose and, later still, in poetry until the Sequence reached its glory in the compositions of Adam of St Victor (cf. the introduction to Corpus Christi and the notes on its hymns), the *Lauda Sion, 74,* and the *Dies irae, 154.* The *Victimae,* which is in rhythmical prose, belongs to the transitional period of the history of the Sequence.

A Sequence is distinguished, musically, from the *alleluia* and the *alleluia* verse by being a syllabic chant, or practically syllabic; and from a hymn by having a new melody for different sections, for instance for each pair of verses or half-verses. (For further information on Sequences consult, besides books on hymns, *Music in the*

Hymn 60

1 *Victimae paschali laudes*
   immolent Christiani.

To the Paschal Victim let Christians offer a sacrifice of praise.

2a *Agnus redemit oves;*
   Christus innocens Patri
   reconciliavit peccatores.

The Lamb redeemed the sheep. Christ, sinless, reconciled sinners to the Father.

2b *Mors et vita duello*
   conflixere mirando;
   dux vitae mortuus regnat vivus.

Death and life were locked together in an unique struggle. Life's captain died; now He reigns, never more to die.

3a *Dic nobis, Maria,*
   quid vidisti in via?

Tell us, Mary. 'What did you see on the way?'

3b *'Sepulcrum Christi viventis*
   et gloriam vidi resurgentis;

'I saw the tomb of the now living Christ. I saw the glory of Christ, now risen. I saw angels who gave witness; the cloths too which once had covered head and limbs.

4a *angelicos testes,*
   sudarium et vestes.

4b *Surrexit Christus spes mea;*
   praecedet suos in Galilaeam'.

Christ my hope has risen. He will go before His own into Galilee.'

5a *(Credendum est magis soli Mariae veraci*
   quam Judaeorum turbae fallaci.)

(The faithful Mary's testimony of itself is preferable to that of the deceitful Jewish crowd.)

5b *Scimus Christum surrexisse a mortuis vere;*
   Tu nobis, victor Rex, miserere.

We know that Christ has indeed risen from the dead. Do You, conqueror and king, have mercy on us.

Hymn 61

Salve, festa dies, toto venerabilis aevo,
   Qua Deus infernum vicit et astra tenet.

Welcome to this day of joy, the day that through eternity will be held in honour, the day when God defeated hell and became master of heaven.

Continued

Middle Ages, by Gustave Reese (Dent), books on the history of plainsong and on the Lutheran chorale, books on the growth of religious drama and on the historical development of the Mass.)

Notes on Hymn 60

Author. Ascribed by tradition to Wipo, chaplain to Conrad II and tutor of Henry III. He died about 1048.

Use. Sequence of the Mass during Easter week. It is in rhythmical prose with four pairs of strophe and antistrophe, the first strophe being, as often, unpaired and stating the subject of the composition. The Missal, by omitting 5a, in effect makes 5b unpaired as well.

The text is divided according to the musical setting; 1a has its own music; 2a and 2b correspond in literary structure and music; likewise 3a and 4a, and 3b and 4b; 5a is of the same structure as 5b and, presumably, had the same music.

A sequence was sung by choir answering choir, perhaps by men answering boys, or tenors answering basses. The melodic range of sequences is accordingly much greater than that of most of the music of the *Graduale.*

1. *immolent;* so that our *sacrificium laudis* may answer our Lord's sacrifice.

2b. *duello,* poetical for *bello. Conflixere = conflixerunt.*

3b. *viventis,* used as a present participle; *resurgentis* used as a past participle; cf. *Christus resurgens* of Rom. 6, 9.

4b. *suos,* the reading of the *Graduale,* must be correct, for the line needs ten syllables. The Missal has *vos,* by attraction, probably, from the Gospel of Easter Sunday. *Galilaeam* is the reading of the liturgical books, but some editors put *Galilaea*—presumably to keep the rhyme, of which the *Victimae* shows many examples. If *Galilaea* be read, it is the equivalent of an accusative.

5a. The author takes only the witness of Mary Magdalene, 3a–4b, and her word by itself, *soli,* is sufficient. Her message, like the angel's, proved to be true, *veraci* (cf. 59, 21) and is sufficient to disprove what the Jews said, *turbae fallaci.* From the author's point of view, 5a is a most necessary part.

Notes on Hymn 61

Author. Fortunatus; see 52. This hymn is formed from one of several poetical letters sent by Fortunatus to Felix, Bishop of Nantes. Its first line is *Tempora florigero rutilant distincta sereno,* and the whole poem runs to 110 lines. (Cf. Migne, PL. 88, 130 or Dreves, *Analecta,* L, 76 or Leo's edition, III, ix.)

In this poem Fortunatus shows a great love of nature and describes with force and beauty the re-

Ecce renascentis testatur gratia mundi
  Omnia cum Domino dona redisse suo.

5 *Namque triumphanti post tristia tartara Christo*
  Undique fronde nemus, gramina flore favent.

Qui crucifixus erat Deus ecce per omnia regnat
  Dantque creatori cuncta creata precem.

Christe, salus rerum, bone conditor atque redemptor,
10 *Unica progenies ex deitate Patris,*

Aequalis, consors, socius, cum Patre coaevus,
  Quo sumpsit mundus principe principium,

Qui genus humanum cernens mersisse profundo,
  Ut hominem eriperes, es quoque factus homo.

15 *Funeris exsequias pateris, vitae auctor et orbis,*
  Intras mortis iter dando salutis opem.

Tristia cesserunt infernae vincula legis
  Expavitque chaos luminis ore premi.

Pollicitam sed redde fidem, precor, alma potestas,
20 *Tertia lux rediit, surge, sepulte meus.*

Solve catenatas inferni carceris umbras,
  Et revoca sursum quidquid ad ima ruit.

Redde tuam faciem, videant ut saecula lumen,
  Redde diem, qui nos te moriente fugit.

25 *Immaculata tuis plebs haec vegetetur in ulnis*
  Atque Deo purum pignus ad astra feras.

Una corona tibi de te tribuatur ab alto,
  Altera de populo vernet adepta tuo.

The beauty of the world today as it springs to life again, is witness that all nature's gifts have returned with nature's Lord. And certainly everywhere trees in leaf and meadow flowers greet Christ as He returns in triumph from the gloom of hell.

It was God that was crucified, but now He rules omnipotent and all creation offers prayer to its creator. Christ Jesus, the world's saviour and man's kindly creator and redeemer, You are the only-begotten of God the Father. The Father's equal, sharer and companion with Him in the Godhead from eternity, at the very beginning You gave the world its being. Moreover, when You saw mankind buried in the depths of sin, You actually became man to rescue man. You, giver of life and creator of the world, allowed men to perform the burial rites over You, trod the road of death and so brought man the help of salvation. The cruel bondage of hell's tyranny disappeared, and the realm of darkness fled in terror before the overwhelming light. Love divine and power eternal, fulfil, I pray You, the word of Your promise. The third day has come again. Arise, my buried Lord. Free those that lie bound in hell's dark prison, and recall heavenwards all that is in danger of falling down to destruction. Show us Your face again that the ages may see its light. Show us again the light of day that disappeared while You were dying.

Let this people of Yours, now freed from sin, grow to vigour in Your arms. Take to heaven this new generation, washed clean by baptism for God. The crown You have won for Yourself be Yours in heaven. May another crown, won for You by Your people, also be Yours.

awakening of nature in the spring. Spring is nature's resurrection and is at once a symbol of our Lord's resurrection and nature's way of greeting the risen Lord. 'Each verse brings a fresh trait, a new point of beauty and exultation, all this rejoicing is brought into connection with the resurrection of Christ', W.

Metre. Elegaic.

Use. Many hymns have been formed from this poem, but none of them are in the Missal or Breviary. They were in use as processional hymns for Easter and the Ascension, the first two lines being used as a refrain. Processional hymns for other feasts were also formed, but they owe nothing to the model except the first line and the elegaic metre.

The text above consists of lines 39, 40, 31–4, 37, 38, 47, 48, 51, 52, 55, 56, 59–62, 65, 66, 73–6 and 107–10 of the original. Of this composite text lines 1–6, 13, 14, 17–24 are the text of the Easter hymn as found, for instance, in *Plainsong for Schools,* Part II; lines 7 and 8 are the second verse of the short Easter hymn in *Laudate Dominum,* compiled by V. G. L.; lines 27, 28, 9–12 form the Ascension hymn in the same book, the second line of the refrain being *qua Deus in caelum scandit et astra tenet.* Lines 15, 16, 25 and 26 are in none of the centos just mentioned, but are in other centos and are added here to help the sequence of thought. All 61 plus another 26 lines can be found in W, *36.*

1. *dies;* cf. *51,* 13–14, notes.

2. After this line, the poem goes on to describe Easter day as *Nobilitas anni, mensum decus, arma dierum,/Horarum splendor, scripula, puncta fovens. Arma* as the protection of each day, and *fovens* as the protection of the minutes, *scripula,* and seconds, *puncta.*

3. *Ecce,* because in the full poem Fortunatus has just described how 'the days grow longer and brighter and the flowers begin to make glad the meadows. . . . The leaves begin to bud, the bees appear, the birds are singing again, and the voice of the nightingale makes sweeter the echoing air', Raby, p. 92.

Renascentis, as nature's awakening is in progress at Easter.

9. *salus;* abstract for *salvator.* Fortunatus often uses abstract for concrete.

11. *consors.* W gives *concors* without noting any variants.

12. *quo* with *principe.* Because of *principium, principe* means beginner, creator rather than king.

13. *Cernens;* the equivalent of a pluperfect, the action being prior to *es factus. Mersisse,* intransitive; *profundo,* used as a noun.

14. *Quoque* 'apparently means "even", "actually", and it qualifies the following words *factus homo'.* So W in his long note on this word.

18. *chaos;* cf. *22,* 7, note. *Premi.* i.e. *se premi* and, notes W, almost equivalent to *quia pressum est.*

19. *pollicitam . . . fidem,* the promised fulfilment—*pollicitam* being used passively. For the promise, cf. Mt. 20, 19.

potestas; abstract for concrete, cf. note on line 9. A similar use of *potestas* in *O pater, o hominum rerumque aeterna potestas,* Verg. *Aen.* X, 18.

20. *lux,* i.e. *dies; meus* = *mi.*

22. *quidquid,* everything else, over and above what is mentioned in line 21. *Ruit,* that is in danger of being lost—present rather than a perfect, W.

24. *diem,* light of day; *fugit,* a perfect—the short *u* being a metrical licence common in Fortunatus. Cf. Mt. 27, 45 for the darkness at the Crucifixion; cf. also *59,* 34, note.

25. The last four lines are the conclusion of the poem and are addressed to Felix. When they are used in a hymn, they are addressed to our Lord.

immaculata . . . haec plebs, i.e. the newly baptized at Nantes. Felix as their bishop must nurture them, *vegetetur,* and *in ulnis* as if they were *infantes.* The same idea recurs in the next line.

26. *pignus,* used collectively for *pignora,* pledges, i.e. children.

27. *una,* because of Felix's own life (or the earthly life of Christ); *de te,* i.e. won by you.

28. *altera,* because of his diocese (or Christ's mystical body). With *vernet* supply *tibi* from the preceding line; *adepta* is used passively. May another crown bloom for you won by your people, W.

Hymn 62

Salutis humanae sator,
Jesu, voluptas cordium,
Orbis redempti conditor
Et casta lux amantium,

5 Qua victus es clementia
Ut nostra ferres crimina,
Mortem subires innocens,
A morte nos ut tolleres?

Perrumpis infernum chaos,
10 Vinctis catenas detrahis,
Victor triumpho nobili
Ad dexteram Patris sedes.

Te cogat indulgentia
Ut damna nostra sarcias
15 Tuique vultus compotes,
Dites beato lumine.

Tu, dux ad astra et semita,
Sis meta nostris cordibus,
Sis lacrimarum gaudium,
20 Sis dulce vitae praemium.

Jesus, author of man's salvation and delight of his heart, founder of the world of the redeemed and pure light of God's lovers, what feeling of pity was it that compelled You to shoulder the burden of our sins and, though sinless, to undergo death to set us free from death? You forced Your way into hell's black realm, struck the chains off those in bondage, entered heaven, a conqueror in noble triumph, and now sit at the Father's right hand. May Your mercy prevail on You to repair the harm we have suffered and to reward us with the light of happiness, our desire to see You satisfied at last. You are our leader and the way to heaven; may You also be the goal on which our hearts are set, our joy in tribulation and life's sweet reward.

Hymn 63

Aeterne rex altissime,
Redemptor et fidelium,
Cui mors perempta detulit
Summae triumphum gloriae,

5 Ascendis orbes siderum,
Quo te vocabat caelitus
Collata, non humanitus,
Rerum potestas omnium,

Ut trina rerum machina
10 Caelestium, terrestrium
Et inferorum condita
Flectat genu jam subdita.

Eternal king, God most high and redeemer of the faithful, the destruction of death gained You a most glorious triumph. You ascend to the starry heavens whither the dominion over all things that God, not man, bestowed on You, was summoning You so that the three parts of creation, heaven, earth and hell, may now in subjection bend the knee before You. The

Notes on Hymn 62

Author. Unknown, of seventh or eighth century.
Use. Hymn at Vespers and Lauds of the Ascension.

1. *sator*, sower, author.

2. *voluptas*, satisfaction, delight (whether bodily or spiritual, whether good or bad). *Omne id, quo gaudemus, voluptas est*, Cic. *Fin.* I, 11, 27; *trahit sua quemque voluptas*, Virg. *Ecl.* 2, 65 (and cf. lessons of Whit Wednesday). Our Lord, now ascended, is the *voluptas cordium*, since in Him should be centred all our hope and love; cf. lines 17–20 and *63, 17–28*.

6. *Ferres* and *subires* are the results of *clementia*, and *tolleres* the result of the two verbs. Cf. Is. 53, 4 and 1 Pet. 2, 24.

9. *chaos*, cf. *61, 18*.

11–12. The ascension is mentioned as the term of the resurrection. So Fortunatus in his Easter hymn mentions the resurrection as the pledge of the ascension; and cf. John, 20, 17.

15. *Compotes*; cf. *35, 15*, note.

16. *Dites, dito*, 1, enrich.

17. *semita = via* of John 14, 6.

18. *meta*, goal, aim. For 17–20, cf. *41, 17–20*, note.

Notes on Hymn 63

Author. Unknown. The question of date is not easy to settle, as the hymn appears in different forms in the MSS. Cf. W. *113*, Julian and B. Unlike *62*, it was not altered much by the revisers—the greatest changes are in the first two verses.

Use. Hymn at Matins for the Ascension.

3. *cui*, to whom the destruction, *perempta*, of death brought a triumph. . . . The first three verses form one sentence.

6–8. whither, *quo*, the sovereignty over all things conferred on You by heaven, *caelitus collata*, not by men, *humanitus*, summoned you. Cf. Mt. 28, 18.

9–11. So that the created, *condita*, threefold fabric of the world, *trina rerum machina*, namely of heaven, earth and hell. The reference here in *trina machina* is to Phil. 2, 10; for the usual meaning in hymns cf. *95, 1–2*.

Tremunt videntes angeli
Versam vicem mortalium;
15 *Peccat caro, mundat caro,*
Regnat Deus Dei caro.

Sis ipse nostrum gaudium,
Manens olympo praemium,
Mundi regis qui fabricam,
20 *Mundana vincens gaudia.*

Hinc te precantes quaesumus,
Ignosce culpis omnibus,
Et corda sursum subleva
Ad te superna gratia,

25 *Ut cum repente coeperis*
Clarere nube judicis,
Poenas repellas debitas,
Reddas coronas perditas.

angels tremble as they see the change in man's destiny. Flesh had sinned, Flesh washes away that sin and God made flesh reigns as God. Ruler of all creation and giver of a joy that is infinitely beyond all earthly ones, be to us our joy and our abiding reward in heaven. We, Your suppliants on earth, beg this favour: pardon all our sins and with grace from heaven lift up our hearts to You so that, when You appear without warning as our judge, resplendent on the clouds of heaven, You will remit the punishment we deserve and give us back our lost crowns.

---

6. PENTECOST

Sancti Spiritus illustratione is the phrase of the Pentecost prayer, almost universally translated as 'by the light of the holy Spirit'. Besides this meaning of 'light', *illustratio,* as a term of rhetoric, signifies a 'vivid representation' which *non tam dicere videtur quam ostendere*—the compelling evidence of the thing itself or of the example used to illustrate a point. This seems an excellent description of the first Pentecost when God showed the faithful beyond all doubt that the Spirit had indeed come. Words were not needed, were not used. The wordless proof and signs were in terms of a mighty wind, the elemental spirit, and fire. The manifestation came suddenly and affected one house only, but all within knew what it was that had happened and were filled with the Spirit. But to the Jews also Pentecost was an *illustratio,* and three thousand were convinced and baptized. The Church puts side by side the texts *replevit totam domum* and *replevit orbem terrarum* and leaves us to see that the one is a commentary on the other.

Just as creation was a unique event, so this vivid and visible manifestation of the Spirit happened but once; but its results will continue to the end of time and into eternity. These results as well as the manifestation are expressed not only in terms of

14. *versam vicem*, the changed lot (state) of men; *vicem*, cf. *20, 2*.

15–16. Flesh (Adam) sins, flesh (Christ) cleanses (man from sin), and the flesh of God (i.e. the God-man) reigns as God.

18. *manens*, abiding—*manens* being used as an adj.; cf. *commune manens gaudium*, quoted in the introduction to this section.

20. *vincens*, surpassing; cf. *vincis, 52, 26*.

21. *Hinc;* (1) therefore, for this cause; (2), possibly, from where we stand, 'on this lowly earth', W.

23. *subleva*, and lift our hearts up to You. *Sursum enim cor non ad Dominum, superbia vocatur; sursum autem cor ad Dominum, refugium vocatur,* St Augustine, 5th lesson of Sunday within octave of the Ascension.

25. *repente* and *nube;* cf. Luke 21, 27 and 34.

---

light, but of fire also, of wind and water. Their exterior expression is, as it was on the first Pentecost day, concerned mostly with the apostolate and preaching; their internal expression is seen in the growth in sanctity of the individual—*verbis ut essent proflui et caritate fervidi, 66, 7–8.*

All this is to be found in the hymns of this section. Pentecost is a feast of light, as the Sequence in particular shows. But it is not a feast of light only; it is the feast of all creation, whose elemental phenomena are used as signs and types of this new creation. If God takes from creatures their spirit, says the Psalmist, they die and go to dust; but if He sends His Spirit, they are created and earth comes to life again. In similar language the Church sings of her creation and birth—significantly changing the *emittes* of the psalm to *emitte*. For in God the Spirit is the eternal 'emanation'—the Fire kindled from eternity by the Light, which is the Father and the Son; but to man He is God's gift, to be man's, if he ask. So the Church sings *Emitte . . . veni . . . visita.* But as the Gift is also the Giver, the Church also sings *lava . . . flecte . . . fove . . . reple.*

> *Laeti bibamus sobriam*
> *Ebrietatem Spiritus.*

I

Hymn 64

Veni, creator Spiritus,
Mentes tuorum visita,
Imple superna gratia,
Quae tu creasti pectora;

5 Qui diceris Paraclitus,
Altissimi donum Dei,
Fons vivus, ignis, caritas
Et spiritalis unctio.

Tu septiformis munere,
10 Digitus paternae dexterae,
Tu rite promissum Patris,
Sermone ditans guttura—

Accende lumen sensibus
Infunde amorem cordibus,
15 Infirma nostri corporis
Virtute firmans perpeti.

Hostem repellas longius
Pacemque dones protinus;
Ductore sic te praevio
20 Vitemus omne noxium.

Per te sciamus da Patrem,
Noscamus atque Filium,
Teque utriusque Spiritum
Credamus omni tempore.

Creator Spirit, come and visit the souls that are Yours; fill with heavenly grace the hearts that You created. You are called by the names of Paraclete, gift of God most high, spring of life, fire, love and the soul's anointing. Seven gifts are Yours to give. You are the finger of the Father's right hand. You, the clear promise of the Father, give men's tongues the grace of speech. Kindle a light in our minds, pour love into our hearts and uphold with Your unfailing strength the frailty of our human nature. Drive our enemy far from us and give us always the gift of peace; so may it be that, with Your grace ever guiding us in this way, we may avoid all that is sinful. Grant that through You we may know the Father and the Son, and may we ever believe You to be the Spirit of both the Father and the Son.

Author. Unknown, but probably of the ninth century.

'There is no evidence to connect the authorship with any known name', W. As no MS of earlier date than the tenth century contains it, a date in the ninth century seems to fit the case. This makes the claim of Rabanus Maurus, 776–856, not impossible. 'By about the beginning of the eleventh century, it is found in MSS representing England, France, Germany with Switzerland, Italy and Spain. Its earliest liturgical use seems to have been at Vespers in Whitsuntide', W. Its use at ordinations is traced back to the eleventh century.

Use. Hymn at Vespers and Terce in Whitsuntide. It is also used at the ordination of priests, the consecration of bishops, the dedication of churches and, in general, on all solemn occasions when the Church needs the grace of the Holy Spirit.

1. *Veni* is the petition *par excellence* of Pentecost, especially in the texts of the Mass. Note the climax *veni, visita* and *imple,* which the rest of the hymn elaborates.

creator. Hymns address God as creator sometimes without distinguishing the Persons, as in *rerum creator, 29,* 2, and sometimes by addressing one of the Persons, e.g. the Son in *Creator alme siderum, 34,* 1 and the Spirit in lines 1 and 4 of this verse. *Creator* also refers here to the 'new creation'—the passage from one creation to the other being common in the Pentecost texts, especially in the adaptation of *Emittes spiritum tuum et creabuntur,* Ps. 103, 30.

2. *visita*. 'Visit' in English is now a weak word, but →

Notes on Hymn 64

it was once, like the Latin *visitare,* a strong word. Its meaning is nearer to our 'visitation' than to 'visit'. The visitation by the Holy Ghost on the first Pentecost was thorough-going enough, transforming completely the Apostles. We ask here that the Holy Ghost will be as uncompromising in His visit to us as He was with the Apostles, for the comfort of the Spirit is the result of His taking possession of our souls and cannot be acquired in any other way. The hymn avoids the natural temptation to pray for the comfort without having to undergo a spiritual transformation. (On the word 'visit', cf. *Hymns and the Faith,* Erik Routley (John Murray), pp. 137, 144 and 209.) Cf. also *19,* 5, note.

5. *Qui.* Some interpret *qui* as a relative and others as the equivalent of a personal pronoun. In either case the verse gives reasons for the petitions of the first verse. Similarly the third verse is treated by some as a complete thing and by others as introducing the next verse. The original text is: *Qui Paraclitus diceris,* where *Paraclitus* is used quantitatively—*cli* being a long syllable. This is the only example in the (unrevised) Breviary.

6. *donum. Accipietis donum Spiritus sancti,* Acts 2, 38; *donum Dei existimasti pecunia possideri,* Acts 8, 20. *Per donum, quod est Spiritus sanctus, multa propria dona dividuntur membris Christi,* S. Aug. *de Trin.* XV, 24; cf. S. Thomas, S.T. I, 38, 2.

7. *fons vivus;* cf. John 4, 10–14 and 7, 38–9, where the words *quam ego dabo* and *nondum enim erat Spiritus datus* connect *fons* with *donum* of the preceding line.

ignis. Cf. *Ignem veni mittere in terram,* Lk. 12, 49 and the use of this text in the second collect of Whit Saturday. *Caritas.* Cf. *Caritas Dei diffusa est in cordibus nostris per Spiritum sanctum, qui datus est nobis,* Rom. 5, 5. The words *datus est* connect with *donum;* and cf. *19,* 7.

8. *spiritalis (=spiritualis) unctio.* To be understood of the mystery of love which anointed us sharers of the 'royal priesthood', and also of all the influence of the Spirit on our minds and heart, according to the words *sed vos unctionem habetis a Sancto, et nostis omnia,* 1 John 2, 20; cf. Pimont, *ad loc.*

10. *digitus.* Original: *dextrae Dei tu digitus,* where

the trochee in the third foot, through the effect of the accent, becomes the equivalent of a spondee and so correct—but not correct enough for the revisers. The original also preserves the rhetorical repetition of *tu.*

In digito Dei of Lk. 11, 20 is *in spiritu Dei* in Mt. 12, 28, and so *digitus=spiritus.* Similarly: *digitum ... pro Spiritu, ut lex digito Dei scripta est,* Ambr. in Ps. 118, 15, 9, with reference to Exod. 8, 19 and Deut. 9, 10. These lines are an echo of Hilary's words: *Tu es digitus, id est potentia dextrae Dei, quia sicut modi digitorum sunt varii, ita varia dona sunt Spiritus sancti.*

11. *rite promissum,* in apposition with *Tu*—You, the clear (express) promise of the Father. *Promissum =promissio* and not, with Pimont, the participle; cf. *Ego mitto promissum Patris mei in vos,* Lk. 24, 49 and *promissionem Patris,* Acts 1, 4. *Rite* is the equivalent of an adjective; cf. *6,* 14 and *7,* 11.

12. *sermone;* cf. Acts 2, 3–4; *guttura,* throats, for *linguas.*

15–16 are from St Ambrose's *Intende qui regis Israel,* where they are addressed to our Lord; as applied to the Spirit, cf. Eph. 3, 16. For *infirma* with a genitive, cf. *49,* 6.

18. *protinus,* in the less common meaning of 'continually' rather than 'forthwith', as in *118,* 19; W.

19. *ductore ... praevio.* Perhaps referring to the guiding cloud in the wilderness, W; or, more probably, to: *spiritum meum ponam in medio vestri; et faciam ut in praeceptis meis ambuletis,* Ezech. 36, 27; *Praevio;* cf. *praeviam, 44,* 6.

21–24. According to W, this is a quasi-doxology. But it looks more like a petition (though mentioning the three Persons), just as *57,* 25–8 is a petition. That it is the last verse of the original does not make it a doxology, for by the ninth century a writer would know that if he did not provide a doxology, one of the traditional ones would be added for liturgical use. Hence the different doxologies which W found added in the MSS after this verse.

23. *Teque,* sc. *esse.* Original: *Te utriusque Spiritum. Utriusque;* cf. *spiritus Patris vestri,* Mt. 10, 20 and *Spiritus Jesu,* Acts 16, 7. These two lines may be a clue to the date of the hymn.

Hymn 65

Jam Christus astra ascenderat,
Reversus unde venerat,
Patris fruendum munere,
Sanctum daturus Spiritum.

5 Solemnis urgebat dies
Quo mystico septemplici
Orbis volutus septies,
Signat beata tempora,

Cum lucis hora tertia
10 Repente mundus intonat,
Apostolis orantibus
Deum venire nuntiat.

De Patris ergo lumine
Decorus ignis almus est,
15 Qui fida Christi pectora
Calore verbi compleat.

Impleta gaudent viscera
Afflata sancto Spiritu,
Vocesque diversas sonant,
20 Fantur Dei magnalia;

Notique cunctis gentibus,
Graecis, Latinis, barbaris;
Simulque demirantibus
Linguis loquuntur omnium.

25 Judaea tunc incredula,
Vesana torvo spiritu,
Madere musto sobrios
Christi fideles increpat.

Sed editis miraculis
30 Occurrit et docet Petrus,
Falsum profari perfidos,
Joele teste comprobans.

Christ had now ascended to the heaven He had left, to send the holy Spirit Who was to be received as the Father's gift. The day appointed was now at hand that would mark the beginning of the age of blessedness, for the cycle of seven days had revolved in the holy number of seven, when suddenly at the third hour of the day a mighty sound is heard on earth, telling the Apostles at prayer that God had come. From the Father's light there comes the kindly, gracious fire of love to fill with burning eloquence those that believed in Christ. And they, their hearts filled with the inspiration of the holy Spirit, rejoice, speak in different tongues and tell of God's wonders. They are understood by men from all parts, whether civilized (Greek or Latin) or not, as they speak, to the universal astonishment of those present, in their respective languages. Then the Jews, still faithless, are possessed by the spirit of blind anger and hate, and accuse Christ's sober servants of being drunk with new wine. But Peter confronts them with his Master's miracles and shows the falsity of what the perfidious Jews are saying, proving it to them from the words of Joel.

Notes on Hymn 65

Author. Unknown, of the fourth or fifth century. The style is not Ambrosian, there being, in the original, seven examples of a spondee in the second foot and a hiatus in line 23.

This hymn and the next are metrical settings of Acts 2, 1–16—this one being completely historical and the next one developing into a prayer in its last two verses. They have little intrinsic value.

Use. Hymn at Matins during Whitsuntide.

3. *fruendum* is probably to be interpreted from the Apostles' point of view—to be received as the Father's gift.

5. *urgebat.* The MSS, but not the different Breviaries, vary between *urgebat* and *surgebat,* and the latter gives the better sense. *Urgebat,* was pressing on, W; drew nigh, B. But the period of waiting was over and the day itself had actually come, cf. Acts 2, 1. *Surgebat,* was beginning; cf. *Lux ecce surgit aurea,* 15, 1 and Verg. *Aen.* 3, 588.

6. *septemplici* is used as a noun and means 'seven' rather than a 'week' because of *mystico;* cf. *sacrum septenarium,* 67, 27.

7. *orbis.* B translates as earth, but W as circuit, i.e. a round of time. In the latter case it is the equivalent of *orbita,* 66, 2 and *circulus,* 66, 15. The expression of numbers brings about curious periphrases; cf. 50, 3–4.

12. *Deum,* i.e. the holy Ghost. There is perhaps a reference to *Deus manifeste veniet,* Ps. 49, 3.

13. *ergo* has no particular force, but merely continues the narrative.

14. *decorus ignis* is practically the equivalent of *sanctus Spiritus* and is qualified by *almus.* For *almus* as a divine attribute, cf. *34,* 1; *61,* 19 and *67,* 7, note.

15. *fida,* believing in. *Fidus* usually governs the dative, but in poetry it may also take a genitive.

16. *verbi.* A capital for *verbi* is incorrect, since the reference is clearly to the gift of eloquence. For a somewhat similar use of *verbi,* cf. *71,* 5.

17. *impleta* takes up *compleat* of line 16, and *afflata* answers *calore verbi.* The first result is *gaudent,* the second *sonant, fantur* etc.

21. *noti* sc. *sunt,* understood by.

22. *barbaris,* i.e. neither Greek nor Latin and therefore uncivilized.

26. *vesana,* maddened; cf. *insanus, 84,* 16 and *amens, 39,* 5.

Torvo spiritu, savage spirit—the opposite of the loving Spirit, and so its fruits will be the opposite of those of the Spirit.

27. *madere musto,* drunk, sodden, with new wine; cf. *66,* 11, from which the revisers took the phrase.

29. *miraculis,* i.e. our Lord's miracles, Acts 2, 22, though some think the reference is to Peter's miracles, Acts 2, 43.

31. *falsum . . . perfidos.* The Spirit is the Spirit of truth, John 14, 17. Unbelief and falsehood are always found where the Spirit does not dwell.

32. The hymn stops abruptly, and some MSS tried to remedy this by adding another verse.

Hymn 66

Beata nobis gaudia
Anni reduxit orbita,
Cum spiritus Paraclitus
Illapsus est apostolis.

5 Ignis vibrante lumine
Linguae figuram detulit,
Verbis ut essent proflui
Et caritate fervidi.

Linguis loquuntur omnium
10 Turbae pavent gentilium;
Musto madere deputant
Quos Spiritus repleverat.

Patrata sunt haec mystice,
Paschae peracto tempore,
15 Sacro dierum circulo
Quo lege fit remissio.

Te nunc Deus piissime
Vultu precamur cernuo,
Illapsa nobis caelitus
20 Largire dona Spiritus.

Dudum sacrata pectora
Tua replesti gratia;
Dimitte nostra crimina
Et da quieta tempora.

The yearly round has brought us once again the day of joy and happiness when the Spirit, the Paraclete, came down upon the Apostles. He took the appearance of a tongue in the form of a fire's quivering flame so that they should be eloquent in speech and on fire with love. The crowds were amazed as the Apostles spoke the languages of all present, while the Jews derided those that were full of the holy Spirit as being drunk with new wine. These things were done in holy mystery when the paschal season was over and the round of days had reached the sacred number that, by law, meant remission and freedom. In profound humility we now ask this of You, most loving God: grant us the gifts of the Spirit—the gifts that come down from heaven. In days gone by You filled with grace Your holy servants' hearts; and now pardon us, Your sinful servants, and grant us peaceful days.

Hymn 67

Veni, sancte Spiritus,
Et emitte caelitus
  Lucis tuae radium:
Veni, pater pauperum,
5 Veni, dator munerum,
  Veni, lumen cordium.

Come, holy Spirit, and from heaven direct on man the rays of Your light. Come, father of the poor; come, giver of God's gifts; come, light of men's hearts. Kindly Paraclete, in Your

Notes on Hymn 66

Author. Unknown, but of about the same date as 65. There is no sufficient evidence to connect it, as some have done, with St Hilary.

Use. Hymn at Lauds during Whitsuntide.

2. *orbita*, circle; cf. *65, 7*, note.

4. *illapsus*, came down upon. But *illabi* rather suggests stealing down, cf. *12, 5*, note—a not very appropriate meaning here. Original: *effulsit in discipulos*.

5–6. The fire with tremulous flame assumed the shape of a tongue, B. Or; the Spirit took the form of a tongue in the quivering light of fire, W.

7. *verbis* refers back to *linguae* and *caritate fervidi* to *ignis*.

11. *deputant*, reckon them, put them down as. *Deputare* sometimes has a sinister meaning, as here, and sometimes a good one, as in *imbuta felle deputans, 82, 7*. *Deputatur in 74, 69* = set aside for, appointed for.

12. *repleverat*; for the expression cf. *repletus Spiritu sancto Petrus*, Acts 4, 8.

13–16. These things were done, *patrata*, in mystic wise, *mystice*, at the fulfilment of the passover season at the sacred number of days when by the law release was made, W.

Mystice, because of the number seven, cf. *65, 6*, note. The paschal season closed after seven rounds of seven days each. The number fifty recalled the year of jubilee or release; cf. Numbers 36, 4; Lev. 25, 8 and Ezech. 46, 17.

circulo, in line 15, is the revisers' substitute for *numero*—hence W's 'sacred number'.

18. *cernuo*, downcast, humble; cf. *2, 31; 71, 13*.

19. *illapsa*; see note on line 14, but the word is appropriate here.

21. *dudum* (with *replesti*, not with *sacrata*), of old, formerly—though its more general meaning is 'a short time ago'. *Sacrata pectora*, referring to the Apostles.

23. *Dimitte*. Original: *Dimitte nunc peccamina*, so that *dudum* and *nunc* answer each other; but *nunc* is still implicit in *dimitte*. *Nostra crimina* in contrast with *sacrata pectora*.

Notes on Hymn 67

Author. ?Stephen Langton.

The style of this sequence is of the twelfth or thirteenth century, and this rules out many who have been suggested as its author. The MSS evidence points the same way. MSS of the eleventh or twelfth century which have the *Veni sancte*, have it as an addition in later writing, but some MSS of the late twelfth and of the thirteenth century have it in the same writing as the rest of the contents—consistent, that is, with a date near to the reign of Innocent III, 1198–1216.

Of all those suggested as author, only Innocent himself and Stephen Langton would fit such a date. Though there is a contemporary reference which

Notes continued on p. 112

Consolator optime,
Dulcis hospes animae,
　　Dulce refrigerium:
10 *In labore requies,*
　　In aestu temperies,
　　　In fletu solatium.

　O lux beatissima,
　Reple cordis intima
15　　*Tuorum fidelium:*
　Sine tuo numine
　Nihil est in homine,
　　Nihil est innoxium.

　Lava quod est sordidum,
20 *Riga quod est aridum,*
　　Sana quod est saucium,
　Flecte quod est rigidum,
　Fove quod est frigidum,
　　Rege quod est devium.

25 *Da tuis fidelibus*
　In te confidentibus
　　Sacrum septenarium;
　Da virtutis meritum,
　Da salutis exitum,
30　　*Da perenne gaudium.*

gracious visits to man's soul You bring relief and consolation. If it is weary with toil, You bring it ease; in the heat of temptation, Your grace cools it; if sorrowful, Your words console it. Light most blessed, shine on the hearts of Your faithful—even into their darkest corners; for without Your aid man can do nothing good, and everything is sinful. Wash clean the sinful soul, rain down Your grace on the parched soul and heal the injured soul. Soften the hard heart, cherish and warm the ice-cold heart, and give direction to the wayward. Give Your seven holy gifts to Your faithful, for their trust is in You. Give them reward for their virtuous acts; give them a death that ensures salvation; give them unending bliss.

Notes continued from p. 111

seems to connect the sequence with Innocent, Dreves and Blume reject such an attribution as 'unverified and unverifiable'. There is the further difficulty that the use of the *Veni sancte* seems to have spread from Paris, while one would have expected Rome if Innocent wrote it—unless he wrote it before he left Paris at the age of 21.

The positive evidence in favour of Stephen Langton is given by a contemporary English Cistercian, who quotes as an authority 'what Master Stephen de Langton, by the grace of God Archbishop of Canterbury, a man worthy of respect for his life and learning, says in praise of the Holy Ghost in a splendid sequence which he composed about the Holy Ghost, namely: *Consolator optime, dulces hospes animae, dulce refrigerium, etc*'. It would seem that Stephen was alive when this quotation was used.

Raby, 342–3, thought the case for Stephen →

'possible and even probable'. Thurston, *Familiar Prayers*, pp. 54 ff. accepted it as practically certain. Grattan Flood, *The Tablet*, 22 May, 1926 and F. M. Powicke in his monograph on Langton, favoured Stephen's authorship (cf. Blakeney, pp. 90, 91).

Metre. Accentual trochaic dimeter catalectic, rhyming aabccb and every third line ending in *ium.* The seven-syllabled lines are a poetic homage to the *septiformis munere.*

Use. As the Sequence of the Mass at Whitsuntide; cf. Note on Sequences, p. 96. The *Veni sancte* shows the musical connection between the alleluia and the sequence, as its melody is clearly derived from the second alleluia of Whitsunday—the first notes of each being the same.

The use of this sequence did not become universal until Pius V, when it displaced another sequence, also of great beauty, the *Sancti Spiritus adsit nobis gratia,* written in rhythmical prose. (For the text, cf. Schuster, II. 392.)

The *Veni sancte* was known in the Middle Ages as the Golden Sequence and has ever been the favourite of contemplative and critic. Gihr devoted 130 pages to it in his book on the Sequences of the Missal and five pages in his book on The Holy Sacrifice of the Mass. In the latter he quotes the famous tribute of Clicthoveus on this sequence. It is worthy of note that in the time of Clicthoveus (early sixteenth century), the author was not known for certain—*auctorem ipsum (quisquis is fuerit)* are his words.

4. *pater pauperum.* The phrase may be suggested by *Oculus fui caeco, et pes claudo. Pater eram pauperum,* Job 29, 16, or perhaps by *patris orphanorum* of Ps. 67, 6—a psalm much used in the Pentecost office and Masses. Commentators, however, refer to Mt. 5, 3 and 2 Cor. 6, 10.

5. *dator munerum.* The Holy Ghost is the distributor of gifts as well as the Gift. *Tu qui dator es et donum,/ Tu qui condis omne bonum,* Adam of St Victor; and cf. *64,* 6, note. The last three verses are a series of petitions for gifts. The fourfold *da* of the last verse is an exact counterpart of the four *veni*'s of the first.

7. Just as the *Veni creator,* after the opening address of petition, turns to the titles of the Holy Ghost, so is it here. All the rest of the sequence from this line may be understood as a development of lines 4–6.

consolator = *paraclitus.* Adam of St Victor sings of the Holy Ghost as *consolator . . . cordium humilium*

and as *consolator alme.*

8. *hospes. Spiritus Dei habitat in vobis,* 1 Cor. 3, 16. The repeated *veni* is an invitation to Him to be our guest; and cf. *64,* 2.

9. *refrigerium,* rest, refreshment—both ideas come in the next three lines.

14. *cordis intima,* a poetic variant of *corda fidelium* and *corda nostra* of the Mass of Whitsunday. *Intima* may also be suggested by the *sui roris intima aspersione* of the Postcommunion of the same Mass.

16. *Numine.* This line and the next have been the subject of much discussion.

Numen, in classical Latin, means a nod, command; hence, divine will, power, sway, command, authority; godhead, divine majesty.

In the hymns *numen* is used regularly for godhead or, as abstract for concrete, for God. It is also used in *perpetuo numine, 136,* 12, for God's power or rule and even, in *Matris sub almae numine, 105,* 1, of our Lady's protection.

Thus there seems to be no reason why *sine tuo numine* cannot mean Without your power, will, protection, aid or grace. The Collect of the third Sunday after Pentecost has: *sine quo nihil validum, nihil sanctum. Sine tuo numine* and *sine quo* are apparently saying that without grace there is in man nothing of real value, nothing but sin. For man's dependence on the Son, cf. John 15, 5; and on the Spirit, cf. among other texts, 1 Cor. 12, 3 and Rom. 8, 14–16 and 26–7.

17. *in homine.* Granting what has been said on line 16, there is no need to emend this to *in lumine* and interpret *in lumine* as *illuminatum,* or to adopt Trench's *Quidquid est in homine.* (Cf. Thurston, *op. cit.,* p. 57.)

18. *innoxium,* blameless, innocent, without sin.

22. *flecte;* cf. *53,* 25, note. Even here *flecte* could mean soften (and thus make flexible) the *hard* heart—*aridum* being of the *dry,* parched, heart.

24. *rege. Quicunque enim spiritu Dei aguntur, ii sunt filii Dei,* Rom. 8, 14. Scriptural references abound for all the lines of this verse.

27. *septenarium;* cf. *septiformis, 64,* 9.

28. 'By means of these gifts we become virtuous, and shall be rewarded with a happy death, *exitum salutis,* the gateway to heaven, *perenne gaudium',* Byrnes.

29. *salutis;* a descriptive genitive—*consisting in* salvation.

7. TRINITY SUNDAY TO ADVENT

The liturgical celebration of the mysteries of our Lord's life is now completed and the feast of Pentecost is over. In terms of hymns this means that the appropriate hymns from the first section of this book now come into use, unless a feast displaces the office of the day. However the first weeks of this period are marked by special feasts, namely those of the Blessed Trinity, of Corpus Christi and of the Sacred Heart. These feasts will accordingly be dealt with in this section. →

Hymn 68

Jam sol recedit igneus The text is that of *28*,
with *amorem* for *lumen* in line 4.
Use. Hymn for Vespers of the Blessed Trinity.

Hymn 69

Summae Parens clementiae
Mundi regis qui machinam,
Unius et substantiae
Trinusque personis Deus,

5 *Da dexteram surgentibus,*
Exsurgat ut mens sobria,
Flagrans et in laudem Dei
Grates rependat debitas.

Deo Patri sit gloria
10 *Natoque Patris unico,*
Cum Spiritu Paraclito,
In sempiterna saecula.

God of infinite mercy, ruler of the world's structure, one in nature and three in persons, stretch out Your right hand to us as we rise. Let our soul rise up recollected and, zealous for God's praise, return Him due thanks. Glory be to God the Father, to the Father's only Son together with the Spirit, the Paraclete, through everlasting ages.

Trinity Sunday

No new hymns were written for this feast when it was introduced by John XXII in 1334, but (certainly from the time of Pius V) the Saturday Vesper hymn was used for Vespers, and two short centos from existing hymns were made for Matins and Lauds—each hymn being, with the doxology, of three verses. This '3' *motif* goes right through the Office, groups of three nouns or verbs constantly recurring.

Another point of interest is that the first four antiphons of Vespers are metrical, the first two being iambic and the next two sapphic—all four already existing as doxologies.

Notes on Hymn 69

Lines 1–4 = *8*, 1–4; 5–8 = *16*, 5–8.

Breviaries give *ut* in line 6 above, but vary between *ut* and *et* in *16*, 6. W mentions no MSS variants for *16*, 6 and prints *et*. It would seem therefore that *et* ought to be used here and in *16*.

Use. Hymn for Matins of the Blessed Trinity.

Hymn 70

Tu, Trinitatis Unitas,
Orbem potenter quae regis,
Attende laudis canticum
Quod excubantes psallimus.

5 Ortus refulget lucifer
Praeitque solem nuntius,
Cadunt tenebrae noctium;
Lux sancta nos illuminet.

Deo Patri sit gloria
10 Ejusque soli Filio,
Cum Spiritu Paraclito,
Nunc et per omne saeculum.

Lord God, one and three, all-powerful ruler of the world, receive the hymn of praise that we sing as we keep watch. The morning star shines clear in the sky and announces the coming of the day; the darkness of night disappears. Shine on us, light most holy. Glory be to God the Father, to His only Son together with the Spirit, the Paraclete, now and for ever.

Corpus Christi

The three hymns and the sequence for this feast were composed by St Thomas Aquinas at the request of Urban IV, who instituted the feast in 1264. There had indeed already been local festivals of Corpus Christi, notably in Belgium, and it is not unlikely that Urban, before he was Pope, knew the office which was in use at Liége. But it does not seem that St Thomas knew this office when he composed the office now in use. Nor is there any evidence for the story, which first appeared in the late sixteenth century, that St Thomas and St Bonaventure composed offices for this feast, and that the latter tore his up on reading that of his competitor.

The Pange lingua and the Verbum supernum are modelled on the hymn of Fortunatus, 53, and the Advent hymn, 35, respectively. St Thomas takes from these more than the opening words, and yet the result is original. There are many imitations of the Passion Pange lingua, but out of the nine mentioned by Daniel, only St Thomas's has really survived. He took from Fortunatus a plan as well as the opening words. Each states the theme of his hymn, outlines the life of our Lord and then describes the events either of the Last Supper or of the Passion; but St Thomas achieves more in his six stanzas than Fortunatus in his ten. Likewise he took a general idea as well as the opening words from the Advent hymn. Both are concerned with the coming of our Lord and with His gift of Himself to man—one with that of the Incarnation and the

Notes on Hymn 70

Lines 1–4 = 7, 1–4; 5–8 = *16*, 9–12.
Use. Hymn for Lauds of the Blessed Trinity.

---

coming at the last day, the other with the sacramental coming which prepares us to receive Him as our *praemium* at the last day *in patria*. The work here, as in the other hymns of the feast, is in a true sense original and far superior to anything on the same subject before or since. The same may be said of St Thomas's use of words and phrases taken from the poems of Adam of St Victor, as is shown in the notes.

Each of these hymns sings of the events of the Last Supper and of their significance, but each according to its liturgical purpose. Vespers is the prelude to a feast, and the *Pange lingua* is well placed at that hour. Its theme is that of the feast and, after stating it briefly, St Thomas invites all to pay homage to so great a sacrament. The homage here is first of all liturgical, through the office and Mass of the feast. The *veneremur cernui* of the hymn is the anticipation of the *adoremus* of the Invitatory of Matins.

The old office hymns for Matins have as one of their ideas the coming of a *new* day together with the praise of God which should be the prelude and the accompaniment of the day. St Thomas adapts this to the feast in the *Sacris solemniis,* whose first stanza urges us to celebrate the festival with joyous praises and to make 'everything *new*'; for it is the festival of the *New* Supper. The fourth verse of this hymn gives what some think to be St Thomas's most lovable picture of our Lord at the Supper as He begins His farewell to the disciples.

In the clear light of Lauds the betrayal and the Cross stand out in startling fashion.

Like St John's account of the Supper, the *Verbum supernum* is full of comfort and is, in a way, a summary of the discourse of our Lord to the disciples as well as of the actual breaking of bread. It is as noteworthy for what it implies, as in the first and fourth verses, as for what it says in the second and third. Nowhere else, except perhaps in the fourth verse of the *Sacris solemniis,* do the details of the scene stand out as clearly as they do here.

The *Lauda Sion,* as is fitting, is a detailed statement of what takes place at Mass and deals with its sacrificial and sacramental aspects. It is severe and exact in its language, rather like the spirit and the liturgically classical language of the Roman rite; but it opens with majestic words of praise and melts away at the end into words of pure love.

Each of these hymns then is adapted to its particular use and to the spirit of the liturgy into which it is introduced. It is a pity that later hymn-writers, revisers and composers of offices did not learn their hymnology as well as their theology from the Angelic Doctor.

To the hymns of Corpus Christi are added in this section the *Adoro te,* the *Ave verum corpus* and the *Sancti venite.*

The *Adoro te* is usually attributed to St Thomas, but there are serious grounds for doubting this.

Only three of the MSS which contain this hymn are older than the fifteenth century, and they belong to the fourteenth century. The early biographers of the saint and the early Dominican tradition are, I believe, silent on St Thomas as author of this hymn. Two of the early MSS, those of Klosterneuburg and Paris, say that St Thomas composed it (or, according to others, recited it) after he had received the Viaticum on his deathbed—a moment described in detail, without any mention of this hymn, by Guglielmo de Tocco.   →

Hymn 71

Pange, lingua, gloriosi corporis mysterium
Sanguinisque pretiosi quem, in mundi pretium,
Fructus ventris generosi rex effudit gentium.

Nobis datus, nobis natus ex intacta virgine
5 *Et in mundo conversatus, sparso verbi semine,*
Sui moras incolatus miro clausit ordine.

Praise, my tongue, the mystery of the glorious Body and of the precious Blood which the king of the nations, fruit of a royal womb, poured out as the world's ransom. To us He was given, to us He was born of a pure virgin. He lived in the world and when He had spread the seed of truth, He closed in a won-

Some have also thought that there are divergencies of thought and expression between the *Summa* of St Thomas and the *Adoro te*. The theologian who wrote *In hoc sacramento nulla est deceptio* (3, 75, 5 *ad* 2) and *In hoc sacramento veritatis sensus non decipitur circa ea quorum judicium ad ipsum pertinet* (3, 77, 7) would, they think, scarcely have written, even in poetry, *Visus, tactus, gustus in te fallitur*. On the other hand there is the strictest possible correspondence between the *Summa* and the *Lauda Sion*. (Cf. also the end of the fifth lesson of the feast.)

Moreover the workmanship seems different from that of St Thomas, and the feeling of the hymn, beautiful though it is, seems to reflect a quite different soul from that of the writer of the last verses of each of St Thomas's compositions.

There is then some case against St Thomas being the author of the *Adoro te*, and Dom Wilmart, to quote but one authority, was very doubtful about it. The common opinion that he did write it may have been spread and confirmed by the Missal which, from 1570 onwards, included it among the thanksgiving prayers after Mass under the title *Rhythmus S. Thomae Aquinatis*. But so many other things in this part of the Missal are now thought to be wrongly ascribed that one may question this ascription as well. The prayer *Gratias tibi ago,* which is also said to be St Thomas's, is to be found in a Psalter copied between 1087 and 1105; and the *Anima Christi,* is much earlier than St Ignatius to whom it is ascribed.

It is only fair to add that Byrnes, a Dominican, gives St Thomas as the author— without any discussion of the arguments for or against.

Nothing need be said in this introduction about the *Ave verum corpus* or the *Sancti venite*.

Note. In this section references such as 5th Saturday indicate the fifth lesson of the office of the Saturday within the Octave of Corpus Christi. The letters ST indicate the *Summa Theologica* of St Thomas.

Notes on Hymn 71

Author. St Thomas Aquinas.

Metre. Three-lined verses in trochaic tetrameter catalectic (accentual), rhyming at the caesura and at the end of the line. Just as the writers of quantitative hymns occasionally substituted one foot for another, so the writers of accentual compositions aimed at a similar variety; e.g. *recúmbens cum frátribus* in line 7. In such places choirs not infrequently try to sing against the accent.

Use. At Vespers of Corpus Christi, at the processions of Maundy Thursday and Corpus Christi and at all other processions of the Blessed Sacrament.

1. *Pange;* cf. *53,* 1. The theme of the hymn as of the feast is the mystery of the Body and Blood of Christ, but especially of the Body. Cf. *ita nos corporis et sanguinis tui sacra mysteria venerari,* collect of the feast.

In supremae nocte coenae recumbens cum fratribus,
Observata lege plene cibis in legalibus,
Cibum turbae duodenae se dat suis manibus.

10 Verbum caro panem verum verbo carnem efficit,
Fitque sanguis Christi merum; et, si sensus deficit,
Ad firmandum cor sincerum sola fides sufficit.

Tantum ergo sacramentum veneremur cernui,
Et antiquum documentum novo cedat ritui;
15 Praestet fides supplementum sensuum defectui.

Genitori Genitoque laus et jubilatio,
Salus, honor, virtus quoque sit et benedictio;
Procedenti ab utroque compar sit laudatio.

drous way the period of His sojourn here. As He is reclining with His brethren on the night of the last supper, He complies completely with the Law in regard to the legal foods and then gives Himself with His own hands as food to the group of twelve. The Word made flesh by a word changes true bread into His flesh, and wine becomes His blood. If man cannot perceive this change, faith of itself is enough to convince the well-disposed. Let us therefore humbly reverence so great a sacrament. Let the old types depart and give way to the new rite. Let faith provide her help where all the senses fail. To the Father and the Son be praise, acclamation, salvation, honour, might and blessing too. To the One who proceeds from them both be given equal praise.

Hymn 72

Sacris solemniis juncta sint gaudia
Et ex praecordiis sonent praeconia;
Recedant vetera, nova sint omnia,
    Corda, voces et opera.

5 Noctis recolitur coena novissima
Qua Christus creditur agnum et azyma
Dedisse fratribus juxta legitima
    Priscis indulta patribus.

Post agnum typicum, expletis epulis,
10 Corpus dominicum datum discipulis,

On this holy festival let our joy pay its tribute and our hymns of praise proclaim the feelings of our inmost hearts. Old rites and habits must depart, and everything must be new—heart, voice and deed.

We are commemorating the Last Supper when, as we believe, Christ gave to His brethren the lamb and the unleavened bread, according to the law given to their fathers in former times. It is our belief that after they had eaten the lamb, which was a type, and when the supper was over, the body of the Lord was

2. *pretium*, ransom; cf. *redemptionem per sanguinem ejus*, Eph. 1, 7, and *77*, 2.

3. *generosi*, noble, of noble family, for Mary was of royal descent. For the word *generosus* cf. Prud. *Cath.* III, 31 and X, 21, and *vos omnes generosos esse volens*, 5th Saturday.

rex. Cf. the lines *Rex sedet in coena, turba cinctus duodena.*/*Se tenet in manibus, se cibat ipse cibus*, quoted in ST. 3, 81, 1. Cf. also *Christum regem adoremus* of the Invitatory of the feast.

4. Like Fortunatus in *53*, St Thomas presses forward to his main theme and only briefly indicates the birth and life of our Lord.

In words this verse owes something to a sequence of Adam of St Victor: *Nobis natus, nobis datur*/*Et nobiscum conversatur*/*Lux et salus gentium*. But St Thomas is more interested in the aspect of *being given*, as is natural on such a feast and is very noticeable in his hymn for Lauds; cf. *73*, 5–8, note. Our Lord explained to Nicodemus that He was the Father's *gift* to the world, John 3, 16.

5. *verbi*, of His preaching, cf. *qui seminat, verbum seminat*, Mk. 4, 14. Much use is made of the word *verbum* in this hymn.

6. *moras*, the period; cf. *5*, 8, note.

7. *fratribus*; our Lord's name for His apostles, Mt. 28, 10 and John 20, 17; cf. Ps. 21, 23 and the Church's echo in *Orate, fratres*.

9. *turbae duodenae*, i.e. the group of twelve; cf. note on *rex*, line 3.

10–11. No translation, in poetry or in prose, seems able quite to meet all the antitheses of this line and a half; cf. Julian.

11. *sensus*. This is commonly taken as the subject of *deficit* and as meaning 'perception' (mental, according to some; of the senses, according to others). Blakeney, however, takes it as the object of *deficit*—which is improbable. The meaning of *sensus* is to be seen in *nam etiam si sensus illud tibi renuntiat, fides tamen te confirmat*, 6th Octave day, where the Greek of St Cyril of Jerusalem for *sensus* is αἴσθησις. Cf. also *11*, 29, note.

12. *sincerum*, true, genuine, well-disposed—not like the men of John 6, 60 and many others since.

13. *Ergo*. As faith is necessary, let us therefore, *ergo*, express it in reverence, *veneremur*, and in humility, *cernui*. *Cernui*; cf. *2*, 31.

14. *documentum*, i.e. the old Law with its sacrifices and the paschal lamb; cf. John 4, 21–3.

15. *sensuum* must here mean the senses of sight, taste etc.; cf. note on line 11.

16–18. Cf. *Qui procedit ab utroque, Genitore Genitoque*, the opening lines of a Pentecost sequence by Adam of St Victor; and, *Amor Patris Filiique*,/*Par amborum et utrique*/*compar et consimilis*, lines 8–10 of the same composition. *Compar*; cf. *4*, 14.

Notes on Hymn 72

Author. St Thomas Aquinas.

Metre. Usually said to be second Asclepiad. But as it is written in accentual verse, it could perhaps be considered as dactylic tetrameter acatalectic, the fourth line excepted. (Cf. the section on Accent and Rhyme in the Introduction.) The caesura occurs regularly after the sixth syllable in the first three lines. Rhyme appears at the caesura and at the end of lines on this plan: ababcbc. There are occasional accentual variations, e.g. *recédant, dedísse, commítti*; see introduction to *71*.

Use. At Matins of Corpus Christi, and in the procession of that day.

K

1. *solemniis*; from *solemnium*, a non-classical, Christian word.

3. *vetera*. The rites of the old Law, but also habits of sin, the leaven of malice and wickedness, 1 Cor. 5, 7–8. *Nova*; the new Law and habits informed by grace.

5. *novissima*, last. But the last is also the newest, *novissima*, and the idea of newness is not far from St Thomas's mind *Nova sint omnia* he had just written.

6. *creditur*. This fact is implied, but not stated, in the Scriptures; cf. Lk. 22, 8.

7. *fratribus*; cf. *71*, 7, note.

Sic totum omnibus, quod totum singulis,
    Ejus fatemur manibus.

Dedit fragilibus corporis ferculum,
Dedit et tristibus sanguinis poculum,
15 *Dicens, 'Accipite quod trado vasculum.*
    Omnes ex eo bibite'.

Sic sacrificium istud instituit,
Cujus officium committi voluit
Solis presbyteris, quibus sic congruit
20   *Ut sumant et dent ceteris.*

Panis angelicus fit panis hominum;
Dat panis caelicus figuris terminum.
O res mirabilis! Manducat Dominum
    Pauper servus et humilis.

25 *Te, trina deitas unaque, poscimus,*
Sic nos tu visita, sicut te colimus;
Per tuas semitas duc nos quo tendimus,
    Ad lucem quam inhabitas.

given to the disciples by our Lord's hands in such a way that the whole was given to all and the whole given to each. He gave them in their weakness His body as food; He gave them in their sorrow His blood as drink and said: 'Receive this cup which I give you, and drink of it—all of you.' In this way He instituted this sacrifice and intended that its performance should be the care of priests alone. And so it is for the priests to receive for themselves and to administer to the rest of the faithful.

The bread of angels becomes man's bread; the bread from heaven puts an end to the types. What marvellous happening is this; the poor, the servant, the lowly feeds upon his Lord.

We ask You, Godhead three and one, to come to us even as we worship You. Guide us along Your paths to our journey's end—to the light in which You dwell.

Hymn 73

Verbum supernum prodiens
Nec Patris linquens dexteram,
Ad opus suum exiens
Venit ad vitae vesperam.

5 *In mortem a discipulo*
Suis tradendus aemulis,
Prius in vitae ferculo
Se tradidit discipulis;

Quibus sub bina specie
10 *Carnem dedit et sanguinem*
Ut duplicis substantiae
Totum cibaret hominem.

Se nascens dedit socium,
Convescens in edulium,

The heavenly Word came forth and yet did not leave the Father's right hand. He went out to His work and came to His life's evening. When He was about to be given over by a disciple to His enemies unto death, He first gave Himself over to His disciples as the food of life. He gave them His flesh and blood under two species for it to be the food of the whole man, who is of twofold nature. By His birth He became man's companion; at this supper He became man's food; in His death He became

11–12. In such a way, *sic,* that the whole, *totum* sc. *corpus,* was given to all and, *quod,* the whole to each. Cf. *se dat suis manibus, 71,* 9, and *71,* 3, note on *rex.*

13. *ferculum,* dish, course, food; *poculum,* cup, drink. *Christus totus/Sub utraque specie,* says *74,* 41–2, and therefore either kind is both food and drink. But not infrequently, especially in the hymns, the two ideas are divided and attached to their appropriate species, for food strengthens us in our weakness, *fragilibus,* and wine cheers us in our sorrow, *tristibus;* and cf. 3 Kings 19, 8 and Ps. 103, 15. *Fragilibus,* because they were to be scandalized in Him and, for a time, scattered; *tristibus,* cf. John 16, 6.

15. *vasculum,* cup, chalice.

21. *angelicus* and *caelicus* of line 22. *Et panem caeli dedit eis. Panem angelorum manducavit homo,* Ps. 77, 24–5. *Angelorum esca nutrivisti populum tuum; et paratum panem de caelo praestitisti illis sine labore, omne delectamentum in se habentem,* Wisdom 16, 20. These texts are about the manna which was 'heavenly' because of its origin and 'angelic' because of its ministers. They are then applied to the Eucharist, the living bread *from heaven,* John 6, 51, and the *bread of angels*

in that the angels feast spiritually on Christ by their direct vision of Him in heaven; cf. ST. 3, 80, 2. They figure prominently in this Office by quotation, as in the versicle at Vespers and the second antiphon at Lauds, and by allusion, as in this hymn.

22. *figuris,* types; but in *75,* 2 *figuris* means appearances. *Terminum,* because all types, the manna, the unleavened bread, the paschal lamb etc., gave way to the reality at this Supper when Christ made all things *new.*

25. *trina deitas,* from *84,* 21; cf. introduction to *84.* St Thomas did not share the scruples of Raban and Hincmar about this phrase. The revisers thought better of changing it here, in spite of the Sorbonne, but changed it in *84.*

26. *Sic . . . sicut.* These words imply that the *effects* of the Eucharistic visit depend in some measure on those who are honoured by it. So the text from Wisdom, quoted in the note on line 21, continues: *et deserviens uniuscujusque voluntati, ad quod quisque volebat convertebatur.*

28. *ad lucem,* explanatory of *quo tendimus;* and cf. ST. 3, 80, 2, *ad* 1.

Notes on Hymn 73

Author. St Thomas Aquinas.

Metre. Iambic dimeter, accentual, with alternating rhyme except in verse 4. There are occasional accentual variations, especially at the beginnings of lines, e.g. *Verbum, venis, suis,* etc.; cf. introduction to *71* and the section on Accent and Rhyme in the general Introduction.

Use. At Lauds of Corpus Christi and at the procession on that day.

1. *supernum.* St Thomas had in mind the original text of *35,* 1–4, namely: *Verbum supernum prodiens, A Patre olim exiens, Qui natus orbi subvenis, Cursu declivi temporis,* where *supernum* is predicative after *prodiens.* St Thomas makes *supernum* an attribute of *Verbum* and gives *prodiens* a meaning different from that of *35. 35* begins with the eternal generation and proceeds to the temporal one. St Thomas's mind is on the God-man entirely. In four short lines he covers

the Incarnation and the whole life of Christ down to its evening, and indeed to *the* evening whose events are now related.

2. *nec . . . linquens;* cf. John 14, 9–11, and St Leo, lesson 5 of Saturday after the Ascension.

3. *opus . . . exiens. Exibit homo ad opus suum, et ad operationem suam usque ad vesperum,* Ps. 103, 23. To describe a human life in terms of a day is common in the hymns, especially in the relation of death and evening; cf. *21* and the Vesper hymns, *22–28.* The idea of evening also belongs to *35;* cf. *35,* 1–4, notes.

5–8. *Tradendus,* used as a future participle; *aemulis,* rivals, enemies (and contrast *aemuli* in *93,* 36); *ferculo,* cf. *72,* 13, for *ferculum,* because of the rhyme; *vitae ferculo* answers *mortem.*

The verse rests on the different meanings of *tradere,* all of which are to be found in 1 Cor. 11, 23–24, and two of which are in the special clauses of

15 *Se moriens in pretium,*
    Se regnans dat in praemium.

man's price; in His kingdom He becomes man's prize.

    O salutaris hostia
    Quae caeli pandis ostium,
    Bella premunt hostilia,
20 *Da robur, fer auxilium.*

Saving victim, opening wide heaven's gate, wars and enemies press hard upon us; give us strength, bring us help.

    Uni trinoque Domino
    Sit sempiterna gloria,
    Qui vitam sine termino
    Nobis donet in patria.

Everlasting praise be to the Lord, one and three. May He give us everlasting life in the land where dwells our Father.

Hymn 74

    Lauda Sion salvatorem,
    Lauda ducem et pastorem
        In hymnis et canticis.
    Quantum potes, tantum aude,
 5 *Quia major omni laude*
        Nec laudare sufficis.

Sion, praise your Saviour. Praise your leader and shepherd in hymns and canticles. Praise Him as much as you can, for He is beyond all praising and you will never be able to praise Him as He merits. But today a theme worthy of particular praise is put before us—the living and life-giving bread that, without any doubt, was given to the Twelve at table during the holy supper. Therefore let our praise be full and resounding and our soul's rejoicing full of delight and beauty, for this is the festival day to commemorate the first institution of this table.

    Laudis thema specialis,
    Panis vivus et vitalis,
        Hodie proponitur:
10 *Quem in sacrae mensa coenae*
    Turbae fratrum duodenae
        Datum non ambigitur.

    Sit laus plena, sit sonora,
    Sit jucunda, sit decora
15   *Mentis jubilatio.*
    Dies enim solemnis agitur
    In qua mensae prima recolitur
        Hujus institutio.

    In hac mensa novi regis
20 *Novum pascha novae legis*
        Phase vetus terminat.
    Vetustatem novitas,
    Umbram fugat veritas,
        Noctem lux eliminat.

At this table of the new King, the new law's new pasch puts an end to the old pasch. The new displaces the old, reality the shadow and light the darkness. Christ wanted what He did

the *Communicantes* and the *Hanc igitur* for Maundy Thursday. This hymn is specially concerned with the idea of giving and each verse, except the first, contains some word meaning 'to give'.

13–16. *Se dedit* must be supplied with *convescens*, and *dedit* with *moriens*. *Edulium*, food. The verse gives a summary of the ways in which our Lord came or gave Himself to mankind. Like the fourth verse of *71*, this verse is most condensed and in perfect form.

20. *robur*, a very hard kind of oak; hardness, strength, power, etc. Cf. *Et ambulavit (Elias) in fortitudine cibi illius usque ad montem Dei*, 3 Kings 19, 8; and, *tamquam leones igitur ignem spirantes ab illa mensa recedamus, facti diabolo terribiles*, 5th Octave day.

23. To sustain our spiritual life on earth is the immediate purpose of this Bread, cf. *vitae ferculo* of line 7; but its consummation is *vitam sine termino; ut si quis ex ipso manducaverit, non moriatur*, John 6, 50.

24. *patria*, i.e. our *Father's* land, where our Lord belongs by right, line 2, and where we belong by grace, lines 7 and 23. Moreover this Bread is the *panis filiorum*, 74, 65.

Notes on Hymn 74

Author. St Thomas Aquinas.

Metre. Trochaic dimeter, accentual, in various groupings.

Verses 1–9 are six-lined and rhyme aabccb; the third and sixth lines are catalectic. The third and fourth verses depart from this general plan in the following details; in the third verse, the fourth and fifth lines are ten-syllabled through the substitution of dactyls; in the fourth verse, all lines are catalectic except the first and second.

Verses 10 and 11 have eight lines and the last verse ten lines, the middle and last line in each case being catalectic. Their rhyme is aaa(a)b, ccc(c)b.

It is an exact metrical copy of Adam of St Victor's *Laudes crucis attollamus*, whose musical setting it uses. The music of the *Laudes crucis* uses the opening notes of the second alleluia of the feast for which it was composed, namely the Finding of the Cross. Cf. Note on Sequences, p. 96 and the introduction to *67*.

Use. Sequence at the Mass of Corpus Christi.

1. The first three verses of the *Lauda Sion*, like those of its model, give the purpose and character of our praise. The first verse is a general invitation to praise our Saviour, leader and shepherd. *Sion* symbolizes the Church on earth; cf. *93*, 2, note.

4–6. *Quantum ... sufficis. Multa dicemus, et deficiemus in verbis ... Glorificantes Dominum quantumcunque potueritis, supervalebit adhuc ... Benedicentes Dominum, exaltate illum quantum potestis; major enim est omni laude*, Ecclus. 43, 29–33. This invitation to praise the Creator and all His wonderful works is applied by St Thomas to our praise of the Saviour. The next verse singles out one particular gift of the Saviour.

7. *specialis* with *laudis*, not with *thema*, which is neuter—a subject worthy of particular praise. With *laudis specialis* compare *speciali gloria* in line 3 of the *Laudes crucis*.

9. *Proponitur* may carry some suggestion of the loaves of proposition.

11. *Turbae fratrum;* cf. *71*, 7 and 9.

12. *Ambigitur*, open to doubt, uncertain; cf. *de veritate carnis et sanguinis non relictus est ambigendi locus*, 7th Wednesday; *quis audebit deinceps ambigere*, 4th Octave day.

13–15 give the character of the praise we should give. Our praise is to be unstinted, full and outwardly expressed, musical, *plena* and *sonora;* the rejoicing of our soul is to be full of delight and beauty, *jucunda* and *decora*. Cf. *laus jucunda, laus sonora*, line 4 of Adam of St Victor's sequence for St Michael.

16–18 give the reason why our praise should have these qualities. *Dies solemnis*, i.e. the festival of Corpus Christi; *in qua*, sc. *die*, the day on which is commemorated the first institution of this table. The relation of this table to the old Law is stated in the fourth verse (*In hac mensa*, line 19) and to the new Law in the fifth verse (*in coena*, line 25).

21. *phase = pascha*.

22–24. Cf. *Umbram fugat veritas, vetustatem novitas,*

25 Quod in coena Christus gessit
   Faciendum hoc expressit
      In sui memoriam.
   Docti sacris institutis
   Panem, vinum in salutis
30   Consecramus hostiam.

   Dogma datur Christianis
   Quod in carnem transit panis
      Et vinum in sanguinem.
   Quod non capis, quod non vides,
35 Animosa firmat fides,
      Praeter rerum ordinem.

   Sub diversis speciebus,
   Signis tantum et non rebus,
      Latent res eximiae.
40 Caro cibus, sanguis potus,
   Manet tamen Christus totus
      Sub utraque specie.

   A sumente non concisus,
   Non confractus, non divisus,
45   Integer accipitur.
   Sumit unus, sumunt mille,
   Quantum isti, tantum ille,
      Nec sumptus consumitur.

   Sumunt boni, sumunt mali,
50 Sorte tamen inaequali
      Vitae vel interitus.
   Mors est malis, vita bonis,
   Vide paris sumptionis
      Quam sit dispar exitus.

55 Fracto demum sacramento
   Ne vacilles, sed memento
   Tantum esse sub fragmento
      Quantum toto tegitur.
   Nulla rei fit scissura,
60 Signi tantum fit fractura,
   Qua nec status nec statura
      Signati minuitur.

at the supper to be repeated in His memory. And so we, in accordance with His holy directions, consecrate bread and wine to be salvation's Victim.

Christ's followers know by faith that bread is changed into His flesh and wine into His blood. Man cannot understand this, cannot perceive it; but a lively faith affirms that the change, which is outside the natural course of things, takes place. Under the different species, which are now signs only and not their own reality, there lie hid wonderful realities. His body is our food, His blood our drink. And yet Christ remains entire under each species. The communicant receives the complete Christ— uncut, unbroken and undivided. Whether one receive or a thousand, the one receives as much as the thousand. Nor is Christ diminished by being received. The good and the wicked alike receive Him, but with the unlike destiny of life or death. To the wicked it is death, but life to the good. See how different is the result, though each receives the same. Last of all, if the sacrament is broken, have no doubt. Remember there is as much in a fragment as in an un- broken host. There is no division of the reality, but only a breaking of the sign; nor does the breaking diminish the condition or size of the One hidden under the sign.

Continued

luctum consolatio, in an Easter sequence of Adam of St Victor.

25–30. What our Lord did at the Supper, He wanted to be repeated *in sui memoriam* and, as 28–30 state, the Church carries out this wish. Lines 28–30 are the link between the first part and what follows.

Verses 6–10 give a precise theological description of lines 29–30. Each verse gives one part of the description, the same truth being expressed in a slightly different form in each half.

31. The description of what takes place necessarily begins with the belief, *dogma,* of transubstantiation.

37. *diversis speciebus* is explained by *utraque specie* of line 42.

38. *signis . . . rebus,* signs only and not the reality of bread and wine; but, which differ in externals only and not in reality, B.

39. *rex eximiae,* i.e. *Christus totus* of line 41; and cf. *72,* 13, note.

46–48. *Isti* answers *mille,* and *ille, unus. Consumitur,* consumed, i.e. lessened, diminished; cf. *Sumptum non consumitur/Corpus salvatoris,* in John of Peckham's *Ave vivens hostia.*

53–54. See how different is the result, *exitus,* of receiving the same sacrament, *paris sumptionis;* cf. 1 Cor. 11, 27 and *72, 26.*

61. *qua* refers to *fractura. Status,* i.e. condition, circumstances; *statura,* literally, stature, size.

62. *signati* (as opposed to *signi* in 60), i.e. the substance of the sacrament, namely Christ.

Ecce panis angelorum
Factus cibus viatorum,
65 Vere panis filiorum,
    Non mittendus canibus.
In figuris praesignatur,
Cum Isaac immolatur,
Agnus Paschae deputatur,
70 Datur manna patribus.

Bone pastor, panis vere,
Jesu, nostri miserere;
Tu nos pasce, nos tuere,
Tu nos bona fac videre
75 In terra viventium.
Tu qui cuncta scis et vales,
Qui nos pascis hic mortales,
Tuos ibi commensales,
Cohaeredes et sodales
80 Fac sanctorum civium.

Behold, the bread of angels is become the pilgrim's food; truly it is bread for the sons, and is not to be cast to dogs. It was prefigured in type when Isaac was brought as an offering, when a lamb was appointed for the Pasch and when manna was given to the Jews of old.

Jesus, good shepherd and true bread, have mercy on us; feed us and guard us. Grant that we find happiness in the land of the living. You know all things, can do all things, and feed us here on earth. Make us Your guests in heaven, co-heirs with You and companions of heaven's citizens.

Hymn 75

Adoro te devote, latens deitas,
Quae sub his figuris vere latitas;
Tibi se cor meum totum subjicit,
Quia te contemplans totum deficit.

5 Visus, tactus, gustus in te fallitur,
Sed auditu solo tuto creditur;
Credo quidquid dixit Dei Filius;
Nil hoc verbo veritatis verius.

In cruce latebat sola deitas,
10 At hic latet simul et humanitas;
Ambo tamen credens atque confitens,
Peto quod petivit latro poenitens.

Plagas, sicut Thomas, non intueor,
Deum tamen meum te confiteor;
15 Fac me tibi semper magis credere,
In te spem habere, te diligere.

I adore You devoutly, Godhead unseen, Who truly lies hidden under these sacramental forms. My soul surrenders itself to You without reserve, for in contemplating You it is completely overwhelmed. Sight, touch and taste are no guide in finding You, and only hearing is a sure guide for our faith. I believe everything that the Son of God has said, and nothing can be truer than this word of the Truth. Only the godhead was hidden on the cross, but here the humanity is hidden as well. Yet I believe and acknowledge them both, and make the same request as did the repentant thief. I do not see the marks of the wounds, as Thomas did, and yet I too own You as 'My God'. Grant that I believe in You more and more, that I put my hope in You and that I love You. Living bread,

63. *angelorum;* cf. *72, 21,* note.

64. *viatorum,* i.e. earthly pilgrims on their way to heaven; cf. *viaticum* and *O esca viatorum,* the first line of a seventeenth(?)-century hymn.

65–66. The 'children' are the worthy recipients, the 'dogs' the unworthy ones; cf. Mt. 15, 26 and Apoc. 22, 15.

67. It was prefigured in type; *figuris,* cf. *72, 22.*

69. *deputatur;* cf. *66,* 11.

71–80. A prayer that all who share this table here

below may be gathered at the heavenly feast and table.

71. *pastor.* St Thomas began with *Lauda .. pastorem,* and to that idea he now returns and develops it in lines 73–75. *Bone pastor;* cf. John 10, 11 ff., and 9th Octave day.

73. *pasce.* Cf. *Tu nos pasce, tu nos munda* in an Easter sequence of Adam of St Victor.

74. *fac,* here and in line 80; cf. note on *109,* 27.

78. Another reading is *tuos ibi* for *tu nos ibi.*

Notes on Hymn 75

Author. ?St Thomas Aquinas; see introduction to this section.

Metre. Trochaic trimeter catalectic, each couplet rhyming.

Use. In the Missal as a prayer after Mass.

1. This line has one too many syllables, and the first syllable of *Adoro* must be taken as an anacrusis, i.e. an up beat before the regular metre begins. Probably the first two lines ought to be:

Adoro devote, latens deitas,

Te qui sub his formis vere latitas.

2. *figuris;* cf. *72,* 22, note. *Latitas,* from *latitare,* lies hidden. *Quae* because of *deitas,* and *latitas* because of *te.*

6. *creditur.* For a similar use, cf. *corde enim creditur,* Rom. 10, 10; for the meaning, cf. *fides ex auditu, auditus autem per verbum Christi,* Rom. 10, 17.

8. Editions vary between *Nihil veritatis verbo verius* and *Verbo veritatis nihil verius.* From a choral point of view almost any order is better than that of the usual text. The same applies to line 24.

9. *latebat . . . deitas;* cf. Mt. 27, 40.

11. *Ambo;* i.e. *deitas* and *humanitas.*

12. *latro;* cf. Lk. 23, 42.

13. *Thomas;* cf. John 20, 29.

14. *Deum . . . meum.* Cf. *Dominus meus, et deus meus,* John 20, 28. Some would read: *Meum tamen Deum.*

O memoriale mortis Domini,
Panis vivus, vitam praestans homini,
Praesta meae menti de te vivere
20 *Et te illi semper dulce sapere.*

Pie pelicane, Jesu Domine,
Me immundum munda tuo sanguine,
Cujus una stilla salvum facere
Totum mundum quit ab omni scelere.

25 *Jesu, quem velatum nunc aspicio,*
Oro fiat illud quod tam sitio;
Ut te revelata cernens facie,
Visu sim beatus tuae gloriae.

that ever recalls the Lord's death and gives life to His servants, grant to my soul to live by You and always to taste Your sweetness. Lord Jesus, loving pelican of heaven, cleanse me, a sinner, with Your blood; for a single drop can save the whole world from all its sin. Jesus, as I look on Your veiled presence, I pray that what I long for so ardently may come about, and that I may see Your face unveiled and be happy in the vision of Your glory.

Hymn 76

Ave verum corpus, natum de Maria virgine,
Vere passum, immolatum in cruce pro homine,
Cujus latus perforatum vero fluxit sanguine,
Esto nobis praegustatum mortis in examine.
5   *O clemens, o pie,*
       O dulcis Jesu, fili Mariae.

Hail true body that was born of Mary, the Virgin, that truly suffered and was offered in sacrifice on the cross for man and that gave forth true blood from its pierced side. Be to us a foretaste of heaven when we are in death's agony, kind, loving and gentle Jesus, son of Mary.

Hymn 77

Sancti, venite, Christi corpus sumite,
   Sanctum bibentes, quo redempti, sanguinem.

Salvati Christi corpore et sanguine,
   A quo refecti laudes dicamus Deo.

5 *Hoc sacramento corporis et sanguinis*
   Omnes exuti ab inferni faucibus.

Dator salutis, Christus, filius Dei,
   Mundum salvavit per crucem et sanguinem.

Come, holy people of God, receive the body of Christ and drink the holy blood of our redemption.

We have been saved by Christ's body and blood; let us give thanks now that we have feasted on Him.

All have been rescued from the jaws of hell by this sacrament of His body and blood.

Salvation's giver, Christ, the son of God, saved the world through His cross and blood.

Continued

18. Or: *Panis veram vitam praestans homini.*

20. *illi,* i.e. *menti; cf.* Ps. 33, 9.

21. *pelicane.* The pelican is an exclusively Christian symbol, the symbol of Christ as Redeemer and in the Eucharist. The symbolism is based on an error in natural history, it being assumed that the pelican was feeding its young with its own blood when in fact it was preening its feathers. Thus: 'And like the kind, life-rendering pelican, Repast them with my blood', *Hamlet* IV, v, 145. The pelican in this form is said, in Christian art and in heraldry, to be 'in her piety'; hence *Pie pelicane.*

24. Or: *Totum mundum posset ab omni scelere; cf.* note on line 8. *Quit,* can, is able.

26-28. It seems that the hymn should end with a question:

> *Quando fiet illud quod tam* (or, *jam*) *cupio*
> *Ut . . . tuae gloriae?*

Cf. *quem nunc velatum in via suscipere propono, revelata tandem facie perpetuo contemplari,* at the end of the prayer ascribed to St Thomas in the *Praeparatio ad Missam* of the Missal.

Notes on Hymn 76

Author. Innocent VI (1352–62).

Metre. Trochaic tetrameter, rhyming at the caesura and at the end of the lines. The last two lines look like a variant of *33,* 10–11.

Use. Nowadays it has no place in the liturgy, but it is one of many short hymns which used to be sung in the Middle Ages after the Consecration, the *Benedictus* not then being divided from the *Sanctus.*

1. *verum corpus.* This takes up the *Hoc est enim corpus meum* and professes that the true body of Christ is now present.

3. *cujus* refers to *corpus.*

Vero fluxit sanguine seems the more probable reading. The hymn is centred round the idea of *verum*—*verum* in line 1, *vere* in line 2 and probably *vero* here. The usual version is *fluxit aqua et sanguine.* But the mention of the water is not really in place here, just as it *is* necessary in *26,* 10. Moreover the usual version is too long by one syllable.

Notes on Hymn 77

Author. Unknown, of Irish origin. It is found in the Bangor (Ireland) Antiphonary, whose date is late seventh century.

Metre. Iambic trimeter, divided regularly after the fifth syllable.

Use. It has no place in the liturgy of today, but was once used as a *Communio.* It is an early example of a metrical *Communio,* but not an unique one; cf. Julian 255 and 993. It seems to have been used mostly in Ireland, and legend connects it with the names of Patrick and Secundinus (Raby, p. 136). The Roman *Communio* is normally a prose text from the Scriptures. Neale's translation of the *Sancti venite* (*Westminster Hymnal,* 179) omits lines 5 and 6.

1. *Sancti* and *sanctum* of the next line recall the liturgical formula *Sancta sanctis.* Holiness is the ruling idea of the hymn; cf. lines 1, 2, 14, 17 and the similar sentiments of 15. For *sancti* applied to Christians cf. St Paul, *passim,* and 1 Pet. 1, 15.

2. *sanguinem.* 'Perhaps *sanguine* (the MSS reading), attracted into the relative clause, is possible . . . But the copyist's eye may have caught sight of *sanguine* in line 3', W. Most editors give *sanguinem,* but W has *sanguine.*

Pro universis immolatus Dominus 10 *Ipse sacerdos exstitit et hostia.*	The Lord was offered in sacrifice for all men, being both priest and victim.
Lege praeceptum immolari hostias, *Qua adumbrantur divina mysteria.*	The Law, foreshadowing the divine mysteries, ordained that sacrifices should be offered.
Lucis indultor et salvator omnium *Praeclaram sanctis largitus est gratiam.*	The giver of light and the saviour of all men has in His bounty bestowed on His holy people a wonderful favour.
15 *Accedant omnes pura mente creduli,* *Sumant aeternam salutis custodiam.*	Let all that believe approach in purity of soul and receive the eternal safeguard of salvation.
Sanctorum custos, rector quoque, Dominus, *Vitae perennis largitor credentibus.*	The Lord is the guardian and guide of holy ones, and the giver of everlasting life to believers.
Caelestem panem dat esurientibus, 20 *De fonte vivo praebet sitientibus.*	He gave the bread of heaven to the hungry and drink from the living spring to the thirsty.
Alpha et ω ipse Christus Dominus *Venit, venturus judicare homines.*	There is come to us the Alpha and Omega, Christ the Lord Himself, Who is to come to judge mankind.

The Sacred Heart

The three hymns for this feast, usually dated eighteenth century, are 'evidently the work of the same author', B. His name is not known. B quotes from Henry, *Eucharistica*, p. 235, the following appreciation: 'Their play of fancy and of imagination, their rhetorical finish, their condensed phraseology, give clear intimations of a skill which has profited by the models constructed by St Ambrose. They abound, too, in Biblical allusions, every stanza recalling some type, or figure, or prophecy, or fulfilment.' However true this may be in other respects, it is scarcely true in the reference to St Ambrose. A hymn is something to be sung, and a good hymn is, among other things, easily singable. St Ambrose's hymns satisfy these requirements,

---

Hymn 78

En ut superba criminum *Et saeva nostrorum cohors* *Cor sauciavit innocens* *Merentis haud tale Dei.*	Look how the proud cruel multitude of our sins has wounded the sinless heart of God, undeserving of such treatment. It was this that

3. *salvati* and *exuti* of line 6 seem to stand for a finite verb and to be first person plural from *dicamus*. Others take *salvati* as a participle and connect it with *venite*.

7. *dator salutis.* An Easter hymn in the same antiphonary addresses our Lord as *Vitaque vitae conditor/ Dator salutis et salus.*

10. *ipse= idem; exstitit= est.*

11. *Lege praeceptum;* it was commanded by law. Phillimore gives *Legem praecepit.*

12. *qua,* sc. *lege. Adumbrantur;* cf. Heb. 10, 1.

13. *indultor,* giver.

15. *Accedant;* al. *accedunt. Creduli,* believing (not used here with the classical meaning of credulous); cf. *praecepit totum per orbem baptizare credulos,* St Hilary.

21. This line requires two syllables between *et* and *ipse. Omega* is too long and *o* is too short. Most editions give *omega* though that name was unknown when this hymn was composed. Probably the disyllable *oo* was meant and 'the letter ω is formed of oo written twice and coalescing' (Gaselee, *An Anthology of Medieval Latin,* p. 23).

---

while these do not; and by that criterion they are not good hymns. St Ambrose would never have written lines such as *78,* 11 or *78,* 17, nor could he be claimed as a model for them.

These hymns were written without any reference to a particular Hour of the Office, and have been used at different Hours at different periods. Thus *79* was once, almost exclusively, the Vesper hymn and *78* the Matins one.

In some Breviaries, other than the Roman, the hymns for this feast are *Summi parentis filio* and *Quicunque certum quaeritis,* of which 'To Christ the prince of peace' and 'All ye who seek a comfort sure' are English versions.

Notes on Hymn 78

Author. Unknown, eighteenth century.
Use. At Vespers of the Sacred Heart.

1. *En ut,* Look how.

5 *Vibrantis hastam militis*
Peccata nostra dirigunt,
Ferrumque dirae cuspidis
Mortale crimen acuit.

Ex corde scisso Ecclesia,
10 *Christo jugata, nascitur;*
Hoc ostium arcae in latere est
Genti ad salutem positum.

Ex hoc perennis gratia
Ceu septiformis fluvius
15 *Stolas ut illic sordidas*
Lavemus Agni in sanguine.

Turpe est redire ad crimina
Quae cor beatum lacerent;
Sed aemulemur cordibus
20 *Flammas amoris indices.*

(Hoc Christe nobis, hoc Pater,
Hoc sancte, dona, Spiritus,
Quibus potestas, gloria
Regnumque in omne est saeculum).

put direction and vigour into the soldier's hesitation; it was man's sin that sharpened the spear's point. The Church, bride of Christ, is born of His pierced Heart; this is the gate in the side of the ark, put there for man's salvation. Seven streams of never-failing grace flow from this Heart that we may wash our soiled robes in the blood of the Lamb. How shameful it would be to return to sins which wound this sacred Heart; how much better to try to reproduce in the burning love of our hearts the flames that are signs of the love of His Heart. Grant this to us, Lord Christ; grant this, Father and holy Spirit. To You belong power, glory and dominion for ever.

Hymn 79

Auctor beate saeculi,
Christe, redemptor omnium,
Lumen Patris de lumine
Deusque verus de Deo,

5 *Amor coegit te tuus*
Mortale corpus sumere
Ut novus Adam redderes
Quod vetus ille abstulerat.

Ille amor, almus artifex
10 *Terrae marisque et siderum,*
Errata patrum miserans
Et nostra rumpens vincula.

Blessed creator of the world and redeemer of all mankind, light from the Father's light and true God from God, love compelled You, Christ, to take a human body that as the second Adam You could restore what the first had taken from us. That love of Yours which was the bountiful creator of earth, sea and the skies, took pity on our first parents' fall and broke the chains that bound us. May that abundant

5. *vibrantis,* trembling, shaking, hesitating.

6. *dirigunt,* put direction, vigour into the shaft, *hastam,* of the spear. Sin also sharpens the spear's point, lines 7–8.

8. *mortale crimen,* man's, mortal's, sin. Mortal sin, B, is ambiguous.

10. *Christo jugata;* cf. *93,* 11, from which the phrase is probably taken.

11. Some take *est* with *positum* (This gate was placed . . .), while others make the lines independent (This is the gate in . . . , placed there).

Hoc praenuntiabat quod Noe in latere arcae ostium facere jussus est, quo intrarent animalia quae non erant diluvio peritura, quibus praefigurabatur Ecclesia, St Aug. in 7th lesson of the octave day.

14. *ceu,* like; cf. *93,* 27. *Septiformis,* referring to the seven sacraments.

15. *stolas;* cf. Apoc. 7, 14 and 22, 14.

19. *aemulemur,* rival, try to imitate.

20. *indices,* signs, proofs.

24. This doxology used to be in the Breviary, and is printed by B and by Daniel. For *79* and *80* the doxology used to be: *Decus Parenti et Filio/Sanctoque sit Spiritui,/Quibus* etc. as above.

Notes on Hymn 79

Author. Same as *78.*

Use. At Matins of the Sacred Heart.

6. *mortale,* man's, a human; cf. *mortale crimen, 78,* 8.

7. *Adam;* cf. Rom. 5, 12–21. In the next line, *vetus ille,* sc. *Adam.*

9. *artifex,* which is in apposition with *amor,* takes up *auctor* of line 1.

Non corde discedat tuo
Vis illa amoris incliti;
15 *Hoc fonte gentes hauriant*
    Remissionis gratiam.

    Percussum ad hoc est lancea
    Passumque ad hoc est vulnera
    Ut nos lavaret sordibus,
20 *Unda fluente et sanguine.*

stream of glorious love never cease to flow from Your Heart; may the nations always draw from this well of love the grace of pardon. It was for this that Your Heart was struck with the lance and for this was it wounded, namely to wash us from our sins in the water and blood that flowed from it.

Hymn 80

Cor, arca legem continens
Non servitutis veteris,
Sed gratiae, sed veniae,
Sed et misericordiae;

5 *Cor, sanctuarium novi*
    Intemeratum foederis,
    Templum vetusto sanctius
    Velumque scisso utilius;

    Te vulneratum caritas
10 *Ictu patenti voluit,*
    Amoris invisibilis
    Ut veneremur vulnera.

    Hoc sub amoris symbolo
    Passus cruenta et mystica,
15 *Utrumque sacrificium*
    Christus sacerdos obtulit.

    Quis non amantem redamet?
    Quis non redemptus diligat
    Et corde in isto seligat
20 *Aeterna tabernacula?*

Your Heart, Jesus, is the ark that holds the law, not indeed the law of man's former slavery, but the law of grace, pardon and mercy. Your Heart is the undefiled sanctuary of the new covenant, a temple holier than the old Jewish one and a veil more profitable than the one that was rent asunder. Love willed that Your Heart be wounded with a blow that disclosed its secrets that we might revere the wounds that are pledges of the love we cannot see. Beneath this symbol of love Christ the Victim suffered in His passion and at the Supper, and beneath it Christ the Priest offered His double sacrifice. Who would not love this Lover in return? Who among the redeemed would not be devoted to His redeemer, or would not choose out for now and into eternity a refuge in that Heart?

17. *percussum*, sc. *cor; ad hoc*, for this reason—referring to the petition of the preceding verse. The language is reminiscent of St Bonaventure: *Ad hoc*

enim perforatum est latus tuum, ut nobis pateat introitus. Ad hoc vulneratum est cor tuum, 9th lesson of the feast.

19. *sordibus*; cf. *sordidam, 78, 15.*

Notes on Hymn 80

Author. See *78.*

Use. At Lauds of the Sacred Heart.

7. temple more holy than the one of old, *vetusto* sc. *templo.* Similarly understand *velo* with *scisso* in the next line.

The Heart is called a temple as signifying here the humanity of our Lord in whom dwelt the fulness of the Godhead; cf. Col. 2, 9. A temple essentially is a place where God dwells; cf. *38,* 14.

8. The Heart is called a veil with reference to the opening of our Lord's side. The torn veil in the Temple exposed to view the mysterious and sacred objects of Jewish worship. The opening of our Lord's side disclosed to men the mysteries of the new Law.

9. *Te* refers to our Lord through the word *Cor,* which is the subject of the address of the first eight lines. *Vulneratum*, sc. *esse*; cf. *79,* 17, note.

10. *ictu patenti*; with an open wound, B. Perhaps *patenti=patefacienti*, i.e. with a wound which disclosed. Thus man would be given visible proof and a visible symbol of His invisible love; cf. the following lines and lesson 6 of the octave day.

St John is the only one to describe the opening of our Lord's side and is also alone in recording that after the resurrection our Lord showed His side as

well as His hands and feet; cf. Luke 24, 40 and John 20, 20 and 27. It is John also who especially connects *caritas* and *amor* with our Lord (cf. lines 9, 11 and 13 of this hymn), and is the special advocate of love of our Lord. Thus devotion to the Sacred Heart may in a special way be traced back to the beloved disciple.

13. *hoc . . . symbolo*, i.e. the Heart.

14. The victim, *passus*, on the cross, *cruenta*, and at the last supper, *mystica. Utrumque* refers to *cruenta* and *mystica.* The identity of Priest and Victim is stated in line 16; cf. also *149,* 13–20.

17–20. The hymn owes much in thought and expression to St Bonaventure; cf. *Vulneratum est ut per vulnus visibile, vulnus amoris invisibile videamus . . . Quis illud cor tam vulneratum non diligat? quis tam amans (sc. cor) non redamet? . . . Nos igitur adhuc in carne manentes, quantum possumus, amantem redamemus,* 9th lesson of the feast.

Non in lines 17 and 18 with the verb, as in the prose passage above.

19. *seligat*, choose out, select; supply *non* from 18.

20. *tabernacula*; cf. 8th lesson of the feast and the beginning of the 9th. *Ad hoc vulneratum est cor tuum, ut in illo ab exterioribus absoluti habitare possimus.*

III

HYMNS OF THE COMMON OF SAINTS

THE hymns of the seasons celebrate, mystery by mystery, the earthly life of the 'light of the world' and end with the sending of 'another Paraclete', who also is a *lumen cordium*. *Tu lux refulge sensibus* and *Accende lumen sensibus*—this, in substance, has been the prayer of the Church year by year from its earliest days. It has been received with favour by God from the very beginning and has been answered in a most striking manner in the person of the saints who, individually or in groups, are the subject of the remaining hymns of this book.

At first there was nothing which corresponded with what we know as the Common of Saints, but as the number of saints gradually increased, it became customary to use a standard office for many individuals of the same class. This standard or common office had previously been composed for one particular saint, and great skill and ingenuity went to its composition. The present Common of Apostles is said to have been originally an office for SS Peter and Paul and, even to most of the antiphons, it is still the basis of their office on 29 June. The Common of Martyrs is clearly derived from offices of SS Stephen, Laurence and Vincent and the Common of Confessors is derived from that of Martyrs, being originally composed for St Martin of Tours (cf. 87).

The hymns which eventually found their way into these Commons are for the most part fairly easy. They are direct and objective in their thought, though to some they may appear a shade reticent. Yet at least there is a refreshing absence of a sentimentality which spoils some modern hymns for saints. They are, however, more unequal in quality than those of the previous sections, and one or two may be thought to be below the general standard of the hymns—which is a pity, since the hymns of this section are among the most used in the Breviary. One would have thought that some of them would have appealed to the revisers as apt material for their correcting pen, yet in fact *comparatively* little was done to them. But the revisers did not leave them altogether untouched. St Ambrose had to be 'corrected'. The *Iste confessor* was greatly altered and the hymn for the Dedication of a Church, which no one ought to have touched, was in fact completely recast in a new metre. →

Just as in the hymns of the seasons one does not find very many references to the hour at which they are used (cf. the Introduction to the last section), so is it with the hymns of the saints, whether from the Common or the Proper. There is little, if anything, about the hours at which they are used and, inevitably in the hymns of the Common, nothing about the seasons. One is more likely to find references to the season during which any feast may occur in the Collects, as an examination of the Collects of saints towards the end of March and the first half of April will show. But the ideas which are fundamental to all the hymns are found here—that God is our creator, our redeemer and our judge and that, by the first two titles, He is the giver of light and of the light of grace.

The metaphor of light is ubiquitous. Our Lady is the *stella maris*, and through her intercession is given *lumen caecis*. She is the *aula lucis fulgida*, resplendent with her own grace and with the presence in her womb of the incarnate God. The apostles, and the martyrs too, are the *vera mundi lumina*. The heavenly Jerusalem is the *caeli corusca civitas*, and it is the Christian's prayer that God will give some of this glory to the dedicated church by filling it *benigno lumine*. To this true light of grace and sanctity is opposed the sham brightness and light of worldly things—the *luculenta praedia* of *89*. These the saints, as true followers of Christ, rejected as *imbuta felle* and *polluta*, and so He became their reward and abiding light. *Lux aeterna lucebit sanctis tuis, Domine,* is the text the Church uses for martyrs during Paschaltide. But that Christ is their reward is also expressed in the hymns under the image of a crown. He is the *sors, corona et praemium* of the martyrs, the *perpes corona praesulum* and the *corona virginum*. All this is summed up in the Invitatory of All Saints: *Regem regum Dominum venite adoremus, quia ipse est corona Sanctorum omnium.*

Finally, just as every season has its own particular lesson and grace, so each group of saints has its own message for us and its own example of sanctity for us to imitate. The hymns, in common with the rest of the office to which they belong, would have us reproduce something of the constancy of the martyrs, the fidelity of the confessors, the purity of the virgins and the resolute single-mindedness of the widows. This we ask through the intercession of the saint of the day, so that phrases like *hac die, hujus gratia* and *hujus oratu* are constantly recurring. The collect of St William, 25 June, well sums up this relationship of the saints to us: 'O God, who to help our weakness hast given us thy saints for our pattern and protection as we tread the path of salvation, grant that we may so revere the merits of the blessed abbot William as to secure his advocacy and to follow in his footsteps' (translation from Burns, Oates Missal).

Reflection may show that the hymns of the days and hours have, *in substance*, more in common with those of the Common of Saints than might appear at first sight and that both sets of hymns are variations on the fragment of an early Christian

---

The Common of Apostles
Hymn 81

Exsultet orbis gaudiis,
Caelum resultet laudibus;
Apostolorum gloriam
Tellus et astra concinunt.

5 *Vos, saeculorum judices*
Et vera mundi lumina,
Votis precamur cordium;
Audite voces supplicum.

Qui templa caeli clauditis
10 *Serasque verbo solvitis,*
Nos a reatu noxios
Solvi jubete, quaesumus.

Praecepta quorum protinus
Languor salusque sentiunt,
15 *Sanate mentes languidas,*
Augete nos virtutibus,

Ut, cum redibit arbiter
In fine Christus saeculi,
Nos sempiterni gaudii
20 *Concedat esse compotes.*

Let earth be glad and rejoice, and heaven re-echo with praise. Earth and heaven in unison sing the Apostles' fame. To you, judges of men and true lights of the world, we tell in prayer our heart's desires; hear your suppliants' words. You shut heaven's gates and with a word undo their bolts; give the word of command, we beg you, for us sinners to be undone from our guilt. As sickness and health are instantly subject to your bidding, heal the sickness of our souls and enrich us with virtue that when Christ comes again at the end of time to be man's judge, He may graciously call us to possess eternal joy.

The Common of one Martyr
Hymn 82

Deus, tuorum militum
Sors et corona, praemium,
Laudes canentes martyris
Absolve nexu criminis.

God, the portion, crown and prize of Your soldiers, we are singing a martyr's praises; free us from the bondage of sin. Your martyr

hymn found in St Paul: *Surge qui dormis, et exsurge a mortuis, et illuminabit te Christus,* Eph. 5, 14.

Notes on Hymn 81

Author. Unknown. Perhaps of tenth century date.

Use. At Vespers and Lauds of feasts of the Apostles, except during Paschaltide. For the Matins hymn, *Aeterna Christi munera,* cf. *85a.* For Apostles' hymns during Paschaltide, cf. *59,* 17–32 and 33–44.

2. *resultet,* re-echo. Cf. *Laetentur caeli et exsultet terra,* Ps. 95, 11.

5. *judices;* cf. *judicantes duodecim tribus Israel,* Mt. 19, 28 and Lk. 22, 30.

6. *lumina;* Christ, the *lux mundi,* says of the Apostles, *Vos estis lux mundi,* Mt. 5, 14.

7. *votis,* desires, yearnings, as expressed in the next line and developed in the rest of the hymn. It is a prayer for help and grace, 9–16, without which man will fare ill at the judgment, 17–20. *Votis;* cf. *12, 9.*

10. *solvitis* and *clauditis,* cf. Mt. 18, 18 and John 20, 23.

11. *a reatu* with *solvi,* not with *noxios.* It displaces the original *a peccatis omnibus.*

13. *Protinus,* immediately, instantly; contrast *64,* 18.

14. *languor* and *languidas* in 15; cf. *10, 6* and *34, 7,* notes.

20. *compotes,* possessed of, sharers in; cf. *35, 15,* note.

Notes on Hymn 82

Author. Unknown, probably sixth century W thinks that *86, 88* and this hymn are all by the same author, because of the similarity of their vocabulary.

Use. At Vespers and Matins of feasts of a Martyr.

2. *sors et corona.* The position of *et* is odd. W suggested that *corona praemium* might be a compound word, *corona-praemium,* expressing a single idea. A hymn for St Luke has the order *Corona, spes et praemium* (Mearns, *Early Latin Hymnaries,* p. 28).

Corona is suggested by *In die illa erit Dominus exercituum corona gloriae,* Is. 28, 5 and is often used in hymns of this section; cf. *86, 2; 90, 1.* The name

5 *Hic nempe mundi gaudia*
Et blanda fraudum pabula
Imbuta felle deputans
Pervenit ad caelestia.

Poenas cucurrit fortiter
10 *Et sustulit viriliter,*
Fundensque pro te sanguinem
Aeterna dona possidet.

Ob hoc precatu supplici
Te poscimus, piissime,
15 *In hoc triumpho martyris*
Dimitte noxam servulis.

reckoned the pleasures of the world and its attractive enticements to sin to be as joyless and bitter as gall and so won through to the joys of heaven. He passed through his tortures bravely and endured them manfully. He shed his blood for You and so obtained his eternal reward. For this reason we turn to You in humble prayer, most loving Lord; forgive Your servants' sins on this day of Your martyr's triumph.

Hymn 83

Invicte martyr, unicum
Patris secutus Filium,
Victis triumphas hostibus,
Victor fruens caelestibus.

5 *Tui precatus munere,*
Nostrum reatum dilue,
Arcens mali contagium,
Vitae repellens taedium.

Soluta sunt jam vincula
10 *Tui sacrati corporis;*
Nos solve vinclis saeculi
Dono superni numinis.

Martyr whom no persecutor could overcome and follower of the Father's only Son, you overcame your enemies and received the honour of a triumph, entering heaven as a conqueror to enjoy its pleasures. Through the merit of your intercession cause our guilt to melt away, keep at a distance from us all infection from sin and drive away life's weariness. The bonds of your dedicated body are now undone. Do you undo us from the bonds of the world by the grace of the God of heaven.

The Common of many Martyrs
Hymn 84

Sanctorum meritis inclita gaudia
Pangamus, socii, gestaque fortia;
Gliscens fert animus promere cantibus
Victorum genus optimum.

Let us sing, fellow Christians, of the glorious joys that the saints gained through their merits, let us sing of their heroic deeds. Our soul is eager and ready to tell in song the noble line of

Stephen, of which *corona* is a Latin translation, also suggested its use for Martyrs.

6. *blanda.* In Christian writers *blandus* is often used in the derogatory meaning of alluring, seductive; but it is sometimes used in a good sense, as in *sermone blando angelus, 59, 21,* note. *Pabula;* cf. *49, 15.*

7. The revisers' *imbuta felle* displaces the original metaphor of the fleeting nature, *caduca,* of earthly joys. *Deputans;* cf. *66,* 11.

8. *caelestia,* sc. *gaudia.*

9. *cucurrit.* He bravely ran the way of torture, B;

he passed through, W. The metaphor is of a toilsome race. W compares the lines about St Agatha: *Inde gavisa magisque flagrans/Cuncta flagella cucurrit ovans.*

13. *Ob hoc,* for this reason. *Precatu,* from *precatus,* 4, prayer—a poetical and post-classical form; cf. *83, 5; 88,* 15.

15. *Hoc triumpho* seems to mean on this day of (his) triumph. *Triumphus* has many shades of meaning in the hymns; e.g. of our Lord's passion, of the death of the martyrs and even, in *53,* 2, of a song of triumph.

Notes on Hymn 83

Author. Unknown. Tenth century, or perhaps earlier (cf. Julian, 1579).

Use. At Lauds of feasts of a Martyr.

3. *triumphas,* receive the honour of a triumph—as explained in the next line. *Hostibus,* the torturers.

5. *precatus;* cf. *82,* 13. *Munere,* by the merit, virtue, favour of.

7. *contagium,* cf. 7, 15, note.

8. *vitae ... taedium,* life's weariness; cf. *ita ut taederet nos etiam vivere,* 2 Cor. 1, 8.

9. *vincula,* the body being considered as a prison; cf. Rom. 7, 24.

10. *sacrati,* dedicated, consecrated, holy—especially as offered to God by martyrdom.

11. *solve;* could be considered as a prayer for a happy death or, more directly, as a prayer to be released from anything which holds us back from God.

Notes on Hymn 84

Author. Unknown, perhaps of the eighth century. The ascription to Raban Maur is impossible. Hincmar in the ninth century several times refers to this hymn in his *De una et non trina Deitate* and says he could not discover who was the author of the hymn which *a quibusdam cantatur vel potius blasphema-*

tur 'Te trina deitas'. Moreover Raban, writing to Hincmar, expressed his disapproval of the phrase *'trina Deitas'.* The revisers removed these words from this hymn, though they left them in *72,* 25.

Metre. Second Asclepiad.

Use. At Vespers of feasts of many Martyrs.

5 *Hi sunt, quos fatue mundus abhorruit;*
Hunc fructu vacuum, floribus aridum
Contempsere tui nominis asseclae,
    Jesu, rex bone caelitum.

    Hi pro te furias atque minas truces
10 *Calcarunt hominum saevaque verbera;*
His cessit lacerans fortiter ungula,
    Nec carpsit penetralia.

    Caeduntur gladiis more bidentium;
Non murmur resonat, non querimonia,
15 *Sed corde impavido, mens bene conscia*
    Conservat patientiam.

    Quae vox, quae poterit lingua retexere,
Quae tu martyribus munera praeparas?
Rubri nam fluido sanguine, fulgidis
20   *Cingunt tempora laureis.*

    Te summa o Deitas unaque poscimus
Ut culpas abigas, noxia subtrahas;
Des pacem famulis, ut tibi gloriam
    Annorum in seriem canant.

warriors. These are the men that the world in its folly rejected. But they were followers of You, Jesus, kind king of those in heaven, and therefore they despised a world that is barren of fruit and blooms only to wither. For Your sake they triumphed over men's rage and savage threats and cruel scourgings. The hook that fiercely tore them to bits effected nothing and left them their spirit unconquered. They are cut down by the sword as if animals for a sacrifice. No sound, no complaint passes their lips. Instead, their soul, dauntless and sure of its cause, keeps their endurance firm and unshaken. What voice, or what tongue can tell the rewards that You prepare for Your martyrs? Red with the blood that is still flowing from their wounds, they crown their heads with shining laurel garlands. We beseech You, mighty Godhead, one in essence, to take away Your servants' guilt, remove all their sins and give them peace that they may sing praise to You for ever.

Hymn 85

The text of the *Aeterna Christi munera* is given here in its unrevised text. The Breviary variants and the two Breviary hymns formed from the text are explained in the notes and under the headings *85a* and *85b*.

Aeterna Christi munera
Et martyrum victorias,
Laudes ferentes debitas,
Laetis canamus mentibus.

5 *Ecclesiarum principes,*
Belli triumphales duces,
Caelestis aulae milites
Et vera mundi lumina,

With joy of heart let us sing a hymn as our tribute of praise to Christ's eternal gifts and the martyrs' victories. Princes of the churches, war-leaders that were honoured with a triumph, picked soldiers of the heavenly court and true lights of the world—they overcame the terrors

1. *meritis,* for the merits, i.e. because they merit our praise, Byrnes; the glorious delights merited by them, B.

3. *gliscens, glisco,* 3, desire, ardently long for; *fert,* hastens, strives, betakes itself; *promere,* tell, relate.

5. *fatue;* cf. *Hi sunt quos habuimus aliquando in derisum* ..., Wisdom, 5, 3. *Abhorruit* answers *contempsere* of line 7.

6. *hunc,* sc. *mundum. Despexit jam quasi aridum mundum cum flore,* Greg. *Dial.* II, 1; cf. also Isaias 40, 6 ff.

7. *contempsere = contempserunt; asseclae,* followers.

9. *furias; furia* or, more usually, *furiae,* passion, rage, fury. *Truces; trux, -cis,* adj., wild, rough, savage, fierce.

10. *calcarunt = calcaverunt; hominum,* explanatory of all the accusatives.

11. *cessit,* yielded, availed nothing. *Ungula,* a steel hook or claw that tore the flesh to bits; cf. *85,* 17, note.

12. *carpsit;* pluck off, i.e. tear away, rob them of. *Penetralia,* the innermost of anything, whether the soul of a person or the sanctuary of a temple. The line could mean that their spirit was unconquered, being a variant of the preceding line; or that they did not die under that torment but lived to be put to death by the sword, as explained in the next verse.

13. *more bidentium,* just like sheep, cattle. *Bidens* means an animal for sacrifice.

15. *mens bene conscia.* The soul self-possessed, happy in the rightness of its cause. 'Their souls, serenely blessed', Neale.

20. *tempora,* heads.

Notes on Hymn 85

Author. St Ambrose.

Though some scholars reject the claim of St Ambrose and classify the hymn as a composition of the fifth century, the balance of opinion seems to be in his favour. The mention of the hymn by St Bede as an *ambrosianus* is of itself no proof that St Ambrose wrote the hymn, for that word is ambiguous in St Bede. Nor is an allusion to the hymn in Maximus of Turin a proof of Ambrosian authorship. Arguments must rest 'on the presence of the hymn in the MSS of the Ambrosian use, and above all on its intimate correspondence in vocabulary, phraseology and thought with the prose works of Ambrose. And these proofs are strong enough to settle the question', W.

The *Aeterna Christi munera* is the oldest of the hymns *In natali martyrum,* and so is the source and inspiration of all other hymns for martyrs. Some verses were eventually taken out to form an Apostles' hymn and the remaining verses used for Martyrs; see *85a* and *b,* below. This division is usually said to have taken place about the tenth century, but it would not be surprising if it happened before that date. If it did, these verses would then be the source of many other hymns in honour of the Apostles.

But the division inevitably spoilt the original hymn and made necessary the substitution of *apostolorum* for *et martyrum* in line 2 and of *ipsorum* or *illorum* for *martyrum* in line 30. These relatively innocuous changes were not to the taste of the revisers who produced the first verses of *85a* and *b.*

1. *munera* and *victorias;* accusatives after *canamus. Munera* has been interpreted as meaning (1) the grace which enabled the martyrs to persevere; (2) the reward which followed their martyrdom; or (3) the martyrs themselves, just as St Paul speaks of

Notes continued on p. 146

Terrore victo saeculi
10 *Poenisque spretis corporis,*
Mortis sacrae compendio
Lucem beatam possident.

Traduntur igni martyres
Et bestiarum dentibus;
15 *Armata saevit ungulis*
Tortoris insani manus.

Nudata pendent viscera,
Sanguis sacratus funditur,
Sed permanent immobiles
20 *Vitae perennis gratia.*

Devota sanctorum fides,
Invicta spes credentium,
Perfecta Christi caritas
Mundi triumphat principem.

25 *In his paterna gloria,*
In his voluntas Spiritus,
Exsultat in his Filius;
Caelum repletur gaudio.

Te nunc, redemptor, quaesumus,
30 *Ut martyrum consortio*
Jungas precantes servulos
In sempiterna saecula.

of the world, despised all tortures inflicted on them and by the short cut of a holy death entered into the light of bliss. They were delivered over to fire and to wild beasts; savage men, armed with hooks of steel, tortured them mercilessly. Their entrails were laid bare and protruded, their holy blood streamed out in profusion; and yet they persevered with the utmost constancy—their reward, eternal life. The devoted faith of these holy men, the immovable hope that was theirs as believers and their perfect love of Christ resulted in triumph over the prince of this world. In their persons the glory of the Father was enhanced, the will of the Spirit was fulfilled and the Son rejoiced; all heaven was filled with joy. We now ask You, our redeemer, to unite us, Your servants and suppliants, to the company of the martyrs for all eternity.

Notes continued from p. 145

apostles, teachers etc. as gifts of God, Eph. 4, 8, 11. In *85a* it is applied to the Apostles.

5. *principes* and the other nominatives are best taken as the subject of *possident*. When the verse is used as part of *85a*, supply *sunt*.

For martyrs as *principes*, cf. *principes populi quos alios nisi sanctos martyres aestimare debemus?*, Ambr. *Ep.* 22, 7. For apostles as *principes*, cf. the use of *constitues eos principes super omnem terram*, Ps. 44, 17, in the office of Apostles. →

6. *triumphales*. *Triumphalis* is normally used of things, but Suetonius has *vir triumphalis* and Livy *senex triumphalis* of one who had had the honour of a triumph. The saints had such an honour at their death.

7. *milites*. St Ambrose is fond of this expression, founded on *Labora sicut bonus miles Christi Jesu*, 2 Tim. 2, 3. Here, in conjunction with *caelestis aulae*, the idea is of *picked* soldiers who guard the royal household. St Ambrose applies it to the Martyrs, and *85a* to the Apostles.

8. *lumina*. 'As Christ is the true light of the world, so His martyrs are also "true lights", in a different and yet in a real sense; cf. (of the martyrs) *ecce veri dies pleni luminis et fulgoris aeterni*, Ambr. *Ep.* 22, 6 and *Christo lucebat martyrum lucerna*, Ambr. *in Ps.* 118, 14, 27', W. For the apostles as lights of the world, cf. *81, 6*, note.

11. *mortis sacrae;* used here of martyrdom, but in *21, 7* in the general sense of a happy death. *Compendio,* by the short cut. The martyrs attain by a swift death what others attain by a long life of service.

12. *lucem*. Another, and common, reading is *vitam,* which most Breviaries, the Roman included, use in *85b*.

13. *igni*. 'Ambrose wishes here to mark a climax; the fire is lifeless, the beasts do but obey the instincts of their nature, man indulges in refinements of cruelty', W. For the tortures mentioned in lines 13–20 Ambrose is an authority in many of his prose works, as are many other writers. And cf. Heb. 11, 36 ff.

15. *ungulis;* cf. *84, 11*, note.

16. *manus* is a nominative, qualified by *armata ungulis. Insani,* mad with rage; cf. *39, 5*, note.

17. *viscera,* i.e. their entrails are laid bare and protrude; cf. *ungulis ita excarnificatus est ut ejus interiora apparerent nuda,* Martyrology, 9 November. There is no allusion to *intentional* disembowelling.

18. *sacratus;* cf. *83, 10*, note.

19. *permanent immobiles*—a common Ambrosian combination. The idea of *immobilis* in Ambrose is always of steadfast perseverance, whether under torture or *in Dei timore*.

20. *gratia,* for the sake of; not, as B, by the grace of.

21. *devota . . . fides,* the devoted (in the true sense of that word) faith.

24. *mundi triumphat principem,* leads in triumph the prince of this world. The transitive use of *triumphare* instead of with *de* or *ex* and the ablative is poetical and post-classical. *Mundi principem;* cf. *princeps hujus mundi,* John 12, 31; cf. also John 14, 30 and 16, 11, and Eph. 6, 12.

For this line the revisers substituted *Mundi tyrannum conterit,* i.e. tramples under foot.

Lines 21–28 follow naturally in the full text, but the transition is abrupt when they only follow 5–8, as in *85a*. 21–24 give the effect on earth of the martyrs' constancy, while 25–28 tell of the effect in heaven. In both verses of the original the second Person is mentioned in the third line of the verse, although out of the order of the Persons in 25–28. This is partly to balance the two mentions of our Lord and also to recall the opening words *Aeterna Christi munera*. The revisers, however, knew better.

25. *In his,* i.e. in the person of these martyrs. This meaning of *in* is not uncommon in Ambrose. *Exsultat* to be taken with *gloria, voluntas* and *Filius*— of the three Persons rejoicing. The divine rejoicing and that of the court of heaven is summed up in line 28.

The Breviary text is: *In his paterna gloria,/In his triumphat Filius,/In his voluntas Spiritus,/Caelum repletur gaudio*. This substitutes triumph for rejoicing, though the revisers rejected *triumphat* in 24. *Triumphat* in itself and by its position in the *second* line is not so easy to adapt to the three nouns as *exsultat* in Ambrose's third line; it also leaves the fourth line largely unexplained. Cf. also note on 24.

29–32. This verse is in the nature of a quasi-doxology rather than of a doxology in the strict sense. But as it is part of Ambrose's hymn, it is never displaced as the last verse of *85b*. In the present Roman Breviary one of the ordinary doxologies is used at the end of *85a*, but unrevised Breviaries normally use this verse, putting *ipsorum* for *martyrum*. The martyrs are witnesses to Christ, they are His gift and He rejoices in them. So we ask Him, as king of the martyrs and as redeemer, to join us to their company.

30. *consortio,* company—common in Ambrose in this connection. Cf. also *intra quorum . . . consortium* in the *Nobis quoque* of the Missal.

Hymn 85a

Aeterna Christi munera,
Apostolorum gloriam,
Palmas et hymnos debitos
Laetis canamus mentibus.

Let us joyfully sing songs of victory and pay our tribute of praise in hymns to commemorate Christ's eternal gifts, the Apostles' glory.

This verse is followed by lines 5–8 and 21–28 of 85.

Hymn 85b

Christo profusum sanguinem
Et martyrum victorias
Dignamque caelo lauream
Laetis sequamur vocibus.

Let us honour in joyous hymns the martyrs' blood shed for Christ, their victories and their triumph that won them heaven.

This is followed by lines 9–20 and 29–32 of 85.

Hymn 86

Rex gloriose martyrum,
Corona confitentium,
Qui respuentes terrea
Perducis ad caelestia,

5 Aurem benignam protinus
Intende nostris vocibus;
Trophaea sacra pangimus,
Ignosce quod deliquimus.

Tu vincis inter martyres
10 Parcisque confessoribus;
Tu vince nostra crimina,
Largitor indulgentiae.

Glorious king of martyrs, crown of them that confess You and leader to heaven of all that despise worldly pleasures, give a ready and gracious hearing to our hymn; our theme is the martyrs' holy triumph, our plea is for pardon for our sins. Your might is displayed in the martyrs, and Your mercy in those that confess You. Exert Your mighty power over our sins and pour out Your mercy on us.

Note on Hymn 85*a*

Use. At Matins of feasts of the Apostles outside Paschaltide.

Note on Hymn 85*b*

Use. At Matins of feasts of many Martyrs.

Notes on Hymn 86

Author. Unknown, probably of sixth century; cf. *82.*

Use. At Lauds of many Martyrs.

2. *corona;* cf. *82, 2,* note. *Confitentium;* cf. *5, 7,* note. The same meaning must be given to *confitentium* and *confessoribus* in line 10. It is at least probable, as W suggests, that the chief reference here is to those singing the hymn, who also by their way of life—*respuentes terrea*—ought to be confessing God.

3. *Terrea* is used, *metri gratia,* for *terrena.*

5. *protinus;* quickly, B; continually, W . Cf. *64, 18* and *81, 13.*

7. *trophaea,* triumphs, victories; cf. *53, 2.*

9. *inter martyres;* original, *in martyribus.* The latter means in the person of the martyrs, like *in his, 85, 25.* *Inter martyres* could be treated as the equivalent of this, making *inter* bear the meaning of *per.*

10. *parcisque;* original, *parcendo. Confessoribus;* cf. note on line 2. The sparing could be because they are not called to martyrdom, B, or because God is merciful to weaker, but not unfaithful, Christians, W—God's mercy being one of the fruits of the martyrs' victory.

12. *Largitor indulgentiae;* original, *donando indulgentiam,* where *donando* balances the original *parcendo* of line 10.

The Common of a Confessor Bishop
Hymn 87

Iste confessor Domini, colentes
Quem pie laudant populi per orbem,
Hac die laetus meruit supremos
    Laudis honores.

5 Qui pius, prudens, humilis, pudicus,
Sobriam duxit sine labe vitam,
Donec humanos animavit aurae
    Spiritus artus.

Cujus ob praestans meritum frequenter
10 Aegra quae passim jacuere membra,
Viribus morbi domitis, saluti
    Restituuntur.

Noster hinc illi chorus obsequentem
Concinit laudem celebresque palmas,
15 Ut piis ejus precibus juvemur
    Omne per aevum.

Sit salus illi, decus atque virtus,
Qui super caeli solio coruscans
Totius mundi seriem gubernat
20   Trinus et unus.

This confessor of the Lord, honoured and lovingly praised by the peoples of the world, on this day merited to receive with joy the highest honour and praise. He was holy, discreet, humble and chaste; and, as long as the breath of life was in him, he led a mortified and blameless life. Because of his outstanding holiness many sick persons from different places were freed of the malady that afflicted them and restored to health. For this reason we as a choir sing his praise and celebrate his renowned victories so that he may help us now and always by his prayers. Salvation, glory and power be to Him that sits in dazzling splendour on the heavenly throne and guides creation on its ordered course, God, three and one.

Hymn 88

Jesu redemptor omnium,
Perpes corona praesulum,
In hac die clementius
Indulgeas precantibus,

5 Tui sacri qua nominis
Confessor almus claruit;
Hujus celebrat annua
Devota plebs sollemnia.

Qui rite mundi gaudia
10 Hujus caduca respuens,

Jesus, redeemer of the world and eternal crown of bishops, show Yourself today even more gracious and kindly disposed to our prayers, for on this day the loving confessor of Your holy name first shone with heavenly glory; and Your devoted people today are keeping his yearly feast. He rightly disdained the fleeting joys of this world and so obtained

Notes on Hymn 87

Author. Unknown, of the eighth century.

It seems to have been written as a hymn in honour of St Martin of Tours and later adopted, with much else from the office of that saint, as part of the office of Bishops. This office was in its turn used as the basis of the office of non-bishops. The *Iste Confessor* loses much of its force when applied to bishops who were not, as was St Martin, famous as wonder-workers, just as it loses much when used for saints who were not bishops and perhaps not even priests. The hymnal seems deficient in the offices of Confessors.

Metre. First Sapphic.

Use. At Vespers and Matins of Confessors, whether bishops or not.

1. The original opening line was: *Iste confessor Domini sacratus*. The office of St Martin was founded on that of the martyrs, and *sacratus* points to this connection; cf. *83, 10*, note.

This hymn was greatly altered by the revisers, only lines 5, 12, 16 and 20 being unchanged.

3-4. The text above is now always used. But if the feast day were the day of the saint's death, it used to be *meruit beatas/Scandere sedes*—the revisers' version of the original text. For the Stigmata of St Francis, 17 September, it is: *meruit beata/Vulnera Christi*.

5-8. A character-sketch of St Martin as an episcopal model after the mind of St Paul. *Oportet ergo episcopum irreprehensibilem esse . . . sobrium, prudentem . . . pudicum*, 1 Tim. 3, 2.

7. *humanos artus*, human limbs, i.e. body; cf. *3, 1*.

8. *spiritus aurae*, breath of life. 'While that life's vigour, coursing through his members,/Quickened his being', Hymner.

9-12. St Martin as a wonder-worker.

11. *Aegra . . . membra* is the subject of the verse.

13. *hinc*, for this reason.

14. *celebresque palmas*, famous, renowned victories. For this meaning of *palmas*, cf. *palmas incessabili devotione venerari* of a collect for Virgin Martyrs and *91, 5*.

17. *illi*, i.e. God; but *illi* in line 13 refers to the saint.

19. *seriem*, order, course; for *seriem* in a temporal sense, cf. *84, 24*.

Notes on Hymn 88

Author. Unknown. It is usually said to be of eighth century date, but if W's surmise is correct, cf. *82*, it must be dated back to the sixth century.

Use. At Lauds of a Confessor Bishop.

2. *perpes*, everlasting; cf. *12, 6*. *Corona*; cf. *82, 2*, note. *Praesulum*, i.e. bishops. *Praesul* is a president, prefect; patron. Its first meaning, according to some, is a dancer, leading dancer.

5. *qua*, sc. *die* of line 3.

7. *hujus*, i.e. the *confessor* of line 6. *Annua* with *sollemnia*.

8. *sollemnia*; cf. *72, 1*, note.

9. *rite*; cf. *caduca rite deputans*, the original text of *82, 7*.

10. *caduca*, fleeting, perishable; *respuens*; cf. *86, 3*.

Aeternitatis praemio
Potitur inter angelos.

Hujus benignus annue
Nobis sequi vestigia,
15 *Hujus precatu servulis*
Dimitte noxam criminis.

an imperishable reward among the angels in heaven. Graciously grant us to follow in his footsteps and through his intercession forgive us our sinful guilt.

The Common of a Confessor not a Bishop
Hymn 89

Jesu, corona celsior
Et veritas sublimior,
Qui confitenti servulo
Reddis perenne praemium,

5 *Da supplicanti coetui,*
Hujus rogatu, noxii
Remissionem criminis,
Rumpendo nexum vinculi.

Anni reverso tempore,
10 *Dies refulsit lumine*
Quo sanctus hic de corpore
Migravit inter sidera.

Hic vana terrae gaudia
Et luculenta praedia
15 *Polluta sorde deputans*
Ovans tenet caelestia.

Te Christe rex piissime
Hic confitendo jugiter
Calcavit artes daemonum
20 *Saevumque averni principem.*

Virtute clarus et fide,
Confessione sedulus,
Jejuna membra deferens,
Dapes supernas obtinet.

25 *Proinde te piissime*
Precamur omnes supplices,
Nobis ut hujus gratia
Poenas remittas debitas.

Jesus, crown most glorious and truth most sublime, You gave an eternal reward to Your humble confessor. Through his intercession grant us, gathered together in prayer, pardon for our guilty faults and break sin's chains that hold us fast. A year has gone by, and the day has once again dawned on which Your holy servant left earth for heaven. He looked on the world's empty joys and unsubstantial possessions as corrupt and base, and now triumphantly rejoices in heaven's joys and blessings. By always being faithful to Your rule, Christ, king most gracious, he set at nought the devils' deceitful schemes and humbled hell's cruel tyrant. He was renowned for his virtue and faith, and steadfast in confessing You; he lived his earthly life in fasting and now shares in the feasts of heaven. Therefore we, Your suppliants, together ask You, most loving God, to remit, as a favour to Your saint, the punishment that our sins deserve.

13. *hujus* here and in line 15 refers to the saint of the day. *Annue*, grant.

14. *sequi* is the object after *annue*; cf. the use of *nescire* in *90, 15*.

15. *precatu*; cf. *82, 13*.

Notes on Hymn 89

Author. Unknown. B puts its date as sixth century. According to Mone 'its metrical form proves it to have been composed in France in the eleventh century', Julian, p. 584. But in the New Supplement to Julian at page 1656 appears the entry 'this hymn was probably written in Italy'. The earliest MSS cited in either place in Julian as containing the hymn are of the eleventh century. The matter is of little importance, but it is an example of the many instances in hymnology where conjectures about the date of a hymn and the country of its origin are numerous and varied.

Use. At Lauds of a Confessor not a bishop. See *87* for Vespers and Matins.

3. *confitenti servulo* = *confessori.* No particular significance is normally attached to the use of *servulus* instead of *servus.* Ambrose uses it more often than not, cf. *85, 31,* and later writers delighted in such forms; cf. e.g. *82, 16; 88, 15.* In *27, 8* it seems to be used purposely.

6. *rogatu,* like *precatu* in *82, 13. Noxii* with *criminis* —the revisers being responsible for the division of the sense between the second and third lines.

11. *quo* referring to *dies.* In *87, 3* and *88, 3 dies* is feminine. *Sanctus hic,* i.e. the saint of the day.

12. On 17 September this line becomes *Christi recepit stigmata,*—*Christi* being dependent on *de corpore.*

14. *luculenta,* deceptive. Classically (and apparently always in a good sense), *luculentus* meant bright, splendid, etc. Later it came to mean bright, showy, deceptive. *Praedia,* goods; literally, farms, estates.

15. *deputans*; cf. *66, 11,* note. *Deputans* is the equivalent of a past participle, but *ovans* is a real present and contemporaneous with *tenet.*

18. *Hic,* sc. *sanctus. Confitendo jugiter,* by unceasingly confessing, i.e. by an unbroken life of virtue.

19. *artes,* wiles; used for the singular *artem,* cf. *53, 8.*

20. *Averni*; cf. *2, 24.*

23. *jejuna,* opposed to *dapes*—fasting to (heavenly, *superna*) feasting; or mortification as opposed to heavenly life. *Membra,* i.e. his body; cf. *87, 10.*

25. According to Daniel I, 110 the original text has the following verse between lines 24 and 25: *Plus currit in certamine/Confessor iste sustinens,/Quam martyr ictum sufferens/Mucrone fundens sanguinem.* No doubt, as Daniel suggested, this rather bombastic verse was omitted as out of place and a reflection on the martyrs.

25. *Proinde*; cf. *hinc, 87, 13.*

M

The Common of Virgins
Hymn 90

Jesu corona virginum,
Quem mater illa concipit
Quae sola virgo parturit,
Haec vota clemens accipe,

5 Qui pergis inter lilia
Septus choreis virginum,
Sponsus decorus gloria
Sponsisque reddens praemia.

Quocumque tendis, virgines
10 Sequuntur atque laudibus
Post te canentes cursitant
Hymnosque dulces personant.

Te deprecamur supplices
Nostris ut addas sensibus
15 Nescire prorsus omnia
Corruptionis vulnera.

Jesus, the virgins' crown, born of that mother who alone gave birth to a child and yet remained a virgin, graciously receive these prayers. You walk among the lilies, surrounded by choirs of virgins—a bridegroom beautiful with glory and giving rewards to His brides. Wherever You go virgins follow, hastening after You with songs of praise and making heaven resound with melodious hymns. We ask and beg You to give us this grace in our life of thoughts—not to have knowledge of anything that may wound or corrupt our virtue.

Hymn 91

Virginis proles opifexque Matris,
Virgo quem gessit, peperitque virgo,
Virginis partos canimus decora
    Morte triumphos.

5 Haec enim palmae duplicis beata
Sorte, dum gestit fragilem domare
Corporis sexum, domuit cruentum
    Caede tyrannum.

Jesus, Son of the Virgin and Your mother's creator, carried in the Virgin's womb and born of the Virgin, we sing of the victory won by a virgin saint's glorious death. This saint was blessed with the grace of a twofold victory. While it was her consuming wish to master in her body its weakness in the face of sin, she mastered in that same body her savage, murderous persecutor. She feared neither death

Notes on Hymn 90

Author. Most probably St Ambrose. 'It is likely enough that he (Ambrose) should have composed such a hymn for the virgins of whom he wrote and thought so much. His characteristic ideas and phrases occur in it, including the *slightly altered* quotation of scripture, which was quite in his manner. . . . It is not (a hymn) in honour of one or more virgins . . . but a beautiful prayer to Christ the heavenly bridegroom,' W.

Use. At Vespers and Lauds of Virgins, whether Martyrs or not.

1. *Jesu*. The first two verses are a double address with *accipe* in line 4 as the main verb. Lines 1–3 are addressed to our Lord as the Virgin's son and lines 5–8 as the heavenly bridegroom, the title *corona virginum* influencing both. The less likely interpretation is to connect verses 2 and 3. *Corona;* cf. *82*, 2.

2. *illa*, pointing to *quae* of line 3—that Mother, or, the Mother herself, who alone . . . The emphatic use of *ille* is common in classical writers.

5. The original has *pascis* here and *pergis* for *tendis* in line 9. *Pascis* is better here, because of *pascitur inter lilia*, Cant. 2, 16; and cf. Cant. 4, 5 and 6, 1. The lily, symbol of purity, is here used of the virgins themselves. *Qui Christi passionem loquuntur et suo ore concelebrant ac mortificationem ejus in suo circumferunt corpore, Christi lilia sunt; specialiter sacrae virgines.* Ambr. *de Inst. Vir.* 93.

6. *septus* (= *saeptus*), surrounded, accompanied by. *Choreis*, dancing choirs or groups.

7. *sponsus decorus;* cf. *quasi sponsum decoratum corona*, Is. 61, 10.

8. *sponsis*, the brides of Christ. *Christus virginis sponsus* and *Mulieris caput vir, virginis Christus*, Ambr. *de Virg.* 1, 22 and 2, 29.

10. *sequuntur.Virgines enim sunt; hi sequuntur Agnum, quocunque ierit*, Apoc. 14, 4. *Laudibus* with *canentes* of line 11.

11. *Cursitant* with *post te;* cf. *post te curremus in odorem unguentorum tuorum*, Cant. 1, 3.

12. *personant;* and make sweet hymns resound. For accusative with *personare*, cf. *19*, 6.

13. *deprecamur*. *Deprecari* is used here rather with the idea that a blessing which is in danger of being lost may be granted, W. These two lines, unrevised, are: *Te deprecamur, largius/Nostris adauge mentibus.*

14. *Addas*, i.e. grant, give, to our thoughts, *sensibus*. But the original *adauge mentibus*, i.e. increase (something already there, which *addas* does not necessarily suggest) in our souls, *mentibus*, is clearly the more fitting thing.

15. *nescire* is the direct object of *addas* (or *adauge*), to be ignorant of, know nothing of, have nothing to do with. Cf. *fraudis venena nescire, 12, 20*, and *sequi* after *annue* in *88*, 14.

Lines 13–16 are the *haec vota* of line 4 and derive from lines 8 and 12.

Notes on Hymn 91

Author. Unknown, perhaps of the eighth century.
Metre. First Sapphic.

Use. At Matins on feasts of Virgins. If the saint is also a Martyr, the whole hymn is used; if not a Martyr, verses 2 and 3 are omitted. Verses 4 and 5 are used at Matins of the Common of Holy Women.

1. *Virginis* and *Virgo* of line 2 refer to our Lady; *virginis* in line 3 to the saint of the day. The hymn is inspired by *90* with the theme of martyrdom added.

3–4. *partos . . . triumphos*, victories won, produced,

by. The original text of line 3 is *Virginis festum canimus tropaeum*, where *tropaeum* gives the clue to the following verses about martyrdom.

If the saint is not a martyr, the lines become *Virginis festum canimus beatae,/Accipe votum.*

5. The double victory is explained by *corporis sexum* and *cruentum tyrannum*. The two graces explain the plural *palmas* in the collect quoted on *87*, 14 and the wording of another collect, *etiam in sexu fragili victoriam martyrii contulisti.*

Unde nec mortem, nec amica mortis
10 *Mille poenarum genera expavescens,*
Sanguine effuso meruit serenum
    Scandere caelum.

nor the countless forms of torture which accompany it, and the sacrifice of her life earned for her entry into the peace of heaven.

 *Hujus oratu Deus alme nobis
Debitas poenas scelerum remitte,
15 *Ut tibi puro resonemus almum*
    Pectore carmen.

*By her intercession, forgive us, loving God, the punishment that our sins deserve, and so with hearts made pure we may sing to You the song of our love. Glory to the Father and to the Son and to the Spirit, the co-equal power of Father and Son—one God, for ever and ever.

Sit decus Patri genitaeque Proli,
Et tibi compar utriusque virtus
Spiritus semper, Deus unus omni
20   *Temporis aevo.*

Common of Holy Women
Hymn 92

Fortem virili pectore
Laudemus omnes feminam,
Quae sanctitatis gloria
Ubique fulget inclita.

Let us all praise a valiant and heroic lady, famed and renowned the world over for her glorious holiness. Wounded by shafts of holy love, she shrank from the world's sinful love and made her way through all difficulties to heaven above. She subdued her body with fasting, but fed her soul on prayer's sweet food; thus she gained the joys of heaven.

5 *Haec sancto amore saucia,*
Dum mundi amorem noxium
Horrescit, ad caelestia
Iter peregit arduum.

Carnem domans jejuniis
10 *Dulcique mentem pabulo*
Orationis nutriens,
Caeli potitur gaudiis.

Rex Christe, virtus fortium,
Qui magna solus efficis,
15 *Hujus precatu, quaesumus,*
Audi benignus supplices.

Lord Christ, our king, strength of all that is strong and only cause of all greatness, to You through the saint's intercession we make our petition. Be gracious to Your suppliants and hear their prayer.

9. *amica mortis*, that accompany death.

11. *serenum* for the *sacratum* or *sacrata* of the older text, either of which points to the theme of martyrdom; cf. *83*, 10.

13. *oratu*; like *rogatu*, *89*, 6 and *precatu*, *88*, 15.

15. *puro* with *pectore*.

Notes on Hymn 92

Author. Cardinal Silvio Antoniano (1540–1603). Antoniano was one of a Commission, whose head was Baronius and of which St Robert Bellarmine was a member, that was responsible for the corrections and changes in the Breviary made by Clement VIII. The Common of Holy Women was added to the Breviary at this time.

Use. At Vespers and Lauds of Holy Women.

1. *Fortem*; cf. *Mulierem fortem quis inveniet*, Prov. 31, 10. This is the key to the whole hymn; cf. *arduum* in line 8, *domans* in line 9 and *fortium* in line 13. *Virili*, manly, heroic.

3. *gloria*; ablative, governing *sanctitatis*.

5. *sancto* for the original *Christi*. *Saucia*, wounded; cf. *78*, 3.

9. *jejuniis* contrasted with *pabulo*; and cf. *89*, 23–4.

The Dedication of a Church

Hymn 93

Caelestis urbs Jerusalem,
Beata pacis visio,
Quae celsa de viventibus
Saxis ad astra tolleris,
5 Sponsaeque ritu cingeris
Mille angelorum millibus.

O sorte nupta prospera,
Dotata Patris gloria,
Respersa Sponsi gratia,
10 Regina formosissima,
Christo jugata principi,
Caeli corusca civitas.

Hic margaritis emicant
Patentque cunctis ostia;
15 Virtute namque praevia
Mortalis illuc ducitur,
Amore Christi percitus
Tormenta quisquis sustinet.

Scalpri salubris ictibus
20 Et tunsione plurima,
Fabri polita malleo
Hanc saxa molem construunt
Aptisque juncta nexibus
Locantur in fastigio.

25 *Alto ex Olympi vertice
Summi parentis Filius,
Ceu monte desectus lapis
Terras in imas decidens,
Domus supernae et infimae
30 Utrumque junxit angulum.

Sed illa sedes caelitum
Semper resultat laudibus,
Deumque trinum et unicum
Jugi canore praedicat;
35 Illi canentes jungimur
Almae Sionis aemuli.

Jerusalem, heavenly city, blest vision of peace! Built from living stones, you are raised on high to the heavens and attended, like a bride, by countless thousands of angels. How happy the bride of such a favoured destiny! Your rich endowment is the Father's glory and your comeliness is from the Bridegroom's grace—queen most beautiful, bride of Christ the King, radiant city of heaven. In this city the gates of glittering pearls stand open for all to enter; for every man that follows the path of virtue must come to those gates—every man that endures sufferings here for love of Christ. Its stones are fashioned by many a stroke and blow of the Saviour-mason's hammer and chisel. Thus shaped they go to the making of this mighty structure, each being fitly joined to each and finding its appointed place in the whole building.

*From the summit of the highest heaven came the sovereign Father's Son, like the stone that was hewn from the mountain and fell to the plains beneath. He was the cornerstone where met the earthly house and the heavenly one. Now that heavenly one is always re-sounding with praises and ever in unceasing song honouring the Triune God. And when we sing our hymns of praise, we are one with heaven, our purpose the same as that of holy

Notes on Hymn 93

Author. Unknown, of date not earlier than the sixth nor later than the eighth century.

Scholars differ about the length of the hymn, some thinking that the last two verses, represented by lines 37–48 of the Breviary text, are additions. Thus Daniel thought that the original hymn had no connection with the dedication of a church but that it was adapted to that purpose by the addition of these two verses (I, p. 240). Trench, p. 318, on the other hand argues against that position. Other reasons, for or against, have to do with supposed differences of style, the presence or absence of these verses in the 'oldest MSS' and such-like considerations.

It seems more probable that these verses are part of the hymn. A lot depends on lines 31–36 which in their original form are:

> *Omnis illa Deo sacra et dilecta civitas*
> *Plena modulis in laude et canore jubilo*
> *Trinum Deum unicumque cum favore praedicat.*

Those who think the hymn ended here say that this is a doxology. But its only connection with a doxology is the mention of the Blessed Trinity and the mention of praise, while a doxology is a giving or expression of praise. Moreover *illa* in both texts clearly contrasts heaven with one particular building on earth (*Hoc in templo* = *Haec templa* of line 37, and *Hic* in both texts of line 43). Finally the verse *Omnis illa* (= *Sed illa*) joins the hymn together. It gives the purpose of the process of building described in verses 4 and 5 and leads to the next verses. The structure on earth whose dedication is being celebrated was built to be the abode of God, a temple, and the place where men may petition Him, lines 37–48 and praise Him, lines 49–54.

Metre. Six-lined verses of iambic dimeter. The original was in three-lined verses of trochaic tetrameter.

The hymn was recast by the revisers 'very much to its disadvantage' (Julian) in 'smooth but comparatively weak iambic dimeters' (Walpole). Trench says: 'This is one of the few [hymns] which have not utterly perished in the process [of being recast]; while if we yet compare the first two rugged and somewhat uncouth stanzas, but withal so sweet, with the smooth iambics which in the Roman Breviary have taken their place, we shall feel how much of their beauty they have lost'.

Use. Verses 1–4 and 9 at Vespers and Matins of the Dedication of a Church, and verses 5–9 at Lauds.

1. *Caelestis:* cf. *Jerusalem caelestem*, Heb. 12, 22 and *Jerusalem novam descendentem de caelo a Deo*, Apoc. 21, 2.

2. *beata.* In the original it is the city which is blessed, not the interpretation of its name: *Urbs beata Jerusalem dicta pacis visio.* Breviaries which use the unrevised text have *Urbs Jerusalem beata*, which may explain the revisers' procedure.

pacis visio. Interpretatur Sion speculatio, et Jerusalem visio pacis, St Aug. *in Ps.* 50, 22. But poets were sometimes forced to neglect this distinction; thus, in line 36, *Sion* refers to heaven, not to the Church militant.

3. *viventibus (saxis). Et ipsi tamquam lapides vivi superaedificamini*, 1 Pet. 2, 5 (and its context, verses 4–8).

5. *ritu*, after the manner of, like; cf. *sicut sponsam ornatam viro suo*, Apoc. 21, 2.

6. *mille . . . millibus*, countless thousands; cf. *multorum millium Angelorum frequentiam*, Heb. 12, 22, and *111*, 5–6.

7. *nupta*, vocative; *prospera* with *sorte*.

8. *dotata*, and *respersa* in line 9, agree with *nupta* and explain *sorte prospera. Patris gloria*, i.e. the Son; cf. *12*, 1, note.

12. *corusca.* Cf. *platea civitatis aurum mundum, tamquam vitrum perlucidum*, Apoc. 21, 21, which inspired the original text: *Plateae et muri ejus ex auro purissimo.*

13. *Hic*, adverb. *Margaritis*, pearls; cf. *duodecim portae, duodecim margaritae sunt*, Apoc. 21, 21.

14. *patent;* cf. *et portae ejus non claudentur per diem;* Apoc. 21, 25.

15. *virtute praevia*, the lead of virtue; cf. *stellam praeviam, 44*, 6.

18. The *premitur* and *pressuris* of the original text point to *in mundo pressuram habebitis*, John 16, 33, and cf. Acts 14, 21. The following text illustrates the original and the revised versions of this verse and the next: *Jerusalem caelestis ut civitas aedificatur, quae tamen*

Haec templa, rex caelestium,
Imple benigno lumine;
Huc, o rogatus, adveni
40 *Plebisque vota suscipe,*
Et nostra corda jugiter
Perfunde caeli gratia.

Hic impetrent fidelium
Voces precesque supplicum
45 *Domus beatae munera*
Partisque donis gaudeant,
Donec soluti corpore
Sedes beatas impleant.

Decus Parenti debitum
50 *Sit usquequaque altissimo,*
Natoque Patris unico
Et inclito Paraclito,
Cui laus, potestas, gloria
Aeterna sit per saecula.

Sion. King of those that dwell in heaven, fill this temple with Your kindly light. Come down to it at our calling, there to receive Your people's prayers, and fill our hearts unceasingly with heavenly grace. Here may the prayers and entreaties of Your suppliants find their answer in graces from our home above and may they find joy and comfort in graces received until, being freed from the body, they take their place among the blessed. Let due glory be given to the Father most high, to His only Son and to the renowned Paraclete. To God be praise, power and glory through everlasting ages.

Common of Feasts of the Blessed Virgin Mary
Hymn 94

Ave maris stella,
Dei mater alma,
Atque semper virgo,
Felix caeli porta.

5 *Sumens illud Ave*
Gabrielis ore,
Funda nos in pace,
Mutans Evae nomen.

Solve vincla reis,
10 *Profer lumen caecis,*
Mala nostra pelle,
Bona cuncta posce.

Monstra te esse matrem,
Sumat per te preces
15 *Qui pro nobis natus*
Tulit esse tuus.

Hail star of the sea, God's loving mother and ever a virgin, heaven's fair gate. You who received that '*Ave*' from Gabriel's lips, establish us in peace, reversing the name '*Eva*'. Break the sinners' fetters, bring light to the blind, drive away our ills and ask for us every blessing. Show yourself a mother. May He who, born for us, deigned to be your Son, receive our prayers

in hac peregrinationis terra, dum flagellis percutitur, tribulationibus tunditur, ejus lapides cotidie quadrantur. Et ipsa est civitas, scilicet sancta ecclesia, quae regnatura in caelo adhuc laborat in terra, Greg. *in Ezech.* 2, 2, 5.

19–24. *Saxa* is the subject of the verse; *polita* and *juncta* with *saxa, plurima* with *tunsione.*

19. *scalpri,* chisel; *salubris* with *scalpri.* The idea underlying *salubris* in the hymns is always that of 'salvation'. Here it may be attached in thought to *ictibus* ('By many a salutary stroke', Irons) or to Christ as the Saviour-mason.

24. *fastigio. Fastigium,* gable, pediment, summit; here, by synecdoche, it may mean the whole building, B, or on high, i.e. in heaven, Irons.

27. *ceu,* like; cf. *78,* 14. Lines 27–8 refer to Daniel 2, 34–45, but the original text is based on 1 Pet. 2, 4 where our Lord is a living stone (on whom we, as living stones, are to be built) and on Eph. 2, 20–1.

30. *utrumque.* Christ is the cornerstone that makes the heavenly and earthly kingdoms one; cf. 1 Pet. 2, 6.

35. *illi* refers to the *illa* of line 31.

36. *aemuli,* rivals, having the same thought or purpose.

Rightly or wrongly, the revisers did not treat this verse as a doxology and wove it even more firmly into the hymn. *Sed* is a most unlikely beginning for a doxology, and *jungimur* echoes *junxit* of line 30.

43. *impetrent,* ask for and obtain.

45. *domus beatae munera,* i.e. gifts *from* heaven; the gift *of* heaven is in line 48.

46. *partis,* granted, received.

47. *soluti,* sc. *fideles* from *fidelium* of line 43.

Notes on Hymn 94

Author. Unknown. It has been ascribed to Fortunatus, to St Bernard and to others—in no case with sufficient justification. It is found in a St Gall MSS, which is probably as early as the ninth century.

It is one of the few unrevised hymns of the Roman Breviary.

Metre. Trochaic dimeter brachycatalectic (accentual).

Use. At Vespers of feasts of our Lady. Its first use, apparently, was for the feast of the Annunciation, but it was soon used universally for all feasts of the Blessed Virgin.

1. *maris stella,* the supposed meaning of the name of Mary. In this verse the poet addresses Mary by four titles, the first for her name, the second for her office, the third for her privilege and the fourth for her place between God and men. The first, through the word *Ave,* is developed in lines 5–12; the second in 13–16; the third in 17–20 and the fourth in 21–24.

4. *caeli porta.* Mary is the gate of heaven primarily because, through her, *God* came on earth; but she is also the gate of heaven in relation to men since she is our mother as well; cf. John 19, 26 and lines 13–16 of this hymn. Cf. also *30,* 1, note.

15. *Pro nobis natus;* cf. *71,* 4.

16. *Tulit = dignatus est; tuus,* sc. *Filius.*

Virgo singularis,
Inter omnes mitis,
Nos culpis solutos
20 *Mites fac et castos.*

Vitam praesta puram,
Iter para tutum,
Ut videntes Jesum
Semper collaetemur.

25 *Sit laus Deo Patri,*
Summo Christo decus,
Spiritui sancto,
Tribus honor unus.

through you. Virgin without equal, gentle beyond all others, win us pardon for our sins and make us gentle and pure. Make it your care that our life is without sin, arrange a safe journey for us so that we may see Jesus and rejoice together for ever. To God the Father be praise, to Christ most high and to the Holy Spirit be glory; to the Three be equal honour.

Hymn 95

(The text below is the unrevised text. Words which are changed and lines which are omitted in the Breviary are bracketed and explained in the notes.)

Quem terra, pontus, (aethera)
Colunt, adorant, praedicant,
Trinam regentem machinam
Claustrum Mariae bajulat.

5 *Cui luna, sol et omnia*
Deserviunt per tempora,
Perfusa caeli gratia
Gestant puellae viscera.

(Mirentur ergo saecula,
10 *Quod angelus fert semina,*
Quod aure virgo concipit
Et corde credens parturit).

Beata mater munere,
Cujus supernus artifex,
15 *Mundum pugillo continens,*
Ventris sub arca clausus est.

(Benedicta) caeli nuntio,
Fecunda sancto Spiritu,
Desideratus gentibus
20 *Cujus per alvum fusus est.*

Mary carried in her womb the ruler of the world's threefold fabric—Him that earth, sea and sky reverence, adore and praise. The Maiden's womb was filled with grace from heaven and received as its burden Him whose will the moon, the sun and all creation obey, each at its appointed time. Therefore let the ages marvel at God's action on her through His angel, at Mary's being with child by accepting the angel's words and at her faith whose reward was the infant Child. How favoured this mother was in her office; for in her womb, as if in the ark, was enclosed the creator from heaven, Who holds the world in the hollow of His hand. The angel declared her blessed, the holy Spirit made her womb fruitful, and from it came forth the Desired of the peoples.

Continued

17. *singularis,* unique; cf. Luke 1, 42.   18. *inter=supra,* beyond.

Notes on Hymn 95

Author. Unknown. It was commonly attributed to Fortunatus, but Leo classified it as falsely attributed to Fortunatus. If it is not by this poet, it is by a very good imitator. From the same unknown source comes another hymn in honour of our Lady, namely the *Agnoscat omne saeculum;* cf. W *38* and *39;* and Raby, pp. 91–2.

Use. Lines 1–8 and 13–20 are used at Matins and lines 21–32 at Lauds of feasts of our Lady. Its first use is said to have been for the feast of the Assumption.

1. *aethera,* n. pl.—a late usage. The Breviary has *sidera. Terra* etc.; cf. *Qui fecit caelum et terram, mare et omnia quae in eis sunt,* Ps. 145, 6; cf. also Exod. 20, 11 and *53,* 21.

This verse and the next begin with the relative clause, the main subject being delayed until the end of the verse. Fortunatus is given to this, even to omitting the antecedent, as happens here in the second verse and at line 25.

The use of groups of three marks the beginning of this hymn—three nouns in lines 1 and 5, three verbs in line 2 and the group of the three first verses. It may be taken as an allusion to the Trinity.

3. *trinam* refers to *terra* etc. of line 1. A reference to the threefold reign of Christ, cf. Phil. 2, 10, would

be out of place here, but is needed in *63,* 9–12. *Machina;* cf. *8,* 2, note.

4. *claustrum,* bolt, bar; figuratively, womb, enclosure. 'Perhaps nowhere else is the word used so absolutely in this sense', W. *Bajulat;* cf. *38,* 11.

6. *deserviunt;* cf. Ps. 118, 91. *Per* is used distributively; *tempora,* seasons, cf. *11,* 3 and *21,* 3.

8. *viscera. Claustrum, viscera, ventris* and *alvum* are used in turn for womb, in each case reserved for the last line of its verse.

9–12. This verse is clearly the third of a group. It is now omitted from all Breviaries, but Daniel quotes Clichtoveus as saying that it was in use in the sixteenth century at a church in Paris for the feast and octave of the Assumption and that it was worthy of being used universally.

13. *munere,* in her office, W; by a (singular) gift, B.

14. *cujus* refers back to *mater* and forward to *ventris. Arca;* cf. *102,* 8, note.

17. *Benedicta* (Breviary, *Beata*), from *Benedicta tu in mulieribus,* Lk. 1, 28.

19. *desideratus. Et veniet desideratus cunctis gentibus,* Agg. 2, 8. *Fusus* from *fundere,* which implies an easy labour; cf. Servius on Verg. *Aen.* VIII, 139.

*O gloriosa (femina),
(Excelsa super) sidera,
Qui te creavit (provide),
(Lactas sacrato) ubere.

25 Quod Eva tristis abstulit,
Tu reddis almo germine;
Intrent ut astra flebiles,
Caeli (fenestra facta es).

Tu regis alti janua
30 Et (porta) lucis fulgida;
Vitam datam per virginem
Gentes redemptae plaudite.

*Lady most illustrious, now in glory far above the stars, you nourished at your virginal breast the One Who created you for that very purpose. You gave back to us through your loving Child what Eve through God's curse had lost for us, and became the opening through which Eve's sorrowing children could find their way into heaven. You are the royal door for the heavenly king and the shining gateway for the light from above. Rejoice, ransomed world, that through the Virgin life has been given to us.

Hymn 96

Memento, rerum conditor,
Nostri quod olim corporis,
Sacrata ab alvo virginis
Nascendo, formam sumpseris.

5 Maria mater gratiae,
Dulcis parens clementiae,
Tu nos ab hoste protege
Et mortis hora suscipe.

Remember, creator of the world, that long ago at Your birth You took our body's form from the Virgin's holy womb. Mary, mother of grace and tender mother of mercy, protect us from our enemies and receive us at the hour of our death.

21. *femina* (Breviary, *virginum*) is the commonest reading of the MSS, though *domina* of breviaries using the old text is found in some MSS. *Femina* refers to Lk. 1, 28, and *domina* to a second meaning given to the name Mary; cf. *94*, 1, note.

22. *excelsa,* vocative; The Breviary has *sublimis* and *inter* for *super.*

23. *provide,* providentially, with a given plan in mind. Breviary: *Qui te creavit, parvulum/Lactente nutris ubere.*

24. The readings of the MSS vary between the text and *Lactasti sacro ubere.* In either case there is a hiatus, which the revisers eliminated. Examples of hiatus, however, are not unknown in Fortunatus. For the line, cf. Lk. 11, 27.

25. *tristis* is contrasted with *benedicta* and *beata.*

27. *flebiles,* mournful, sorrowful—balancing *tristis* of line 25.

28. *fenestra,* window, gate, way. 'St Fulgentius, d. 523, was the first to style Mary a "window of heaven" . . . but, basically, the word has the sense of *porta*', Byrnes, p. 269.
Breviary: *Caeli recludis cardines,* you open the gates of heaven.

29. *janua* and *porta* of next line; cf. Ezech. 44, 2.

30. *porta.* Breviary has *aula,* i.e. the hall, palace of Mary's womb.

31. *datam, sc. esse.*

32. *plaudite* is used figuratively to mean rejoice, give thanks.

Notes on Hymn 96

The Little Office of our Lady uses *94–5* at the same hours as the ordinary office, and uses this hymn at the Little Hours and at Compline.

The first four lines are 9–12 of *37*. The second verse has been said to be the last verse of *95*—an opinion for which there seems to be no justification. This verse was *added* to the two divisions of *95* and thus became, in fact, the last or last but one verse of those hymns. It is still used by the Dominicans as the verse before the doxology. For a similar thing in the Roman Breviary, cf. *57, 25–28,* note.

IV

HYMNS OF THE PROPER OF SAINTS

As most of what was said about the hymns of the Common of Saints also applies to the hymns of this section, little need be added in this introduction. While some of the hymns of the Proper of Saints are famous and while many of them are quite easy, there are some which are neither famous nor easy. Some of the difficulties are due to the vocabulary, and others arise from involved and complex constructions. Sometimes verses are puzzling and seem harder than they are because one must know or be able to work out the biographical incident to which they refer. For this reason references are often given to the life of the saint in the second nocturn; indeed, in some cases, as for instance in that of St Venantius in May, the composition of the hymns and the lessons seem to be dependent on one another.

The fundamental ideas of creation, redemption and judgment appear in these hymns as they do in the others, and scarcely a hymn which does not mention light. The theme of the judgment finds its climax in the *Dies irae* with which, appropriately enough, this collection of hymns for the Christian year ends.

Practically one third of the hymns in this part are in Mary's honour—for her Immaculate Conception, her Sorrows, her Assumption and as Queen of the Rosary —and practically all of them have been written within the last two or three cen-

---

8 Dec. *The Immaculate Conception*
Hymn 97

Praeclara custos virginum,
Intacta mater numinis,
Caelestis aulae janua,
Spes nostra, caeli gaudium,

5 *Inter rubeta lilium,*
Columba formosissima,
Virga e radice germinans
Nostro medelam vulneri,

Glory and protector of virgins, sinless mother of God, entrance to the court of heaven, hope of earth and joy of heaven! Lily among thorns, dove most beautiful, rod from Jesse's root whose flower was healing for man's

166

turies. In addition the two hymns for the Servite Founders, *104* and *105*, and that for the Servite St Juliana, *116*, touch on the Sorrows of our Lady, and a hymn for St Mary Magdalen, *127*, and the two for All Saints, *152* and *153*, each devote a verse to the Mother of God. These hymns then occupy quite an amount of the hymnal and form an important part of Marian liturgical literature. Like other hymns they portray truths of the faith and reflect the feelings of the Christian soul. But as they are modern compositions they do these things in a different way from such hymns as the *Ave maris stella* and the *Quem terra, pontus, aethera*. It would be ungracious and in one or two cases unjust to condemn the modern approach without some qualification, and yet one is tempted to say that our Lady survives the modern hymns but lives in the old ones. Probably one of the reasons, among many, why there is such a difference between the old and the modern is that the old were written *ex corde* while the modern were written to order. (This also applies to many of the modern hymns for other Saints as well.) A poet like Fortunatus rejoiced in an occasion for poetry and lost himself in the occasion. But no Fortunatus has appeared among the more recent writers, and the occasion is nearly lost in the writer. Official poets too often cease to be poets when exercising their office.

Note: For the sake of those who have no Breviary or are not familiar with the structure of the Office, it may be worth pointing out that three hymns, for Vespers, Matins and Lauds, have to be provided for each feast. Only the special hymns for a feast are put in this section, and the number of hymns is made up by using, when necessary, the corresponding hymns from the Common of Saints. Thus 8 December uses *94* for Vespers, *97* for Matins and *95*, 21–32 for Lauds.

Notes on Hymn 97

Author. Unknown, seventeenth century, though Julian, p. 1612, suggested Benedict XIV (1675–1758). The office of the Purity of the Blessed Virgin, in which this hymn first appeared, was approved by Benedict in 1751 for use in Portugal and was printed in full in his *Opera Omnia;* but that does not prove that he wrote the hymn.

Use. At Matins of the Immaculate Conception.

1. Lines 1–10 are an address to our Lady under various titles, and lines 11–16 are a series of petitions.

2. *intacta*, sinless; applied to our Lady the word may mean virginal or sinless.

5. *rubeta*, thorns; cf. *sicut lilium inter spinas*, Cant. 2, 2. *Rubeta*, literally, means bramble bushes, whose unripe fruit is red (*ruber*).

6. cf. *columba mea, formosa mea*, Cant. 2, 10; and *columba mea, immaculata mea*, Cant. 5, 2.

7. *Virga. Egredietur virga de radice Jesse, et flos de adice ejus ascendet*, Is. 11, 1. According to the Hebrew text *virga* refers to the power and *flos* to the beauty of the Messias, but Christian application of the text, as in these lines, applies *virga* to our Lady and *flos* to our Lord.

Turris draconi impervia,
10 *Amica stella naufragis,*
    Tuere nos a fraudibus
    Tuaque luce dirige.

    Erroris umbras discute,
    Syrtes dolosas amove,
15 *Fluctus tot inter, deviis*
    Tutam reclude semitam.

wounds! Tower that is proof against the devil's assaults and star that is welcomed by the ship-wrecked, protect us from our treacherous foe and guide us by your light. Dispel the mists that make man lose the way, keep us away from treacherous shoals and show a way to safety to those who are off their course.

---

18 Jan. *St Peter's Chair at Rome*

As all the feasts of SS Peter and Paul, separately or together, have for their hymns sections of two long hymns, it is easier for their treatment and understanding to deal

---

Hymn 98

Decora lux aeternitatis auream
Diem beatis irrigavit ignibus,
Apostolorum quae coronat principes
Reisque in astra liberam pandit viam.

5 *Mundi magister atque caeli janitor,*
    Romae parentes arbitrique gentium,
    Per ensis ille, hic per crucis victor necem
    Vitae senatum laureati possident.

    *Beate pastor, Petre, clemens accipe
10 *Voces precantum, criminumque vincula*
    Verbo resolve, cui potestas tradita
    Aperire terris caelum, apertum claudere.

    *Egregie doctor, Paule, mores instrue
    Et nostra tecum pectora in caelum trahe,
15 *Velata dum meridiem cernat fides*
    Et solis instar sola regnet caritas.

A beauteous light streams down from the eternal God to grace with happiness the golden day that brought reward to the Princes of the Apostles and gave sinners a clear road to heaven. Earth's teacher and heaven's door-keeper, founders of Rome and judges of the world, they take their place, laurel-crowned, in heaven's assembly—the one triumphant through being beheaded, the other through being crucified.

*Peter, blessed shepherd, mercifully receive your suppliants' prayers and with a word undo the chains of sin, for to you was entrusted the power of opening heaven to men and of shutting the open gate of heaven.

*Paul, teacher without equal, fashion our lives aright and carry off our hearts with yours to heaven till faith, whose vision now is veiled, beholds the noonday glory, and love, sun-like, is sole master of our hearts.

Continued

9. *turris,* i.e. the tower of David of Cant. 4, 4. Mary's fulness of grace causes her to be likened to the high, strong and beautifully decorated tower of David and makes her proof against all attacks of the devil.

10. *stella;* cf. *94,* 1. *Amica naufragis,* welcome, dear, to the shipwrecked; cf. *amica* in *91, 9.*

11. *fraudibus, sc. draconis.* The petitions derive mostly from the ideas of *turris* and *stella.*

13. *erroris,* wandering, losing the way; *discute,* disperse, dispel; cf. *13,* 13.

14. *Syrtes,* sandbanks, shoals; here, metaphorically, of anything which could treacherously (*dolosas*) bring us to spiritual shipwreck.

---

with them in one place. These two hymns are *Aurea luce et decore roseo* and *Felix per omnes festum mundi cardines,* from which come respectively the *Decora lux* and the *Miris modis* of the Roman Breviary.

Notes on Hymn 98

Author. ?Elpis. This Elpis is often said to be the wife of Boethius, but that lady's name was Rusticiana (daughter of the senator Symmachus); cf. W *126.* The hymn has also been attributed to a Sicilian poetess, also called Elpis, 'as remarkable for her piety as for her wit' (*Manual of Patrology,* Cayré; Eng. Trans. I, p. 213). But this attribution is extremely doubtful as is also the statement that it was *she* who was Boethius's wife. Still 'an Elpis may quite well have written the hymn; for why should it be attributed to a name otherwise unknown, and to a woman?', W.

Metre. Iambic trimeter.

Use. 18 Jan., 22 Feb. and 1 Aug., Lauds: verses 3 and 6.

25 Jan., Vespers and Matins, and 30 June, Matins: verses 4 and 6;

29 June, Vespers: verses 1, 2, 5 and 6; and

29 June, Lauds: verses 3, 4 and 6.

The hymn was much altered by the revisers and became more difficult and less beautiful in the process. This fact and the further fact that the hymn is never used in its entirety in any one office combine to make the Breviary sections a stumbling-block to many.

The original hymn consists of six verses: the first

N

is about the feast day of the two Saints, the second about the Saints themselves, the third and fourth about St Peter and St Paul respectively, the fifth is a prayer to the two Saints and the sixth a doxology. All this is represented in the Breviary, except that the fifth verse has been replaced by one from *Felix per omnes mundi cardines,* which is as follows:

> *O Roma felix, quae tantorum principum*
> *Es purpurata pretioso sanguine;*
> *Excellis omnem mundi pulchritudinem,*
> *Non laude tua sed sanctorum meritis,*
> *Quos cruentatis jugulasti gladiis.*

The fifth line of this was omitted to give it a place in a hymn of four-lined verses, and the order of the third and fourth lines was inverted. This shortened form, first added, so it is said, by Pius V, was in turn changed by the revisers.

1. *Decora lux.* The original *Aurea luce et decore roseo,/Lux lucis, omne perfudisti saeculum* refers to Christ, the Dawn, which leads to a reference to the dawning of the Apostles' day. Apart from the dawn-metaphor, *aurea* well suits this hymn since to Prudentius, Ausonius and others it was a special epithet of Rome.

2. *beatis,* used actively; making happy, bringing joy.

O Roma felix, quae duorum principum
Es consecrata glorioso sanguine.
Horum cruore purpurata ceteras
20 Excellis orbis una pulchritudines.

Sit Trinitati sempiterna gloria,
Honor, potestas atque jubilatio,
In unitate, quae gubernat omnia,
Per universa saeculorum saecula.

How happy, Rome, your fortune in being dedicated to God in the Princes' noble blood; for clad in a robe dyed purple with their blood, you far outstrip in beauty all else the world can show.

To God, in essence one, in persons three, the ruler of the universe, be eternal glory, power and acclamation through all the ages of ages.

Hymn 99

Miris modis repente liber, ferrea,
Christo jubente, vincla Petrus exuit.
Ovilis ille pastor et rector gregis
Vitae recludit pascua et fontes sacros,
5 Ovesque servat creditas, arcet lupos.

*Quodcunque in orbe nexibus revinxeris,
Erit revinctum, Petre, in arce siderum;
Et quod resolvit hic potestas tradita,
Erit solutum caeli in alto vertice:
10 In fine mundi judicabis saeculum.

Patri perenne sit per aevum gloria;
Tibique laudes concinamus inclitas,
Aeterne Nate; sit, superne Spiritus,
Honor tibi decusque: sancta jugiter
15 Laudetur omne Trinitas per saeculum.

Set free in a wonderful and unexpected way, Peter at Christ's command puts off his chains. Now he, the shepherd of the fold and ruler of the flock, brings us to the pastures of life and to the springs of holiness. He guards the sheep entrusted to him and keeps the wolves away.

*Anything that you fasten on earth with chains, will be bound, Peter, in the starry heights; anything that you loosen on earth with the power given to you, will be loosed on heaven's topmost peak. At the end of time you will judge the world.

To the Father be glory through never-ending ages. To you, eternal Son, be our song of triumphant praise. To you, heavenly Spirit, be honour and renown. May the holy Trinity be unceasingly praised through every age.

5. *mundi magister;* cf. *doctor gentium,* 1 Tim. 2, 7, and *magister gentium,* 2 Tim. 1, 11. *Caeli janitor;* cf. Mt. 16, 19.

6. *arbitrique gentium* in place of the original *judices saeculi;* cf. *81, 5,* note.

8. *vitae senatum,* i.e. heaven's assembly; cf. *patrum senatum, 59, 7.*

9. *Beate* (for the original *Jam, bone*) at least gives St Peter the epithet which tradition, following our Lord's example, reserved for him; Mt. 16, 17. *Pastor;* cf. John 21, 15 and 1 Pet. 5, 1–4.

10. *precantum* (the form *precantium* is used in *110, 26*) instead of a relative clause. The verse is based on

Mt. 16, 19, though *vincula* probably refers also to Acts. 12, 1–11.

13. *instrue,* instruct, fashion. The word is inspired by its use in *quae te possunt instruere ad salutem,* 2 Tim. 3, 15.

14. *trahe.* Probably an allusion to St Paul's ecstasies, 2 Cor. 12, 2, and to his command *quae sursum sunt quaerite,* Col. 3, 1.

20. *una.* Rome is famous by the single fact of the Apostles' martyrdom; cf. lessons 5 and 6 of 4 July. For *una* cf. the use of *sola* in *45, 1.*

23. *quae* refers to *Trinitati in unitate.*

Notes on Hymn 99

Author. ?Paulinus of Aquileia, *circa* 730 to 802. It has also been ascribed to Elpis, cf. preceding hymn. The style of the original seems to suggest the later date though 'there is no direct evidence that these verses are the work of Paulinus', Raby, p. 169, note 3.

Metre. Iambic trimeter.

Use. 18 Jan., and 22 Feb., Vespers and Matins, and 1 Aug., Matins: verses 2 and 3;

1 Aug., Vespers: verses 1 and 3.

The hymn has the same kind of difficulties as the preceding hymn and, though of nine verses in the

original instead of six, has the same general plan. The Breviary only uses the two verses about St Peter and the doxology (verses 4, 5 and 9 of the original), and the verse about Rome provides the fifth verse of *98.*

2. *vincla;* cf. Acts 12, 1–11, which explains the use of this verse on 1 Aug.

3. *ovilis;* this is more likely to be, as it is in the original, from the noun *ovile* than from the adj. *ovilis.*

8. *hic,* adverb and = *super terram* of Mt. 16, 19.

12. *Tibi* refers to *Aeterne Nate* of the next line; *tibi* in line 14 refers back to *superne Spiritus.*

25 Jan. *The Conversion of St Paul*
Egregie doctor, Paule, mores instrue. Cf. *98, 13–16 and 21–24*
30 Jan. *St Martina, Virgin and Martyr*

Hymn 100

Martinae celebri plaudite nomini
Cives Romulei, plaudite gloriae;
Insignem meritis dicite virginem,
    Christi dicite martyrem.

5 *Haec dum conspicuis orta parentibus*
Inter delicias, inter amabiles
Luxus illecebras, ditibus affluit
    Faustae muneribus domus,

Vitae despiciens commoda, dedicat
10 *Se rerum Domino, et munifica manu*
Christi pauperibus distribuens opes
    Quaerit praemia caelitum.

*Non illam crucians ungula, non ferae,
Non virgae horribili vulnere commovent;
15 *Hinc lapsi e superum sedibus angeli*
    Caelesti dape recreant.

Quin et deposita saevitie leo
Se rictu placido projicit ad pedes;
Te, Martina, tamen dans gladius neci
20   *Caeli coetibus inserit.*

Te thuris redolens ara vaporibus,
Quae fumat, precibus jugiter invocat,
Et falsum perimens auspicium, tui
    Delet nominis omine.

25 **Tu natale solum protege, tu bonae*
Da pacis requiem Christiadum plagis;
Armorum strepitus et fera proelia
    In fines age Thracios.

Et regum socians agmina sub crucis
30 *Vexillo, Solymas nexibus exime*

Give praise, men of Rome, to Martina's renowned name and fame. Sing of a virgin, noted for her virtue; sing of a martyr who died for Christ. As she was the daughter of distinguished parents and surrounded by pleasures and by luxury's attractive charms, she had in abundance the riches of a prosperous family. Yet she renounced the world's comforts, consecrated herself to the world's creator, and with generous heart distributed her wealth to Christ's poor, seeking no reward save in heaven.

*Neither the torturer's hook nor wild beasts nor the scourges' terrible wounds made any impression on her will to endure; but angels came down from the home of the blessed and refreshed her with heavenly food. Nay more, even the lion, forgetful of its savage nature, in gentle friendliness lay quiet at her feet. However the sword, Martina, brought you to death and thus enrolled you among the saints of heaven. The altar, from which arise fragrant clouds of incense, calls on you unceasingly in prayer. It destroys and completely removes, by the happy omen of your name, the ill-omen of idolatry.

*Protect your native land and give all Christian nations the respite of true peace. Banish the tumult of arms and the savagery of wars into far-distant lands. Unite the forces of Christian princes under the standard of the Cross and free Jerusalem from its bondage. Avenge innocent blood and overthrow com-

Continued on p. 173

Notes on Hymn 100

Author. Urban VIII (1586–1644).

Metre. Second Asclepiad.

Use. Verses 1–6, inclusive, and the last verse at Matins; the last four verses at Lauds. In some places, however, it has to be divided into three sections, each ending with lines 37–40.

3–4. *virginem ... martyrem*—the double palm of *91, 5.*

13–14. *Ungula, ferae* and *virgae* are subjects of *commovent. Ungula;* cf. *84,* 11.

21–24. *Ara,* the subject, is personified and is qualified by the participles and the relative clause. *Auspicium* is divination by the flight of birds; here, with *falsum,* it stands for idolatry, false worship. *Omen* is divination *quod fit ore* (*omen* = *os-men*); hence, foreboding, sign, token. The name Martina, derived from Mars, the god of war, was a happy omen of the warfare waged by the saint on idolatry. There is an implied contrast between the Christian and pagan altar and use of incense, as well as a reference

to the pagan altars overthrown at Martina's intercession; cf. lesson 5.

25. *natale solum,* native land; cf. *24,* 2, note.

26. *Christiadum,* a Greek form latinised; cf. *106,* 2. *Plagis,* districts, i.e. nations; cf. *25,* 2, note.

28. *Thracios,* i.e. afar; to distant lands.

30. *Solymas;* cf. *Solymis, 106,* 11. The shortened forms of Jerusalem are *Solyma,* n. pl., or *Solyma, -ae* (sing. or plur.) and, as an adjective, *Solymus, -a, -um.*

32. *robur,* power, i.e. of the Turks; cf. *73,* 20. *Funditus,* completely.

33. *columen,* support, prop, i.e. strength or pillar of strength; cf. *107,* 2.

38. *dexter.* To stand on a person's right hand was to protect his unprotected side. Moreover the first martyr, St Stephen, saw 'Jesus standing on the right hand of God', Acts 7, 55.

39. *jubar,* light (cf. *11,* 8), explained by the next line.

40. *beas,* from *beo,* 1, make happy.

Continued from p. 172

Vindexque innocui sanguinis hosticum
   Robur funditus erue.

Tu nostrum columen, tu decus inclitum,
Nostrarum obsequium respice mentium;
35 *Romae vota libens excipe, quae pio*
   Te ritu canit et colit.

A nobis abigas lubrica gaudia,
Tu qui martyribus dexter ades, Deus,
Une et trine; tuis da famulis jubar
40   *Quo clemens animos beas.*

pletely the enemies' power. You are a pillar of strength to us, our glory and our fame; look with favour on the homage we pay you. Rome, as is her duty, honours you in song and ceremony; do you graciously receive her prayers. God, one and three, the martyrs' protector at their right side, drive from us all sinful pleasures. Give your servants that light that in your mercy is man's crowning happiness.

11 Feb. *The Apparition of the Immaculate Virgin at Lourdes*

Hymn 101

Te dicimus praeconio,
Intacta mater numinis;
Nostris benigna laudibus
Tuam repende gratiam.

5 *Sontes Adami posteri,*
Infecta proles gignimur;
Labis paternae nescia
Tu sola, Virgo, crederis.

Caput draconis invidi
10 *Tu conteris vestigio,*
Et sola gloriam refers
Intaminatae originis.

O gentis humanae decus,
Quae tollis Hevae opprobrium,
15 *Tu nos tuere supplices,*
Tu nos labantes erige.

Serpentis antiqui potens
Astus retunde et impetus,
Ut caelitum perennibus
20 *Per te fruamur gaudiis.*

We sing of you, sinless mother of God, in words of praise. In gracious acknowledgement of them, show us your favour in return. We, Adam's guilty race, are from birth a sin-infected people, while you alone—this is our faith—are free from Adam's sin. You crush under your heel the envious serpent's head, and none but you can point to the distinction of a sinless descent. You are the glory of mankind and take away Eve's reproach. Guard us who pray to you and give us courage when we falter. Since you are powerful, blunt the old serpent's crafty deceits and open attacks so that through you we may enjoy the eternal joys of the blessed.

Hymn 102

Aurora soli praevia,
Felix salutis nuntia,
In noctis umbra plebs tua
Te, Virgo, supplex invocat.

5 *Torrens nefastis fluctibus*
Cunctos trahens voragine,
Leni residit aequore
Cum transit arca foederis.

Dum torret arescens humus,
10 *Tu rore sola spargeris;*

To you, Virgin, does your people, surrounded by the darkness of night, address its humble prayer—you, the dawn that comes before the Sun and the auspicious herald of salvation. The torrent, whose evil waves sweep all mankind into the abyss, grows calm and its waters become smooth as the ark of the covenant passes over. While the rest of the earth is scorched and dried up, you alone are wet with

Notes on Hymn 101

Author. Unknown.

Use. At Matins.

2. *intacta,* sinless, immaculate; cf. 97, 2.

5. *Sontes,* from *sons, -tis,* guilty.

7. *nescia,* free from; cf. *nescire, 90,* 15. This line is predicative after *crederis,* which is passive as in 9, 17.

11. *refers;* apparently with the idea of boast of, point to.

16. *labantes,* those who totter, waver; cf. 11, 25.

17. *serpentis antiqui;* cf. Apoc. 12, 9.

18. *astus,* 4, craft, cunning; *retunde,* blunt, restrain, check.

Notes on Hymn 102

Author. Unknown.

Use. At Lauds.

1. *Aurora,* i.e. our Lady, though in the hymns our Lord is usually the *aurora.* The reference to dawn is apt at Lauds.

soli . . . nuntia. Mary, from the moment of her immaculate conception until the Annunciation, was the dawn which preceded the Sun, *soli praevia,* and the herald of our salvation.

3. *noctis umbra.* Unless this is figurative, it must refer to the fact that Lauds is sung before the full light of day has come.

5–8. The reference is to Josua 3, 14–17. *Voragine=in voraginem,* abyss, whirlpool; *leni . . . aequore,* i.e. grows calm. *Arca.* The ark was a symbol of the divine presence. Mary, as the living ark in which God was to dwell, was not engulfed in the sea of sin.

Tellure circum rorida,
Intacta sola permanes.

Fatale virus evomens
Attollit anguis verticem;
15 *At tu draconis turgidum*
Invicta conteris caput.

Mater benigna, respice
Fletus precesque supplicum,
Et dimicantes tartari
20 *Victrix tuere ab hostibus.*

dew. Though the earth all around is wet with dew, you alone remain untouched. The serpent lifts up its head and empties out its deadly poison; but you, unscathed, crush the dragon's head and humble its pride. Be graciously mindful, Mother, of your suppliants' tears and prayers. As you triumphed over sin, preserve us from our enemies as we battle with them.

Hymn 103

Omnis expertem maculae Mariam
Edocet summus fidei magister;
Virginis gaudens celebrat fidelis
    Terra triumphum.

5 *Ipsa se praebens humili puellae*
Virgo spectandam, recreat paventem
Seque conceptam sine labe, sancto
    Praedicat ore.

O specus felix, decorate divae
10 *Matris aspectu! veneranda rupes,*
Unde vitales scatuere pleno
    Gurgite lymphae.

Huc catervatim pia turba nostris,
Huc ab externis peregrina terris
15 *Affluit supplex et opem potentis*
    Virginis orat.

Excipit Mater lacrimas precantum,
Donat optatam miseris salutem;
Compos hinc voti patrias ad oras
20 *   Turba revertit.*

Supplicum, Virgo, miserata casus,
Semper o nostros refove labores,
Impetrans maestis bona sempiternae
    Gaudia vitae.

The supreme teacher of the faith proclaims Mary to be free from all sin, and the faithful of the world celebrate in joyous song the praises of the Virgin's triumph. The Virgin presented herself before the eyes of the lowly Bernadette, reassured the frightened girl and from her holy lips came the words that she was conceived without sin. How happy the cave that was honoured with the presence of God's mother! How worthy of man's veneration the rock from which living waters gushed forth in full flood. To this place come, as in duty bound, large crowds of suppliants from our own land, and to it come suppliant pilgrim crowds from abroad. Here, French and foreigner alike, implore the mighty Virgin's help. Their Mother catches the tears that her suppliants shed and makes a gift to the afflicted of the peace of mind they desire. Then, their wish granted, the pilgrims return to their homes. In your compassion, Virgin, for the misfortunes of those that pray to you, bring us at all times help and comfort in our labours, and through your intercession obtain for us the happy gift of everlasting life.

11. *Tellure . . . rorida,* abl. absol; though the earth all round, *circum,* is wet with dew. *Intacta;* cf. *97,* 2. For lines 9–12 cf. Judges 6, 36–40.

14. *verticem,* i.e. head; cf. *140,* 18.

19. *tartari.* Some take this with *ab hostibus,* but it seems more probable that it is to be taken with *victrix.*

Notes on Hymn 103

Author. Unknown, French (cf. line 13).

Metre. First Sapphic.

Use. At second Vespers, *94* being used at first Vespers.

1–4. The definition in 1854 of the Immaculate Conception. *Expertem,* free from, without.

5–8. The apparitions at Lourdes.

9–12. The cave at Lourdes. *Aspectu,* i.e. apparition; *vitales lymphae,* living waters; *scatuere, scateo,* 2, gush forth.

13–16. The pilgrimages to Lourdes. *Catervatim,* adverb from *caterva,* in troops, crowds. The French pilgrimages, *nostris,* are a special manifestation of *pietas* to our Lady, while other pilgrimages are foreign, from abroad, *peregrina.* In a general sense any pilgrimage is *peregrina* and ought to be *pia. Affluit,* hastened, flocked, to; contrast *affluit, 100, 7.*

17–20. The effects of the pilgrimages. *Salutem.* The usual meaning of *salus* in the hymns is health of body or health of soul, i.e. salvation, but neither of these meets the case here. As the word seems to apply to all pilgrims, a general phrase such as 'peace of mind', i.e. a healthy reconciliation to God's will, seems to be required.

21–24. A prayer to our Lady. *Casus;* cf. *12, 15,* note.

12 Feb. *The Seven Founders of the Servite Order*
Hymn 104

Bella dum late furerent, et urbes
Caede fraterna gemerent cruentae,
Adfuit Virgo, nova semper edens
    Munera matris.

5 En vocat septem famulos, fideles
Ut sibi in luctu recolant dolores,
Quos tulit Jesus, tulit ipsa consors
    Sub cruce Nati.

Illico parent Dominae vocanti;
10 Splendidis tectis opibusque spretis,
Urbe secedunt procul in Senari
    Abdita montis.

Corpora hic poenis cruciant acerbis,
Sontium labes hominum piantes;
15 Hic prece avertunt lacrimisque fusis
    Numinis iram.

Perdolens mater fovet atque amictum
Ipsa lugubrem monet induendum;
Agminis sancti pia coepta surgunt,
20   Mira patescunt.

Palmes in bruma viridans honores
Nuntiat patrum; proprios Mariae
Ore lactenti vocitant puelli
    Nomine Servos.

25 *Sic patres vitam peragunt in umbra,
Lilia ut septem nivei decoris,
Virgini excelsae bene grata, Petro
    Visa nitere.

Iamque divina rapiente flamma,
30 Cursitant urbes, loca quaeque oberrant,
Si queant cunctis animis dolores
    Figere matris.

Hinc valent iras domuisse caecas,
Nescia et pacis fera corda jungunt,

While wars were raging all over Italy and its cities mourned the blood that brothers shed in conflict with brothers, the Virgin appeared and showed, as she always does, fresh tokens of a mother's love. She summons seven who waited on her in prayer, bidding them be faithful to her command of recalling in sorrowful contemplation the sufferings that Jesus bore and that she in person shared at the foot of her Son's cross. Immediately they obey their Lady's summons. They turn their backs on their magnificent palaces and wealth and, leaving the city of Florence far behind, hide themselves in the caves of Monte Senario. Here they inflict cruel punishments on themselves, atoning for the sins of guilty men; here by their prayers and tears they turn aside from men God's anger. The sorrowful Mother encourages them and tells them to wear a habit of mourning. Thus the dutiful beginnings of the holy company prosper, and men come to hear of marvellous happenings. A vine puts forth green leaves in winter, thus telling the glory of these men. Unweaned children call them by name as Mary's own 'Servi'.

*The fathers so spend their time of retirement from the world that they seem to Peter of Verona in a vision to be like seven pure white lilies, well pleasing to the Virgin in heaven and dazzling in their beauty. And now, under the impulse of divine love, they hasten from city to city and make their way over all the countryside with the intention of implanting in all souls the sorrows of their Mother. By this means the preaching of the holy men avails to tame senseless anger; it unites savage hearts that are blind to peace, uplifts the

Notes on Hymn 104

Author. Eugenius M. Poletti (1869–1940), a Servite, though according to some this and *105* are by the same author, Tarozzi.

Metre. First Sapphic.

Use. Lines 1–24 at Matins, 25 to the end at Lauds.

1–2. Feuds and dissensions among Italian cities were common occurrences from the eleventh to the thirteenth century. *Cruentae* with *urbes* and qualified by *caede fraterna.*

9. *Dominae* because they were *Servi.*

11. *urbe,* i.e. Florence.

14. *sontium;* cf. *101, 5.*

18. *lugubrem* (with *amictum*), because the Servite habit is black.

19. *agminis sancti,* i.e. the Servite Order; *surgunt,* prosper.

20. *mira,* miracles, two of which are now related; *patescunt,* become manifest, public.

21. 'The miracle of the vine occurred in March while the mountain was still covered with hoar frost. The vine which had been planted in the pre-ceding year, grew miraculously in a single night, and was covered at once with foliage, flowers and fruit—a symbol of the speedy increase of their little company, as was revealed to the Bishop of Florence', B.

22. On two occasions children called them *Mariae servi,* one of the children afterwards becoming the famous Servite, St Philip Benizi.

27. *Petro,* i.e. St Peter of Verona, O.P.

28. *visa,* were seen by Peter in a vision. The vision was of a mountain, covered with flowers, among which were seven lilies of dazzling brightness.

30. *loca,* opposed to *urbes* and indicating less populated places.

33. *Hinc.* For this reason (namely because they preached the sorrows of Mary) the Saints' words, *dicta piorum,* availed to tame. . . . By punctuation *dicta* is the subject of all the verbs, though some restrict it to *revocant.*

34. *nescia* with *pacis;* cf. *101, 7.*

35 *Erigunt maestos, revocant nocentes*
   Dicta piorum.

At suos virgo comitata servos
Evehit tandem superas ad oras;
Gemmeis sertis decorat per aevum
40   *Omne beatos.*

Eia nunc coetus gemitum precantis
Audiant, duros videant labores,
Semper et nostris faveant benigno
   Lumine votis.

sorrowing and calls sinners back to repentance. When at length death comes to them, the Virgin accompanies her '*Servi*', brings them to heaven and adorns them, blessed now for ever, with jewelled garlands. May they hear our sighs as we are gathered together to pray, regard us as we make our laborious efforts and always favour our prayers with their kindly help.

Hymn 105

Matris sub almae numine
Septena proles nascitur;
Ipsa vocante, ad arduum
Tendit Senari verticem.

5 *Quos terra fructus proferet*
  Dum sacra proles germinat,
  Uvis repente turgidis
  Onusta vitis praemonet.

Virtute claros nobili
10 *Mors sancta caelo consecrat;*
   Tenent Olympi limina
   Servi fideles virginis.

Cohors beata, Numinis
Regno potita, respice
15 *Quos hinc recedens fraudibus*
   Cinctos relinquis hostium.

Ergo per almae vulnera
Matris rogamus supplices,
Mentis tenebras disjice,
20 *Cordis procellas comprime.*

Tu nos, beata Trinitas,
Perfunde sancto robore,
Possimus ut feliciter
Exempla patrum subsequi.

A company of seven souls comes into being under the protection of its loving Mother, and at her bidding makes the difficult ascent to the top of Monte Senario. A vine is in a moment heavy with swelling grapes—a sign of the fruits the earth will yield when the company of saints begins to put forth its buds. A holy death puts these men in God's presence, famed for their noble virtue; the Virgin's faithful servants attain the abode of heaven. O happy company, now that you have obtained the kingdom of God, look down on those whom, at your departure from this world, you left behind surrounded by their enemies' wily snares. We therefore make this earnest prayer through our loving Mother's wounds: dispel the darkness from our souls and hold in check our passions.

Implant in our whole being, blessed Trinity, a holy strength that we may be able to follow with happy success the example which these fathers have given.

38. *tandem,* i.e. at their death. The seven died on different days, but were honoured as a group and, in 1888, canonized as a group.

39. *sertis,* cf. *47, 2.*

Notes on Hymn 105

Author. Vincent Tarozzi (1848–1918), a Servite.
Use. At second Vespers.

1. *numine,* protection; but *Numinis* in line 13, God, and cf. *104, 16.*

5. Order: *Vitis repente onusta uvis turgidis praemonet fructus quos. . . .*

10. *caelo,* i.e. to God. *Consecrat;* cf. *106,* 13, note.

20. *procellas,* storms, passions.

24. *patrum,* i.e. the Seven Founders; likewise in *104,* 22 and 25.

22 Feb. *St Peter's Chair at Antioch*
Quodcunque in orbe nexibus revinxeris; cf. *99, 6–15*
Beate pastor, Petre, clemens accipe; cf. *98, 9–12 and 21–24*
19 March *St Joseph*
Hymn 106

Te Joseph celebrent agmina caelitum
Te cuncti resonent christiadum chori,
Qui clarus meritis junctus es inclitae
   Casto foedere Virgini.

5 *Almo cum tumidam germine conjugem*
Admirans, dubio tangeris anxius,
Afflatu superi Flaminis angelus
   Conceptum puerum docet.

Tu natum Dominum stringis, ad exteras
10 *Aegypti profugum tu sequeris plagas;*
Amissum Solymis quaeris et invenis,
   Miscens gaudia fletibus.

Post mortem reliquos sors pia consecrat
Palmamque emeritos gloria suscipit;
15 *Tu vivens, superis par, frueris Deo,*
   Mira sorte beatior.

Nobis, summa Trias, parce precantibus,
Da, Joseph meritis, sidera scandere,
Ut tandem liceat nos tibi perpetim
20   *Gratum promere canticum.*

Let the choirs of angels sing your praises, Joseph, and all the choirs of the Christian world make your name resound, to honour you for your unique merits and for your union in chaste wedlock with the glorious Virgin. When you were astonished at your wife being pregnant with her loving Child, and doubt and anxiety filled your soul, an angel told you that the Child was conceived by the breath of the heavenly Spirit. You took your Lord in your arms at His birth and waited on His direction on the journey into exile in far-off Egypt. You searched Jerusalem for Him, when He was missing, and on finding Him your tears of sorrow became tears of joy. A loving providence puts other men in God's presence when they are dead and glory is the welcome for those who win the palm of victory. But through a wonderful act of providence you were more fortunate, for in your life here below you enjoyed God's presence, the equal of those in heaven.

Mighty God, three in one, spare us, Your suppliants. Grant through Joseph's merits that we enter heaven where we may then unceasingly sing in Your honour our hymns of joy and gratitude.

Author. Probably the Spanish Carmelite Juan de la Concepcion of the seventeenth century.

It is most unlikely that any of hymns *106–108* were written before the seventeenth century. They are not among the known hymns of the fifteenth or sixteenth centuries, have no place in the breviaries of that time and are not in the Breviary of St Pius V

(1568). Gerson therefore must be ruled out as a possible author.

The Carmelite nun, Sister Clare Mary, was greatly responsible for Clement X raising the rank of St Joseph's feast on 19 March to that of a double of the second class and providing a revised office for that feast. This office of 1671 was the same as that of the →

Notes on Hymn 106

Breviary of 1568, except for three new antiphons and three new hymns, which were *106–108*. Behind the scenes Sister Clare seems to have persuaded the Carmelite friar Juan de la Concepcion, then in Rome, to compose an entirely new office. This office for the *Patronage* of St Joseph was sanctioned in 1680 for use by the Carmelites and, like the Roman office of 1671, contained these hymns. Later Clement XI composed the present office for 19 March—a masterpiece of composition, as Batiffol rightly says in his *History of the Roman Breviary*, p. 254, n. 4. The present office of the Solemnity is *substantially* the same as that of 1680.

A Carmelite life of Sister Clare, first published in 1681, and the Jesuit Patrignani's book on devotion to St Joseph (Florence, 1707) state that Juan composed the office of 1680. The interest of Sister Clare and the testimony of Patrignani are confirmed in a memorandum drawn up in 1714 by the future Benedict XIV and later inserted by him in his *De Servorum Dei Beatificatione*, Bk. IV, Part II, ch. xx, especially sections 17 and 20.

No authority asserts explicitly that Juan is the author of all or any of these hymns. But as Patrignani says that 'L'Uffizio *tutto proprio* del Santo' was Juan's work, the authorship of the hymns seems to be included in this statement. It is also clear that whatever the date of the composition of the *office* of 1680, the *hymns* had certainly been composed by 1671, for they are part of the office approved in that year. Further, as the decree of 1714 does not include hymns among the new elements of Clement XI's office, it must be presumed that Clement is not their author, though he has been claimed as such.

The history of devotion to St Joseph seems to point in the seventeenth century to a Spaniard and to a Carmelite as the composer of these hymns, and Juan is the only person at present known who fits both conditions. A further pointer to his authorship is a similarity of style between these hymns and some that he certainly wrote in honour of St Teresa. The influence of Urban VIII is perceptible in *106* which has many points of resemblance with *Martinae celebri, 100*.

Dom Wilmart dealt with the complicated subject of the offices of St Joseph and the authorship of these hymns, especially *106*, in the *Revue Grégorienne*, January 1926, pp. 1–12, where all the authorities are to be found. It is clear that if his conclusions are correct, they do away with all the various suggestions found, for example, in Julian and amplify B's 'Unknown, seventeenth century'.

Metre. Second Asclepiad.

Use. At Vespers of 19 March, and at Vespers and Matins of the Solemnity.

2. *christiadum;* cf. *100, 26*.

3. *clarus meritis.* St Matthew, 1, 19, calls him a 'just man'. The office of 19 March underlines his fidelity, cf. *108*, 19, note. Both his feasts and that of the Holy Family honour his privileged position in the plan of man's redemption.

10. *profugum* sc. *Dominum* after *sequeris.* The phrase is an adaptation of the Chapter for None on 19 March: *Profugum justum deduxit Sapientia* and implies the Divinity of the Child. *Plagas* with *exteras;* cf. *100, 26*.

11. *amissum* sc. *Dominum; Solymis,* cf. *100, 30,* note.

13. *Sors pia* is an officially approved emendation of *mors pia.* The juxtaposition of *Post mortem* and *mors pia* is a literary conceit with little meaning.

Some think the allusion in *mors* to St Joseph as the patron of a holy death ought to have been kept, Wilmart, for example, suggesting *Mortales reliquos mors pia consecrat.* Others criticise the change to *sors* because, so they think, *sors* and *sorte* in line 16 have somewhat different meanings. But it would seem that in the text as emended *sors* and *sorte* both refer to God's providence, like *sors reduxerit* in *18, 14*. Thus in place of the reference to St Joseph there has been put a contrast between God's dealings with the rest of mankind, *sors pia,* and His dealing with St Joseph, *mira sorte.*

consecrat. Consecrare means, among other things, to deify, place among the gods. Thus *consecrat* here means 'puts in God's presence' and balances *frueris,* 'enjoy God's presence'; and cf. *Mors sancta Deo consecrat, 105,* 10. 'Out of God's presence satisfied/Into God's presence passed away' says Mgr Knox's hymn in honour of the Saint (*Westminster Hymnal, 140*).

Hymn 107

Caelitum Joseph decus, atque nostrae
Certa spes vitae columenque mundi,
Quas tibi laeti canimus, benignus
    Suscipe laudes.

5 Te sator rerum statuit pudicae
Virginis sponsum voluitque Verbi
Te patrem dici, dedit et ministrum
    Esse salutis.

Tu redemptorem stabulo jacentem,
10 Quem chorus vatum cecinit futurum,
Aspicis gaudens humilisque natum
    Numen adoras.

Rex Deus regum, dominator orbis,
Cujus ad nutum tremit inferorum
15 Turba, cui pronus famulatur aether,
    Se tibi subdit.

Laus sit excelsae Triadi perennis,
Quae tibi praebens superos honores,
Det tuis nobis meritis beatae
20   Gaudia vitae.

Joseph, glory of those in heaven, sure hope of those on earth, strong support of the world, graciously accept the hymn of praise that we sing to you with joyful heart. The creator of all things appointed you the pure Virgin's husband, wished you to be known as the father of the Word and made you an instrument of man's salvation. The prophets had sung of the coming of the Redeemer, but you had the joy of seeing Him as He lay in the stable and humbly adored the infant God. God, the king of kings and lord of the world, submits Himself to your authority, though the power of hell trembles at His word and heaven adores and serves Him. Everlasting praise be to the most high Trinity that gave you the honours of heaven. May we, through your merits, receive the joys of the blessed.

Hymn 108

Iste, quem laeti colimus fideles,
Cujus excelsos canimus triumphos,
Hac die Joseph meruit perennis
    Gaudia vitae.

5 O nimis felix, nimis o beatus,
Cujus extremam vigiles ad horam
Christus et Virgo simul adstiterunt
    Ore sereno.

Hinc stygis victor, laqueo solutus
10 Carnis, ad sedes placido sopore
Migrat aeternas, rutilisque cingit
    Tempora sertis.

Joseph, honoured and praised by the joyful faithful for his glorious triumphs, on this day entered into the joys of everlasting life. How singularly fortunate and blessed he was, for at his last hour Christ and the Virgin stood side by side to watch over him, their faces full of peace and comfort. Triumphant over hell and his soul freed from the body's prison, calmly and peacefully he leaves this world for his eternal home, and there puts on his crown of

Notes on Hymn 107

Author. Probably Juan de la Concepcion, cf. *106*.
Metre. First Sapphic.
Use. At Matins of 19 March, and at Lauds of the Solemnity.

2. *columen,* pillar, support, with reference to St Jospeh being patron of the Church.

6. *dedit* sc. *te,* gave you, made you to be, an instrument, *ministrum;* cf. *nati in salutem gentium, 46,* 14.

Notes on Hymn 108

Author. Probably Juan de la Concepcion, cf. *106*.
Metre. First Sapphic.
Use. At Lauds of 19 March.

3. *Hac die*. The date of St Joseph's death is not known, but 19 March has been assigned as the day of its commemoration. As this hymn is concerned only with his death, it is not used for the Solemnity.

9. *Hinc,* from this world. Or perhaps *hinc* is not local, but connects the two verses.

12. *tempora,* cf. *84,* 20; *sertis,* cf. *47,* 2 and *117,* 37.

o

Ergo regnantem flagitemus omnes,
Adsit ut nobis veniamque nostris
15 *Obtinens culpis, tribuat supernae*
  Munera pacis.

Sint tibi plausus, tibi sint honores,
Trine, qui regnas, Deus, et coronas
Aureas servo tribuis fideli
20 *Omne per aevum.*

shining garlands. And so let us implore him, now enthroned in heaven, to be with us at death, to obtain us pardon for our sins and the gift of heavenly peace. Praise and honour be to You, blessed Trinity and ruler of heaven and earth, Who gives to the faithful servant a crown of gold as his ageless reward.

---

24 March. *St Gabriel*
Christe sanctorum decus angelorum; cf. 112
Placare Christe servulis; cf. 152a
The Seven Sorrows of the Blessed Virgin Mary
Hymn 109

Stabat mater dolorosa
Juxta crucem lacrimosa
  Dum pendebat Filius;
Cujus animam gementem,
5 *Contristatam et dolentem*
  Pertransivit gladius.

O quam tristis et afflicta
Fuit illa benedicta
  Mater unigeniti!
10 *Quae maerebat et dolebat*
Pia mater dum videbat
  Nati poenas incliti!

Quis est homo qui non fleret
Matrem Christi si videret
15 *In tanto supplicio?*
Quis non posset contristari,
Christi matrem contemplari
  Dolentem cum Filio?

The sorrowful mother was standing in tears beside the cross on which her Son was hanging. Her soul was full of grief and anguish and sorrow, for the sword of prophecy pierced it. How sad now and how unhappy at the fate of her only Son was that mother, once called blessed; how the faithful mother grieved and lamented as she saw her glorious Son so shamefully treated. Who is there who would not weep, were he to see Christ's mother in such great suffering? or who could help feeling sympathy with the mother, were he to think of her sorrowing with her Son? Yet she actually saw Jesus in agony and broken by the scourging

19. *servo ... fideli.* This refers in the first instance to St Joseph and then, collectively, to all faithful servants of God. The life and reward of St Joseph are summed in the Vesper Chapter of 19 March: *Vir fidelis multum laudabitur, et qui custos est Domini sui, glorificabitur.*

Notes on Hymn 109

Author. Jacapone da Todi (Tuderti of the Breviary and Martyrology).

The authorship of this poem, perhaps the most famous and certainly the tenderest of all the hymns of the Middle Ages, has been much disputed. It has been ascribed to St Gregory, St Bernard, St Bonaventure, John XXII and Gregory XI. But the real claim seems to lie between Innocent III, who died in 1216, and Jacapone, who died in 1306, with the balance of opinion apparently in favour of the latter. 'It is impossible to prove that Jacapone composed the Stabat Mater, but there is no positive evidence for its ascription to any other poet', Raby, p. 439.

Jacapone, also called Jacobus de Benedictis, born at Todi in Umbria about 1230 and by profession a lawyer, on the death of his wife joined the Franciscans. Besides being a well-known lampoonist and satirist, he became famous as a composer of *Laude*, one of which, the *Donna del Paradiso*, has the same inspiration and feeling as the *Stabat Mater*. This is one of the reasons why he is also looked on as the author of the *Stabat*. It is in any event a fact that the earliest ascription of the *Stabat* is to Jacapone.

The masterly use of rhyme suggests a later rather than an earlier date, and the personal note as in *me sentire vim doloris/Fac, ut tecum lugeam* points to a Franciscan tradition; and both these considerations favour Jacapone rather than Innocent. The curious idea was once advanced that the *Stabat* was a prayer

that one should undergo the *stigmata*. But the lines just quoted show it to be a prayer that we may suffer with our Lady even as she suffered with our Lord in her Compassion. The idea of compassion is Bernardine, as may be seen from lessons 4–6 of the feast, but this does not prove St Bernard to be the author. It is one of the things, like devotion to the name of Jesus (see introduction to *41*), which the Franciscans inherited from St Bernard and popularised. St Bernard was in many things a forerunner of the Franciscans.

Metre. Six-lined verses in trochaic dimeter (accentual), the third and sixth lines being catalectic, the rest acatalectic. Each verse rhymes aabccb.

Use. In the *Breviary.* At Vespers lines 1–30, at Matins 31–42 and at Lauds 43–60 for the feast in Passiontide. It had no place in the Breviary until 1727.

In the *Missal* it is the Sequence for the feast in Passiontide and on 15 September. Strictly speaking, there should be no sequence during Passiontide (or at a Requiem Mass), since the alleluia verse is not sung (cf. Note on Sequences), 'but the Missal of Pius V had sanctioned several exceptions to this rule which had already been consecrated by the Church's use', Schuster, IV, p. 89.

Certain textual differences, mentioned in the notes, are given by some editors as the correct text. Most of these variants were, apparently, once part of the

Pro peccatis suae gentis
20 *Vidit Jesum in tormentis*
        Et flagellis subditum.
    Vidit suum dulcem Natum
    Moriendo desolatum
25   *Dum emisit spiritum.*

25 *Eja, Mater, fons amoris,*
    Me sentire vim doloris
        Fac, ut tecum lugeam.
    Fac ut ardeat cor meum
    In amando Christum Deum
30   *Ut sibi complaceam.*

    *Sancta Mater, istud agas,
    Crucifixi fige plagas
        Cordi meo valide.
    Tui Nati vulnerati,
35 *Tam dignati pro me pati,*
        Poenas mecum divide.

    Fac me tecum pie flere,
    Crucifixo condolere
        Donec ego vixero;
40 *Juxta crucem tecum stare*
    Et me tibi sociare
        In planctu desidero.

    *Virgo virginum praeclara
    Mihi jam non sis amara,
45   *Fac me tecum plangere.*
    Fac ut portem Christi mortem,
    Passionis fac consortem
        Et plagas recolere.

    Fac me plagis vulnerari,
50 *Fac me cruce inebriari*
        Et cruore Filii.
    Flammis ne urar succensus,
    Per te, Virgo, sim defensus
        In die judicii.

—and this because of the sins of her own people. She saw her dear Son all the time He was dying and abandoned until He yielded up His soul. Come then mother from whom all love springs, make me understand the meaning of your sorrow that I may mourn with you. Make my heart burn with love of Christ, my God, that He may look on me with favour.

*Holy mother, do this for me. Pierce my heart once and for ever with the wounds of your crucified Son. Let me share with you the pain of your Son's wounds, for He thought it right to bear such sufferings for me. Grant that my tears of love may mingle with yours and that, as long as I live, I may feel the pains of my crucified Lord. To stand with you beside the cross and be your companion in grief is my one wish.

*Virgin without equal among virgins, do not now turn down my request; grant that I may mourn with you. Grant that I carry about the dying state of Christ; grant that I be a sharer of His passion; grant that I relive His wounds. Grant that I be wounded with His wounds; grant that I drink to my soul's content of the chalice of His cross and blood. Be a defence to me, virgin Mary, on the judgement day, and I will not burn and be consumed in the fires of

Missal text; cf. e.g. the text as given in the *Missale Romanum*, Antwerp, 1762. Yet Palestrina's setting, as given in Alfieri's edition, is of the text as given above. The only major difference is in the last verse, in which the text now in use seems inferior.

1. *Stabat.* Verses 1, 2 and 4 give the scene as described in John 19, 25. The author scarcely thinks of our Lord as God or as the Son of God for the purpose of this poem; line 29 is about the only mention of the divinity. His mind is fixed almost entirely on our Lord as Mary's son, on her sorrow as His mother and on her further sorrow that her own race were responsible for His death; cf. notes on lines 9 and 19.

2. *lacrimosa. Stabat et sancta mater juxta crucem Filii, et spectabat virgo sui unigeniti passionem. Stantem illam lego, flentem non lego,* Ambr. *De ob. Valent.* 39. But the 'sorrowful' mother appears in St Bernard in lessons 4–6 of the feast, and again in this poem.

5. *contristatam* (al. *contristantem,* mourning); either, compassionate, like *contristari* in line 16 (the emphasis being on *con*), or sorrowful, as in *contristatus incedo.* The latter is more probable here.

8. *benedicta,* purposely contrasted with *tristis et afflicta,* just as *poenas* is with *incliti* in line 12.

9. *unigeniti.* This would seem to refer to our Lord as Mary's only son, just as it clearly does in the sentence from St Ambrose quoted in the note on line 1. *Plangent eum quasi unigenitum* says the antiphon of Holy Saturday Lauds, which is derived from Zach. 12, 10 where *unigenitum* and *primogenitum* are used synonymously. *Primogenitus* is the Vulgate word in Mt. and Lk. for our Lord as Mary's son. Editors and translators, however, are practically unanimous in giving *unigeniti* here its more normal meaning of 'only-begotten' and Breviary editors indulge their usual passion for capital letters by giving *Unigeniti.* But Mary's sorrow is a *mother's* sorrow, and *unigeniti* here is answered by *nati incliti* in line 12.

10. *quae;* either a relative, or, better, 'how she grieved'.

11. *pia mater;* either the subject of the verbs or an 'aside' of the poet. *Quae maerebat et dolebat/Et tremebat cum* (or *dum*) *videbat* is the other text.

16. *Quis non,* i.e. *Quis posset non,* Who would be able not to, could refrain from. *Contristari;* cf. note on *contristatam,* line 5.

17. *Christi.* The other version is *piam matrem,* which is better because of *matrem Christi* in line 14.

Contemplari = si contemplaretur, balancing *si videret* of line 14.

19. *suae.* Almost without exception this is said to mean 'His people', with reference to Mt. 1, 21. This use of *suae* would then be like that of *sibi* in line 30. But as *suum* in this same verse is used normally and not as in late Latin, *suae* would seem to be used in the same way here and refer to 'her people'. It was an added grief to Mary that her own people, who were also her Son's people, were responsible for her sufferings and bereavement.

20. *vidit.* With the supposed case of a man looking at Mary in her suffering is contrasted the actual occurrence of Mary watching her Son die.

21. *flagellis.* Not the actual scourging, as *subditum* shows, but its results; cf. *133, 9.*

23. *moriendo* (al. *morientem*), to be taken as a present participle.

26. *vim* is perhaps used here in its meaning of essence, nature, meaning, purport. *Vim doloris* and *fons amoris* then explain one another, for her love is the explanation of her sorrow and her compassion. We also must *love,* cf. line 29, and then sorrow and compassion will develop in us, cf. lines 31 foll.

27. *Fac;* used, not as meaning 'suppose', but as the equivalent of *effice,* bring it about, grant etc. Constr. with acc. and infin., as here, or with *ut* as in the next line. Both have a dependent *ut* clause here, *ut tecum* and *ut sibi.*

30. *sibi,* to Him (Christ). In late Latin and the Vulgate *sibi* is often used for *ei* or *ipsi. Complaceam.* The Father, looking down from heaven, said: *Hic est filius meus, in quo mihi bene complacui.* By association, *complaceam* may suggest here our Lord looking down on us with pleasure, just as He found comfort and pleasure in His mother on Calvary.

31. *istud* (al. *illud*), as explained by *fige* and *divide.*

33. *valide,* strongly; deeply, indelibly, enduringly.

35. *tam* (al. *jam*). Some take this with *dignati,* others with *pati.*

37. *Fac me vere tecum flere* is the other version.

41. Or; *Meque tibi,* or *Te libenter.*

43. *praeclara,* unique, peerless; cf. *singularis, 94,* 17.

44. *amara,* bitter, unfavourable, ill-disposed.

46. *portem ... mortem. Semper mortificationem Jesu in corpore nostro circumferentes,* 2 Cor. 4, 10. 'Dying state' is the Knox version of *mortificationem.* The point of the verse is sharing in the sufferings of the *dying* Christ, not in the *death* as a completed state.

55 *Christe, cum sit hinc exire,*
   Da per Matrem me venire
     Ad palmam victoriae.
   Quando corpus morietur,
   Fac ut animae donetur
60   *Paradisi gloria.*

hell. When it is time, Lord Christ, for me to leave this world, give me through Your mother's prayers the palm of victory. When my body is dead, grant that my soul be given the glory of paradise.

---

13 April. *St Hermenegild*

Hymn 110

Regali solio fortis Iberiae,
Hermenegilde, jubar, gloria martyrum,
Christi quos amor almis
Caeli coetibus inserit,

5 *Ut perstas patiens, pollicitum Deo*
Servans obsequium, quo potius tibi
Nil proponis, et arces
Cautus noxia quae placent.

Ut motus cohibes, pabula qui parant
10 *Surgentis vitii, non dubios agens*
Per vestigia gressus,
Quo veri via dirigit.

*Nullis te genitor blanditiis trahit,
Non vitae caperis divitis otio
15 *Gemmarumve nitore*
Regnandive cupidine.

Diris non acies te gladii minis,
Nec terret perimens carnificis furor;
Nam mansura caducis
20 *Praefers gaudia caelitum.*

Nunc nos e superum protege sedibus
Clemens, atque preces, dum canimus tua
Quaesitam nece palmam,
Pronis auribus excipe.

Valiant Hermenegild, shining light of Spain's royal house and glory of the martyrs that have won their place in heaven through their love of Christ, how steadfastly you persevered, faithful to the allegiance you promised to God; for nothing was dearer to you than His service and you kept away from you all sinful pleasures. How readily you curbed the passions as being occasions for sin, never hesitating to walk in the direction that the way of truth made clear.

*Your father could not move you by any flattering or coaxing. Neither the leisure of a life of luxury, nor wealth, nor the thought of becoming king could entice you. The naked sword, angry threats, the executioner's death-dealing fury did not frighten you, for you preferred heaven's abiding joys to the fleeting ones of earth. Now that you are in heaven, graciously protect us and with ready ear listen to our prayers as we sing of the triumph your death earned for you. Everlasting glory to the

47. *fac* (sc. *me*) *consortem. Fac;* cf. line 27, note. *Passionis ejus sortem* is the other version of this line.

48. *recolere,* recall to mind. But the metaphors of these three lines are so physical, that *recolere* perhaps means exercise, practise again, renew.

49. *vulnerari;* al. *verberari.*

50. *fac me cruce;* al. *cruce hac. Inebriari;* cf. *12, 24,* note. The Cross is thought of as a *calix inebrians* (cf Ps. 22, 5).

51. *et cruore;* al. *ob amorem.*

52. The other text, *Inflammatus et accensus,* has the quite different idea of being inflamed and on fire with the love of Christ.

55-57. The other text is:

> *Fac me cruce custodiri,*
> *Morte Christi praemuniri,*
> *Confoveri gratia.*

The poem as a whole is about *Mary's* sorrows or to Mary, mostly in the form of the *Fac* petitions. A direct prayer to Christ, such as *Christe, cum sit hinc exire,* breaks that unity. The lines quoted above lead logically to the lines *Quando corpus* . . . , but the lines *Christe* . . . *victoriae* add little to the idea of the last three lines. The line *Ad palmam victoriae* is also the only instance of departure from rhyme, while *gratia* preserves the rhyme.

Notes on Hymn 110

Author. Urban VIII. St Hermenegild (or Hermengild) was martyred in 586. His feast in the Roman Breviary and Missal dates from Urban VIII.

Metre. Third Asclepiad.

Use. Verses 1, 2, 3 and 7 at Vespers and Matins, and verses 4–7 at Lauds.

1. *fortis,* vocative with *Hermenegilde.*

5. *Ut,* here and in line 9, = How; cf. *78,* 1.

6. *quo.* Order: *quo nil potius tibi proponis.* The relative implies the other term of the comparison, namely *quam obsequium.*

9. *qui* refers to *motus.*

11. *per vestigia* = on the path.

12. *quo,* whither.

13. The saint was martyred because he refused his father's command that he receive Communion from an Arian bishop; cf. second nocturn lessons.

17. *acies,* sharp edge.

22. *preces* with *excipe* of line 24.

23. *quaesitam,* gained, earned; cf. *16, 17.*

25 *Sit rerum Domino jugis honor Patri,*
   Et Natum celebrent ora precantium,
   Divinumque supremis
   Flamen laudibus efferant.

Father, Lord of the world. May your suppliants honour in song the Son and glorify the holy Spirit with the highest praise.

Solemnity of St. Joseph
Te Joseph celebrent agmina caelitum. Hymn 106
Caelitum Joseph decus, atque nostrae. Hymn 107

3 May. *The Finding of the Holy Cross*
Vexilla regis prodeunt. Hymn 52
Pange lingua gloriosi lauream certaminis. Hymn 53

8 May. *The Apparition of St Michael, Archangel*

Hymn 111

Te splendor et virtus Patris,
Te vita, Jesu, cordium,
Ab ore qui pendent tuo,
Laudamus inter angelos.

5 *Tibi mille densa millium*
  Ducum corona militat,
  Sed explicat victor crucem
  Michael salutis signifer.

Draconis hic dirum caput
10 *In ima pellit tartara,*
   Ducemque cum rebellibus
   Caelesti ab arce fulminat.

Contra ducem superbiae
Sequamur hunc nos principem
15 *Ut detur ex Agni throno*
   Nobis corona gloriae.

Deo Patri sit gloria
Qui, quos redemit Filius
Et sanctus unxit Spiritus,
20 *Per angelos custodiat.*

Jesus, the radiance and power of the Father and life of all hearts, we offer You our praise in company with the angels who ever wait on Your wishes. An army of thousands upon thousands in close array fights for Your cause, but Michael, their victorious leader and the standard-bearer of salvation, unfurls the standard of the Cross. He casts the wicked dragon into the depths of hell and hurls Satan and his rebel followers like lightning from high heaven. Let Michael be our leader in the battle with the prince of pride that the Lamb, enthroned in heaven, may reward us with the crown of glory. Glory be to God the Father. May He guard through His angels those whom the Son has redeemed and the holy Spirit has anointed.

26. *ora* is the subject of the two verbs; *precantium*, cf. *98*, 10, note.

Notes on Hymn III

Author. Unknown. The usual ascription to Raban Maur is doubtful, cf. Julian, p. 1531.

Use. At Vespers and Matins of St Michael, 8 May and 29 September.

The September feast is the main one, its full title being St Michael and All Angels. The feast of the Guardian Angels on 2 October is modern and emphasises something already present in the September feast; cf. *ab his in terra vita nostra muniatur* of the collect of 29 September.

Because the September feast is in honour of All Angels as well as St Michael, all the angels are mentioned in this hymn and individual angels in the next. For the same reason this hymn asks the angels to guard us and the next hymn asks them to help us. Finally the same reason explains the collect *Deus qui, miro ordine* which puts in lapidary form the whole theology of the angels.

The original of this hymn is in trochaic tetrameter, its first line being *Tibi Christe splendor Patris, vita,*
virtus cordium.

1. *splendor*, cf. *12*, 1, note; *virtus*, cf. 1 Cor. 1, 24. But the original says our Lord is *virtus cordium*, not *virtus Patris*.

3. *ab ore pendent*, pay close attention to, wait for a person's command or wish.

4. *inter*; cf. *In conspectu angelorum psallam tibi*, Ps. 137, 2.

6. *corona*, assembly, host.

9. *hic*, and *hunc* in line 14, refer to Michael.

12. *fulminat. Fulminare*, hurl lightnings, strike with lightning. *Videbam satanam sicut fulgur de caelo cadentem*, Lk. 10, 18.

19. *unxit*; cf. *quomodo unxit (Jesum) Deus Spiritu sancto*, Acts 10, 38. Similarly the members of the kingly and priestly people of Christ must be anointed with the holy Ghost, especially through Baptism, Confirmation and, for the clerical members, through Holy Orders.

Hymn 112

Christe, sanctorum decus angelorum,
Gentis humanae sator et redemptor,
Caelitum nobis tribuas beatas
　　Scandere sedes.

5 *Angelus pacis Michael in aedes*
Caelitus nostras veniat, serenae
Auctor ut pacis lacrimosa in orcum
　　Bella releget.

Angelus fortis Gabriel, ut hostes
10 *Pellat antiquos et amica caelo,*
Quae triumphator statuit per orbem,
　　Templa revisat.

Angelus nostrae medicus salutis
Adsit e caelo Raphael, ut omnes
15 *Sanet aegrotos dubiosque vitae*
　　Dirigat actus.

Virgo dux pacis genetrixque lucis
Et sacer nobis chorus angelorum
Semper assistat, simul et micantis
20　　*Regia caeli.*

Christ, glory of the holy angels, creator and redeemer of mankind, grant that we may ascend to heaven to live there with the blessed.

May Michael, the angel of peace, come from heaven into our homes, bringing fair peace with him and banishing wars to hell.

May Gabriel, the angel of strength, come to banish our old enemies and to revisit the temples, dear to heaven, which Christ in triumph has placed in all parts of the world.

May Raphael, the angel-physician of man's health, be with us to heal all that are sick and to guide all who are in doubt and uncertainty.

May the Virgin, queen of peace and the Mother of light, together with the holy company of angels and the radiant court of heaven ever be our help and defence.

---

18 May. *St Venantius, Martyr*

Hymn 113

Martyr Dei Venantius,
Lux et decus Camertium,
Tortore victo et judice,
Laetus triumphum concinit.

5 *Annis puer, post vincula,*
Post carceres, post verbera,
Longa fame frementibus
Cibus datur leonibus.

Venantius, martyr in God's cause, honour and glory of Camerino, overcame his torturers and judge and now, one of heaven's choir, sings his song of triumph. Though but a boy, he was put in chains, imprisoned and scourged, and then thrown to be eaten by hungry, roaring lions. But the savage beasts

Notes on Hymn 112

Author. Unknown. The ascription to Raban is doubtful.

Metre. First Sapphic.

Use. The whole hymn is used at Lauds of 8 May and 29 September. Verses 1, 3 and 5 are used at Vespers and Matins of St Gabriel, 24 March, and verses 1, 4 and 5 at Vespers and Matins of St Raphael, 24 October.

1. *decus angelorum.* This is a hymn to Christ, not to the angels. The petitions of later verses, connected with individual angels, are (more obviously in the original) addressed to Him.

3. *caelitum* is the key to the hymn. Each verse has some mention of heaven and is an appeal to heaven for help. The revised version makes more of the idea of peace than does the original.

5. *pacis.* Michael is called the angel of peace because his victory established peace in heaven; cf. Apoc. 12, 8. *Sub tutela Michaelis/Pax in terra, Pax in caelis,* Adam of St Victor.

9. *fortis.* Gabriel means *fortitudo Dei;* cf. third nocturn lessons of 24 March and lesson 5 of 29 September. Understand *veniat* before *ut.*

11. *triumphator* seems to refer to Christ, though some refer it to Gabriel. The idea of the line is foreign to the original text.

12. *templa revisat,* just as he visited the Temple, Lk. 1, 11–19.

13. *medicus.* Raphael means *medicina Dei;* cf. second nocturn lessons of 24 October.

15. *sanet.* Gabriel restored sight to the elder Tobias and was a guide (*dirigat* in line 16) to the younger one. Cf. also the antiphon *In viam pacis* in the *Itinerarium.*

19. *assistat,* in the general sense of be our help, not in the particular sense of *assistitur* of St Michael's collect or of *assistebant* of Dan. 7, 10.

20. *regia,* court.

Notes on Hymn 113

Author. Unknown, of the seventeenth century. It is said that Clement X (1670–76), who was previously bishop of Camerino, ordered the hymns for St Venantius to be added to the Breviary. For the strange story of confusion connected with St Venantius and his *cultus,* see Thurston, *Lives of the Saints,* V, p. 225.

Use. At Vespers.

2. *Camertium,* gen. pl. *Camers* and *Camertinus* both mean an inhabitant of Camerino in Umbria, while *Camerinus* refers to Cameria in Latium. The Breviary lessons have caused confusion by using *Camers* and *Camerinus* as synonyms. Bagshawe's translation of this line 'Who Latium light and glory brings' is wrong and Caswell's 'Camertium's light, her joy and prize' is very odd.

4. *triumphum,* perhaps a song of triumph here, cf. 53, 2.

5. *puer.* Venantius was fifteen when martyred in A.D. 250.

Sed ejus innocentiae
10 Parcit leonum immanitas,
    Pedesque lambunt martyris,
    Irae famisque immemores.

    Verso deorsum vertice
    Haurire fumum cogitur;
15 Costas utrimque et viscera
    Succensa lampas ustulat.

    Sit laus Patri, sit Filio,
    Tibique sancte Spiritus:
    Da per preces Venantii
20 Beata nobis gaudia.

spared the innocent boy's life and licked the martyr's feet, quite forgetful of their rage and hunger. Then he was hung head downwards and so could not avoid the fire's choking fumes; flaming torches on each side of him burned his ribs and body. Praise be to the Father, Son and holy Ghost. Grant us through Venantius' prayers the joys of heaven.

Hymn 114

    Athleta Christi nobilis
    Idola damnat gentium,
    Deique amore saucius
    Vitae pericla despicit.

 5 Loris revinctus asperis,
    E rupe praeceps volvitur;
    Spineta vultum lancinant,
    Per saxa corpus scinditur.

    Dum membra raptant martyris,
10 Languent siti satellites;
    Signo crucis Venantius
    E rupe fontes elicit.

    Bellator o fortissime,
    Qui perfidis tortoribus
15 E caute praebes poculum,
    Nos rore gratiae irriga.

Christ's noble champion rejects paganism and its idols and, a victim of God's love, treats with contempt all the risks and dangers to his life. Bound with rough thongs, he is pushed down from the top of a cliff and, as he rolls down, the briars tear his face and the rocks bruise his body. When the soldiers that are dragging him about become weak from thirst, Venantius with a sign of the cross brings a stream of water from the rock. Valiant warrior, that so provided drink for the faithless tormentors, comfort us with the refreshing stream of grace.

· 15. *utrimque,* on each side.

16. *lampas,* sing. for plur. For the incident, cf. lesson 4.

17–20. These lines are also used as the doxology of the next two hymns.

Notes on Hymn 114

Author. Unknown; cf. *113.*

Use. At Matins.

1. *Athleta,* champion; cf. *121, 2.*

3. *saucius,* wounded by, a victim of; cf. *92, 5.*

4. *pericla=pericula.*

7. *spineta,* from *spinetum, -i,* thorn.

10. *satellites,* attendants, soldiers; cf. *39, 7.* For the incident cf. lesson 6.

15. *caute,* from *cautes, -is,* rock.

Hymn 115

Dum nocte pulsa lucifer
Diem propinquam nuntiat,
Nobis refert Venantius
Lucis beatae munera.

5 *Nam criminum caliginem*
Stygisque noctem depulit
Veroque cives lumine
Divinitatis imbuit.

Aquis sacri baptismatis
10 *Lustravit ille patriam;*
Quos tinxit unda milites
In astra misit martyres.

Nunc angelorum particeps,
Adesto votis supplicum;
15 *Procul repelle crimina*
Tuumque lumen ingere.

While the day-star has bidden night be gone and gives news of the approach of day, Venantius brings us the gift of heavenly light. For he broke the darkness of sin and the night of paganism and brought his fellow-citizens into the light of the true God. He purified his country with the waters of holy baptism, and the soldiers that baptism had made clean went, through him, to heaven as martyrs. And now that you share with the angels the joys of heaven, graciously listen to our earnest prayer: banish sin far from us and shine on us the light of your holiness.

19 June. *St Juliana Falconieri*
Hymn 116

Caelestis Agni nuptias,
O Juliana, dum petis,
Domum paternam deseris
Chorumque ducis virginum.

5 *Sponsumque suffixum cruci*
Noctes diesque dum gemis,
Doloris icta cuspide
Sponsi refers imaginem.

Quin septiformi vulnere
10 *Fles ad genu Deiparae;*
Sed crescit infusa fletu
Flammasque tollit caritas.

When it was your desire, Juliana, to be a bride of the Lamb of heaven, you left your father's house and became the leader of a new Order of nuns. Day and night you mourned your Spouse fastened to the Cross until, pierced with a sword of sorrow, you bore His image. You also knelt in tears at Mary's feet, grieving over her seven Sorrows; but your God-given love grew stronger through your tears and its flame mounted higher to

Notes on Hymn 115

Author. Unknown; cf. *113.*

Use. At Lauds.

1. *lucifer,* day-star; cf. *11, 9,* note. The many re-ferences to light suit a Lauds hymn.

6. *Stygis,* hell. The classical name is apt here, for it refers to the pagan darkness of Camerino.

Notes on Hymn 116

Author. Francesco Maria Lorenzini (1680–1743).

Use. At Vespers and Matins. The office of St Juliana, foundress of the Third Order of Servites, was granted to the Servites and to the city of Florence in 1728 and to the whole Church ten years later. The saint died in 1341. For the Servites and the con-templation of the sufferings of our Lord and the sorrows of our Lady, see *104.*

9. *Septiformi,* i.e. the seven sorrows of Mary.

11–12. 'But love infused, by tears grows strong,/ And higher still doth lift its flame', Mulcahy. But B understands *doloris* after *flammas* and translate 'rendered more keen the poignancy of thy grief'.

Hinc morte fessam proxima
Non usitato te modo
15 Solatur et nutrit Deus,
Dapem supernam porrigens.

Aeterne rerum conditor,
Aeterne Fili par Patri
Et par utrique Spiritus,
20 Soli tibi sit gloria.

heaven. For this reason God miraculously consoled you when you lay exhausted and near to death, and fed you by giving you the Bread of heaven. Eternal maker of the world, eternal Son, the Father's equal, and Spirit equal to both—to You alone be glory.

---

24 June. *St John the Baptist*

Hymn 117

Ut *queant laxis* resonare *fibris*
Mira *gestorum* famuli *tuorum,*
Solve *polluti* labii reatum,
    Sancte Joannes.

5 Nuntius celso veniens Olympo
Te patri magnum fore nasciturum,
Nomen et vitae seriem gerendae
    Ordine promit.

Ille promissi dubius superni
10 Perdidit promptae modulos loquelae,
Sed reformasti genitus peremptae
    Organa vocis.

Ventris obstruso recubans cubili
Senseras regem thalamo manentem;
15 Hinc parens nati meritis uterque
    Abdita pandit.

Free from guilt your servants' unclean lips, holy John, that they may be able to sing with clear voices the wonders of your life. A messenger came from high heaven and disclosed in turn to your father the greatness that would be yours at birth, the name you were to bear and the course of life you were to lead. As Zachary hesitated to accept God's message, he was deprived of the power of ready speech; but when you were born you restored to him the use of speech that he had lost. While still in the hidden home of your mother's womb, you recognized your King as He waited in Mary as in an inner room. Thus both parents, through their child's merits, revealed hidden truths.

Continued

15. *solatur*. Unable to receive Communion because of her sickness, Juliana asked the priest to put the Host on her breast. This he did, and *eodem*

momento divinus panis disparuit, et Juliana sereno ac ridenti vultu exspiravit, lesson 6.

20. *tibi*, i.e. to You, God, one in three Persons.

Notes on Hymn 117

Author. ?Paul the Deacon (720–99), historian of the Lombards and friend of Charlemagne.

'Almost, but not quite, certainly by Paul,' says the editor of the *Oxford Medieval*. Raby, however, says: 'The court poems and a few epitaphs exhaust the limited scope of Paul's achievement. . . . It is only a late and uncertain testimony which makes him the author' of this hymn, p. 166. The author, whoever he was, certainly belonged to the Carolingian age.

Metre. First Sapphic.

Use. The first four verses at Vespers, the second four at Matins and the last five at Lauds. The Vespers and Matins sections have in the Roman Breviary the usual Sapphic doxology *Sit decus Patri genitaeque Proli*, whose unrevised form is given in the *Oxford Medieval* in place of the verse *Laudibus cives*. Raby, however, prints the verse *Laudibus cives* as part of the hymn, and it shows every sign of having been written by the author of the rest of the hymn. Daniel, I. 210, adds after this verse a doxology beginning: *Gloriam Patri resonemus omnes*.

1. *Queant*; cf. *quit*, *75*, *24*. *Laxis fibris*; (1) with loosened tongue and throats—Zachary's lips and tongue were loosened to praise God after John's birth; (2) suggesting a good, pleasant voice; (3) connected in thought with the next lines, for God's praise is better sounding if it comes from one who is pleasing to God. The hymn is said to have been written in gratitude for its author having been cured of a throat malady, and from early times St John has been honoured as the patron of singers and invoked in case of throat ailments. *Famuli*, the choir and, in general, the Church.

3. *solve*, loosen, i.e. remove, cleanse; *polluti*; cf. *pollutus labiis*, Is. 6,5.

The Romanized syllables of this verse suggested to Guido of Arezzo the (continental) names of the notes of the musical scale, as each half-line of the melody begins on the next ascending note of the scale. The *name* of the seventh note, *si*, is sometimes said to be formed from the initial letters of *Sancte Joannes* in the fourth line; but the *note* itself is not used in the melody.

5–8. cf. Luke 1, 13–17.

9. *ille*, i.e. Zachary.

10. *modulos*, measure, music, melody; here, use, power.

13. *obstruso* or *abstruso*, hidden, secret; and cf. *38*, 19–20 and *138*, 7–8. The reference is to the Visitation. (*Obstruso* of some Breviaries must be wrong.) *Recubans* instead of the original *positus*.

14. *thalamo*. The word is suggested by *sponsus procedens de thalamo suo*, Ps. 18, 6.

15. *parens . . . uterque*, i.e. Zachary, lines 9–12, and Elizabeth, lines 13–14; *nati* refers to the *genitus* of line 11; *hinc* indicates what happened to the parents because of their son John. Both Elizabeth and Zachary were filled with the holy Ghost and then *spoke* the hidden things of God; Lk. 1, 41–45 and 67–69. The hymn keeps close to the life of John to the exclusion of all else and obviously has in mind the gift and use of *speech* in relation to John. This must therefore rule out the interpretation of *parens uterque* as referring to Mary and Elizabeth. Moreover *uterque* would scarcely refer to *two* ladies and *nati* has no qualification which would refer it to someone other than

P

*Antra deserti teneris sub annis,
    Civium turmas fugiens, petisti,
    Ne levi posses maculare vitam
20   Crimine linguae.

    Praebuit durum tegumen camelus
    Artubus sacris, strophium bidentes,
    Cui latex haustum, sociata pastum
        Mella locustis.

25 Ceteri tantum cecinere vatum
    Corde praesago jubar affuturum;
    Tu quidem mundi scelus auferentem
        Indice prodis.

    Non fuit vasti spatium per orbis
30 Sanctior quisquam genitus Joanne,
    Qui nefas saecli meruit lavantem
        Tingere lymphis.

*O nimis felix meritique celsi,
    Nesciens labem nivei pudoris,
35 Praepotens martyr nemorumque cultor,
        Maxime vatum.

    Serta ter denis alios coronant
    Aucta crementis, duplicata quosdam,
    Trina te fructu cumulata centum
40   Nexibus ornant.

    Nunc potens nostri meritis opimis
    Pectoris duros lapides revelle,
    Asperum planans iter et reflexos
        Dirige calles,

45 Ut pius mundi sator et redemptor,
    Mentibus culpae sine labe puris,
    Rite dignetur veniens beatos
        Ponere gressus.

    Laudibus cives celebrent superni
50 Te, Deus simplex pariterque trine,
    Supplices et nos veniam precamur;
        Parce redemptis.

*You left the busy cities, when still a child, and chose to live in desert caves to avoid the discredit of even the slightest sin of speech. The camel provided your holy body with coarse clothing, and oxen your belt. A spring gave you your drink, honey and locusts your food. All other prophets had spoken in their messages of the future coming of the Light, but you pointed out with your finger the One that takes away the sin of the world. In the whole wide world there was no child of man more holy than John, found worthy as he was to baptize Him Who washes man clean of sin.

*Mightiest of martyrs, lover of solitude, greatest of prophets, how exceedingly favoured you were and how great your merit, for your snow-white purity was unsullied by any sin. Some receive a single crown for their harvest of thirtyfold, others a double crown for their sixtyfold; but a triple crown is your reward for the heaped-up return of a hundredfold increase. And now in virtue of your rich merits take from our heart its stony insensibility, make its roughness smooth and its crookedness straight that when our loving creator and redeemer comes He may make His way, as befits Him, through a soul free of sin's guilt and stain. May the citizens of heaven sing their praise to You, one God in three Persons. But we on earth ask and beg for Your pardon. Spare us for You redeemed us.

John or to someone with John. The confusion perhaps arises from referring *hinc* only to lines 13 and 14.

19. *levi*, with *crimine*, slightest sin of the tongue. The 'tongue' and 'speech' *motifs* are still present.

21-24. *Praebuit* is the verb of all the verse. *Bidentes*, animals for sacrifice—sheep, oxen, swine and later signifying mostly sheep. But here it means the animals who provided the *leathern* girdle of Mt. 3, 4—which B's 'sheep' could scarcely have done. *Cui=et tibi; sociata=et*—both used for metrical reasons only.

26. *corde praesago*, with prophetic spirit, explaining *vatum*, but not adding anything not already in *vatum*.

28. *prodis*, cf. John 1, 29.

30. *sanctior quisquam*, cf. Mt. 11, 11.

32. *tingere lymphis*, bathe with water, baptize.

33. *nimis*, exceedingly; cf. *108*, 5.

35. *nemorum, nemus*, grove, forest; place of solitude. It displaces *eremique*. The hermits took St John's way of life as their model.

37-40. A ˙difficult verse. The thirty, sixty and hundredfold of Mt. 13, 8 is joined with the idea of a single, double and triple crown. The triple crown is that of martyr, hermit and prophet, as mentioned in lines 35-36. Order: *Serta aucta ter denis incrementa coronant alios, quosdam duplicata (serta coronant); te ornant trina fructu cumulata serta centum nexibus*, B.

Chaplets, enriched by thirty-fold return,
Crown some; while others, double garlands honour;
Triple wreaths, fruit-heaped in an hundred foldings,
    Thy brows adorn. (Mulcahy.)

41. *nunc*. What John had once done by his preaching, may he now do by his intercession.

47. *rite*, fitly, duly, rightly. Here it suggests something that becomes our Lord as God.

52. *redemptis*. *Visitavit et fecit redemptionem plebis suae*, Lk. 1, 68.

29 June. *Saints Peter and Paul*
Decora lux aeternitatis, auream: Hymn *98*, 1–8 and 17–24
Beate pastor, Petre, clemens accipe: cf. *98*, 9–16 and 21–24
30 June. *Commemoration of St Paul*
Egregie doctor, Paule, mores instrue; cf. *98*, 13–16 and 21–24
1 July. *The Most Precious Blood*

Hymn 118

Festivis resonent compita vocibus,
Cives laetitiam frontibus explicent,
Taedis flammiferis ordine prodeant
  Instructi pueri et senes.

5 *Quem dura moriens Christus in arbore*
Fudit multiplici vulnere sanguinem,
Nos facti memores dum colimus, decet
  Saltem fundere lacrimas.

Humano generi pernicies gravis
10 *Adami veteris crimine contigit;*
Adami integritas et pietas novi
  Vitam reddidit omnibus.

Clamorem validum summus ab aethere
Languentis Geniti si Pater audiit,
15 *Placari potius sanguine debuit*
  Et nobis veniam dare.

Hoc quicunque stolam sanguine proluit,
Abstergit maculas, et roseum decus,
Quo fiat similis protinus angelis
20 *Et Regi placeat, capit.*

A recto instabilis tramite postmodum
Se nullus retrahat, meta sed ultima
Tangatur: tribuet nobile praemium
  Qui cursum Deus adjuvat.

25 *Nobis propitius sis, Genitor potens,*
Ut quos unigenae sanguine Filii
Emisti, et placido Flamine recreas
  Caeli ad culmina transferas.

Let the streets resound with festive hymns and the people's joy be seen in their faces as young and old, each in his rank and carrying a flaming torch, walk in procession. Yet while we are mindful of His passion and pay honour to the blood that Christ shed from His many wounds as He hung upon the cruel tree, it is but right that at least we should shed tears. The old Adam's sin resulted in death and misery to mankind, but the new Adam's sinlessness and loving-kindness gave life back to all men. If the sovereign Father heard from heaven the great cry of His Son in His agony, much more ought He to be appeased by His blood and so give us pardon. Everyone that washes his soul's robe in this blood, frees it of all its filth and gives it a beauty and fragrance that immediately make him like the angels and pleasing to his King. Henceforth let no one, in fickle inconstancy, leave the path of right, but keep to the course until he reach the finishing post in triumph; and God, Who assists man on his way, will give him a glorious prize. Father of might be merciful in our favour and bring from earth to the heights of heaven those that You have bought with the blood of Your only-begotten Son and have created anew through the Spirit of peace.

Notes on Hymn 118

Author. Unknown, seventeenth century.

Metre. Second Asclepiad.

Use. At Vespers.

1. *compita*, crossways, streets.

2. *frontibus*, i.e. faces; *explicent*, manifest, display.

5. *dura* . . . *arbore*; cf. *53, 25–27*.

6. *fudit* . . . *sanguinem* is answered by *fundere lacrimas* in line 8.

10. *Adami veteris*; cf. Rom. 5, 12–21.

13. *clamorem validum*. The phrase is from *cum clamore valido*, Heb. 5, 7 but the cry referred to is probably 'Father, forgive them', Lk. 23, 34.

15. *Potius*, far more; cf. Heb. 9, 14.

19. *protinus*, forthwith, as in *ut protinus des mihi*, Mk. 6, 25; cf. *64*, 18, note.

21. *postmodum*, henceforth, in the future, i.e. because of the grace received.

22. *meta*, goal, finishing-post, cf. *62*, 18 and Phil. 3, 13 foll.

26. *unigenae*, only-begotten.

27. *emisti*; cf. 1 Pet. 1, 18–19. *Recreas*; cf. *64*, 4, note and Titus 3, 5.

Hymn 119

Ira justa conditoris imbre aquarum vindice
Criminosum mersit orbem, Noe in arca sospite:
Mira tandem vis amoris lavit orbem sanguine.

Tam salubri terra felix irrigata pluvia,
5 *Ante spinis quae scatebat, germinavit flosculos*
Inque nectaris saporem transiere absinthia.

Triste protinus venenum dirus anguis posuit
Et cruenta belluarum desiit ferocia:
Mitis Agni vulnerati haec fuit victoria.

10 *O scientiae supernae altitudo impervia!*
O suavitas benigni praedicanda pectoris!
Servus erat morte dignus, rex luit poenam optimus.

Quando culpis provocamus ultionem judicis,
Tunc loquentis protegamur sanguinis praesentia;
15 *Ingruentium malorum tunc recedant agmina.*

Te redemptus laudet orbis grata servans munera,
O salutis sempiternae dux et auctor inclite,
Qui tenes beata regna cum Parente et Spiritu.

The creator's righteous anger engulfed the sinful world in an avenging flood of water, only Noe in the ark being saved. But at long last by a wonderful display of love He washed the world in His blood. The happy earth, made fruitful by the rain of salvation, has grown flowers where once briars abounded; the bitterness of wormwood has given place to the sweetness of nectar. The dread serpent at once laid aside his deadly poison and wild beasts lost their savage nature; this was the victory that the gentle Lamb won by His wounds. How unfathomable the depth of God's knowledge! How great the praise due to the mercy of His loving heart! The slave was under sentence of death, but his gracious King paid the penalty for him. When our sins call down the Judge's vengeance, may we at that hour find protection in the pleadings of this blood, and may the hosts of evil that threaten us leave us and depart. May the world of Your redemption treasure the gifts that deserve its thanks and give praise to You, leader and glorious author of man's salvation, Who with the Father and the Spirit rules the kingdom of the blessed.

Hymn 120

Salvete Christi vulnera,
Immensi amoris pignora,
Quibus perennes rivuli
Manant rubentis sanguinis.

5 *Nitore stellas vincitis,*
Rosas odore et balsama,
Pretio lapillos indicos,
Mellis favos dulcedine.

Per vos patet gratissimum
10 *Nostris asylum mentibus;*

All hail, wounds of Christ, pledges of a measureless love; from you there flow endlessly the red streams of His blood. You surpass the stars in brilliance, roses and balsam in fragrance, jewels from India in worth and honeycombs in sweetness. Through you there lies open for our souls entrance to a welcome

Notes on Hymn 119

Author. Unknown, seventeenth century.

Metre. Trochaic tetrameter.

Use. At Matins.

3. *vis amoris* contrasted with *ira, lavit* with *mersit* and *sanguine* with *aquarum.* Moreover redemption is universal, while only Noe and those in the ark were saved at the flood.

4. *salubri . . . pluvia,* i.e. Christ's blood. *Salubri,* cf. *93,* 19 note.

7. *protinus;* cf. *118,* 19. *Posuit,* laid aside.

8. *desiit;* cf. Isaias 65, 25.

14. *loquentis,* pleading; cf. *sanguinis aspersionem melius loquentem quam Abel,* Heb. 12, 24.

17. *salutis . . . auctor;* cf. *37,* 9, note.

Notes on Hymn 120

Author. Unknown, seventeenth century.

Use. At Lauds.

5. *vincitis,* surpass; cf. *45,* 6 and *52,* 26.

6. *balsama,* neuter plural.

Non huc furor minantium
Unquam penetrat hostium.

Quot Jesus in praetorio
Flagella nudus excipit!
15 Quot scissa pellis undique
Stillat cruoris guttulas!

Frontem venustam, pro dolor,
Corona pungit spinea,
Clavi retusa cuspide
20 Pedes manusque perforant.

Postquam sed ille tradidit
Amans volensque spiritum,
Pectus feritur lancea
Geminusque liquor exsilit.

25 Ut plena sit redemptio
Sub torculari stringitur
Suique Jesus immemor
Sibi nil reservat sanguinis.

Venite quotquot criminum
30 Funesta labes inficit:
In hoc salutis balneo
Qui se lavat mundabitur.

Summi ad Parentis dexteram
Sedenti habenda est gratia,
35 Qui nos redemit sanguine
Sanctoque firmat Spiritu.

refuge, and no angry foe can ever pursue us there with his menaces. How many the stripes Jesus received, all naked in Pilate's hall; how many the drops of blood that His torn skin lets fall all round Him. And now a crown of thorns pierces His noble brow, and nails with blunted points bore their way through His hands and feet. And after He had breathed His last, all love and sacrifice to the end, His side is pierced by a soldier's lance, and there gushes forth the twofold stream of water and blood. To pay our ransom in full, Jesus is crushed completely in the wine-press and, forgetful only of Himself, is drained of His blood to the very last drop. All that are corrupted by sin's deadly infection, come to these healing streams; for if a man bathe himself at this atoning spring, purity of soul will be his.

Thanks are due to Him Who sits at the Father's right hand, for He has redeemed us by His blood and strengthens us by the holy Spirit.

---

7 July. *SS Cyril and Methodius*

Hymn 121

Sedibus caeli nitidis receptos
Dicite athletas geminos, fideles,
Slavicae duplex columen decusque
    Dicite gentis.

5 Hos amor fratres sociavit unus
Unaque abduxit pietas eremo
Ferre quo multis celerent beatae
    Pignora vitae.

Sing, faithful, of two great champions that are now in heaven's shining city; sing of the twofold strength and glory of the Slav people. These two brothers were one in their love of God; one also in their pity for men that induced them to leave their monastic retreat and hasten to bring to many assurance of a future life of blessedness. Through them the gracious light of heaven shone in all parts of

11. *huc,* i.e. the *asylum* of line 10.

17. *pro dolor,* an interjection of wonder or sorrow, but little more here than a verse-filler.

26. *torculari,* winepress—used in Scripture to denote tribulation, e.g. Is. 63, 1–3; *stringitur,* i.e. crushed, pressed.

30. *inficit,* corrupts, infects.

34. *gratia.* The singular, *gratia,* rather than the plural, is used with *habere.*

Notes on Hymn 121

Author. Unknown, nineteenth century. This hymn and the next 'have been improperly ascribed to Leo XIII, who extended the feast of SS Cyril and Methodius to the whole Church in 1880, at which time the hymns were probably written', B.

Metre. First Sapphic.

Use. At Vespers and Matins.

2–3. *Geminos* and *duplex;* Cyril (827–69) and Methodius (826–85) were brothers who became first monks, then bishops and the 'Apostles of the Slavs'. *Fideles,* vocative; *columen;* cf. *100,* 33.

6. *abduxit . . . eremo,* drew them from their solitude, i.e. their monastery.

8. *pignora,* pledges, tokens, assurance.

Luce quae templis superis renidet
10 Bulgaros complent, Moravos, Bohemos;
Mox feras turmas numerosa Petro
    Agmina ducunt.

Debitam cincti meritis coronam
Pergite o flecti lacrimis precantum;
15 Prisca vos Slavis opus est datores
    Dona tueri.

Quaeque vos clamat generosa tellus
Servet aeternae fidei nitorem;
Quae dedit princeps, dabit ipsa semper
20   Roma salutem.

Gentis humanae sator et redemptor,
Qui bonus nobis bona cuncta praebes,
Sint tibi grates, tibi sit per omne
    Gloria saeclum.

Bulgaria, Moravia and Bohemia; in a short time they bring great crowds of savage pagans as a notable addition to Peter's flock. You are now enjoying your well-earned reward; but at all times listen with pity to our suppliant prayers; for the gift of faith you brought the Slavs centuries ago now needs your protection. Indeed may any land, of true Christian stock, that turns to you for help keep its faith unsullied; and Rome, the first to give salvation, will continue to give it. May man through all eternity sing his gratitude and praise to You, creator and redeemer of mankind, Goodness itself and the source of all goodness we have.

Hymn 122

Lux o decora patriae
Slavisque amica gentibus,
Salvete, fratres, annuo
Vos efferemus cantico.

5 Quos Roma plaudens excipit,
Complexa mater filios,
Auget corona praesulum
Novoque firmat robore.

Terras ad usque barbaras
10 Inferre Christum pergitis;
Quot vanus error luserat,
Almo repletis lumine.

Noxis soluta pectora
Ardor supernus abripit;
15 Mutatur horror veprium
In sanctitatis flosculos.

Et nunc, serena caelitum
Locati in aula, supplici

To the brothers that brought lustre and glory to their native land and shone like a friendly beacon to the Slavs—all hail; we will sing you our yearly hymn of praise. When you visited Rome, she gave warm approval of your work, received you with a mother's love, added to your dignity by making you bishops and strengthened your resolve with new determination. You set out for distant and uncivilized peoples to bring Christ to them, and fill with the light of faith those that folly and error had once deceived. A zeal for heavenly things took possession of hearts now freed from sin; where once vice and its thorns had ruined men's souls, holiness now yielded its welcome flowers. Now that you are safe in the peace and glory of

13. *coronam*, i.e. with the crown your merits earned. *Cingere* may, in the passive, govern the accusative in poetry.

15. *Prisca*, for the hymn was written about a thousand years after the Saints' missionary work.

17. *Quaeque*, cf. *2*, 13; *generosa*, cf. *71*, 3. Noble as having the faith and therefore part of Christ's *genus*, the Church.

Notes on Hymn 122

Author. Unknown; cf. *121*.

Use. At Lauds.

2. *amica*, friendly, kind to; cf. *91*, 9.

5. *Quos Roma*; cf. lesson 5.

7. Gives the added honour, *auget*, of the bishop's mitre; the two were made bishops on a visit to Rome. Distinguish *corona praesulum* here from that of *88*, 2.

9. *ad usque*; cf. *38*, 2.

15–16. Cruel thorns (of sin, and with reference to Gen. 3, 18) give way to flowers of holiness; for the same metaphor, cf. *119*, 4–6.

Adeste voto; Slavicas
20 *Servate gentes numini.*

Errore mersos unicum
Ovile Christi congreget;
Factis avitis aemula
Fides virescat pulchrior.

25 *Tu nos, beata Trinitas,*
Caelesti amore concita,
Patrumque natos inclita
Da persequi vestigia.

heaven, listen to our earnest prayer. Keep the Slav peoples faithful to God. May those that are now sunk in error be gathered into Christ's one and only fold. May their faith rival in its results the accomplishments of former times and grow with an even greater beauty. Inflame us, blessed Trinity, with heavenly love and grant that the sons may follow their fathers' glorious example.

8 July. *St Elizabeth of Portugal*
Hymn 123

Domare cordis impetus Elisabeth
Fortis, inopsque Deo
Servire, regno praetulit.

En fulgidis recepta caeli sedibus
5 *Sidereaeque domus*
Ditata sanctis gaudiis,

Nunc regnat inter caelites beatior
Et premit astra, docens
Quae vera sint regni bona.

10 *Patri potestas, Filioque gloria,*
Perpetuumque decus
Tibi sit alme Spiritus.

Elizabeth thought the resolute curbing of her passions and the service of God in a spirit of poverty of more importance than her queenly dignity. As a result she has been welcomed into the dazzling court of heaven and made rich with the holy joys of her home on high where, happier than any on earth, she is a queen among the blessed in heaven, the stars a royal carpet for her feet—her life and its reward a lesson of what is the true happiness of a ruler. To the Father be power, to the Son glory and to You, loving Spirit, everlasting honour.

Hymn 124

Opes decusque regium reliqueras,
Elisabeth, Dei dicata numini.
Recepta nunc bearis inter Angelos;
Libens ab hostium tuere nos dolis.

5 *Praei, viamque dux salutis indica:*
Sequemur: O sit una mens fidelium,

You despised, Elizabeth, riches and royal dignity, devoting yourself to the service of God. Now, in the angels' company, you enjoy the vision of God; graciously protect us from our deceitful enemies. Be our guide and leader, and show us the way that leads to salvation; we will follow you. Let dissension have no place

26. *concita, concitare*, rouse, urge on, quicken.

Notes on Hymn 123

Author. Urban VIII.
Metre. Third Archilochian.
Use. At Matins. In some places at Vespers also.
3. *regno praetulit;* put before her queenly state the curbing, *domare*, . . . and the serving of God. . . .
4. *recepta;* cf. *121*, 1.
8. *premit*, treads the stars.

Notes on Hymn 124

Author. Urban VIII.
Metre. Iambic trimeter.
Use. At Lauds.
2. *numini*, will, command; cf. *105*, 1.
3. *bearis;* cf. *100, 40*.
4. *libens*, willingly, graciously. *Hostium;* the saint was renowned as a peacemaker; cf. the collect and the lessons of the second nocturn.
5. *Praei*, go before, guide, lead.
6. *Una mens* is another reference to her power as a peacemaker.

Odor bonus sit omnis actio, tuis
Id innuit rosis operta caritas.

Beata caritas, in arce siderum
10 *Potens locare nos per omne saeculum:*
Patrique Filioque summa gloria,
Tibique laus perennis alme Spiritus.

among the faithful. Let each act of ours give something of the fragrance of Christ; for this is the meaning of the roses that once concealed your charitable deeds. How blessed is the reward of charity; it can ensure us a place in heaven for ever. To the Father and to the Son be infinite glory; to You, loving Spirit, everlasting praise.

---

22 July. *St Mary Magdalen*
Hymn 125

Pater superni luminis,
Cum Magdalenam respicis,
Flammas amoris excitas
Geluque solvis pectoris.

5 *Amore currit saucia*
Pedes beatos ungere,
Lavare fletu, tergere
Comis et ore lambere.

Adstare non timet cruci,
10 *Sepulcro inhaeret anxia,*
Truces nec horret milites;
Pellit timorem caritas.

O vera, Christe, caritas,
Tu nostra purga crimina,
15 *Tu corda reple gratia,*
Tu redde caeli praemia.

Source and giver of heavenly light, with a glance You lit a fire of love in Magdalen and thawed the icy coldness of her heart. Wounded by love of You, she ran to anoint Your sacred feet, wash them with her tears, wipe them with her hair and kiss them with her lips. She was not afraid to stand by the Cross; in anguish of soul she stayed near Your tomb without any fear of the cruel soldiers, for love casts out fear. Lord Christ, love most true, cleanse us from our sins, fill our heart with grace and grant us the reward of heaven.

Hymn 126

Maria castis osculis
Lambit Dei vestigia,
Fletu rigat, tergit comis,
Detersa nardo perlinit.

Mary Magdalen kisses God's feet in holy love. She washes them with her tears, wipes them with her hair and, that done, anoints them with precious ointment.

---

7. *odor bonus;* cf. *Christi bonus odor sumus,* 2 Cor. 2, 15.

8. *rosis operta;* cf. lesson 5.

9. *caritas* links the two verses; the reward of charity, *in arce . . . saeculum,* leads to the doxology of the last two lines.

Notes on Hymn 125

Author. St Robert Bellarmine, cf. *137.*

Use. At Vespers.

1. The hymn is addressed to Christ as the *Pater* or source of all grace.

5. *saucia;* cf. *92, 5.*

9. *adstare;* cf. John 19, 25.

10. *inhaeret;* cf. Mt. 27, 61 and 28, 1.

12. *pellit. Perfecta caritas foras mittit timorem,* 1 John 4, 18.

Notes on Hymn 126

Author. Unknown. Ascribed without reason to St Gregory. It is taken from a hymn of twelve verses, *Magnum salutis gaudium,* for Palm Sunday, W *104.* The second verse in the Breviary is one of the usual doxologies.

The same poet seems to have written the hymn for Holy Thursday, *Hymnum dicamus Domino,* W *105,* whose fourth and fifth verses form the fifth Responsory of Matins for that day, *Judas mercator pessimus.*

Use. At Matins.

4. *detersa,* i.e. *vestigia* of line 2.

Hymn 127

Summi Parentis unice,
Vultu pio nos respice,
Vocans ad arcem gloriae
Cor Magdalenae poenitens.

5 Amissa drachma regio
Recondita est aerario,
Et gemma, deterso luto,
Nitore vincit sidera.

Jesu, medela vulnerum,
10 Spes una poenitentium,
Per Magdalenae lacrimas
Peccata nostra diluas.

Dei parens piissima,
Hevae nepotes flebiles
15 De mille vitae fluctibus
Salutis in portum vehas.

Uni Deo sit gloria
Pro multiformi gratia,
Peccantium qui crimina
20 Remittit et dat praemia.

Only-begotten of God most high, You called the penitent Magdalen to the glory of heaven; look on us too with kindly favour. The coin that was lost is put back in the royal treasury; the gem is wiped clean of all dirt and now surpasses the stars in brilliance. Jesus, healing for all man's wounds and the penitents' one hope, wash away our sins in token of Magdalen's tears. Most loving Mother of God, bring us, Eve's sorrowful children, through life's many storms to the haven of salvation. Glory to God, simple in essence and most varied in grace, Who pardons man his sin and rewards the just.

---

1 August. *St Peter in Chains*
Miris modis repente liber ferrea. Cf. 99, 1–5 and 11–15
Quodcunque in orbe nexibus revinxeris. Cf. 99, 6–15
Beate pastor, Petre, clemens accipe. Cf. 98, 9–12 and 21–4

6 August. *The Transfiguration of our Lord*

Hymn 128

Quicumque Christum quaeritis,
Oculos in altum tollite;
Illic licebit visere
Signum perennis gloriae.

5 Illustre quiddam cernimus,
Quod nesciat finem pati,

All you who look for Christ, lift up your eyes on high, for there you may see a sign of eternal glory. We see a brilliant Something that

Notes on Hymn 127

Author. St Odo of Cluny (879–942). He composed another hymn in honour of St Mary Magdalen, the *Lauda mater ecclesia,* which is still in use among the Dominicans.

Use. At Lauds.

5. The saint's soul is typified first by the drachma and then by the gem. Just as a coin has the image of the king on it, so the soul is made to the image of its King.

7. *deterso,* cf. *126, 4.*

8. *vincit;* cf. *120, 5.*

14. *nepotes,* descendants; *flebiles;* cf. *95, 27.*

Notes on Hymn 128

Author. Prudentius, cf. *13.* The hymn consists of lines 1–4, 37–44 and 85–88 of *Cathemerinon* XII, cf. *39.* Prudentius's hymn is about the Epiphany and has been applied in this selection to the Transfiguration. This feast was not added to the calendar until 1457 so that there are very few, if any, old hymns which have it as their subject. But after 1457 many hymns seem to have been written, and Paul IV removed some uncouth (*absonos*) ones which had been assigned to the feast (Batiffol: *History of the Breviary,* p. 194).

Use. At Vespers and Matins.

2. *in altum.* In the original this refers to the star that guided the kings to Bethlehem, as is clear from the next verse in Prudentius *Haec stella,* i.e. *45, 5–8.*

4. *signum,* sign, evidence, token, glimpse.

5. *illustre quiddam.* Prudentius applies to the star properties which belong to Christ as God. Here the properties are referred to His transfigured body.

Q

Sublime, celsum, interminum,
Antiquius caelo et chao.

Hic ille rex est gentium
10 *Populique rex Judaici,*
Promissus Abrahae patri
Ejusque in aevum semini.

Hunc et prophetis testibus
Isdemque signatoribus,
15 *Testator et Pater jubet*
Audire nos, et credere.

knows no end, exalted, most high and bound-less, older than the heavens or the primitive chaos. This is the king of the nations and king of the Jewish race, who was promised to our father Abraham and to his seed for ever. With the prophets as witnesses and signatories, the Testator and Father bids us hear Him, and believe.

Hymn 129

Lux alma, Jesu, mentium,
Dum corda nostra recreas,
Culpae fugas caliginem
Et nos reples dulcedine.

5 *Quam laetus est, quem visitas,*
Consors paternae dexterae,
Tu dulce lumen patriae,
Carnis negatum sensibus.

Splendor paternae gloriae,
10 *Incomprehensa caritas,*
Nobis amoris copiam
Largire per praesentiam.

Jesus, kindly light of our souls, when You bring new life to our hearts, You drive away sin's gloom and fill us with consolation. How happy the man that is host to You, for You are the companion of the Father at His right hand. You are the light that consoles heaven, but is unseen by man on earth. Radiance of the Father's splendour and love unfathomable, bestow on us by Your presence an abundance of love.

15 August. *The Assumption of the Blessed Virgin Mary*
Hymn 130

O prima, Virgo, prodita
E conditoris spiritu,
Praedestinata Altissimi
Gestare in alvo Filium;

5 *Tu perpes hostis femina*
Praenuntiata daemonis,
Oppleris una gratia
Intaminata origine.

Virgin, you were the first to receive the creator's breath of grace, destined as you were to carry in your womb the Son of the Most High. You, the woman of whom it was fore-told that she would be the devil's unrelenting enemy, were conceived without sin and, alone among mortals, filled completely with grace. You conceived the Life in your womb and by giving the divine Victim a body for His

9. *Hic ille.* As often, *ille* is little more than the definite article; This is the king. . . . The apparent emphasis on *hic* and *hunc* of line 13 is due to the omission of the intervening ten verses.

13–16. The Father gave testimony at our Lord's baptism and at the Transfiguration. Prudentius probably had the baptism in mind, for the baptism of Christ is one of the things commemorated on the feast of the Epiphany; cf. *44, 5*, note. *Testator* of the original would seem to mean one who gives testimony, though some think it refers to the Father giving the Son the nations for His inheritance, Ps. 2, 8. Here the whole verse is applied to the Transfiguration. This verse gives the only instance of an actual changing of the wording to adapt it for use on this feast.

Prophetis, Moses and Elias. *Signatoribus,* those who attest or confirm a will or statement, usually by seal or signature. The metaphor of lines 13–16 is taken from the formalities of a Roman will.

Notes on Hymn 129

Author. Whoever was the author of the *Dulcis Jesu memoria;* cf. intro. to *41–43.* The hymn is a cento of lines rather than of verses, but there is little point in giving a full list of the lines used. The lines of the first verse are, in order, line 1 of verse XI (of the composite text of the *Dulcis Jesu*), *42, 5, 43, 15* and *43, 16.* These lines were in turn altered by the revisers. The four-lined rhyme of the original has necessarily disappeared.

Use. At Lauds.

1. *Lux alma. Lux* is explained by line 3, and *alma* by line 4.

8. *sensibus;* here, apparently, of the bodily senses. For the word, cf. *71, 15,* note; for the idea, cf. 1 Cor. 2, 9.

9. This line was borrowed from *12, 1* by the centonist and kept by the revisers. Other Breviaries, for instance the Dominican, have *aeternae gloriae,* perhaps to avoid repeating *paternae.*

Notes on Hymn 130

Author. This and the next two hymns are by Vittorio Genovesi, S.J. As with other modern hymns, the studied effects of the Humanists replace the lyricism and inspiration of the older hymns. A verse translation of these hymns may be found in the Irish Ecclesiastical Record, November 1951.

Use. At first Vespers, the *Ave maris stella* being used at second Vespers.

1. *prodita,* come forth from; cf. *26, 7.*

5. *perpes,* unceasing, unrelenting; cf. *88, 2.* Cf. Gen. 3, 15 for lines 5–6.

7. *oppleris, oppleo,* 2, filled completely. *Una,* unique, alone; cf. *una, 98, 20* and *sola, 101,* 8 and 11.

8. *intaminata origine;* cf. *101,* 11–12.

Tu ventre Vitam concipis
10 Vitamque ab Adam perditam,
Diae litandae victimae
Carnem ministrans, integras.

Merces piaclo debita,
Devicta mors te deserit
15 Almique consors Filii
Ad astra ferris corpore.

Tanta coruscans gloria,
Natura cuncta extollitur,
In te vocata verticem
20 Decoris omnis tangere.

Ad nos triumphans exsules,
Regina, verte lumina,
Caeli ut beatam patriam
Te consequamur auspice.

sacrifice, restored to man the life that Adam had lost. Death, the penalty that sin must pay, enjoyed no victory over you and gave up its claim to you. Thereupon you hastened away bodily to heaven above to be your loving Son's companion. All nature, shining in the light of glory so great, is thereby raised up and is called in you to reach the summit of all grace and beauty. Queen, in your triumph, turn your eyes to us in our exile that through your protection we may come to heaven, our homeland and our bliss.

Hymn 131

Surge! Jam terris fera bruma cessit,
Ridet in pratis decus omne florum,
Alma quae Vitae genitrix fuisti,
    Surge, Maria!

5 Lilium fulgens velut in rubeto,
Mortis auctorem teris una, carpens
Sontibus fructum patribus negatum
    Arbore vitae.

Arca non putri fabricata ligno
10 Manna tu servas, fluit unde virtus
Ipsa qua surgent animata rursus
    Ossa sepulcris.

Praesidis mentis docilis ministra,
Haud caro tabo patitur resolvi;
15 Spiritus imo sine fine consors
    Tendit ad astra.

Rise up, for the cheerless winter is now over and the fields are gay with beautiful flowers of all kinds. Rise up, Mary, the loving mother of Life Himself. You alone, as radiant in your glory as a lily among brambles, trod under foot the author of death and plucked from the tree of life the fruit that was denied to our guilty parents. Like a casket of imperishable wood, you preserved the Manna from heaven, the source of the power by which dead bones, now given life again, rise from their tombs. Your body, ready servant of the will that ruled it, did not suffer being broken up by corruption, but instead made its way to heaven to be for

11. *diae=divae; litandae, lito,* 1, sacrifice under favourable auspices; bring an offering to, make atonement, purify. The line is dative after *ministrans.*

12. *integras, integro,* 1, make whole, renew, restore; it governs *vitam.*

13. *piaclo=piaculo.* The line explains *mors* of line 14.

16. *ferris,* active used as middle; took yourself, hastened.

22. *verte lumina* equals the *oculos . . . converte* of *33, 7.*

24. *consequamur,* arrive at, attain to—as often in the Collects; *te auspice,* with you as our leader, protector.

Notes on Hymn 131

Author. See *130.*

Metre. First Sapphic.

Use. At Matins.

1. *bruma,* winter; cf. *104, 21. Surge . . . et veni; jam enim hiems transiit,* Cant. 2, 10–11.

2. *ridet,* is smiling, glad—the subject being *decus omne. Flores apparuerunt in terra nostra,* Cant. 2, 12.

5. *in=inter; rubeto,* cf. *97, 5,* note.

6. *teris;* cf. *conteret caput tuum,* Gen. 3, 15 and *conteris, 101,* 10. *Una;* cf. *130, 7.*

7. *sontibus;* cf. *sontes, 101, 5.*

9. *arca;* box, casket, vessel. The reference is not to the Ark, but to the vessel of manna which was kept before the testimony, the Ark; Exod. 16: 33. The whole line is in apposition with *tu* of line 10.

13–16. The subject of the whole verse is *caro. Tabo,* from *tabum, -i,* corruption.

Surge! Dilecto pete nixa caelum,
Sume consertum diadema stellis
Teque natorum recinens beatam
20   *Excipe carmen.*

Laus sit excelsae Triadi perennis,
Quae tibi, Virgo, tribuit coronam
Atque reginam statuitque nostram
     Provida matrem.

ever your soul's partner. Rise up. Enter heaven on the arm of the Son you loved. Receive in heaven the diadem of stars and from earth the hymn that your children sing to honour you as blessed. Everlasting praise be to the most high Trinity that gave you, Virgin, a crown and with kindly providence made you our queen and mother.

Hymn 132

Solis, o Virgo, radiis amicta,
Bis caput senis redimita stellis,
Luna cui praebet pedibus scabellum,
     Inclita fulges.

5 *Mortis, inferni domitrixque noxae,*
Assides Christo studiosa nostri,
Teque reginam celebrat potentem
     Terra polusque.

Damna sed perstat soboli minari
10 *Creditae quondam tibi dirus anguis;*
Mater, huc clemens ades et maligni
     Contere collum.

Asseclas diae fidei tuere,
Transfugas adduc ad ovile sacrum,
15 *Quas diu gentes tegit umbra mortis*
     Undique coge.

Sontibus mitis veniam precare,
Adjuva flentes, inopes et aegros,
Spes mica cunctis per acuta vitae
20   *Certa salutis.*

You are radiant in your glory, Virgin Mary, with the sun as your mantle, a crown of twelve stars on your head and the moon as your footstool. Conqueror of death, hell and sin, you now sit at Christ's side, ever zealous on man's behalf, while earth and heaven sing the praises of their powerful queen. But the deadly serpent still persists in his threats to do hurt to the people once entrusted to your care. In your mercy, mother, come and help us, and crush the head of our deadly enemy. Keep guard over those that faithfully accept God's message, and lead back to His holy fold those that have strayed from it. Bring together from all parts of the world nations that sin's death has for so long hidden in its darkness. Graciously obtain pardon for sinners; bring help to the sorrowful, the poor and the afflicted. Be to all men in life's severe trials the light that promises sure hope of salvation.

18. *stellis;* cf. Apoc. 12, 1.

19–20. *te* with *beatam* and *recinens* with *carmen.*

24. *provida,* referring to *Triadi.*

Notes on Hymn 132

Author. See *130.*

Metre. First Sapphic.

Use. At Lauds.

1. *Solis.* For lines 1–3, cf. Apoc. 12, 1.

2. *redimita;* cf. *redimitur, 47,* 2.

6. *assides;* cf. *assidet, 47,* 25. In *47* the word is used of our Lady at home, ready to care for Jesus and Joseph; here of our Lady in heaven, ready to help us.

8. *polus;* cf. *11,* 10, note.

9. *damna,* object of *minari. Soboli* with *creditae quondam tibi.*

12. *contere;* cf. *131,* 6, note.

13. *asseclas,* followers of; cf. *84,* 7. *Diae;* cf. *130,* 11.

14. *transfugas,* deserters (from the faith).

19. *acuta vitae;* cf. *acuta rerum, 47,* 31.

The doxology which follows line 20 is the same as *131, 21–24.*

14 September. *The Exaltation of the Cross*
Vexilla regis prodeunt. Hymn 52
Pange lingua gloriosi lauream certaminis. Hymn 53
15 September. *The Seven Sorrows of the Blessed Virgin Mary*
Hymn 133

Jam toto subitus vesper eat polo
Et sol attonitum praecipitet diem,
Dum saevae recolo ludibrium necis
    Divinamque catastrophen.

5 *Spectatrix aderas supplicio parens,*
  Malis uda, gerens cor adamantinum,
  Natus funerea pendulus in cruce
    Altos dum gemitus dabat.

Pendens ante oculos Natus, atrocibus
10 *Sectus verberibus, Natus hiantibus*
  Fossus vulneribus, quot penetrantibus
    Te confixit aculeis.

Heu! sputa, alapae, verbera, vulnera,
Clavi, fel, aloe, spongia, lancea,
15 *Sitis, spina, cruor, quam varia pium*
    Cor pressere tyrannide.

Cunctis interea stat generosior
Virgo martyribus: prodigio novo,
In tantis moriens non moreris parens,
20   *Diris fixa doloribus.*

Sit summae Triadi gloria, laus, honor,
A qua suppliciter, sollicita prece,
Posco virginei roboris aemulas
    Vires rebus in asperis.

Let evening without warning darken the whole sky and the sun make the terrified light of day disappear in an instant, as I reflect on the mockery of that cruel death and the climax in the tragedy of God. You, His mother, were there to witness His sufferings, overwhelmed with grief but with a heart that nothing could daunt. Your Son meanwhile was hanging on the cross of death and in His agony uttered deep groans. All torn by the inhuman scourging and His body all broken with gaping wounds, your Son hung there before your eyes. How often did this sight pierce your heart right through. Spittle, blows, lashes, wounds, nails, gall, aloes, sponge, lance, thirst, thorns and blood—how each of these in its special way oppressed your loving heart. Yet through it all the Virgin stands there, more courageous than any martyr; for though each suffering of His was a death-stroke to you, yet by a unique grace you, His mother, did not die but were transfixed in soul by each cruel sorrow. To the most high Trinity be glory, praise and honour, and with earnest and fervent prayer I ask to be given in life's calamities strength like to the Virgin's constancy.

Notes on Hymn 133

Author. Callisto Palumbella, Servite, eighteenth century; the next two hymns are also said to be his.

Metre. Second Asclepiad.

Use. At Vespers. This hymn was once assigned to Matins, for which the mention of *vesper* makes it unsuited.

1. The mention of evening suits Vespers and also suggests the sudden darkness (cf. *praecipitet* of the next line) which covered the whole earth at the Crucifixion. *Polo;* cf. *132*, 8.

2. *Praecipitet,* throw headlong; or, with the idea of speed, dispatch, hasten.

4. *Catastrophen,* a Latinised form of the Greek, signifies the turning point of an action or plot in tragic drama; the tragedy which involved God, the divine tragedy.

5. *Parens;* You, His mother; or, according to others, *parens* is vocative. *Supplicio,* cf. *109,* 15, as explained by line 7.

6. *malis uda;* your eyes wet with tears because of His sufferings, *malis;* cf. *109,* 2, note. *Gerens,* with a heart. . . .

13. For the first such list of the incidents of the Passion, cf. *53,* 19.

15. *quam* with *pressere* (= *presserunt*), how they weighed on, oppressed; *varia* with *tyrannide.*

17. *generosior,* better-born and *therefore* more courageous than all the martyrs; cf. *71,* 3, note. This verse would have pleased St Ambrose more than the second verse; cf. *109,* 2, note.

18. *prodigio novo,* by a new miracle, unique grace. The martyrs suffered and died, while Mary suffered much more intensely and yet lived.

23. *aemulas,* cf. *93,* 36 and *122,* 23.

Hymn 134

O quot undis lacrimarum, quo dolore volvitur,
Luctuosa de cruento dum revulsum stipite
Cernit ulnis incubantem virgo mater filium.

Os suave, mite pectus et latus dulcissimum
5 *Dexteramque vulneratam et sinistram sauciam*
Et rubras cruore plantas aegra tingit lacrimis.

Centiesque milliesque stringit arctis nexibus
Pectus illud et lacertos, illa figit vulnera:
Sicque tota colliquescit in doloris osculis.

10 *Eia mater obsecramus per tuas has lacrimas*
Filiique triste funus vulnerumque purpuram,
Hunc tui cordis dolorem conde nostris cordibus.

Esto Patri Filioque et coaevo Flamini,
Esto summae Trinitati sempiterna gloria
15 *Et perennis laus honorque hoc et omni saeculo.*

What a flood of tears flowed from the eyes of the Virgin Mother, what a weight of sorrow crushed her heart as she mournfully looks upon her Son after He had been taken from the tree of His passion and was lying in her arms. In her desolation she bathes with her tears His beautiful face, His gentle breast, His side that is man's comfort, His wounded hands and His feet all red with blood. Again and again she holds tightly to herself His breast and arms, and has eyes for nothing but His wounds. And in this state of mind she wholly melts away in the kisses of a bereaved mother. Therefore we ask you, Mother, by these your tears, by your Son's cruel death and by the blood of His wounds, plant well in our hearts the grief that afflicted yours. To the Father and the Son and the co-eternal Spirit, to the most high God in three Persons, be everlasting glory, eternal praise and honour in this and in every age.

Hymn 135

Summae Deus clementiae
Septem dolores Virginis
Plagasque Jesu Filii
Fac rite nos revolvere.

5 *Nobis salutem conferant*
Deiparae tot lacrimae,
Quibus lavare sufficis
Totius orbis crimina.

Sit quinque Jesu vulnerum
10 *Amara contemplatio,*
Sint et dolores Virginis
Aeterna cunctis gaudia.

God of infinite mercy, grant that we reflect with due devotion on the seven sorrows of the Virgin and on the wounds of her Son, Jesus. May the many tears of God's mother win us salvation, for with them You can wash away the sins of the world. May the bitter contemplation of Jesus' wounds and the Virgin's sorrows be to all men the source of eternal joys.

Notes on Hymn 134

Author. As *133*.

Metre. Trochaic tetrameter.

Use. At Matins, though it was formerly the Vesper hymn.

1. *volvitur.* The subject of this and *cernit* is *virgo mater.*

2. *stipite;* cf. *53*, 18, but here it *is* used as an ablative.

4. *dulcissimum.* Our Lord's side is man's comfort and an object of his love because of all that the piercing of the side means to him.

5. *vulneratam* and *sauciam* have the same meaning.

6. *rubras . . . plantas,* feet red with blood; *aegra,* in her desolation.

8. *figit* is probably used here in its classical meaning of regarding earnestly and = *figit oculos in illa vulnera,* Byrnes. But B has 'imprints on herself these wounds'.

9. *tota colliquescit,* wholly melts away. *Colliquescere,* a rare word, may have been suggested by *tamquam cera liquescens* of Ps. 21, 15.

12. *conde,* plant well; cf. *fige plagas, 109, 32.*

Notes on Hymn 135

Author. As *133*.

Use. At Lauds.

7. *quibus,* sc. *lacrimis; sufficis,* sc. *Deus* of line 1; *lavare,* 'by accepting Mary's pain vicariously for us', Byrnes.

10. *amara,* bitter, sorrowful; not, unfavourable, as in *109, 44.*

Sequence: Stabat mater dolorosa. 109

29 September. *Dedication of St Michael*
Te splendor et virtus Patris. 111
Christe, sanctorum decus angelorum. 112

2 October. *The Guardian Angels*

Hymn 136

Custodes hominum psallimus angelos,
Naturae fragili quos Pater addidit
Caelestis comites, insidiantibus
Ne succumberet hostibus.

5 *Nam, quod corruerit proditor angelus,*
Concessis merito pulsus honoribus,
Ardens invidia pellere nititur
Quos caelo Deus advocat.

Huc custos igitur pervigil advola,
10 *Avertens patria de tibi credita*
Tam morbos animi quam requiescere
Quidquid non sinit incolas.

Sanctae sit Triadi laus pia jugiter,
Cujus perpetuo numine machina
15 *Triplex haec regitur, cujus in omnia*
Regnat gloria saecula.

We sing of the angels, guardians of men, that the heavenly Father has given as an additional help to our weak nature that it may not yield to enemies ever ready to attack. For since the traitor angel fell headlong to his destruction and was rightly deprived of the honours that once were his, he has been on fire with envy and endeavouring to hurl to their destruction those that God is inviting to heaven. Therefore fly to us here, ever-watchful guardian, and ward off from the land entrusted to your care all spiritual illness and everything that denies its people peace of soul. Loving praise be for ever given to the holy Trinity, whose power rules the threefold fabric of the world and whose glory and kingdom lasts for all eternity.

Hymn 137

Aeterne rector siderum
Qui, quidquid est, potentia
Magna creasti nec regis
Minore providentia,

5 *Adesto supplicantium*
Tibi reorum coetui,
Lucisque sub crepusculum
Lucem novam da mentibus:

Eternal ruler of the stars, Who with mighty power created and with a no less mighty providence rules all that is, listen to us sinners, here gathered together, as we pray to You. The light of day is now fading; grant new light to

Notes on Hymn 136

Author. Unknown. Roth in his *Lat. Hymnen* (1887) says that this hymn is in MSS 852 of the Darmstadt Library, in a hand of the beginning of the sixteenth century; this would make the usual ascription to St Robert Bellarmine impossible. Cf. Julian, 1558, and the introduction to the next hymn.

Use. At Vespers and Matins.

5. *Nam* introduces the reason for verse 1, especially for the word *insidiantibus. Quod,* because, since.

10. *patria.* That angels guard individual nations and communities is implied in Exod. 23, 20 and Dan. 10, 13. That they guard individuals is clear from Mt. 18, 10. *Avertens.* 'The primary office of the angel guardian is to preserve our souls from sin; the secondary office is to preserve us from lesser evils (cf. verses 3 to 5 of the next hymn)', Byrnes.

14. *numine,* will, power, rule—as explained in the first verse of the next hymn; *machina triplex,* cf. 63, 9, note.

Notes on Hymn 137

Author. Unknown. Under the heading *Orbis patrator optime* (the first line of the unrevised text) Julian says 'Cardinal Bellarmine?', but under *Aeterne rector siderum* gives Bellarmine as the author without hesitation. Daniel IV, p. 306, quotes one editor as saying that the author is unknown and another as claiming Bellarmine. B and Mulcahy are in favour of Bellarmine and Byrnes says it is ascribed to that saint. But the Rev. J. Brodrick, S.J., the biographer of the saint, in a letter to the author said: 'I remember going into this question very carefully at the time of writing his life and deciding that he was not the author of any hymns except the one to St Mary Magdalen', i.e. *125.*

Use. At Lauds.

4. The collect of the day also refers to God's *ineffabili providentia.* The reviser's first line, substituting stars for the world, is singularly inept.

7. *crepusculum,* twilight, dusk, and opposed to *diluculum,* dawn; cf. 12, 26–28. *Crepusculum* is not a

Tuusque nobis Angelus
10 Electus ad custodiam,
Hic adsit, a contagio
Ut criminum nos protegat.

Nobis draconis aemuli
Versutias exterminet,
15 Ne rete fraudulentiae
Incauta nectat pectora.

Metum repellat hostium
Nostris procul de finibus,
Pacem procuret civium
20 Fugetque pestilentiam.

our souls. May Your angel that was chosen as our guardian, be present here to protect us from sin's contamination. May he keep far from us the wily and envious devil that our unwary hearts be not ensnared in the net of his deceitfulness. May he take from our land all fear of invasion, be the cause of peace among its inhabitants and banish plague and disease.

---

7 October. *The Most Holy Rosary*
Hymn 138

Caelestis aulae nuntius,
Arcana pandens numinis,
Plenam salutat gratia
Dei parentem virginem.

5 Virgo propinquam sanguine
Matrem Joannis visitat,
Qui clausus alvo gestiens
Adesse Christum nuntiat.

Verbum quod ante saecula
10 E mente Patris prodiit,
E matris alvo virginis
Mortalis infans nascitur.

Templo puellus sistitur
Legique paret legifer;
15 Hic se redemptor paupere
Pretio redemptus immolat.

Quem jam dolebat perditum
Mox laeta mater invenit
Ignota doctis mentibus
20 Edisserentem Filium.

A messenger of the heavenly court reveals God's hidden plan and addresses the Virgin that is to be God's mother with the words 'full of grace'. The Virgin visits her relative, the Baptist's mother; and he, leaping with joy in his mother's womb announces Christ's presence. The Word that proceeded from the Father's thought before time began, is now born from the Virgin Mother's womb—a mortal, wordless babe. As a little child He is presented in the temple, the Lawgiver obeying His law. Here the Redeemer offers Himself and is redeemed at a pauper's price. His mother grieves over the loss of her Son, but to her joy soon finds Him instructing the ignorance of the Rabbis.

synonym of *diluculum,* though it has to be interpreted here as if it were. The hymn is misplaced, just as *133* once was, and, like *133,* ought to have been put at Vespers.

11. *hic,* adverb; *contagio,* cf. 7, 15, note.

13. *aemuli,* envious; for a similar use, cf. *73,* 6 and

contrast *133,* 24, note.

18. *finibus;* for a similar prayer, cf. *152,* 22. 'This stanza cites what has been called "the trinity of evil": invasion from without, discord from within, and the terrible curse of plague', Byrnes.

Notes on Hymn 138

Author. Ascribed to Augustine Ricchini, O.P. (1695–1779).

Use. At first Vespers. Its five verses tell in order of the five Joyful Mysteries of the Rosary.

7. *qui clausus,* i.e. t he Baptist; cf. *38,* 19–20 an *117,* 13–14.

12. *mortalis* answering *ante saecula* and *infans,* not able to speak, wordless, answering *Verbum.*

Hymn 139

In monte olivis consito
Redemptor orans procidit,
Maeret, pavescit, deficit,
Sudore manans sanguinis.

5 A proditore traditus
Raptatur in poenas Deus
Durisque vinctus nexibus
Flagris cruentis caeditur.

Intexta acutis sentibus
10 Corona contumeliae
Squalenti amictum purpura
Regem coronat gloriae.

Molis crucem ter arduae
Sudans, anhelans, concidens,
15 Ad montis usque verticem
Gestare vi compellitur.

Confixus atro stipite
Inter scelestos innocens,
Orando pro tortoribus
20 Exsanguis efflat spiritum.

As the Redeemer prays on the olive-covered hill, He falls prostrate and becomes sad, fearful and faint as blood, like a sweat, comes out of Him. God is handed over by the traitor, hurried off to His passion, bound with rough cords and torn with cruel scourges. A crown of mockery, woven of sharp thorns, is put on the head of the King of glory—His regal attire a filthy purple robe. Sweating, gasping and stumbling on the way, He is brutally forced to carry to Calvary's summit a cross that is too heavy for His weakness. The Holy One is fastened to the shameful cross, a criminal on either side of Him. At last, drained of blood and praying for those that caused His death, He breathes out His last breath.

Hymn 140

Jam morte victor obruta
Ab inferis Christus redit
Fractisque culpae vinculis
Caeli recludit limina.

5 Visus satis mortalibus
Ascendit ad caelestia
Dextraeque Patris assidet
Consors paternae gloriae.

Quem jam suis promiserat,
10 Sanctum daturus Spiritum,
Linguis amoris igneis
Maestis alumnis impluit.

Death now overcome, Christ returns from hell and, breaking the bonds of sin, opens the gate of heaven. After He had been seen by men for a time long enough for His purpose, He ascends to heaven and sits at the Father's right hand, sharing His glory. And when He is ready to give the holy Spirit that He had promised to His own, He sends the Spirit on His sorrowing disciples in fiery tongues of love. The Virgin,

Notes on Hymn 139

Author. Ascribed to Augustine Ricchini, O.P.

Use. At Matins. Its subject is the five Sorrowful Mysteries.

3. *maeret,* cf. *coepit,* ... *maestus esse,* Mt. 26, 37; *pavescit,* cf. *coepit pavere,* Mk. 14, 33; *deficit,* grows faint, and cf. *sensus deficit, 71,* 11.

4. *manans,* dripping with; cf. Lk. 22, 44.

9. *sentibus, sentis,* thorn, thorn-bush.

13. *crucem,* after *gestare; ter arduae,* of exceeding heavy weight; cf. *ter beata, 151, 9.*

Notes on Hymn 140

Author. Augustine Ricchini, O.P.

Use. At Lauds. Its theme is the Glorious Mysteries.

5. *Visus satis,* having appeared for a sufficient time, i.e. to convince the Apostles that He had really risen from the dead and to instruct them about His Kingdom; cf. Acts 1, 3 and lesson 4 of the Ascension.

10. *daturus,* referring to Christ, the subject of this verse.

12. *Impluit,* rains down upon, i.e. pours forth, sends down.

R

Soluta carnis pondere
Ad astra Virgo tollitur,
15 Excepta caeli jubilo
Et angelorum canticis.

Bis sena cingunt sidera
Almae parentis verticem;
Throno propinqua Filii
20 Cunctis creatis imperat.

freed from the burden of the flesh, is taken up
to heaven, which welcomes her with shouts of
joy and angelic song. Twelve stars are the
loving mother's crown as, next to her Son's
throne, she reigns as the Queen of all creation.

Hymn 141

Te gestientem gaudiis,
Te sauciam doloribus,
Te jugi amictam gloria,
O virgo mater pangimus.

5 Ave redundans gaudio,
Dum concipis, dum visitas,
Et edis, offers, invenis
Mater beata Filium.

Ave dolens et intimo
10 In corde agonem, verbera
Spinas crucemque Filii
Perpessa, princeps martyrum.

Ave in triumphis Filii,
In ignibus Paracliti,
15 In regni honore et lumine,
Regina fulgens gloria.

Venite gentes, carpite
Ex his rosas mysteriis,
Et pulchri amoris inclitae
20 Matri coronas nectite.

Virgin mother, we sing of the times when
joy filled your soul or sorrow wounded your
heart, and of the eternity that robes you with
glory. Hail, blessed mother; your joy knew no
bounds when you conceived in your womb,
visited Elizabeth, gave birth to your Son,
offered Him in the temple and found Him
when lost. Hail, queen of martyrs; full of
sorrow, you suffered in your inmost heart all
the anguish of the agony in the garden, the
scourging, the crowning with thorns and your
Son's cross. Hail, queen of shining glory, in
your Son's triumphs, in the fires of Pentecost
and in the honour and light of the heavenly
kingdom. Come, nations of the world, gather
flowers from this rose-garden of mysteries, and
weave rose-garlands for her who gave birth to
all noble love.

---

11 October. The Motherhood of our Lady

Hymn 142

Caelo redemptor praetulit
Felicis alvum virginis

The Redeemer preferred to heaven the
favoured Virgin's womb, where He took a

15. *excepta,* received, welcomed.   17. *bis sena,* cf. *132, 2.*

Notes on Hymn 141

Author. According to Byrnes, himself a Dominican, this hymn is to be ascribed to Eustace Sirena, O.P. (died 1769). B and others ascribe it to Ricchini, to whom the three preceding hymns are also ascribed.

Use. At second Vespers. Its subject is the Rosary and the fifteen mysteries, and so is a summary of *138–40* and of the antiphons of this office.

1–4. An address to our Lady under her title of the Rosary, the first three lines mentioning in turn the Joyful, Sorrowful and Glorious Mysteries. *Jugi,* everlasting, eternal.

5–8. The Joyful Mysteries, each being indicated by the verbs *concipis* etc. *Edis,* from *edere,* give birth. *Filium* is the object of all the verbs except *visitas.*

9–12. The Sorrowful Mysteries, the fourth and fifth being indicated by *crucem Filii. Princeps Martyrum;* cf. *133,* 17–20.

13–16. The Glorious Mysteries, *triumphis* indicating the first two.

17–20. The Rosary itself. *Rosas,* from the Rosary as from a rose-garden, *(rosarium). Et . . . nectite;* and weave garlands of roses for the glorious mother of fair love. Cf. *Ego mater pulchrae dilectionis,* Ecclus. 24, 24.

Notes on Hymn 142

Author. Unknown. According to Mulcahy, it is an 'Old Ambrosian hymn', while Julian, p. 1612, says it is 'presumably by Benedict XIV' on the grounds that it is printed in the *Opera Omnia* of that pope.

The case is the same as that of *97.* Like the office of the Purity of the Blessed Virgin, that of the Motherhood was approved by Benedict XIV for use in Portugal. It was afterwards in use in various local

Ubi futura victima
Mortale corpus induit.

5 *Haec virgo nobis edidit*
Nostrae salutis auspicem,
Qui nos redemit sanguine
Poenas crucemque pertulit.

Spes laeta nostro e pectore
10 *Pellat timores anxios;*
Haec quippe nostras lacrimas
Precesque defert Filio.

Voces parentis excipit
Votisque Natus annuit;
15 *Hanc quisque semper diligat*
Rebusque in arctis invocet.

Sit Trinitati gloria,
Quae matris intactum sinum
Ditavit almo germine;
20 *Laus sit per omne saeculum.*

human body for the sacrifice He was to offer. This Virgin gave birth to the source of our salvation; and He redeemed us by His blood, enduring sufferings and the cross. May she, the hope that brings man joy, cast fear and care from our souls; may she offer to her Son our sorrow and our prayers. The Son listens to His mother's words and grants her wishes; may all men ever love this mother and ask her help in all their trials. Glory be to God in three Persons, Who enriched with loving fruit the mother's virginal womb. Praise be to Him for ever.

Hymn 143

Te mater alma numinis
Oramus omnes supplices
A fraude nos ut daemonis
Tua sub umbra protegas.

5 *Ob perditum nostrum genus*
Primi parentis crimine,
Ad inclitum matris decus
Te rex supremus extulit.

Clementer ergo prospice
10 *Lapsis Adami posteris;*
A te rogatus Filius
Deponat iram vindicem.

Loving mother of God, we ask you in humble prayer to protect us and give us shelter from the devil's wily attacks. For the sake of our race that our first parent's sin brought to dishonour, the king of heaven raised you up to the noble dignity of being His mother. Therefore show your loving care to Adam's fallen children, and may your Son, at your request, lay aside His avenging anger.

breviaries and its use was extended to the whole Church in 1931.

Use. At Matins.

4. *mortale corpus,* man's flesh; cf. *79, 6,* note.

Each verse, naturally, mentions the mother and the Son—the Son being the subject of the first verse and of the beginning of the fourth, and the mother of the second and third verses.

6. *auspicem,* author, founder, beginning; and cf. *130, 24.*

9. *Spes laeta;* let joyous hope—referring back to the last verse and forward to line 11. But some think it is personified, being the equivalent of *causa nostrae laetitiae* of the Litany. *Haec* in line 11 either refers to *Haec virgo* of line 5 or to *spes* in 9, if the latter be personified. A reference to line 9 is more natural.

18. *quae, sc. Trinitas.*

Notes on Hymn 143

Author. Unknown. See preceding hymn.
Use. At Lauds.

5. For the sake of our race, disgraced by. . . .

15 October. *St Teresa of Avila*
Hymn 144

Regis superni nuntia
Domum paternam deseris,
Terris Teresa barbaris
Christum datura aut sanguinem.

5 *Sed te manet suavior*
Mors, poena poscit dulcior;
Divini amoris cuspide
In vulnus icta concides.

O caritatis victima,
10 *Tu corda nostra concrema*
Tibique gentes creditas
Averni ab igne libera.

You leave your father's house, Teresa, as a herald of the heavenly king, to bring to pagan lands the gift of Christ or of your life. But a less cruel death is in store for you and a more exquisite pain marks you as its victim; for death will lay you low when the shaft of God's love has pierced and wounded you. Victim of love, set our hearts on fire with love and save from hell's fire the nations that have been entrusted to you.

Hymn 145

Haec est dies qua candidae
Instar columbae caelitum
Ad sacra templa spiritus
Se transtulit Teresiae,

5 *Sponsique voces audiit,*
'Veni soror de vertice
Carmeli ad Agni nuptias,
Veni ad coronam gloriae'.

Te, sponse Jesu, virginum
10 *Beati adorent ordines*
Et nuptiali cantico
Laudent per omne saeculum.

This is the day when Teresa's soul went in the form of a white dove to the sacred temples of heaven; this the day when it heard the Bridegroom's summons: 'Come, sister, from Carmel's height to the nuptial of the Lamb. Come, receive your crown of glory.' May the choir of virgins adore You, Jesus, the Bridegroom, and praise You for ever in their own song of love.

Notes on Hymn 144

Author. Urban VIII.

Use. At Vespers and Matins.

2–3. Teresa, aged seven, and her little brother set out to convert the Moors, *barbaris,* or to die at their hands. An unromantic uncle brought the children back; cf. lesson 4.

5–6. *mors* and *poena* are explained by the next two lines, *suavior* and *dulcior* by comparison with the opening lines.

5–8. *Manet* et *concides,* because the incident is viewed from Teresa's seventh year. The reference is to the transverberation, as it is called, of the Saint's heart. '*Tanto autem divini amoris incendio cor ejus conflagravit, ut merito viderit Angelum ignito jaculo sibi praecordia transverberantem',* lesson 5.

10. *concrema,* inflame, fire with love; but cf. *35,* 6, note.

Notes on Hymn 145

Author. Urban VIII.

Use. At Lauds.

2. *instar,* after the fashion of, like.

6. *vertice Carmeli;* because the Carmelite order was founded on Mount Carmel in 1156, and also because the individual convents are called Carmel and in them the nuns aspire to the heights of holiness from which God calls them, as He did St Teresa, to heaven.

8. *coronam; veni . . . sponsa mea . . . veni, coronaberis,* Cant. 4, 8; and cf. *90,* 1.

9. Some punctuate this line with a comma after *virginum* instead of after *Jesu.*

10. *ordines;* cf. *choreis virginum, 90,* 6.

11. *cantico;* cf. Apoc. 14, 3–5 and *90,* 9–12.

20 October. *St John of Kenty* (Cantius)
Hymn 146

Gentis Polonae gloria
Clerique splendor nobilis,
Decus Lycaei et patriae
Pater, Joannes inclite,

5 *Legem superni numinis*
Doces magister, et facis.
Nil scire prodest; sedulo
Legem nitamur exsequi.

Apostolorum limina
10 *Pedes viator visitas;*
Ad patriam ad quam tendimus
Gressus viamque dirige.

Urbem petis Jerusalem,
Signata sacro sanguine
15 *Christi colis vestigia*
Rigasque fusis fletibus.

Acerba Christi vulnera,
Haerete nostris cordibus
Ut cogitemus consequi
20 *Redemptionis pretium.*

Most famous and renowned John, Poland's glory, the priesthood's shining honour, distinguished son of the University of Cracow and father of the fatherland, you taught and observed the law of the God of heaven. Merely to know the law is no use; so let us try to obey it faithfully. You went on foot to visit the Apostles' tombs; so guide our footsteps and show us the way as we journey to our Father's land. You visited Jerusalem, honoured the road, once stained with holy blood, where Christ had walked, and washed it with tears of devotion. Bitter wounds of Christ, take deep root in our hearts that our thoughts be directed to appreciating how much our redemption cost Him.

Hymn 147

Corpus domas jejuniis,
Caedis cruento verbere,
Ut castra poenitentium
Miles sequaris innocens.

5 *Sequamur et nos sedulo*
Gressus parentis optimi;
Sequamur ut licentiam
Carnis refraenat spiritus.

Rigente bruma, providum
10 *Praebes amictum pauperi,*

You tamed your body with fasting and scourged it unto blood that, though of blameless life, you might be a follower in the army of penitents. Let us then be earnest followers of our good father, John, that our soul may curb the wanton licence of the flesh. In the depth of winter your loving care found clothing

Notes on Hymn 146

Author. Unknown, eighteenth century. This hymn, *147* and *148* are probably divisions of one long hymn.

Use. At Vespers.

3. *Lycaei,* i.e. of the University of Cracow, where St John was a professor of theology.

6. *doces . . . facis;* cf. *simul docens scilicet et faciens,* lesson 4. The fact that the Saint put his faith and his theological learning into practice is emphasized in the lessons of the office and in the text of the Mass. One practical manifestation, namely through works of bodily mercy, is also emphasized in the lessons and in *147* and *148*. The two things are connected in the Introit by an application of Ecclus. 18, 13: *Qui misericordiam habet, docet et erudit quasi pastor gregem suum.*

7. *nil scire prodest;* of no avail at all is knowledge (without putting it into practice). *Quid proderit, si fidem quis dicat se habere, opera autem non habeat,* James 2, 14—from the epistle of the Mass.

9. *limina.* The saint made four pilgrimages to Rome and one to Jerusalem. Those to Rome suggest the prayer of lines 11–12, and that to Jerusalem the prayer of 17–20.

10. *pedes, -itis,* adj., on foot.

18. *haerete,* take root in, stay deep within.

19. *cogitemus,* have in mind; cf. *nil perenne cogitat, 22,* 11. *Consequi,* probably in the sense of understand, appreciate. But others take it in the more usual sense of gaining, attaining, like *consequamur* in *130,* 24 and often in the Collects. *Consequi* is the object of *cogitemus.*

Notes on Hymn 147

Author. Unknown; cf. *146*.

Use. At Matins.

8. *refraenet;* cf. *refraenans, 18,* 5.

9. *rigente bruma,* in the depth of winter; *bruma,* cf. *103,* 21. For the incident, cf. lesson 5.

Sitim famemque egentium
Esca potuque sublevas.

O qui negasti nemini
Opem roganti, patrium
15 *Regnum tuere, postulant*
Cives Poloni et exteri.

Sit laus Patri, sit Filio
Tibique sancte Spiritus;
Preces Joannis impetrent
20 *Beata nobis gaudia.*

for the poor and relieved with food and drink the hunger and thirst of those in need. You never refused anyone who asked for help; hear now the prayer of Poland and Christendom: 'Protect your native land'. Praise to the Father, to the Son and to You, holy Spirit; may the prayers of John obtain for us the happiness of heaven.

Hymn 148

Te deprecante, corporum
Lues recedit, improbi
Morbi fugantur, pristina
Redeunt salutis munera.

5 *Phthisi febrique et ulcere*
Diram redactos ad necem,
Sacratas morti victimas,
Ejus rapis e faucibus.

Te deprecante, tumido
10 *Merces abactae flumine,*
Tractae Dei potentia
Sursum fluunt retrogradae.

Cum tanta possis, sedibus
Caeli locatus, poscimus;
15 *Responde votis supplicum*
Et invocatus subveni.

O una semper Trinitas,
O trina semper Unitas,
Da, supplicante Cantio,
20 *Aeterna nobis praemia.*

Through your intercession, pestilence departed, terrible plagues were put to flight and the former blessing of health returned. You snatched from the jaws of death those that were doomed to be its victims, since consumption, fever or ulcers had brought them near to death. Through your intercession, the merchandise that was carried away on the swollen river floats back upstream by God's mighty power, and finds its former home. Since your power is so great, we ask you, now enthroned in heaven, to listen to your suppliants' prayers and to come to their aid when they call on you. Trinity forever One and Unity forever Three, grant us, through John's prayers, the reward of eternity.

13. *negasti nemini;* cf. lesson 5.

17–20. The doxology of *146* is found elsewhere in the Breviary, e.g. in *51*, but this hymn and the next have each their own doxology. The one here is a variant of *113*, 17–20.

Notes on Hymn 148

Author. Unknown; cf. *146*.

Use. At Lauds.

2. *lues*, pestilence; *improbi morbi*, terrible plagues.

5–7 are the object of *rapis*, 7 being in apposition with 5 and 6. *Redactos*, brought to death by consumption . . .; *sacratos*, given over to, doomed to. *Ejus* in line 8 refers to *morti* of 7.

24 October. *St Raphael, Archangel*
Christe sanctorum decus angelorum. Hymn *112*
Placare Christe servulis. Hymn *152b*
Last Sunday in October. *Christ the King*

Hymn 149

Te saeculorum principem,
Te, Christe, regem gentium,
Te mentium, te cordium
Unum fatemur arbitrum.

5 *Scelesta turba clamitat,*
 'Regnare Christum nolumus';
 Te nos ovantes omnium
 Regem supremum dicimus.

 O Christe, princeps pacifer,
10 *Mentes rebelles subjice*
 Tuoque amore devios
 Ovile in unum congrega.

 Ad hoc cruenta ab arbore
 Pendes apertis brachiis
15 *Diraque fossum cuspide*
 Cor igne flagrans exhibes.

 Ad hoc in aris abderis
 Vini dapisque imagine,
 Fundens salutem filiis
20 *Transverberato pectore.*

 Te nationum praesides
 Honore tollant publico,
 Colant magistri, judices,
 Leges et artes exprimant.

25 *Submissa regum fulgeant*
 Tibi dicata insignia
 Mitique sceptro patriam
 Domosque subde civium.

We acknowledge You, Christ, to be lord of the ages, king of the nations and only master of man's soul and heart. The wicked mob screams out, 'We don't want Christ as king', while we, with shouts of joy, hail You as the world's supreme king. Christ, peace-bringing prince, subject rebellious souls to Your rule, and in Your love lead back to the one fold those that have strayed from it. For this, with arms outstretched, You hung, bleeding, on the cross, and the cruel spear that pierced You, showed man a heart burning with love. For this, You are hidden on our altars under the form of bread and wine, and pour out on Your children from Your pierced side the grace of salvation. May the rulers of the world publicly honour and extol You; may teachers and judges reverence You, may the laws express Your order and the arts reflect Your beauty. May kings find renown in their submission and dedication to You. Bring under Your gentle rule our country and our homes.

Notes on Hymn 149

Author. Unknown.

Use. At Vespers.

6. *nolumus;* cf. *nolumus hunc regnare super nos*, Lk. 19, 14; also John 19, 15.

11. Some put a comma after *devios* and translate: those who have strayed from your love; others translate: and in your love bring back.

15. *fossum*, agreeing with *cor* in line 16.

22. *tollant*, exalt, extol. Understand *te* with *colant* and *exprimant*.

Hymn 150

Aeterna imago Altissimi,
Lumen, Deus, de lumine,
Tibi, redemptor, gloria,
Honor, potestas regia.

5 Tu solus ante saecula
Spes atque centrum temporum,
Cui jure sceptrum gentium
Pater supremum credidit.

Tu flos pudicae virginis,
10 Nostrae caput propaginis,
Lapis caducus vertice
Ac mole terras occupans.

Diro tyranno subdita,
Damnata stirps mortalium,
15 Per te refregit vincula
Sibique caelum vindicat.

Doctor, sacerdos, legifer
Praefers notatum sanguine
In veste, 'Princeps principum
20 Regumque rex altissimus'.

Tibi volentes subdimur
Qui jure cunctis imperas;
Haec civium beatitas
Tuis subesse legibus.

Eternal image of God most high, Yourself God and light of light, to You, our redeemer, be glory, honour and kingly power. Before time began You were its only hope and goal, and to You the Father entrusted as Your right absolute dominion over the peoples. You are the flower that came from the pure virgin, the head of our race and the stone that fell from the mountain and filled the earth with its mighty mass. Through You the condemned race of men, subject to a cruel tyrant, broke the chains that bound it and claimed heaven for its own. You, man's teacher, priest and lawgiver, display on Your garment the title written in blood: 'Prince of Princes and king of kings, most high'. To You, Who by right claim rule over all men, we willingly submit ourselves; to be subject to Your laws means happiness for a country and its people.

Hymn 151

Vexilla Christus inclita
Late triumphans explicat;
Gentes adeste supplices
Regique regum plaudite.

5 Non ille regna cladibus,
Non vi metuque subdidit;
Alto levatus stipite,
Amore traxit omnia.

Christ triumphantly unfurls His glorious banners everywhere; come, nations of the world, and on bended knee acclaim the King of kings. Not by bloodshed did He bring the peoples under His rule, not by force or fear; but by love, as He hung aloft on the cross, did He draw all things to Himself. How great is the

Notes on Hymn 150

Author. Unknown.
Use. At Matins.

1. *imago;* cf. *12,* 1–4; also *imago Dei invisibilis,* Col. 1, 15.

5. *solus,* sc. *eras.*

8. *supremum,* with *sceptrum,* the supreme rule. Were this an old hymn, the MSS would almost certainly vary between *supremum* and *supremus. Credidit,* entrusted; cf. *creditas, 144,* 11.

9. *flos,* from Is. 11, 1; cf. *97,* 7, note.

10. *caput;* cf. *primogenitus omnis creaturae,* Col. 1, 15.

11. *lapis;* cf. Dan. 2, 29–45 and *93,* 27. The reference here is to Christ in His Church which is the kingdom that 'shall consume all these kingdoms and itself shall stand forever', Dan. 2, 44.

18–20. Cf. *Et vestitus erat veste aspersa sanguine . . . Et habet in vestimento et in femore suo scriptum: Rex regum et Dominus dominantium,* Apoc. 19, 13 and 16.

Notes on Hymn 151

Author. Unknown.
Use. At Lauds.

2. *lute,* widely, everywhere; cf. *104,* 1.

7–8. *levatus . . . traxit. Si exaltatus fuero a terra omnia traham ad meipsum,* John 12, 32.

O ter beata civitas
10 Cui rite Christus imperat,
Quae jussa pergit exsequi
Edicta mundo caelitus.

Non arma flagrant impia,
Pax usque firmat foedera,
15 Arridet et concordia,
Tutus stat ordo civicus.

Servat fides connubia,
Juventa pubet integra,
Pudica florent limina
20 Domesticis virtutibus.

Optata nobis splendeat
Lux ista, rex dulcissime;
Te, pace adepta candida,
Adoret orbis subditus.

happiness of a country that rightly owns the rule of Christ and zealously carries out the commands God gave to men. No wicked wars rage in that country, but peace is the strength of all its treaties, the happiness of concord is there and its civic life stands secure. The plighted word keeps marriage unbroken, the children grow up with virtue intact and homes where purity is found, abound also in the other virtues of home life. Beloved King, may the light from You that we desire, shine on us in all its glory; may the world receive the gift of peace, be subject to You and adore You.

---

1 November. *All Saints*

Hymn 152

Placare Christe servulis
Quibus Patris clementiam
Tuae ad tribunal gratiae
Patrona virgo postulat.

5 Et vos, beata per novem
Distincta gyros agmina,
Antiqua cum praesentibus,
Futura damna pellite.

Apostoli cum vatibus
10 Apud severum judicem
Veris reorum fletibus
Exposcite indulgentiam.

Vos purpurati martyres,
Vos candidati praemio
15 Confessionis, exsules
Vocate nos in patriam.

Chorea casta virginum
Et quos eremus incolas

Be merciful, Christ, to Your servants, for whom our advocate, the Virgin, asks the Father's mercy at the throne of grace. Blessed hosts of angels, divided into nine choirs, drive away from us past, present and future evils. Apostles and prophets, obtain from the just Judge by your prayers pardon for sinners who are truly contrite. Red-robed martyrs and white-robed confessors, call us back from our exile to our Father's land. Choirs of chaste virgins and all those who exchanged their

12. *caelitus,* from heaven, by God; cf. *63, 6.*

14. *usque,* like *usquequaque* in *93, 50;* on all occasions, at all times.

20. *domesticis virtutibus;* stigmatized by Mgr Knox as 'easily the worst line in Latin poetry'. It has some close rivals in this hymn and in the preceding one.

21. *optata* with *lux,* i.e. Christ, the *Aurora* of Lauds. On this day we hope He will come with the blessings and graces enumerated in this hymn.

23. *adepta,* deponent used as passive; cf. *61, 28. Candida,* because white is the traditional colour of peace. Byrnes suggests it may mean a *bloodless* peace, to be obtained by obeying God's law and not by the bloodshed of lines 5 and 6.

Notes on Hymn 152

Author. ?Rabanus Maurus. The ascription of this and the next hymn to Rabanus is called in question by some editors.

The sixth verse is an addition to the original hymn. 'When the celebration of All Saints was extended to the Frankish Empire in 825, after having been observed in Rome for two centuries, this stanza was added with reference to the Normans and Saracens who were laying waste the northwest of Gaul and the south of Italy' (Baudot: *The Roman Breviary,* p. 68).

Use. At Vespers and Matins. See also *152a* and *b.*

1–4. This hymn and the next mention our Lord and our Lady in the first verse and then recount the different classes of saints in the other verses. A similar arrangement is to be found in the Responsories of Matins.

13. *purpurati* and *candidati.* According to Apoc. 7, 9–14, all the saints are *amicti stolis albis,* and according to *9, 9* the martyrs are. Here *candidati* is used of the bloodless (cf. *candida, 151,* 23) triumph of the confessors as opposed to the martyrs' shedding of their blood. Red and white are also used by St Bede in the 5th lesson of the feast to mark the triumph of martyrs and of virgins: *Floribus ejus nec rosae nec lilia desunt . . . coronas vel de virginitate candidas, vel de passione purpureas. In caelestibus castris pax et acies habent flores suos, quibus milites Christi coronantur.*

Transmisit astris, caelitum
20 Locate nos in sedibus.

Auferte gentem perfidam
Credentium de finibus
Ut unus omnes unicum
Ovile nos pastor regat.

desert home for heaven, find place for us in the heavenly mansions. Drive the faithless race far from Christian lands that the one Shepherd may rule us all as His only fold.

Hymn 152a

Placare Christe servulis
Quibus Patris clementiam
Tuae ad tribunal gratiae
Patrona virgo postulat.

5 Nobis adesto Archangele,
Robur Dei qui denotas;
Vires adauge languidis,
Confer levamen tristibus.

Et vos, beata per novem
10 Distincta gyros agmina,
Antiqua cum praesentibus,
Futura damna pellite.

Auferte gentem perfidam
Credentium de finibus
15 Ut unus omnes unicum
Ovile nos pastor regat.

Deo Patri sit gloria
Qui, quos redemit Filius
Et sanctus unxit Spiritus,
20 Per angelos custodiat.

Be merciful, Christ, to Your servants for whom our advocate, the Virgin, asks the Father's mercy at the throne of grace. Be present to us, Gabriel; your name means Power of God. Bring increase of healthy vigour to the sick and give comfort to the sorrowful. Blessed hosts of angels, divided into nine choirs, drive away from us past, present and future evils. Drive the faithless far from Christian countries that the one Shepherd may rule us all as His only fold. Glory be to God the Father. May He guard through His angels those whom the Son has redeemed and the holy Spirit has anointed.

Hymn 152b

5 Nobis adesto Archangele,
Dei medelam denotans;
Morbos repelle corporum,
Affer salutem mentibus.

Be present to us, Raphael; your name means Healing of God. Drive away all bodily sickness and bring health of grace to our souls.

---

17. *chorea*, choir; cf. *90, 6*.

18. And those whom the desert has sent to heaven to live there. *Eremus* points first of all to the hermits (the *anachoritae* of the antiphon of the feast), but it must also mean monks and then religious in general. The original is: *Chori sanctarum virginum/Monachorumque omnium.*

Notes on Hymn 152*a*

Use. At Lauds of St Gabriel, 24 March. Verses 1, 3 and 4 are verses 1, 2 and 6 of *152*, while the doxology is that of *111*. The second verse is proper to the feast.

6. *robur Dei;* cf. *112, 9,* note.

Notes on Hymn 152*b*

Use. This hymn which is the same as *152a,* except for lines 5–8, is used at Lauds of St Raphael, 24 October.

6. *Dei medelam.* cf. *112, 13,* note.

Hymn 153

Salutis aeternae dator,
Jesu, redemptis subveni;
Virgo, parens clementiae,
Dona salutem servulis.

5 Vos, angelorum millia
Patrumque coetus, agmina
Canora vatum—vos, reis
Precamini indulgentiam.

Baptista Christi praevius
10 Summique caeli claviger
Cum ceteris apostolis
Nexus resolvant criminum.

Cohors triumphans martyrum,
Almus sacerdotum chorus
15 Et virginalis castitas
Nostros reatus abluant.

Quicunque in alta siderum
Regnatis aula principes,
Favete votis supplicum
20 Qui dona caeli flagitant.

Jesus, giver of eternal salvation, help Your redeemed people; Mary, mother of mercy, obtain the gift of salvation for your servants. Angels in your thousands, company of patriarchs and choir of prophets, ask pardon for us sinners. May the Baptist, Christ's forerunner, the heavenly key-bearer and the other Apostles free us from the chains of our sins. May the triumphant multitude of martyrs, the choir of holy priests and the chaste virgins wash away our guilt. Do all of you, now reigning as princes in heaven, give favourable ear to your suppliants' prayers as they ask most earnestly for heaven's graces.

2 November. *All Souls*

Hymn 154

Dies irae, dies illa
Solvet saeclum in favilla,
Teste David cum Sibylla.

Quantus tremor est futurus,
5 Quando judex est venturus,
Cuncta stricte discussurus.

Tuba mirum spargens sonum
Per sepulcra regionum
Coget omnes ante thronum.

A day of wrath that day will be. It will dissolve the world into glowing ashes, as David and the Sibyl have testified. How great a dread there will be when the Judge comes to examine all things in strict justice. The trumpet's wondrous call will sound in tombs the world over and urge everybody forward to the

Notes on Hymn 153

Author. ?Rabanus Maurus. Like *152* it has been extensively revised.

Use. At Lauds.

2. *Jesu;* cf. *152,* 1, note.

6. *Patrum = patriarcharum* of the original.

7. *canora,* lit. melodious; (cf. *10,* 3). *Canorus, canor* and *canere* are, in Christian and classical Latin, connected with prophets and oracles; cf., about St John the Baptist, *Salvatorem mundi et cecinit adfuturum et adesse monstravit,* the Secret prayer of 24 June, and *Ceteri tantum cecinere vatum, 117, 25.*

9. *praevius = praecursor;* for the word, cf. *praeviam, 44,* 6 etc.

15. *virginalis castitas = virgines castae.*

17. The unrevised text of 17–18 is *Monachorum suffragia/Omnesque cives caelici.* The Breviary text only represents the second of these lines. The *Monachi,* who were disguised in *152,* 18, have now been removed altogether. But if Rabanus wrote these two hymns, he would almost certainly have included monks, and for that matter so would almost any hymn-writer of the time.

Notes on Hymn 154

Author. Thomas of Celano (1200–55), a Franciscan, friend and biographer of St Francis.

Juxta est dies Domini magnus; juxta est, et velox nimis; vox diei Domini amara, tribulabitur ibi fortis. Dies irae dies illa, dies tribulationis et angustiae, dies calamitatis et miseriae, dies tenebrarum et caliginis, dies nebulae et turbinis, dies tubae et clangoris super civitates munitas, et super angulos excelsos, Sophonias 1, 14–16.

From the noble language of this passage of the Vulgate came the Responsory *Libera me Domine de morte aeterna,* the alphabetical hymn, of early date, *Apparebit repentina dies magna Domini,* the alphabetical *Altus prosator* of St Columba and many other hymns of later date and of varying quality. But the most famous of its offspring is the *Dies irae,* whose language, metre and music combine to make it the most majestic of all the hymns.

Besides using Sophonias, the poets turned to other parts of the Old Testament, to the second letter of St Peter and, above all, to the Gospels. Thus the writer of the *Apparebit repentina dies magna Domini* uses St Matthew as much as Sophonias, though the idea of the suddenness of the last day is also found in the prophet: *consummationem cum festinatione faciet cunctis habitantibus terrae,* Soph. 1, 18.

The writer of the *Dies irae* was in the first place indebted to these passages of the Scriptures, but he also seems to have called on some poems on the same

10 *Mors stupebit et natura,*
   Cum resurget creatura
   Judicanti responsura.

   Liber scriptus proferetur
   In quo totum continetur
15 *Unde mundus judicetur.*

   Judex ergo cum sedebit,
   Quidquid latet apparebit;
   Nil inultum remanebit.

   Quid sum miser tunc dicturus?
20 *Quem patronum rogaturus?—*
   Cum vix justus sit securus.

   Rex tremendae majestatis,
   Qui salvandos salvas gratis,
   Salva me, fons pietatis.

25 *Recordare, Jesu pie,*
   Quod sum causa tuae viae,
   Ne me perdas illa die.

   Quaerens me sedisti lassus;
   Redemisti, crucem passus;
30 *Tantus labor non sit cassus.*

   Juste judex ultionis,
   Donum fac remissionis
   Ante diem rationis.

   Ingemisco tamquam reus,
35 *Culpa rubet vultus meus;*
   Supplicanti parce, Deus.

   Qui Mariam absolvisti
   Et latronem exaudisti,
   Mihi quoque spem dedisti.

40 *Preces meae non sunt dignae,*
   Sed tu bonus fac benigne
   Ne perenni cremer igne.

   Inter oves locum praesta
   Et ab haedis me sequestra,
45 *Statuens in parte dextra.*

throne. Death and nature will stand amazed when creation rises again to give answer to its Judge. Then will be brought out the book in which is written the complete record that will decide each man's fate. And when the Judge is seated, all secret sin will be made known, and no sin will go without its due punishment.

In such a plight what can I then plead? Or whom can I ask to plead for me, when the just man will be saved only with difficulty? King of dread majesty, You give salvation's grace to all that will be saved. Save me, fount of pity.

In Your pity, Jesus, call to mind that I am the reason why You became man. Do not cast me from You on that day. It was me You were seeking out when, exhausted, You sat by the well; me that You redeemed when You suffered on the cross. Do not allow such toil to have been in vain. Just and avenging Judge, grant me the grace of pardon before that day of reckoning comes.

I groan like one condemned and am red with shame for my sins; spare Your suppliant servant. You forgave Mary and granted the robber's prayer, and thus gave me hope as well. Though my prayers do not deserve to be heard, yet in Your goodness graciously bring it about that I do not burn in the unquenchable fire.

Give me a place among Your sheep, separate me from the goats and set me on Your right

subject already in existence, for verbal similarities are sometimes very striking. The unity which the writer achieves in his poem is due partly to the simplicity and nobility of its language and partly to the personal note which is the mark of the Franciscan tradition (cf. Raby, p. 450, and the introduction to *109*). So it would seem that we must look among the Franciscans or those most in contact with their tradition for the writer of the *Dies irae;* and the only person so far suggested who would fulfil these requirements is Thomas of Celano.

St Gregory the Great may be ruled out at once as its author. St Bernard's case might on some grounds seem plausible (cf. *109*); yet it must be admitted that the poem is too austere for St Bernard—apart from the fact that it is not known until the thirteenth century. But it is most unlikely that such a poem, if really the work of one as well known as St Bernard, should lie, literally, unsung for a century.

Metre. Trochaic dimeter acatalectic, accentual, in three-lined verse with two-syllabled rhyme. The grouping of three eight-syllabled trochaic lines in a verse is something unique in the hymns, and the triple rhyme which results has 'been likened to blow following blow of the hammer on the anvil' (Trench). The music of the vowels in lines such as *Tuba mirum spargens sonum* is also worthy of note.

In spite of these qualities, the *Dies irae* did not please those who were bitten by the bug of classicism. One such sufferer, appalled at its debased Latin, re-wrote the first verse in this way:

> *Illa dies, extrema dies et sacra furori!*
> *O quam terribili complebit lumine terras*
> *Qua, subito emotis convulsus sedibus orbis*
> *Ibit in ultrices, flamma evertente, favillas.*
> *Credite, divino verax ita carmine vates*
> *Regius et veteres olim cecinere Sibyllae.*

(cf. *Le Bréviaire Expliqué,* by C. Villi, C.SS.R., I, pp. 185–6). Anyone who is depressed by the revised text of the Breviary hymns may look at this and find some consolation in the fact that P. du Cerceau was not one of the revisers.

The last six lines of the Missal text of the *Dies irae* are an addition to the original work. Of these the first four are eight-syllabled, forming one verse in which each couplet rhymes. It is taken from a twelfth-century (or earlier) hymn, its fourth line being changed from *Tu peccatis parce Deus* to *Huic*

ergo parce Deus. The last two lines are seven-syllabled, without rhyme.

Use. Sequence at Requiem Masses, for which purpose it was adapted by the addition of the last six lines; (cf. Note on Sequences, p. 96, and *109*). Some have regretted its inclusion in the Requiem since the keynote of the Mass is peace, joy and light while the sequence strikes a discordant note of gloom and fear. Others, however, think it is well placed in the Requiem.

The last lines apart, the poem is a *pia meditatio* on death and judgement. Its first liturgical use, according to common opinion, was for the first Sunday of Advent, though it has been suggested that it was a Trope of the Responsory *Libera me Domine*. There is certainly some musical kinship between the two. It is well suited to Advent when the Church is thinking also of our Lord's coming as judge (cf. *34–6*), and to the mass of the first Sunday of Advent. As far as the present gospel readings go, it would suit the last Sunday after Pentecost as well as, if not better than, the first Sunday of Advent.

The words of the poem have fascinated and been the despair of translators (cf. B and Trench), and the music has found its way into Berlioz's 'Fantastic' Symphony, Saint-Saen's 'Danse Macabre' and Liszt's 'Totentanz'.

The plan of the *Dies irae* is very simple. The first six verses describe the judgement, and the poet introduces himself into the scene of judgment in the seventh and asks who will be able to help him *then*. As no one can, since all are to be judged, now is the time to prepare for that day. He prays to our Lord Who will then appear as the *Rex tremendae majestatis* but who is now a *fons pietatis* to mankind. The first reason for mercy is the Incarnation—*quod sum causa tuae viae*—together with His labours and death —*tantus labor non sit cassus*. The other reason is the repentance of the sinner—*Ingemisco tamquam reus . . . mihi quoque spem dedisti*. The verses *Juste judex* and *Preces meae* are the prayers which end each of the sections. As a result of God's mercy in his regard, he hopes to be with God when the judgement is over, lines 43–8, and the last verse is the cry of humble hope which sums up the whole hymn—*Gere curam mei finis*.

1. *dies illa*. These words are for the prophet, Soph. 1, 15, and for the poet the real subject, *dies irae* being in apposition in the poem. The words *dies illa* or *dies*

Notes continued on p. 256

Confutatis maledictis,
Flammis acribus addictis,
Voca me cum benedictis.

Oro supplex et acclinis,
10 Cor contritum quasi cinis;
Gere curam mei finis.

Lacrimosa dies illa
Qua resurget ex favilla
Judicandus homo reus:
15 Huic ergo parce Deus.

Pie Jesu Domine,
Dona eis requiem.

hand. When the accursed have been silenced and sentenced to the acrid flames, call me along with the blessed. In humility and abasement I make this prayer. My sin is burnt to ashes in the fire of my sorrow. Take care of me when my end is come.

That day when guilty man rises out of the ruins of the world for judgement, will be a day of tears and mourning. Spare him on that day, Lord God.

Jesus, Lord, of Your mercy grant them rest.

Notes continued from p. 255

ista are common in the Vulgate for the last day. Another poet contrasts that day with the day of eternity. *Terret me dies terroris,/Irae dies et furoris,/ Dies luctus et maeroris,/Dies ultrix peccatoris,* and: *Dies illa, dies vitae,/Dies lucis inauditae . . . Appropinquat enim dies,/In qua justis erit quies.*

2. *solvet. Adveniet autem dies Domini . . . in quo . . . elementa calore solventur, terra autem et quae in ipsa sunt*

opera, exurentur, 2 Pet. 3, 10; cf. also verse 12. *favilla, -ae,* hot cinders, glowing ashes.

3. *David,* who is taken as representative of revelation in either testament. The primary reference is probably to Sophonias, but the poet's *solvet in favilla* is so reminiscent of 2 Pet. 3, 10 that some, quite unnecessarily, suggested *Teste Petro* for *Teste David.*

Sibylla, as representative of natural religion, →

though the Sibylline oracles were once credited with a more than natural authority. The destruction of the world by fire is found in the oracle connected with the name of Hystaspes, while in the later oracles the destruction of the world by water, fire and such-like disasters is a common theme. St Justin in his Apology says that both Sybil and Hystaspes foretold the destruction by fire, and St Augustine in the *De civitate Dei* quotes the verses of the Erythraean Sybil as foretelling the end of the world. The passage in question begins with these lines, in which also was discovered the acrostic on the Holy Name:

> Judicii signum: tellus sudore madescet,
> E caelo rex adveniet per saecla futurus,
> Scilicet ut carnem praesens ut judicet orbem.

(Cf. Trench, p. 303; Raby, pp. 443 and 446; Arendzen: *Men and Manners in the Days of Christ*, pp. 136–188; Schuster, I, p. 360).

A dislike of putting the Sybil alongside David led to the alternative line: *Crucis expandens vexilla,* referring to *Et tunc parebit signum Filii hominis in caelo,* Mt. 24, 30. But such a line is clearly out of keeping with the rest of the poem; cf. Trench, p. 303 and Arendzen, p. 188.

4. *tremor;* cf. Luke 21, 25–7.

6. *stricte,* closely, accurately, minutely; *discussurus,* future of purpose.

7. *tuba. Dies tubae et clangoris,* Soph. 1, 16; *cum tuba et voce magna,* Mt. 24, 31. The *Apparebit repentina* thus pictures the scene: *Clangor tubae per quaternas terrae plagas concinens,/Vivos una mortuosque Christo ciet obviam.*

10. Cf. *Et dedit mare mortuos . . .; et mors et infernus dederunt mortuos . . .; et judicatum est de singulis secundum opera ipsorum,* Apoc. 20, 13.

13. *liber. Et vidi mortuos, magnos et pusillos, stantes in conspectu throni, et libri aperti sunt; et alius liber apertus est, qui est vitae; et judicati sunt mortui ex his quae scripta erant in libris,* Apoc. 20, 12; cf. also Mal. 3, 16–18.

16. *sedebit.* Probably *censebit* ought to be read here; *censebit,* rate, value, assess (the deeds of men).

17–18. Whatever is hidden will then be brought to light; nothing (that is sinful) will remain (hidden and so) unpunished.

This is a commonplace in medieval hymns. *Cui latebit nil occultum,/Et manebit nil inultum,* Trench, p. 293; and: *Ante Dei potero consistere quomodo vultum,/*

Cum nihil occultum, cum nihil remanebit inultum?, Radewin, quoted Raby, p. 447.

20. *patronum,* advocate, counsel. *Quem nunc sanctorum mihi deprecer esse patronum,* Raby, p. 447. The time for gaining merit will have passed, and, as all are to be judged, no one will be free to be a man's advocate; and even the just will encounter difficulties.

21. *vix. Et si justus vix salvabitur, impius et peccator ubi parebunt?,* 1 Pet. 4, 18.

22. *Rex tremendae majestatis* looks back to the first six verses, while *fons pietatis* looks forward to the rest of the poem, being immediately taken up by *Jesu pie.* Cf. *pia Deitas, tremenda majestas* in the prayer ascribed, wrongly, to St Ambrose in the preparatory prayers of the Missal.

26. *viae,* i.e. of the incarnation and His life on earth.

28. *sedisti lassus. Fatigatus ex itinere, sedebat sic supra fontem,* John 4, 6. On this St Augustine said: *Tibi fatigatus est ab itinere Jesus,* and the poet: *Quaerens me.*

30. *cassus,* fruitless, in vain.

33. *rationis,* reckoning. *Reddent rationem de eo in die judicii,* Mt. 12, 56; cf. also Rom. 14, 12.

34. *reus;* in this context, meaning condemned rather than accused.

42. *igne;* cf. Mt. 25, 41.

46. *confutatis,* silenced. No further answer on the part of the wicked will be possible when they hear *Quamdiu non fecistis . . . nec mihi fecistis.* For them there only remains: *Ibunt hi in supplicium aeternum,* Mt. 25, 45–6. *Maledictis;* the *maledicti* of Mt 25, 41.

49–51. This final prayer looks to our Lord as the *Rex* and *fons pietatis* and to the repentance of the sinner, lines 34–9.

supplex, kneeling; *acclinis,* bending low; in complete submission.

cor . . . cinis. The idea seems to be that the sinful desires of the heart are reduced to powder, burnt up in contrition till nothing but their ashes is left. *Cinis* seems to be an echo of *favilla* in line 2. The line is in loose apposition with the subject of *oro.*

gere curam, governing a genitive; cf. *gerunt curam/ nascentis Ecclesiae,* in Adam of St Victor's sequence for St Andrew.

53. *favilla,* from the ashes, ruins, of the world; cf. line 2.

54. *reus,* sinner, guilty; contrast line 34.

INDEX OF LATIN AUTHORS

Ascriptions which seem to be mere guess-work, as often happens in relation to SS Ambrose, Gregory and Bernard, are not mentioned here. Those for which certainty cannot be claimed are given by the hymn number preceded by a question mark.

INDEX OF FIRST LINES

Portions of a hymn which serve in the Breviary as separate hymns are indicated by asterisks.